# AMERICAN BANKING STRUCTURE

# American Banking Structure

GERALD C. FISCHER

NEW YORK AND LONDON

*Columbia University Press*

1968

*Gerald C. Fischer is Research Professor of Business Administration at Temple University*

TO ALYSON

# FOREWORD

IN 1963 A FEW BANKERS and staff personnel of the American Bankers Association conceived the idea of a major research effort in the area of banking structure. At that time the question of branch versus unit banking was particularly acute. The rapid evolution of banking technology, a shortage of qualified management personnel, the enlarged financing requirements of the economy, and changes in banking regulation at the Federal level all made it appear that the Government and the banking industry might soon be forced to make a choice regarding the form of banking structure that would prevail nationally.

With this background, the ABA, through its Committee on Banking and Financial Research, began to plan a research program designed to provide information that would be needed for an intelligent appraisal of the problem. The first step was the commissioning of a survey of the evolution of American banking structure which would be designed to trace the history of developments in this area—legislative and judicial, theoretical and factual. It was hoped that such a study would provide, in a single source, a substantial amount of material on subjects of importance in this field which would be useful to bank regulatory officials, to bank officers and their legal counsel, and to banking scholars.

The ABA found that Gerald Fischer, a finance professor who had served as a consultant to the Association in the banking structure area, had already begun a study of developments in this field. However, the study which was being prepared by Dr. Fischer under a Ford Foundation faculty research grant was far more limited in scope than the survey envisaged by the ABA, and therefore, the Association provided sufficient funds to permit a substantial expansion of his original work. Ultimately, in terms of financial support, the ABA and the Ford Foundation contributed about equally, although this had not been planned as such, nor had the two sponsors approached the project jointly.

While members of the ABA research staff and the Banking and

Research Committee discussed the general outline of this book with Professor Fischer, the Association and the author agreed initially that the work was to be carried out exactly as it was under the terms of the Ford Foundation grant. This meant that the specific content of the study and its findings would be determined exclusively by the author. The only request made by the ABA was that Dr. Fischer primarily emphasize the evolution and regulation of banking structure in the United States, rather than attempt to evaluate the performance of alternative banking structures. It was felt that this delimitation was necessary to avoid duplication of effort because the Association's program of research in this field called for a major factual study of the effects of bank structure to follow Professor Fischer's work. In 1966 the National Bureau of Economic Research was commissioned to do this project.

Since the inception of Professor Fischer's study, the nature of the banking structure problem has changed somewhat. It now appears unlikely that a choice of a monolithic banking structure will have to be made for the nation as a whole. Technology has been adapted so that it is not exclusively available to large units. Enlargement of correspondent banking services and new management methods have made technically possible the survival of units once thought to be uneconomic. On the legislative side, the tide has turned, and the states have shown an active interest in refurbishing their banking codes under pressure from alert bankers. This change in the nature of the question on banking structure, however, has made no less urgent the need for clear thought on the subject. Rather, many levels of Government are free to make their own decisions about banking structure intelligently and without inexorable pressure of developments. The disappearance of need for a nationwide commitment to a single structure means that, more than ever, a clear understanding of how the present system developed is necessary in making future decisions about the type of banking that will prevail. The area for conscious and free decision making has thus increased, with consequent need for greater knowledge. In answering this need, I believe Professor Fischer's study has made a major contribution.

The American Bankers Association is pleased to have had a part in making this important survey of developments in the all-important field of banking structure. It acknowledges the assistance of others, particularly the Ford Foundation, in making possible the early work on this project, even though at that stage the ultimate form of this study was not seen. Most of all, of course, credit must be given the author for imagination, perseverance, thoroughness, and sheer energy in following leads to make a coherent story of how the present banking structure evolved. The completeness of this job is attested by the ability of the work to stand on its own as a manuscript for publication by Columbia University Press.

*Charls E. Walker*
Executive Vice President
The American Bankers Association

December 1967

# ACKNOWLEDGMENTS

I AM VERY GRATEFUL to the Ford Foundation, which granted me a faculty research fellowship, and to the American Bankers Association, which assisted in financing this study. I also sincerely appreciate the cooperation of the Administration of the Graduate School of Business and of my former colleagues in the Finance Department at Indiana University, who made it possible for me to devote a considerable period of time to this research. Jon Prager and my other graduate assistants were very helpful, and my secretaries, Mrs. Kay Miller and Mrs. Rosalie Hutchinson typed most of the manuscript and aided me in innumerable ways. But surely my greatest debt is to my banking students at Indiana whose questions and comments regarding points in a number of the chapters of this book (which were distributed to them in mimeographed form) made me aware of at least some of its shortcomings.

Numerous individuals and organizations provided information or counsel while this book was in progress. I am particularly indebted to the following: the staff members of the federal banking agencies and the Department of Justice; Thomas Atkinson, William Brown, and Mrs. Gertrude Williams, of the American Bankers Association (ABA); Albert Cox, Jr., Carter Golembe, and Leslie Peacock, who were formerly employed by the ABA; Fred Bateman, David Martin, and Ross Robertson of Indiana University; Theodore Flechsig of the FDIC research division; Tynan Smith of the Federal Reserve Board staff; Herbert Schoepke of the Department of Justice; and Donald Rogers of the Association of Registered Bank Holding Companies.

Naturally, the conclusions, opinions, and other statements in this publication are those of the author and are not necessarily those of the above.

Finally, I would like to express my gratitude to my wife and daughter for their patience and encouragement while this book was being written.

*Gerald C. Fischer*

# CONTENTS

FOREWORD   vii

ACKNOWLEDGMENTS   x

CHAPTER 1   *Introduction*   1

CHAPTER 2   *Unit and Branch Banking*   8

    DEVELOPMENT OF UNIT AND BRANCH BANKING BEFORE 1900   9

    GROWTH OF UNIT AND BRANCH BANKING   29

    BRANCH BANK OPERATIONS   41

    LEGISLATION AND REGULATION   42

CHAPTER 3   *Chain, Group, and Correspondent Banking*   72

    INTRODUCTION   72

    MULTIPLE-UNIT BANKING   73

    CHAIN BANKING   82

    BANK HOLDING COMPANIES   95

    THE FUTURE OF MULTIPLE-UNIT BANKING   108

    CORRESPONDENT BANKING   110

CHAPTER 4   *Mergers and Acquisitions*   122

    MERGER MOVEMENTS   123

    REGULATION   137

    THE EFFECT OF BANK MERGERS AND ACQUISITIONS   165

CHAPTER 5   *Chartering*                                       174

   DEVELOPMENTS IN THE NINETEENTH
   CENTURY                                                175

   DEVELOPMENTS 1900–1935                                  184

   DEVELOPMENTS 1936–1966                                  210

CHAPTER 6   *Commercial Banking and the Federal
Antitrust Laws: Interbank Cooperation*                        238

   INTRODUCTION                                           238

   PRICE FIXING: BACKGROUND                               246

   PRICE FIXING: FEDERAL BANK ANTITRUST
   CASES                                                  256

   TYING ARRANGEMENTS AND EXCLUSIVE
   DEALING                                                263

   INTERLOCKING DIRECTORATES                              267

CHAPTER 7   *Commercial Banking and the Federal
Antitrust Laws: Mergers*                                      276

   INTRODUCTION                                           276

   ANTITRUST LAW AND THE BANK MERGER
   ACT OF 1960                                            286

   ANTITRUST IMPLICATIONS OF THE 1966
   AMENDMENTS                                             310

CHAPTER 8   *Banking Concentration*                           327

   CONCEPT OF THE BANKING MARKET                          333

   THE IMPORTANCE OF BANKING
   CONCENTRATION                                          347

CHAPTER 9   *Closing Observations*                            382

BIBLIOGRAPHY                                                  393

INDEX                                                         413

# AMERICAN BANKING STRUCTURE

# CHAPTER 1

# Introduction

"FEW INDEED ARE the areas that have been left untouched by industrial dispersion, revolutionary changes in production and marketing techniques, population shifts, and new highway and other transportation systems. This is the time . . . to take a new hard look at our existing banking structures. Our sights should go higher than the emotional issues of fifty years ago. Instead we must look realistically at the form of multi-office banking now existing in our respective states and determine whether it is still the most appropriate and best form."[1] These remarks, which were made by the president of the American Bankers Association early in 1966, reflect an enormous change not only on the part of prominent members of the banking industry, who speak candidly about issues in this very delicate area, but also on the part of bankers in general, who have begun to gather facts and to weigh alternatives regarding questions which in the recent past would have been settled by emotion, not by investigation.

Committees have been formed in many states to develop information concerning various types of bank organization. And some of these groups have been organized by bankers' associations in those states which historically have been classified as "bastions of independ-

[1] Excerpts from a speech by Archie K. Davis before the midwinter meeting of the Ohio Bankers Association. Quoted in the *American Banker*, February 21, 1966.

1

ent banking," as well as in those states which have for some time permitted at least limited branching. In addition, bank-sponsored research in this field is being carried out at a number of leading universities, and the American Bankers Association recently awarded a substantial grant to the National Bureau of Economic Research (NBER) for the stated purpose of developing additional knowledge in the area of bank structure.

Nevertheless, there are still many individuals, including a number of prominent state banking officials, who prefer the status quo and strenuously object to even studying alternative banking systems. For example, this writer received the following communication from the Superintendent of Banks of a leading unit-bank state a short time ago:

I am not aware of any need or public demand for changes in the laws relating to banking or bank supervision, at least in my state. In my view, big bankers and a federal supervisory agency are the principal agitators for change. The agitators are trying to ram branch banking down our throats here and in other nonbranch states. They also want to authorize nonbanking activities that are unlawful, unwarranted, and unsound . . . to the detriment of the dual banking system that has operated success-fully for more than 100 years.

The argument developed by this official regarding the situation in his state may be valid. Moreover, were this position supported by convincing evidence, it would merit very serious consideration by the Congress, if its members were weighing the possibility of freeing national banks from state branch restrictions. But the almost classic defense he presents in support of his position (to take the other side one would seemingly have to be "for" big bankers and federal govern-ment as opposed to state power and against the dual banking system) may no longer be sufficient to win the day in the federal legislature or in most state legislatures. This does not mean to imply that the present bank structure in many parts of this country will necessarily change radically, but it does suggest that if an existing system prevails it will do so at least partly because careful analysis has revealed that on balance it has merit, not because it is an inviolable piece of Americana.[2]

[2] The standard rejoinder to this is that once branch banking is given a foothold it is only a matter of time before statewide branching and nationwide branching will follow. The most pessimistic unit-banking advocate should at

## FUNCTION OF THIS SURVEY OF BANK STRUCTURE

This book was written to provide background material for investigations of banking structure, such as those which are being conducted by state study groups or the NBER, and for work in this general area which may be undertaken by academic or government economists. It has also been designed for the banker, the lawyer, and the student of banking who may have a professional or a personal interest in this relatively new and most exciting field of research. With this type of audience in mind, great pains have been taken to document statements made and to cite other works which may expand upon a given point or lead the reader to still other sources. For example, the chapters which may be of particular interest to those concerned with antitrust questions (6–8) include frequent references to relevant case law and detailed lists of articles in leading economic and legal periodicals which are related to the topics in question.

Extensive bibliographical material is also provided in the sections of this study which trace the history of unit, branch, chain, correspondent, and group banking. Of course, the development of some of these forms of bank organization (particularly branch banking) has already been analyzed in other publications; hence, part of the research done concerning the evolution of this nation's banking structure may appear to be merely an unnecessary duplication of effort. Yet a careful perusal of the present literature in this field has revealed that none of these works has brought together the material needed in this book; that there is considerable disagreement among the existing studies regarding many of the important "facts" concerning the development of banking in this country; and that some of the finest studies have neglected to provide more than a handful of footnotes to aid the investigator who wanted to verify a statement or pursue a given argument somewhat further. Therefore, to minimize error and to assist those who desire more information about the points made, whenever possible the original documents or publications were carefully examined in gathering historical data for these chapters, and a relatively large amount of bibliographical information has been included.

---

least have some doubts concerning the accuracy of this statement if he examines Table 2.3.

CONCEPT OF BANKING STRUCTURE

Banking structure is a dynamic rather than a static concept.[3] It includes much more then the congeries of banking institutions which exists at a point in time, for it encompasses the forces of law and tradition as well as the way in which banks are organized. Moreover, in its broadest sense, banking structure might include not only banks but all financial intermediaries, public and private, whose product markets even slightly overlap those of commercial banking.

However, for the purposes of this book the concept of banking structure had to be narrowed considerably. In this study only commercial banking will be considered as the relevant line of commerce to be analyzed, and a fairly standard industrial organization definition of market structure will be employed—"those characteristics of the organization of a market which seem to influence strategically the nature of competition and pricing within the market." The characteristics primarily emphasized in this book include the degree of seller concentration (described by the number and the size distribution of banks in the market); the degree of product differentiation (the extent to which the "output" of one bank may be viewed as nonidentical to that of another bank), and the condition of entry into the market.[4]

ORGANIZATION OF THIS STUDY

With this basic idea of market structure in mind, the book was organized as follows:

Chapters 2 and 3 provide a general discussion of the types of multiple-office and multiple-unit banking found in the market place. Chapter 2 reviews unit and branch banking, and Chapter 3 considers the "hybrid" forms of bank organization: chains and groups, and correspondent banking. The historical development, growth, regulation, and current dimensions of each of these various institutions is presented. Also, some information concerning bank holding company operations and correspondent banking has been gathered, for the willingness of the general public to accept one form of bank organiza-

---

[3] See Howard Crosse's discussion of banking structure in his *Management Policies for Commercial Banks*, pp. 12–13.

[4] Bain, *Industrial Organization*, p. 7.

tion as a substitute for another (cross elasticity of demand) will depend heavily upon the ability of one system to offer products or services comparable with those of its competitor.[5] (The problem of the homogeneity of banking products and services is examined further in Chapter 8 in the review of some of the findings of banking structure research.)

Chapters 4 (chartering) and 5 (mergers) are concerned with the influence upon competition and pricing of some of the "internal factors" (that is, factors which affect the ability of the banking industry, including the standard banking agencies, to regulate itself). In terms of economic theory, in addition to product homogeneity noted above, other elements which may affect the ability of a market to be self-regulating are the number of firms serving the market and the ability of new firms to enter the industry and to compete with the existing firms. Both of these factors are considered in Chapters 4 and 5, which examine some of the variables which may tend to increase or reduce the number of competitors in a banking market, including failures, mergers, and the formation of new banks.

Chapters 6 to 8 continue the analysis of the major forces influencing competition and pricing within banking markets, but these chapters primarily emphasize some of the more important "external factors," namely the federal antitrust laws. Chapter 6 discusses those factors which could most directly affect price, such as interlocking directorates, and clearing house and "gentlemen's" agreements. It also traces the evolution of the "rule" that only nonprice competition should exist among commercial banks. Chapters 7 and 8, on the other hand, return to the problem of the number of competitors and banking concentration, and the efforts of the Justice Department to try to ensure that the quantity of independent alternative sources of bank services in a market will not be reduced to the point that competition may be substantially lessened. Both chapters explore the relevant antitrust statutes in the directorate, price-fixing, and merger fields, and their application to commercial banking is illustrated by analyses of some of the recent court decisions in the areas in question.

There are many topics in each of these chapters which merit additional examination. This writer is well aware of a number of these

[5] *Ibid.*, p. 8. The extent of buyer concentration will not be considered in this book although it is often important in market structure studies.

omissions, particularly the lack of analysis of competition with other financial intermediaries and the very limited discussion of deposit insurance which contributes to bank homogeneity. These two items were among those covered in the tentative outline for this study, for this work as originally designed would have included much more extensive analysis of the implications and measures of banking concentration and the product and geographic market concepts.[6] However, since this book was prepared with the close cooperation of the American Bankers Association (ABA), with an awareness of other research efforts currently in progress, and with the knowledge that a forthcoming series of ABA financed National Bureau of Economic Research projects[7] supposedly would be directed toward questions such as the above, the discussion relative to these items, when possible, was held to a minimum. Thus, while some of the detail which is absent from this work is missing because of time constraints or the failure of this investigator to realize the contribution which it might have made to this study, material has frequently been excluded by design.

THE NEED FOR ADDITIONAL BANK STRUCTURE RESEARCH

In 1929 the American Bankers Association's Economic Policy Commission, in its *Study of Group and Chain Banking,* observed: "In this investigation the Commission entered an unexplored region. There were no landmarks to go by. There was no established body of reliable facts to build on. There was a confusion of rumors and a chaos of misinformation." Three decades later, in a debate concerning the content of a study of "Chicago Banking" in which there were many points of dispute, both sides were in agreement that the area of bank structure remained sadly neglected.[8] In part this reflected the difficulty of doing research in this field, but it also indicated the lack

[6] The difficulty of this research is not underestimated.

[7] The possible relationship of this study to others which were expected to develop from the ABA sponsored research was not as tenuous as it may appear from this statement, for this writer prepared the original plans regarding organization and research objectives for the ABA project.

[8] Jacobs and Lerner, "Chicago Banking: A Critical Review," *Journal of Business* (October 1962), pp. 414, 419; and "Reply" to this article by Irving Schweiger, *ibid.,* p. 420.

of interest which long prevailed among scholars in considering banking institutions as business firms.

Instead of examining the banking industry by employing the type of analysis developed by industrial organization specialists, banking professors, in all but a few instances, prior to the mid-1950s devoted their research efforts almost entirely to money and monetary policy and gave little serious thought to commercial banking competition. However, this situation has changed tremendously in recent years, and much of the credit for this expansion of banking structure research must go to the Department of Justice, the Supreme Court, and the Office of the Comptroller of the Currency, for these three governmental bodies introduced a degree of uncertainty into the staid banking industry which disturbed bankers but excited scholars.

The series of projects which has been undertaken and the numerous publications devoted to bank structure questions which have been issued during the last decade provide some measure of the interest which has been stimulated in this area. But, despite the vast amount of work which has already been done, tremendous opportunities remain for investigation in this field. For, as Robert Holland, Adviser to the Board of Governors, has remarked: "Banking markets provide many clear issues, both in theory and in policy, that are crying for resolution."[9] At present the bank supervisor must make decisions regarding banking competition knowing surprisingly little about how, with whom, or where banks compete. The legislator must write laws and the courts must interpret these statutes with the public interest in mind, and yet the available information concerning so fundamental a question as the performance by different forms of bank organization and by size of bank is extremely limited. It is hoped that this book by bringing together much of the available knowledge in this field, by providing a reasonable amount of new data not readily available before, by tracing the evolution of American bank organization, and by including an inordinate amount of reference material may assist not only the academic, the banker, and the lawyer but all individuals concerned with the continuing search for solutions to a vast array of bank structure questions.

[9] Holland, "Research into Banking Structure and Competition," *Federal Reserve Bulletin* (November 1964), p. 1398.

# CHAPTER 2

———◆———

# *Unit and Branch Banking*

AT THE BEGINNING of the colonial period in American history, there was perhaps less money in circulation here than in any other civilized community of the Western world.[1] Barter was common and numerous commodities and even wampum were in effect legal tender in some of the colonies. There were no banks of discount and deposit,[2] and many of the normal banking functions were performed by merchant houses for their customers as a part of their trading business.

Occasionally, historical works mention "banks" which existed in the colonies during the first half of the eighteenth century. However, these institutions were extremely crude by present-day standards, and it could be argued that they were banks in name only. Instead of being convenient institutions for receiving deposits, making discounts, and negotiating drafts, these "banks" amounted to little more than public and private issues of bills of credit,[3] or as they were described by one author—"simply a batch of paper money."[4] As a result, banking

[1] Nussbaum, *A History of the Dollar*, p. 3.
[2] Collins, *Rural Banking Reform*, pp. 2, 21.
[3] A private bank in the American colonies was an emission of notes by private individuals to supply a supposed deficiency of the medium of exchange; in some cases there was a promise of redemption. A public bank was an emission of circulating notes by a provincial government with the promise of redemption from the proceeds of taxes at a fixed time.
[4] Dewey, *Financial History of the United States*, p. 24.

8

structure was of little or no concern, for the issuers of the bills rarely (if ever) had permanent places of business.[5]

## DEVELOPMENT OF UNIT AND BRANCH BANKING
### BEFORE 1900

In 1781 the firm which many authors term "the first genuine bank" in the colonies or in the "Confederation," the Bank of North America, was formed under a resolution by the Continental Congress.[6] However, at the time, there was considerable doubt regarding the power of the Congress to permit the establishment of a bank, and the institution also obtained a charter from the Pennsylvania legislature.[7] As a result, the Bank of North America held concurrent charters issued by both federal and state authorities; and if the Bank of Massachusetts and the Bank of New York had not been formed in 1784 this country could have had a dual banking system but only one bank.

Although the problem of branching by the Bank of North America does not appear to have been an important issue (the ordinance under which it was incorporated did not mention branching), even at this early date the question of "money power" was raised and great concern was expressed regarding the possible political influence this bank might enjoy. Thus, from the beginning of banking history in the

[5] *Ibid.* The most notable of these banks, the Massachusetts Land Bank, was outlawed by the British government in 1741. [See White, *Money and Banking,* pp. 262–66.] In 1751 Parliament passed an act prohibiting the New England colonies from erecting new land banks or making paper currency legal tender, and in 1764 this prohibition was extended to all colonies. [See Morison and Commager, *The Growth of the American Republic,* pp. 105–106; and Dewey, *Financial History of the United States,* p. 29.]

[6] Robert Morris had attempted to organize a bank as early as 1763, and Alexander Hamilton had at least considered the establishment of a bank in 1779, but nothing came of these plans at the time. [See Eliason, *The Rise of Commercial Banking in the United States,* pp. 19–21.] The Bank of Pennsylvania was formed in 1780; however, it was organized only to help finance the war, and all of its funds were used for that purpose. [*Ibid.*]

[7] Pennsylvania later repealed the bank's charter (1785). The bank continued to operate, nevertheless, and applied to Delaware for a charter which was granted in 1786. Its directors contemplated moving the bank to some point in that state, but Pennsylvania, fearing it might lose the bank, granted it a new charter. White, *Money and Banking,* p. 270.

United States, one finds opposition to banks by those who feared
these institutions might lead to an undesirable concentration of economic resources.

A considerable confusion has arisen regarding this point, for authors have frequently mistaken this general opposition to banks for a
specific opposition to branch banks. A careful review of the literature
devoted to this period revealed a substantial number of attacks upon
banks but little comment about branching in particular as a means of
further concentrating control of banking resources.[8] One of the few
important statements against multiple-office banking which was found
was Alexander Hamilton's criticism of possible branching by the
[First] Bank of the United States.[9] Hamilton felt the bank should not
establish branches, but his attack did not stem from a fear that this
authority might tend to increase the bank's monopolistic power.[10]
Instead, he opposed this form of organization because he felt that
possibly some weakness in a branch might endanger the whole system. Some critics have argued that part of his hostility toward branching by the proposed bank might have arisen not because of a fear that
competition would be diminished but that it might be increased, for if
new national bank branches were placed in operation one would
almost inevitably have been located in New York where it was likely
to compete with the Bank of New York, an institution with which
Hamilton was closely associated.

Precedent for such anticompetitive action had already been set by
the Bank of North America. The directors of this firm in 1784 feared
if there were two banks in Philadelphia they "might act in opposition
to each other, and would be sure eventually to be of mutual disadvantage."[11] Therefore, these men skillfully prevented the formation of a

[8] Others have also noted there was little consideration of branching. See for
example, Miller, *Banking Theories in the United States,* p. 162.

[9] Holdsworth and Dewey, *The First and Second Banks of the United States,*
p. 13.

[10] *Ibid.,* p. 36. His position on this question changed in a relatively few years.
Finding the branch operations were successful, in 1794 he urged the bank to
open an additional branch at Alexandria, Virginia. *Ibid.,* p. 40.

[11] Lewis, *A History of the Bank of North America,* p. 52. Another writer
observed while describing New York State banking in the 1820s: "Since Olcott
controlled so many banks and at the same time would not allow any more
banks to be chartered, he had forced the business community into dependence
on him for loans." Wilburn, *Biddle's Bank,* p. 114.

new bank by offering its subscribers shares in the Bank of North America at very favorable terms. As a result the bank's comfortable monopoly position remained undisturbed.[12] It is interesting to ponder how today's Department of Justice would have handled this eighteenth-century "Philadelphia case."

## BANKS OF THE UNITED STATES

*First Bank.* Although Alexander Hamilton's original plan for the First Bank of the United States did not contemplate the formation of branches, at least initially,[13] the act incorporating the bank included a provision making it lawful for the directors to establish offices for the purpose of discount and deposit anywhere within the United States.[14] In the light of Hamilton's misgivings regarding the organization of branches, it was thought at first the directors would not use this authority.[15] Nevertheless, they decided to open branches at Baltimore, Boston, Charleston, and New York as soon as possible after operations began. In addition, other offices were set up at Norfolk, Savannah, Washington, and New Orleans, making in all eight branches[16] (excluding the head office). No difficulties of any great moment appear to have arisen because of these additional offices, and Hamilton's doubts regarding them were dispelled. But, for reasons largely unrelated to the fact that the Bank had branches, when its charter expired in 1811 it was not renewed.[17]

*Second Bank.*[18] The provisions of the charter of the Second Bank of the United States were more explicit in regard to the formation of

[12] This writer does not mean to pass judgment on the merits of having two banks in Philadelphia or a branch in New York at the time, for perhaps the city could not have supported two banks. It is only hoped that these illustrations may show that arguments against branching and free entry as potential sources of monopoly power should not always be accepted without question.

[13] Holdsworth and Dewey, *The First and Second Banks of the United States,* pp. 36, 39.

[14] 1 Stat. 191, ch. 10, § 7 (XV) (1791). This section was amended to permit branching by the bank in United States territories and dependencies as well. 2 Stat. 274, ch. 32 (1804).

[15] Chapman and Westerfield, *Branch Banking,* p. 26.

[16] Holdsworth and Dewey, *The First and Second Banks of the United States,* p. 38.

[17] Federal Reserve Board, Committee Reports, "Branch Banking," p. 33.

[18] The best study of the operations and development of this bank is Catterall's *The Second Bank of the United States.*

branches than those found in the act incorporating the "First Bank." In the case of the "First Bank" the authority to establish additional offices was permissive, but the "Second Bank" was required to set up branches under certain conditions. The branch provision of the act chartering the "Second Bank" stated that it must locate an office of discount and deposit in the District of Columbia if Congress required it, and establish an office in any state in which 2,000 of the bank's shares were subscribed or held if the legislature of the state applied for it. In addition, on their own initiative the directors could establish offices anywhere within the United States or its territories.[19]

The Second Bank of the United States had organized nineteen branches in fourteen different states by the fall of 1817. Eight others were later established, which provided representation for the bank in every state on the Atlantic Seaboard except New Jersey and Delaware, and every district in the interior except Illinois and Indiana.[20] In addition, by the early 1830s applications for branches from at least thirty cities were under consideration.

Unfortunately, the losses of the branches were ten times those of the headquarters' bank,[21] and Hamilton's apprehensions regarding the establishment of additional offices by the "First Bank" in 1791 were proved to be more than justified by the experience of the "Second Bank." In some cases the main office could not control the operations of the branches because communication and transportation facilities were so poor. In other instances local directorates simply defied the "parent" board and carried out their own policies in direct violation of specific orders.[22] Ironically, while this action may have weakened the bank, it also gained popular support for this institution, for the "excessive" lending by a number of branches seems to have contributed significantly to the development of industries in some areas.[23]

Jean Wilburn, in her book *Biddle's Bank,* suggests the West and

[19] 3 Stat. 266, ch. 44, § 11 (XIV) (1816).
[20] Two of the offices were discontinued and one office was moved from Middletown to Hartford, Connecticut. Holdsworth and Dewey, *The First and Second Banks of the United States,* pp. 195–96.
[21] *Ibid.,* p. 196.
[22] Mussey, ed., *Reform of the Currency,* Vol. I, No. 2, p. 208.
[23] Catterall, *The Second Bank of the United States,* p. 401. But some writers have suggested that this lending may have been related to efforts by the Bank to obtain support in its recharter battle.

Southwest gained considerably from the existence of the "Second Bank." Professor Wilburn based this conclusion on numerous statements to this effect in the memorials or petitions sent to Congress by state banks, state legislatures, and groups of citizens who were concerned about the rechartering of the Bank. For example, the Louisiana State Bank and the Bank of Orleans memorials noted that the Southwest and West had benefited in the development of their resources by the Bank's lending to planters, merchants, and mechanics.[24] Other memorials noted the great harm that would result from the withdrawal of capital from the West if the bank were not rechartered, for "Westerners on their own individual responsibility . . . cannot get loans from the East; only through the medium of the Bank can they get the use of surplus capital from the East." Furthermore, the Wilburn study argues that the long-accepted idea that the South and Southwest strongly opposed the Bank while New England and the Middle States actively supported it is false.[25]

However, a reviewer has raised some significant questions regarding the Wilburn book. He has suggested that while there are many interesting points discussed in this monograph, "it does not seem that the documentation supports the strength with which the conclusions are drawn."[26] The critic indicates that the author may have replaced one straw man, the rather exhaustive lists of opponents of the Bank who took so long to eliminate it, with another, a small group of people who in an election year could thwart the will of the people.

Regardless of the position in this debate which may be correct, the fact that in 1832 the bill to recharter the Second Bank of the United States passed the House 107 to 85 and the Senate 28 to 20 is not disputed. And, considering Jackson's popularity at the time, it is not surprising that the legislators were unable to muster a two-thirds majority to overcome the President's veto. Thus, this was clearly a victory for Old Hickory, but it may be much less certain than has usually been assumed that it was also a victory for democracy, for if Professor Wilburn is correct: "The least . . . that we have a right to

[24] Wilburn, *Biddle's Bank,* pp. 46–48.

[25] *Ibid.,* p. 85. This is a major change from accepted interpretation of the demise of the Second Bank.

[26] Review of *Biddle's Bank* by Stanley Engerman in *The National Banking Review* (March 1967).

claim is that there was stronger pro-Bank than anti-Bank feeling among the people of the United States at that time."[27]

*Third Bank.*[28]    After the inauguration of William Henry Harrison, an attempt was made to establish a bank following the general pattern of the first two Banks of the United States. The Whig party had a large majority in Congress, and, under the leadership of Henry Clay, its members were determined to organize a national bank. To accomplish this objective, a bill was introduced entitled an "Act to incorporate the subscribers to the Fiscal Bank of the United States," which in many ways resembled the act incorporating the Second Bank of the United States. The bill was passed by both houses of Congress and was sent to the President for signature.

In the interim, Vice President Tyler had become President following the death of Harrison. Considerable controversy developed between the new Whig President and the "Whig Congress," and as a result he vetoed the bank bill. In his veto message Tyler indicated that his chief objection to the bill was that it created "a national bank to operate per se over the Union," and he went on to declare his unalterable opposition to any bank created by Congress with the power to establish branches in the states independently of their consent." The original bill to charter the new bank had included a provision which might have made it satisfactory to Tyler, for it provided that branches could be established by the bank only if the states in which they were to be located would assent. But this bill was smothered in a Senate Committee, which declared in its report that "the Constitutional power of Congress to establish branches anywhere where the interests of the United States called for them must be affirmed and established."[29]

As a result of the Tyler veto of this bill and the emphasis of the

[27] Wilburn, *Biddle's Bank,* pp. 6, 119, 133–34. About one-half of the Senators who voted against the Bank were actually men who were known to be, or had expressed themselves to have been, in favor of the Bank. *Ibid.,* p. 11.

[28] The material in this section is drawn from Knox, *A History of Banking in the United States,* pp. 87–90; and Sumner, "A History of Banking in the United States" in *A History of Banking in All Leading Nations,* Vol. I, pp. 347–50.

[29] Sumner, "A History of Banking in the United States," p. 348. The Clay bill apparently was amended to give state legislatures the right to refuse to give assent, but Congress would have retained the power to override the refusal. *Ibid.*

branch problem in his message, some authorities have concluded the chartering of the new bank hinged directly on this issue. However, even if this were true, the debate as in the past was not based on the merits of branches but on the question of state versus federal sovereignty in the establishment of these branches. Moreover, still another bill was passed by Congress which appeared to be in conformity with Tyler's views on the formation of additional offices; yet, he also vetoed this bill, which casts at least some doubt on the significance of the branch issue. In any event this ended the attempts to establish another "great national bank" in this period.

## STATE BANKS

With the exception of the Bank of North America, the First and Second Banks of the United States, and private banks, all of the banks in operation in this country prior to the passage of the National Currency Act[30] in 1863 were initially state chartered.[31] The first state banks to be established were the Bank of New York and the Bank of Massachusetts, both formed in 1784. Shortly thereafter a number of other state institutions were organized, including: the Maryland Bank (1790); Bank of Providence (1791); Bank of Albany (1792); Bank of South Carolina (1792); Union Bank of Boston (1792); and the Hartford Bank (1792). By 1800 it has been estimated there were 28 state chartered banks in operation, and during the next few decades their number increased rapidly, reaching 208 by 1815 and 329 by 1830.[32]

*Branch banking.* During the early years of banking in the United States, the right of a bank to establish branches was rarely questioned; in fact, it was considered the natural means of providing banking facilities to smaller communities. As early as 1792 both a Boston and a Richmond bank had been given the authority to establish branches; the Bank of Pennsylvania (1793) could establish branches anywhere in the state; and the Vermont State Bank (1806) had a number of additional offices. Branch powers were also enjoyed by banks in about

[30] 12 Stat. 665, ch. 58 (1863).

[31] The Bank of New York also might be considered an exception to this for it operated 7 years (1784–1791) with no charter. White, *Money and Banking,* pp. 272–73.

[32] *Historical Statistics of the United States, 1789–1945,* pp. 254, 261.

a dozen other states, including Indiana and Illinois, both of which forbade the establishment of a bank unless it was a state bank with branches.[33]

An unpublished Federal Reserve Board study prepared several decades ago considered the question of the general attitude toward branching in the early 1800s and it concluded that branches per se were not the object of disapproval.[34] In support of this thesis the researchers at the Board cited a number of standard works on banking history and reviewed the highly successful operations of four outstanding "branch banks" formed between 1834 and 1858—the State Banks of Indiana, Iowa, Missouri, and Ohio.[35] However, it should be emphasized that with the exception of the Bank of Missouri these banks differed considerably from modern branch systems. Their branches typically were locally organized, had their own capital and stockholders, accounted for their own earnings, and paid their own dividends. The actual banking business of the Banks of Indiana, Iowa, and Ohio, for example, was carried on entirely by the individual branches with a central board merely supervising, examining, and controlling.[36] As a result some authorities tend to view the so-called "branches" of these state banks not as branches but as individual units of a state banking system, with the central board performing the function of bank commissioner.[37]

Branch banks were numerous in the South Atlantic and East South Central states prior to the Civil War. Unlike the Banks of Indiana, Iowa, Missouri, and Ohio mentioned above, these institutions rather closely resembled present-day branch systems. The branches had little or no independence, and although on occasion capital may have been assigned to them, they were nonetheless merely offices of a single corporation.[38] Most of these banks with branches were created by special charter which stipulated branches were to be operated at

[33] Chapman and Westerfield, *Branch Banking*, p. 37, and Dewey, *State Banking before the Civil War*, pp. 137–39.

[34] Federal Reserve Board, Committee Reports, "Branch Banking," p. 38.

[35] *Ibid.*, pp. 39–41.

[36] *Ohio Archaeological and Historical Publications* (Columbus: Ohio State Archaeological and Historical Society, 1915), Vol. XXIV, p. 481.

[37] In many ways the branch systems in a number of other states resembled these, including Illinois, Kentucky, Delaware, Tennessee, Vermont, and possibly Michigan.

[38] Federal Reserve Board, Committee Reports, "Branch Banking," p. 44.

designated points, apparently with the objective of making adequate banking facilities available throughout a state.

It is difficult to explain why this "modern form" of branch banking should have been relatively common in the South while it was practically nonexistent in the North. Some authors have concluded that Scottish banking, as described in the writings of Adam Smith, made a particularly strong impression in the southern states;[39] while other writers simply argue that this phenomenon is only another example of the "economic differentiation between North and South." But, regardless of the origin of the southern systems, as in the case of the large midwestern state banks discussed earlier, the Federal Reserve Board in its studies of branch, chain, and group banking found no record of contemporary dissatisfaction with them.[40]

*Banks or no banks.* There seems to have been much less opposition to branching by state banks and by the First and Second Banks of the United States in the first half of the nineteenth century than some writers have suggested. But, while the strength of the antibranch forces may have been exaggerated, the magnitude of the antibank movement has not been overemphasized for there was a great antagonism toward banking in general in this interval.[41] In fact groups opposed to banks gained sufficient popular support in many areas to secure the passage of new, more restrictive banking statutes.[42] In some cases these laws merely limited state participation in banking, but in a surprising number of instances these statutes went so far as to prohibit the chartering of banks. By the mid-1800s, Arkansas, Iowa, Louisiana, and Texas by constitutional amendment had outlawed the establishment of banking corporations, and California and Oregon had disallowed the formation of banks of issue, although banks of discount and deposit were still permitted.[43]

While the critics of banking were associated with laws which re-

---

[39] Bryan, *History of State Banking in Maryland,* pp. 13–14; and Starnes, *Sixty Years of Branch Banking in Virginia,* p. 27.

[40] Federal Reserve Board, Committee Reports, "Branch Banking," p. 46.

[41] Helderman, *National and State Banks,* p. 103.

[42] Andrew Jackson remarked in a letter in 1837: "You know I hate the paper system, and believe all banks to be corruptly administered." *Ibid.,* p. 101.

[43] *Ibid.,* Ch. V discusses this at some length. One study found that in 1852 banking was illegal in nine states. Miller, *Banking Theories in U. S.,* p. 21.

stricted bank chartering, they were also influential in securing the passage of laws which vastly increased bank incorporation. These statutes, which are usually referred to as free banking acts, involved a compromise between two interest groups within the antibank movement—the anticorporation element which viewed virtually all charter and license arrangements as monopolistic[44] and the bullionists who called for the elimination of paper money and banks of issue. To satisfy the former, laissez-faire group, the free banking laws made entry into this industry relatively easy. And, to calm the fears of the latter, hard money advocates, these statutes required that notes issued by the "free banks" had to be secured.[45]

## NATIONAL BANKS

In the long run it was the free banking laws, not the statutes outlawing bank charters, which were to have the greatest impact upon the structure of American banking, for the free bank principle was incorporated in the national banking legislation. Representative E. G. Spaulding is reported[46] to have contributed significantly to the first draft of the bill which in time would become the National Currency Act, and he has indicated that in preparing the bill he used the New York free banking law sent to him from Albany.[47] Surprisingly, neither the New York law, the 1863 National Currency Act,[48] nor the

[44] Historiography has tended to label the Equal Rights (Locofoco) Party in New York in the 1830s as a major contributor to free banking. If this thesis were accurate, it is of some importance that the Locofocos were not concerned with branch or unit banking but with restrictions upon entry. They attacked not only chartered banks but licensed ferry boats since they felt both represented vested interests. [Hershkowitz, "The Locofoco Party of New York," *New York Historical Society Quarterly,* 1962, pp. 309 ff.] However, a recent scholarly study has concluded that although the Locofocos and their radical Democratic allies strenuously agitated against monopoly and called for free banking, "they failed to originate, direct, or monopolize the agitation," and "the 1838 law violated some of their most cherished doctrines of political economy." The author considers the legislation to be basically Whig not Democratic. Benson, *The Concept of Jacksonian Democracy,* pp. 97–104.

[45] Helderman, *National and State Banks,* p. 14.

[46] The original author of the bill is still in doubt. The contributions of Silas Stilwell, Edward Jordan, and Samuel Hooper, among others, may have been very great. See Davis, *The Origin of the National Banking System,* p. 139.

[47] Spaulding, *History of the Legal Tender Paper Money,* p. 12.

[48] The National Currency Act, 12 Stat. 665 (1863).

1864 National Bank Act[49] (which superseded the latter statute), specifically mentioned branch banking; yet it is these three laws which must be given the bulk of the credit (or blame) for the establishment of a unit banking system in the United States.

*National banking law branch provisions.*[50]  There were two main provisions of the National Bank Act which, although they did not mention branches, were interpreted as precluding their establishment by national banks. The first, Section 6 mentioned above, stated that the persons forming the association had to specify *"the place* where its operations of discount and deposit are to be carried on, designating the state, territory, or district, and also the particular county or city, town, or village." [Emphasis added] Apparently this national bank provision was taken directly from a passage which appeared in many of the free banking laws of the states, and these state laws were typically modeled on the New York legislation. The relevant provision in the New York law, in turn, can be traced to the special charters under which all except the earliest banks in this state were created prior to 1838. These documents were drawn uniformly and they specified the place of business, but, according to an unpublished Federal Reserve study, this provision was found in the charters of banks with branches as well as those without any. Similarly, in some states such as Ohio, which had both a state bank with many offices and a free banking statute, the reference to "the place of business" is found in the law, and it applies to branches of the state bank as well as to unit banks.[51]

As early as 1865 this section (§ 6) of the National Bank Act was interpreted by a Comptroller of the Currency as prohibiting the establishment of additional offices by national associations. On August 18, 1865, Comptroller Freeman Clarke notified a state bank officer that the latter's bank would not be able to continue to operate both of its offices if it entered the national system. Clarke's letter indicated that he reached this conclusion because "the sixth Section [of the National Bank Act] requires that they shall specify in their

---

[49] The National Bank Act, 13 Stat. 99 (1864).

[50] Federal Reserve Board, Committee Reports, "Branch Banking," pp. 52–70, contains a lengthy discussion of this topic.

[51] *Ibid.*, p. 55.

organization certificate the particular place (not places) at which their operations of discount and deposit shall be carried out."[52]

In this instance the banking offices were definitely located in two different places—Hagerstown and Williamsport, Maryland. Furthermore, the communications between the Comptroller's office and the bank in question provide no hint that the capital of the bank was "joint and assigned to and used by the mother bank and branches in definite proportions" as required by an 1865 amendment to the National Bank Act[53] if a state bank converting to a national charter was to retain its branches.[54] Thus, since the offices were unquestionably operating in different places and there was no reference to a specific allocation of capital to the additional office, it would appear that the Comptroller had no alternative but to reject the "branch" request.

The second provision of the National Bank Act, which has been interpreted as prohibiting branches, and the one which usually receives greatest emphasis, is found in Section 8 and reads in part: "and its usual business shall be transacted at an *office* or banking house located in the place specified in its organization certificate." [Emphasis added] This passage too seems to have evolved from the New York free banking statute, or more precisely from the wording of an 1848 amendment to this Act, and the factors which led to the inclusion of this provision in the New York law would also appear to explain why it was inserted in the National Bank Act.

---

[52] Answer to letter from D. Weisel of the Washington County Bank, Maryland, from Freeman Clarke, August 18, 1865. Miss Abby Gilbert and Professor J. A. Batchelor kindly called this to my attention, having uncovered it in their research for the Comptroller's office. In regard to the meaning of the word "place" in the National Bank Act, three decades later the Supreme Court in *McCormick* v. *Market Bank* [165 U.S. 538, 549 (1896)] noted the "place" specified in its organization certificate refers to "the city or town in which . . . its office or banking house is located;" thus, the word place alone did not seem to restrict the bank to a single point in a community.

[53] 13 Stat. 469 (1865).

[54] This provision was included in the act which imposed a discriminatory tax on state bank notes and which thereby brought nearly all chartered commercial banks into the national system within a few years. In 1863 there were 1,466 state chartered banks in operation and 66 national banks; in 1864 there were 1,089 state and 467 national; in 1867 there were 272 state and 1,636 national banks. (These data do not include the many private banks which remained in operation.)

Millard Fillmore, Comptroller of New York State at the time the 1848 amendment to the free bank act was passed, summarized its objectives as follows:[55]

A practice had grown up under the general banking law, of establishing banks in obscure places, in remote parts of the state where little or no business was done, with a view of obtaining a circulation merely, and doing no other business. This circulation was then redeemed in New York or Albany by the agents of the bank, at one-half of one per cent discount, and again put in circulation without being returned to the bank, thereby enabling the bank to redeem its own paper at a discount, and then again put in circulation in the same place where it was redeemed. The object of the present law appears to be to break up that practice, and to ensure obedience to its requirements, the legislature has enacted that the president and cashier shall in every report made to this office, state that their business has been transacted at the place required by that act, and that such report shall be verified by their oaths. A strict compliance with this rule will hereafter be exacted from every bank and individual banker subject to its provisions.

Banks in many other states also located their headquarters in rural areas to avoid having to redeem their currency; however, these so-called "wildcat banks" usually had only one office, in contrast to the New York banks with their distant head office and "shaving shop" outlet in the city.[56] The undesirable activities of these remote institutions were considered in Congressional debate prior to the passage of the National Currency Act,[57] and this question was stressed by the Comptroller of the Currency, Hugh McCulloch, in his general regulations issued in 1863. It would seem reasonable to conclude the primary concern in this period was the accessibility of the head office for the redemption of currency—not the status of a bank as a branch or unit institution.[58]

[55] Fillmore, "The Banking System of New York," *Bankers Magazine* (June 1848), p. 744.

[56] For example, see Sumner, *A History of Banking in the United States,* pp. 246, 444–45; Collins, *Rural Banking Reform,* p. 13; and Dewey, *State Banking before the Civil War,* pp. 80, 100–104.

[57] *Congressional Globe,* 37th Cong., 3rd Sess., February 10, 1863, pp. 846–48. At about the time Spaulding is reported to have prepared a draft of the National Currency Act, he strongly criticized the activities of the "shaving shops of New York, Boston, and Philadelphia." Gresham, *The Greenbacks,* p. 56.

[58] McCulloch, "The National Banking Law of 1863," *Bankers Magazine* (July 1863), p. 9. It should also be mentioned that the term "office" may have

Over the years there has been considerable debate regarding a change which was made in the section of the National Currency Act, which appears to have been framed to prevent the organization of "wildcat banks." Section 11 of the 1863 Act provided ". . . and *their* usual business shall be transacted in banking *offices* located at the *places* specified respectively in its certificate of association and not elsewhere." [Emphasis added] In 1864 in Section 8 of the National Bank Act, which corresponds to Section 11 of the earlier law, the following wording was used: ". . . *its* usual business shall be transacted at an *office* or *banking house* located in the *place* specified in its organization certificate." [Emphasis added] Some writers interpret the wording in the Currency Act with its plurals as permissive in regard to branching. Other authors suggest the change to the singular in the National Bank Act has considerable significance since they feel it was made to emphasize that these federally chartered institutions were to have only one office. It is this writer's opinion, after carefully reviewing the material available, that this revision was little more than the correction of a grammatical error. The original mistake might easily have been made if the New York statutes were used in framing the national legislation, which certainly seems to be the case;[59] and the lack of debate concerning both 1863 and 1864 terminology would

---

been used in the nineteenth century to refer to both the head office or headquarters of branch systems and the single office of unit banks. For example, Sumner, in his *History of Banking in the United States* written in the 1890s, in discussing the State Bank of Indiana on page 255 stated: "Ten districts were to be formed with one branch in each . . . the *office* of the bank was to be located in Indianapolis." [Emphasis added]

[59] The bulk of Section 11 of the National Currency Act (1863) appears to have been taken almost verbatim from § 18 of the New York free banking act of 1838. However, the last clause in Section 11 seems to be drawn from an 1848 amendment to the 1838 New York law, which read in part" . . . and the usual business of banking of said *associations,* or individual banker, shall be transacted at the place where such banking association, or individual banker, shall be located agreeable to the location specified in the *certificate* [of association] . . . and not elsewhere." In the 1863 federal law the last clause of Section 11 reads: ". . . and *their* usual business shall be transacted in banking offices located at the places specified respectively in *its certificate* of association, and not elsewhere." The New York law switched from singular references in 1838 to a confused combination of singular and plural references in 1848, and in rewording these sections for the National Currency Act an error in grammar could have been introduced very easily.

lead to the conclusion that the wording was never meant to be anything but *singular*.[60]

Branch banking was mentioned for the first time in the National Bank Act in the 1865 amendment taxing institutions which paid out state bank notes. As noted earlier, this legislation also contained a section[61] permitting state banks with more than one office which met certain capital requirements to convert to national banks and retain their branches. The 1865 branch provision was adopted without any recorded objection and only its author's discussion.[62] Furthermore, the tone of his remarks would lead to the conclusion that there was little or no opposition to branches.

Additional research may uncover information which was overlooked in this study, but from the evidence available this writer would have to conclude, as the Federal Reserve Board's research staff did in the early 1930s, that:[63]

The provisions which effectively prevented branch banking from developing under the national bank legislation, till amended in 1927, had no connection with branching. They originated as measures to control note issue, and were intended, according to the explanation made at the time, to prevent the practice under free banking "of establishing banks in obscure places, in remote parts of the state where little or no business was done, with a view of obtaining a circulation merely, and doing no other business."

The relevance of this conclusion in the 1960s may be seriously questioned, for the power of a national bank to establish branches was denied by the United States Supreme Court, at least by implication, in the *First National Bank in St. Louis* case in 1924,[64] and the McFadden Act and Banking Act of 1933 establish the current authority for national banks to organize branches. But, since a landmark

[60] E. G. Spaulding, who was chairman of the subcommittee of the House Ways and Means Committee in which the bill originated, in a speech before the House of Representatives, January 12, 1863, stated: "This bill in all its essential features is like the free banking law of the State of New York."

[61] 13 Stat. 469 (1865), § 7.

[62] *Congressional Globe*, 38th Cong., 2d Sess., March 3, 1865, pp. 1281 ff.

[63] Federal Reserve Board, Committee Reports, "Branch Banking," pp. 65–66. Chapman and Westerfield [*Branch Banking*] and Southworth [*Branch Banking in the United States*] reach the same conclusions.

[64] *First National Bank in St. Louis* v. *State of Missouri*, 263 U.S. 640, 657–58 (1924).

Supreme Court decision relating to the branching powers of federally chartered banks was handed down as recently as December 1966,[65] and because a number of similar actions are still being tried in the courts, it would seem that not only this brief survey but a much more thorough investigation of this subject is warranted.

*Effect on branch bank development.* The 1865 amendment to the National Bank Act brought nearly all state *chartered* commercial banks into the national system. However, the major "branch" institutions of the Midwest, whose offices functioned much more like unit banks than branches, did not each join as a branch system; instead apparently the individual "branches" obtained federal charters and entered as unit banks. In the South, where multiple-office banking in the modern sense was primarily concentrated, a number of the banks were destroyed by the Civil War and the carpetbaggers; others were dissolved by state authorities; and still others became national associations as unit rather than branch banks. This last action, not only by the southern banks but by other "real branch" systems, was encouraged by the provision in the 1865 legislation which specified that a definite allocation of capital had to be made to each branch, and by the requirement that the circulation redeemable at each branch was to be regulated by the amount of capital assigned to it. In the North and East, the banks which were in operation when the free banking laws were passed usually found it was to their advantage to give up their existing charters and to obtain charters under the new laws. Furthermore, it was in these areas that free banking was strongest and branch banking had nearly disappeared before the national banks began operation.[66]

Of course, free banking was not concentrated exclusively in the North and East. In fact, in the quarter century between the passage of the 1838 New York legislation and the formation of the national banking system, free banking had become extremely popular through-

[65] *First National Bank of Logan* v. *Walker Bank and Trust Company; First Security Bank of Utah* v. *Commercial Security Bank;* and *James J. Saxon, Comptroller of the Currency* v. *Commercial Security Bank,* 385 U.S. 252 (1966).

[66] Southworth, *Branch Banking in the United States,* pp. 13–14.

out the nation. Many hypotheses are offered to explain its growth:[67] (1) Its chartering requirements were not only democratic, permitting relatively free entry into the field, but they appear to have been ideally suited for a period characterized by individual enterprise and opposition to monopoly. (2) These laws made the formation of new banks relatively easy at a time when travel and communications problems made the operation of large (or merely widespread) branch systems extremely difficult. (Thus, freedom of entry into the industry was granted when any economies of scale which might have been enjoyed by large banks were probably at a minimum.[68] (3) The same conditions which adversely affected the functioning of branch banks (poor transportation, etc.) encouraged a spirit of parochialism in the towns and forced communities to be as self-sufficient as possible; hence, local banks were not only desirable but necessary.

On the other hand, while the above factors may help explain why large branch systems were eliminated with the growth of free banking, it would be fair to ask what happened to limited branching, since most of the points made are applicable only to inter-city and not to intra-city branches. But this ignores the fact that the branches operated before the Civil War were almost without exception located outside the town in which their head office was established,[69] and the great development of branches within cities did not come until after 1900.

THE BRANCH BANKING QUESTION

From the early 1860s to the 1890s there was almost no mention of branch banking in Congressional debates[70] and very little discussion of the subject in general.[71] in 1887 and 1888 the Comptroller of the Currency did recommend that national banks be allowed to establish

[67] Pontecorvo, in his "Patterns of Ownership of Commercial Banks" [Bankers Magazine (Winter 1966), p. 30], and Chapman and Westerfield, in their book on Branch Banking, [p. 46] have some interesting thoughts on the evolution of unit banking.

[68] There may have even been diseconomies of scale in many cases.

[69] Federal Reserve Board, Committee Reports, "Branch Banking," p. 69.

[70] This conclusion is found in a number of standard works, such as Chapman and Westerfield, Branch Banking, p. 62.

[71] One of the earliest was Dunbar's article on "The Bank Note Question" in the Quarterly Journal of Economics (October 1892), pp. 55–77.

additional offices with limited functions in the head-office city, but apparently this suggestion was given little consideration.[72] However, during the next few years branch banking received much more attention because of a growing concern with providing safe and adequate banking facilities for small towns, and frequent references to multiple-office banks could be noted in the statements of leading public officials. In 1895 both Secretary of the Treasury Carlisle and President Cleveland suggested that branching by national banks be permitted.[73] Similar comments were made in succeeding years by other important members of the executive branch of government, by speakers at American Bankers Association (ABA) conventions, and by a small number of contributors to scholarly journals.

Probably the most surprising factor to the present-day researcher is not that branch banking was advocated but that papers supporting multiple-office systems could be presented at sessions of the ABA and at other meetings with little or no criticism of them in the discussions which followed. In fact, the first major diatribe in opposition to branch banks this writer has been able to uncover was found in an 1898 minority report accompanying a banking bill. It would seem that the main elements in this bank legislation were the "asset currency"[74] and branch provisions which followed recommendations made by the Indianapolis Monetary Commission,[75] and the minority statement attacked the bill on both points. In regard to branch banking in particular, it stressed the great service the local bank performs for its community, and warned: ". . . Our choice must be made between one great 'United States Bank' with ten thousand branches, and on the other hand ten thousand independent banks."[76]

Comptroller of the Currency Dawes, in his *Annual Report* in 1898, voiced strong opposition to the "asset currency" provisions in this bill

[72] Comptroller of the Currency, 25th *Annual Report,* 1887, pp. 4, 17, 26; and 26th *Annual Report,* 1888, p. 4.

[73] Federal Reserve Board, Committee Reports, "Branch Banking," pp. 73–76.

[74] "Asset currency" refers to issuing bank notes which have a first lien against the general assets of banks. U. S. Congress, House, Report No. 1575, Part I, *Strengthening the Public Credit,* 1898, p. 30.

[75] *Report of the Monetary Commission of the Indianapolis Convention,* pp. 66, 67, and 71.

[76] U. S. Congress, House, Report No. 1575, Part 2, *To Secure to the People a Sound Currency,* 1898, pp. 44–46.

and gave only qualified approval to the branch provisions. In regard to branching, Dawes supported the formation of branches in communities of 2,000 inhabitants or less but he argued against large-scale branching.[77] Apparently the Comptroller's opposition was sufficiently important to delay any action on the bill, and ultimately it was withdrawn from the calendar. The following year, 1899, Dawes did not even mention the branch banking provisions in the 1898 bill in presenting further recommendations as to how the banking needs of the small communities could best be met. Instead of suggesting that branches be authorized for this purpose, he advised that the capital requirements of national banks which were to be located in towns with only a few thousand in population be reduced. As a result, a provision permitting the establishment of new national banks with capital stock of only 25 thousand dollars in communities of 3,000 inhabitants or less was included in the Gold Standard Act passed March 14, 1900,[78] and thus one of the strongest arguments in support of branch banks at the time—the need for banking facilities in rural areas—was substantially weakened.

Despite the passage of the 1900 legislation, a number of bills advocating branch banking remained before Congress, and there was considerable and rather vehement discussion concerning them in 1900 and 1902. However, by the following year support for this legislation had nearly vanished, except for occasional academic mention of the question.[79] This no doubt occurred because those people who supported branch banking were by and large individuals who advocated currency reform, and their interest in multiple-office banking had arisen primarily because it appeared to fit in well with their plans for improving the money supply. But, when very serious resistance to branching developed, this cause was dropped and an alternative route to the currency reform goal was sought.

So little attention was paid to branching thereafter that it was not even considered in the National Monetary Commission's recommen-

---

[77] Comptroller of the Currency, 36th *Annual Report,* 1898, p. xi. Comptroller Eckels in 1896 requested that the National Bank Act be amended to permit national banks "to establish branch banks in towns and villages where no national bank is established and where the population does not exceed 1,000 inhabitants." Comptroller of the Currency, 34th *Annual Report,* 1896, p. 100.

[78] 31 Stat. 45, 48 (1900).

[79] Federal Reserve Board, Committee Reports, "Branch Banking," p. 94.

dations in 1911.[80] Nevertheless, it should be kept in mind that between the early 1890s and the date of the Commission's report the number of banks in the United States had risen from less than 10,000 to over 25,000. Many of the small communities, which the proponents of branching had argued were in need of banking service, now apparently had their own banks. Furthermore, with the establishment of these small banks, not only was the need for branches reduced but a major force which would resist any future expansion of branching was being developed.

Thus, while this early branch banking movement lost its momentum after having accomplished very little, the developments associated with it were extremely important from the viewpoint of banking structure. In contrast to the 1800s, when criticism was directed primarily toward banks in general or paper money, by the early 1900s the attacks were clearly aimed at branch banking. Supporters of single-office banks, such as the former Comptroller of the Currency Charles G. Dawes, by 1902 had established the arguments of the "unit banker" which were to be heard throughout the twentieth century:[81]

Most of the arguments for branch banking assume that a community can be as well served by an agent acting at a distance under delegated authority as by an independent local institution possessing full authority and power to pass upon local questions. Now the record of corporation development in the United States indicates that the process of centralization and consolidation which is going on, is accompanied by the absorption into head offices of an increasing number of functions formerly exercised by independent institution[s]. . . . The tendency would be to curtail the number of small loans where personality and character are elements in the consideration of loan applications by the local banker. . . . The man, in other words, who goes to work in fields of undeveloped resources, is the very one whose credit is to be curtailed and his chance to found or increase a business injured by the branch banking system. In this country we are leading the world commercially, because under our law and government we have made it our special effort to protect the rights, interests, and opportunities of the individual and of the small enterprise.

On the other side, advocates of branch banking such as Dawes'

[80] National Monetary Commission, *Report of the Commission,* Vol. VII, January 9, 1912.

[81] "Proceedings of the American Bankers Association 28th Annual Convention," *Commercial and Financial Chronicle,* Supplement, 1902, November 22, 1902, p. 62.

successor as Comptroller, William B. Ridgely, had also presented by 1902 the basic arguments for multiple-office banks:[82]

I believe in branch banking. Theoretically, it is the best system, as it is more economical, more efficient, will serve its customers better, and the organization can be such as to secure in most respects better management. Owing to co-operation between its branches, it can be made safer than any system of independent banks. If I were outlining a new system for a country in which there was none, I would adopt this system, and I regret that it was not adopted or permitted in the beginning of the National Banking System. I believe the National Banks would be stronger and better today if branches had been permitted and the system had been developed with the branch feature an essential part of it.

And, Professor H. Parker Willis, who was later to assist Carter Glass in drafting some of the most important banking legislation of this century remarked:[83]

Country bankers foresee danger to themselves in the possibility of inroads upon their fields of effort, should the larger institutions of the cities be permitted to establish branches and compete with them in their home market on equal terms. They know that such a policy would result in a reduction of interest rates in their towns and that their chances for the profitable use of their funds might thereby be somewhat diminished unless they were prepared to go as far as their new rivals in serving customers cheaply. The usual complaint against such proposals is that they would result in building up a money power which would crush the small banks out of existence. A more absurd reversal of the actual facts in the case could scarcely be imagined. What the establishment of branches would actually do would be to destroy the local money power which now practically stifles many forms of legitimate industry by the pressure of excessive interest rates, and by other even less justifiable means.

Thus, although the major conflict over branching did not develop for nearly two decades, by the early 1900s the battle lines were drawn in a controversy which continues to the present time.

## GROWTH OF UNIT AND BRANCH BANKING

Both unit and branch banking in the United States have experienced many changes since 1900, but their individual development has

[82] *Ibid.*, p. 59.
[83] Willis, "The Demand for Centralized Banking," *Sound Currency* (March 1902), pp. 23–24.

differed considerably in this period. During the first two decades of this century, the number of unit banks grew tremendously while branch banking registered only modest increases (in absolute terms). However, after 1921 the pattern was far different, for the number of unit banks began a steady decline which has continued to the present time. On the other hand, it was not until the late 1920s that a substantial reduction in the number of multiple-office banks occurred, and the decline lasted only from 1928 through 1934. Since then branch bank expansion has progressed without interruption for over thirty years.

The changing roles of unit and branch banks in the American financial system between 1900 and 1967 are examined in this section. Initially, the general experience of both forms of bank organization is reviewed briefly and then the growth of intracity and intercity or "outside the city" branching are each analyzed in some detail.

GENERAL DEVELOPMENT

*1900–1935.* In 1900 the United States was definitely a unit banking nation, for less than 2 percent of the offices and loans and investments of all banks were controlled by branch institutions. (See Table 2.1) But during the next two decades there was a substantial growth in branch assets, and by 1920 multiple-office (branch) banks held nearly 15 percent of the total loans and investments of all commercial banks. In this same interval the number of branches expanded tremendously; yet, the ratio of the number of branch offices to total offices remained relatively small, for on the average about 1,000 new banks were chartered each year between 1900 and 1920. This pattern changed considerably between 1920 and 1935, as the number of commercial banks was reduced by roughly one-half, from 30,300 to 15,500, and the number of branches rose by nearly 2,000. As a result, by the mid-1930s over one-fifth of all banking offices were affiliated with multiple-office institutions, and the branch bank had become the dominant form of bank organization in terms of total assets, controlling more than one-half of all loans and investments of commercial banks in the United States.

The substantial decrease in the number of banks between 1920 and 1935 resulted primarily from the 15,000 bank suspensions in this fifteen-year span. But, it is often argued that the general growth of branching in this period also contributed substantially to the decline

TABLE 2.1.   COMMERCIAL BANK OFFICES IN THE UNITED STATES, 1900–1966[a]

| Year[b] | Unit Banks | Branch Banks | Total Number of Banks | of Branches[c] | Total Banking Offices Number | Percent Branch Bank Offices[d] |
|---|---|---|---|---|---|---|
| 1900 | 12,340 | 87 | 12,427 | 119 | 12,546 | 1.6 |
| 1905 | 17,956 | 196 | 18,152 | 350 | 18,502 | 3.0 |
| 1910 | 24,222 | 292 | 24,514 | 548 | 25,062 | 3.4 |
| 1915 | 26,993 | 397 | 27,390 | 785 | 28,175 | 4.2 |
| 1920 | 29,761 | 530 | 30,291 | 1,281 | 31,572 | 5.7 |
| 1925 | 27,722 | 720 | 28,442 | 2,525 | 30,967 | 10.5 |
| 1930 | 22,928 | 751 | 23,679 | 3,522 | 27,201 | 15.7 |
| 1935 | 14,666 | 822 | 15,488 | 3,156 | 18,644 | 21.3 |
| 1940 | 13,575 | 959 | 14,534 | 3,531 | 18,065 | 24.9 |
| 1945 | 13,110 | 1,016 | 14,126 | 3,723 | 17,849 | 26.6 |
| 1950 | 12,905 | 1,241 | 14,146 | 4,721 | 18,867 | 31.6 |
| 1955 | 12,121 | 1,659 | 13,780 | 6,710 | 20,490 | 40.8 |
| 1960 | 11,143 | 2,329 | 13,472 | 10,216 | 23,688 | 53.0 |
| 1965 | 10,664 | 3,140 | 13,804 | 15,486 | 29,290 | 63.6 |
| 1966 | 10,457 | 3,313 | 13,770 | 16,648 | 30,418 | 65.6 |

[a] Not all these figures correspond to those in Tables 4.1 and 4.2, primarily because the statistics for more recent years include the "Total United States *and* Other Areas" in the Chapter 4 Tables. They include U. S. possessions and territories in the Pacific and the Panama Canal Zone which are usually excluded from the Federal Reserve Board data. In addition, 4.1 and 4.2 include facilities at military and other government establishments while this table does not. Some differences over the years also stem from agency definitions of banks, etc. since Tables 2.1 and 2.2 are Federal Reserve data and Tables 4.1 and 4.2 are FDIC data.

[b] Data prior to 1935 are not for any uniform month, but from 1935 to 1966 December statistics were consistently available.

[c] Excludes facilities at military and other government establishments; 224 in 1945; 122 in 1950; 213 in 1955; 267 in 1960; 270 in 1965; and 260 in 1966.

[d] Includes head offices.

*Sources: Historical Statistics of the United States: Colonial Times to* 1957, pp. 631–35; *Federal Reserve Bulletin;* and Federal Reserve Board. The above data for the current year usually appear in the February and April issues of the *Federal Reserve Bulletin.*

in the number of operating banks. This conclusion would appear to be rather simple to defend, for there were roughly 7,000 commercial bank mergers[84] in this interval, and a large number of these firms

[84] Throughout this study the terms merger, consolidation, absorption, and acquisition will be used interchangeably unless otherwise noted.

became branches of multiple-office institutions. Nevertheless, after an extensive study of banking developments in the 1920s and early 1930s, the Federal Deposit Insurance Corporation reported:[85]

Expansion of branch banking systems was not a primary force in these bank absorptions. The number of banks absorbed was much larger than the increase in the number of branches operated and a relatively small proportion of the absorptions occurred in the same States as most of the increase in branches. Moreover, during most of the period from 1920 to 1934, the number of absorptions appears to have been related to the number of suspensions. Both tended to rise during the 1920's and both increased with the onset of the depression, though absorptions dropped back to earlier levels as the depression continued. Also, the majority of the absorptions occurred in the same States as the majority of suspensions. Many, if not most, of the absorption transactions of that period appear to have been alternatives either to failure or to voluntary liquidation. To the extent that this was true, bank absorptions were not a direct cause of decline in the number of banks but, instead, only the means by which many banks, which would have ceased business in any event happen to have left the banking scene.

Thus, in analyzing the reasons behind developments in bank structure, great care must be taken to avoid confusing the factors which merely facilitate a given change, such as branch banking in this instance, with those that initiate it.

*1935–1966.* The reorganization of the banking structure which began in the depression was largely completed by the mid-1930s. Nevertheless, between 1935 and 1950 the American financial system continued to shift toward multiple-office institutions as the number of unit banks declined slowly to about 13,000 and the number of branch bank offices (including head offices) advanced from 4,000 to over 6,000. But, surprisingly, the loans and investments of branch institutions as a percentage of the total for all commercial banks fell from 54 percent to about 52 percent, despite the increase of more than 2,000 in the number of branch offices. This phenomenon can probably be explained by the general decline in the market shares of the largest banks and expansion of the market shares of the smaller banks during World War II.[86]

[85] *FDIC Annual Report* for the year ended December 31, 1960, p. 34.

[86] Between 1940–1945 the share of total deposits held by the 100 largest banks fell from 57 to 48 percent and the share held by banks ranking 301 and over rose from 31 to 38 percent. *American Banker,* March 21, 1962, p. 53.

From 1950 through 1966 the number of commercial banking offices in the United States expanded from less than 19,000 to over 30,400; yet there were only a few years during this period in which a net gain was registered in the number of banks in operation. On balance, during these sixteen years, the number of unit commercial banks declined by approximately 2,500 to 10,457 while the number of banks maintaining branches rose from 1,241 to 3,313 and the number of branches increased from 4,721 to 16,648. Although recent data are not available, it would seem reasonable to estimate that the loans and investments of branch institutions currently amount to approximately 70 percent[87] of the total of these assets for all commercial banks. Thus, by the mid-1960s both the assets of branch banks and the number of branch bank offices were about double those of unit banks. Therefore, this country's unit banking system would perhaps better be termed a "local banking system," emphasizing the limited areas served by most banks rather than the form of bank organization.

INTRACITY BRANCHING

In 1860 there were only nine places[88] in the United States with a population of 100 thousand or more, but by the turn of the century there were 38. Yet, in 1900 there were only 25 head-office-city branches in this country—a figure which a person exposed to the branch banking of the 1960s in many states may find incredible. Furthermore, the paucity of branches would not appear to have been attributable to branch restrictions, for a survey of banking laws prepared by the Comptroller of the Currency in 1895 revealed that branching was permitted in twenty states, and in a second survey in 1902 the findings were much the same. Thus, it would seem reasonable to assume that the type of banking engaged in at the time, which today would probably be classified primarily as wholesale banking, simply did not require more than one outlet in a given community.

[87] Loan and investment data for branch banks at various times may be found in *Historical Statistics of the United States: Colonial Times to 1957*, p. 636; and in U. S. Congress, House, Staff Report on *Banking Concentration and Small Business*, 1960, p. 14. The current figure was estimated from the FDIC *National Summary of Accounts and Deposits*, June 30, 1966, which showed branch banks held about 70 percent of all commercial bank deposits.

[88] The term "place" is used here in the technical sense (that is, as used in *U. S. Census of Population*), not as a colloquial expression.

After 1900 the status of intracity branching changed very rapidly. (See Table 2.2) That year only 25 of 119 commercial bank branches in operation were located within the head-office city, but by 1910 intracity branches comprised nearly one-half of the 548 branch offices, and by the mid-1920s this figure had risen to over two-thirds of the 2,525 branches then in existence.[89] This growth was concentrated primarily in a handful of states: Massachusetts, Michigan, New York, Ohio, and Pennsylvania. The pattern of urban branching development was very similar in each state. It began about 1900, showed a steady subsequent growth, involved little controversy, and was typically limited to a single city.

While it is not difficult to cite a number of variables which probably contributed to this expansion of intracity branching, it is almost impossible to rank them according to their importance. Nevertheless, it would seem at least to this writer that high on any list of contributing causes would have to be the urbanization of America and the tremendous expansion of the nonfarm household as both a potential and an actual source of funds for the commercial bank.[90] Numerous other developments, many of which are directly related to the above, might be noted which stimulated the commercial banks' interest in branching in the early decades of this century, such as: the rising household income; the decline of the circulation function and the continued growth of deposit banking; the lower reserve requirements against time deposits of member banks under the Federal Reserve Act and of additional nonmember banks under state law after 1913;[91] the increase in the size of many of the banks' business customers and the banks' natural desire to emulate this growth; and very importantly, even four or five decades ago, the congestion of traffic in large cities due to the use of the automobile for local transportation.[92]

[89] This growth was particularly concentrated in some of the large cities. See Federal Reserve Board, Committee Reports, "Branch Banking," pp. 99–100.

[90] Nonfarm households supplied 22 percent, 30 percent, and 36 percent of operating commercial bank funds in 1900, 1912, and 1929, respectively. There was little percentage change in the use of bank funds by this sector until the 1920s. Goldsmith, *Financial Intermediaries in the American Economy since 1900*, p. 159.

[91] *The Banking Situation in the United States*, pp. 104–105.

[92] Collins, *Rural Banking Reform*, p. 88. By 1916 automobile output passed the 1.5 million mark; and the Comptroller of the Currency in his 62nd *Annual Report* [1924, p. 4] notes: "In certain of the larger cities of the United States

TABLE 2.2. LOCATION OF COMMERCIAL BANKING OFFICES IN THE UNITED STATES, 1900–1966[a]

| Year | All Commercial Banks[b] | Banks Maintaining Branches | | | Number of Branches[c] | Branch Banks / Location of Offices (including head offices) | | |
|---|---|---|---|---|---|---|---|---|
| | | Total | National | State | | Head Office City (A) | Outside Head Office City (B) | % (B/A) |
| 1900 | 12,427 | 87 | 5 | 82 | 119 | 112 | 94 | 83.9 |
| 1905 | 18,152 | 196 | 5 | 191 | 350 | 331 | 215 | 64.9 |
| 1910 | 24,514 | 292 | 9 | 283 | 548 | 563 | 277 | 49.2 |
| 1915 | 27,390 | 397 | 12 | 385 | 785 | 832 | 350 | 42.0 |
| 1920 | 30,291 | 530 | 21 | 509 | 1,281 | 1,303 | 508 | 39.0 |
| 1925 | 28,442 | 720 | 130 | 590 | 2,525 | 2,445 | 800 | 32.7 |
| 1930 | 23,679 | 751 | 166 | 585 | 3,522 | 3,140 | 1,133 | 36.0 |
| 1935[d] | 15,488 | 822 | 181 | 641 | 3,156 | 2,470 | 1,508 | 61.0 |
| 1940[d] | 14,534 | 959 | 200 | 759 | 3,531 | 2,562 | 1,928 | 75.2 |
| 1945[d] | 14,126 | 1,016 | 222 | 794 | 3,723 | 2,631 | 2,108 | 80.1 |
| 1950 | 14,146 | 1,241 | 324 | 917 | 4,721 | 3,276 | 2,686 | 82.0 |
| 1955 | 13,780 | 1,659 | 543 | 1,116 | 6,710 | 4,450 | 3,919 | 88.0 |
| 1960 | 13,472 | 2,329 | 905 | 1,424 | 10,216 | 6,283 | 6,262 | 99.7 |
| 1965 | 13,804 | 3,140 | 1,331 | 1,809 | 15,486 | 8,767 | 9,859 | 112.5 |
| 1966 | 13,770 | 3,313 | 1,406 | 1,907 | 16,648 | 9,351 | 10,610 | 113.5 |

[a] These data do not all correspond with those found in Tables 4.1 and 4.2. For an explanation see Table 2.1.

[b] Data from 1935 to 1966 are for the year end; earlier data are not as of any uniform month.

[c] Facilities excluded.

[d] Some data concerning the location of offices had to be estimated; however, the possible error at a maximum would be under 1 percent of the total offices in any year.

Sources: Historical Statistics of the United States: Colonial Times to 1957, p. 635; Federal Reserve Bulletins: October 1938, p. 880; May 1941, pp. 460–61; June 1946, pp. 672–73; May 1951, pp. 586–87; April 1956, pp. 398–99; April 1961, pp. 486–87; April 1966, pp. 600–601; and Federal Reserve Board. The data for the current year usually appear in the April issue of the Federal Reserve Bulletin.

The Federal Reserve Board in its study of branch, chain, and group banking in the 1930s described the intracity branch development as follows: "In New York as elsewhere it was proved by the banks possessing branches that the business of small customers was profitable, if properly cultivated and handled, and eventually some of the typical Wall Street banks decided also to go into this wider market which existed among the great mass of individuals, employees, and tradesmen of small means."[93] Thus, in a very broad sense one might draw something of a parallel between the growth of urban branch banks and the development of mass distribution through chain stores of standard, low-priced merchandise or the tendency of large firms in other industries to diversify, thereby participating in several different customer markets at the same time.

The importance of the relatively small customer to the commercial bank by the early 1900s should not be underestimated. One report revealed that eight million of the eleven million checking deposits in this country in 1909 had balances of less than 500 dollars each, and they represented mostly personal and farm accounts.[94] One of the researchers studying this phenomenon concluded that the habit of paying by check had probably reached down in some measure to all economic classes of the community whose income was 1,000 dollars or more, provided they were other than what is classified as manual laborers.[95]

In the 1920s intracity branching was further stimulated by several actions taken by the federal government. The first, in 1922, involved an administrative ruling by the Comptroller of the Currency which permitted national banks to open additional offices in the home-office city for the accommodation of customers in making deposits and

---

topographical conditions and changes in city structure, lack of parking facilities, etc., have made it difficult for outlying customers of a bank to reach the banking house."

[93] Federal Reserve Board, Committee Reports, "Branch Banking," p. 110. With the growth of population, neighborhood business increased and tradesmen in Cleveland in 1900, for example, set up or expanded community shops which needed banking services. Jollie, *On the Grow with Cleveland,* p. 16. Also see New York State Superintendent of Banks, *Annual Report* for the fiscal year 1905–1906, p. xxx.

[94] Trescott, *Financing American Enterprise,* p. 145.

[95] *Ibid.* This work includes the quotation from the original study.

cashing checks *if* state banks could establish intracity branches in the same community. The second was the passage of the McFadden Act in February 1927, which allowed a national bank to establish branches in its home-office city if branches were permitted there by state law. No doubt these changes strongly influenced branch development between 1920 and 1930, for the number of intracity branches (excluding head offices) rose from 773 to 2,389, while the number of branches outside the head-office city increased from 508 to 1,133. However, by the late 1920s, with the collapse of rural banking, the growth of "outside" branches began to exceed the expansion of "inside" branches despite the above-mentioned changes in regulation and legislation, and in the early 1930s the number of intracity branches declined markedly and remained at this relatively low level for over two decades until the postwar branch banking movement began.

## INTERCITY ("OUTSIDE") BRANCHING

The lack of interest in establishing intercity branches as late as the 1890s is not difficult to explain, for many of the arguments presented in the discussion of the disappearance of branch banking by the mid-1860s were as applicable three decades later. This is well-illustrated by Frederick Lewis Allen's description of American life about 1900:[96]

It is hard for us today to realize how very widely communities were separated from one another when they depended for transportation wholly on the railroad and the horse and wagon—and when telephones were still scarce, and radios non-existent. A town which was not situated on a railroad was really remote. A farmer who lived five miles outside the county seat made something of an event of hitching up and taking the family to town for a Saturday afternoon's shopping. (His grandchildren make the run in a casual ten minutes, and think nothing of it.) A trip to see friends ten miles away was likely to be an all-day expedition, for the horse had to be given a chance to rest and be fed. No wonder that each region, each town, each farm was far more dependent upon its own resources—its own produce, social contacts, amusements—than in later years. For in terms of travel and communication the United States was a very big country indeed.

[96] Allen, *The Big Change*, p. 8.

Moreover, some "intercity branches" (this term as used in this chapter unfortunately had to include branches limited to the immediate vicinity of the head office as well as distant branches because of a lack of detailed branch location data in these early periods) faced many problems which intracity systems or even metropolitan area branches usually did not encounter. For example, the markets served by urban and suburban branches were more compact; the banks which initiated the expansion were typically larger; competition among the city banks was often already severe and there was less fear of disturbing the status quo; and the opposition to "absentee management" carried less weight when a bank was branching only within its own locality.[97]

Despite these many obstacles, intercity branching did expand during the first quarter of the twentieth century, but it grew at a much slower pace than intracity branching. The development of intercity branches was particularly advanced in California, and they existed also in Georgia, Louisiana, Maine, Maryland, North Carolina, South Carolina, Tennessee, and Virginia. However, in contrast to the relatively large California systems, nearly all of the branch institutions in the other states cited were limited to less than a half dozen branches.[98]

The importance of intercity branching began to increase quite substantially by the mid-1920s. The ratio of intercity branches to total branches had fallen steadily from 1900 to 1925, but between 1925 and 1930 the trend was reversed, and from that time to the present the growth of multiple-office banking has been dominated by branches located outside the head-office city. There are many possible explanations for this growth of intercity or suburban branches. Until 1920 the central city usually grew much more rapidly than the surrounding area. Since then, however, this trend has been reversed; and the cities have grown much less rapidly than the nation as a whole, and only about one-third as fast as their own suburban areas.[99] This general population growth and movement out of the city was accompanied by a substantial shift from so-called wholesale banking to retail banking, and branches were established in large numbers as

[97] Federal Reserve Board, Committee Reports, "Branch Banking," p. 111. See Chapman and Westerfield, *Branch Banking,* for a detailed discussion of the growth of California branching.
[98] *Ibid.,* pp. 111–12.
[99] Davis and Hughes, *American Economic History,* p. 293.

banks attempted to follow their customers or to acquire new customers in these seemingly very profitable lines. One might add that the
people moving to the suburbs often preferred to do business with
branches of city banks which were known to them rather than with
independent suburban banks.[100]

In terms of aggregate statistics, it would seem that there was very
little change in the status of branch banking in the early 1930s, for the
number of branch banks increased by only about one-tenth, while the
number of branches declined by a similar amount. However, these
modest differences in branch data do not reveal a very important shift
from intracity to intercity or suburban branching which was in progress at the time. In a five-year period, the number of branches
located in the head-office city declined by about 750 while the number
of "outside" branches rose by 375. The reduction of urban branches
between 1930 and 1935 in large part reflected the vast increase in city
bank suspensions in this period, while the expansion of branch systems into wider areas could be traced to the weakness of small rural
banks. The expansion of "outside" branches was also facilitated by
changes in federal law in the Banking Act of 1933 and by amendments to the laws of at least fifteen states in this interval
(1930–1935) which broadened branch powers for many institutions.

Although there was a modest increase in the number of branches
located both inside and outside the head-office city between 1935 and
1950, the major branch banking movement of recent years did not get
underway until the early 1950s. By that time the continued growth of
income and population and the migration into the rapidly growing
suburbs had encouraged many banks to establish *de novo* branches or
to merge with institutions already in operation on the outskirts of
cities. A study published several years ago in the *Federal Reserve
Bulletin* described this growth as follows:[101]

In the areas surrounding urban centers in particular there has been a great
expansion both in business activity and in the demand for checking and
consumer loan services, some by people who only a few years ago might
not have been customers of banks. Therefore, city banks seeking these

---

[100] U. S. Congress, Senate, *Recent Developments in the Structure of Banking*,
1962, p. 3.
[101] "Changes in Banking Structure," *Federal Reserve Bulletin* (September
1963), p. 1192.

customers have sought to establish new banks or to merge with banks in the suburbs, when permitted by law.

The development of metropolitan area branches is well-illustrated by the more detailed data concerning branch locations which has been made available in recent years. From shortly after the end of World War II through 1951 the percentages of total branch offices which were located in the head-office city and head-office county (excluding the city) remained relatively stable at about 43 percent and 26 percent respectively. However, since 1951 the head-office city's share of branch offices has declined to about 36 percent at the end of 1966 while the head-office county's share has risen to over 32 percent. Branches located outside the head-office county have accounted for 31 or 32 percent of all branch offices throughout the postwar period, with 14 to 15 percent designated as branches in contiguous counties and all other branches accounting for about 17 percent.

Thus, the growth of "outside" branching as a percentage of all commercial bank branches during the past two decades has been concentrated almost exclusively within the head-office county. And, ironically, when one considers the violent opposition to this expansion of branching today, some of the most bitter opponents of multiple-office banking in the past might not have even classified these localized systems as branch banks.[102] Nevertheless, those who strongly support unit banking argue:[103]

> The time to stop a trend is in its early day. Branch banking in a small way doesn't look particularly obnoxious. Branching confined to a city isn't offensive. Branching within a county or contiguous counties has no appearance of monopolistic danger. However, these small steps are, we believe, in the wrong direction.

Naturally, this statement reflects a fear which is not uncommon among unit bankers that any expansion of branching may in time lead to the elimination of the small bank and the establishment of "a few giant financial institutions with subsidiaries scattered nationwide."

To prevent the development of "a monolithic banking structure," a leader of the Independent Bankers Association has suggested to his members that they "try to secure most protective legislation" and "not

[102] See, for example, Comptroller of the Currency, 62d *Annual Report,* 1924, p. 3.
[103] *Independent Banking: An American Ideal,* p. 8.

permit any erosion in the statutes now protecting our old system of banking."[104] At best this is only a short-run solution or perhaps no solution at all, for such legislation merely impedes the growth of branch banking—it does not solve the many basic problems which appear to have contributed to the decline of the unit bank in recent years. Moreover, regardless of the political pressure exerted by the supporters of the single-office bank, in the longer run the banking system of the United States is unlikely to return to unit banking and it will surely not maintain the status quo; thus, time would seem to be on the side of the branch banker. But, although branching is very likely to continue to expand in the future, the history of American banking would seem to suggest there is little or no danger that the growth of individual multiple-office institutions will not be regional instead of national; and the possibility of the eventual establishment of a nationwide "money monopoly" or oligopoly is very remote indeed.

## BRANCH BANK OPERATIONS[105]

In discussing the operations of branch banks, it would be most convenient to contrast local branching with branch systems which serve very wide areas. But, unfortunately, for over a century America has had little general experience with even relatively broad branching. In fact, of the 2,797 commercial bank branches located in counties which were noncontiguous to the head-office county at the end of 1966, four-fifths of them were found in only six states—three adjoining West Coast States: California (47%), Oregon (5%), and Washington (4%), and three adjacent East Coast states: North Carolina (14%), South Carolina (5%), and Virginia (5%). On the other hand, there were 33 states which had only ten branches or less in this noncontiguous county category.[106]

Of course, other attributes, such as deposit size or number of

[104] *Ibid.,* p. 9. The comment was made by Ben DuBois.

[105] Federal Reserve Board, Committee Reports, "Branch Banking," Chapter IX, contains a lengthy discussion of this topic.

[106] "Banks and Branches," *Federal Reserve Bulletin* (April 1967), pp. 658–59.

offices, might be employed instead of geographic location in studying branch operations, but it would seem that regardless of the criteria used vast differences still remain within given classifications. This variation often appears to be primarily related to the philosophy of the management of a given institution, but no doubt numerous other factors[107] could also be found which may significantly affect the functioning of a particular branch organization. Therefore, in this book there has been no attempt to provide capsule descriptions of "typical" branch operations, since the functions which appear to be most common among branch systems are well known and they have been spelled out on many occasions.[108] Any discussion of branch operations as contrasted with the performance of other forms of bank organization will be limited to Chapter 8, which includes a brief review of the possible effects of bank mergers.

## LEGISLATION AND REGULATION

### FEDERAL ACTION

While the National Bank Act did not expressly prohibit branching, this statute was interpreted by the Comptrollers of the Currency until 1922 as implying that branches could not be established.[109] There appears to have been very little interest in branching until the 1890s,[110] when the Comptroller began to receive a considerable number of inquiries from national banks regarding their ability to establish branches. At that time the Comptroller asked the Attorney General for his views on this question, and he reported that it was not the intent of the law for national banks to do business in that manner.[111] This also appears to have been the opinion of the federal

[107] This writer traveled many thousands of miles visiting banks in a great variety of market situations, and this conclusion is based upon his observation of bank operations and discussions with bank officers.

[108] See, for example, Chapman and Westerfield, *Branch Banking,* Chapters VI–XII.

[109] *Ibid.,* p. 87.

[110] "Official Bulletin of New National Banks," *Bankers Magazine* (August 1877), p. 154, however, notes that some time before at least one national bank established a branch—the Waynesville National Bank in Ohio in 1877.

[111] "Financial Facts and Opinions," *Bankers Magazine* (January 1892), p. 528. In 1896 Comptroller Eckels stated: "The construction placed upon the

lawmakers in this period, for in at least two instances special legislation was deemed necessary to allow the establishment of national bank branches. In 1892 Congress authorized a national bank in Chicago to open a branch on the World's Fair Grounds, and it permitted banks in Missouri in 1904 to locate branches on the Louisiana Purchase Exposition grounds in St. Louis.[112] The existence of the branch bank in each instance was limited to a period of two years.

*Wickersham opinion.* In 1911 Comptroller of the Currency Lawrence O. Murray requested the Attorney General to express his views regarding the branching powers of national banks. Attorney General Wickersham in his opinion recognized the probable power of a national bank to establish an agency to carry on the business of banking, but he felt that the power to branch was not implied in the National Bank Act. He approached the problem from the aspect of a single board of directors operating two banks on the capital of one, and from this analysis he concluded that if this were allowed it would vitiate the capital requirements of the act.[113] Some years later, Charles W. Collins, in his book *The Branch Banking Question,* indicated that because Wickersham did not have before him the city branch developments of the 1920s his opinion had no bearing on the problems in the later period.[114]

Except for an occasional speech, the subject of branch banking was rarely considered at American Bankers Association meetings between 1903 and 1916. However, in 1915 the Federal Reserve Board recommended that legislation be passed which would permit national banks to operate branches within the city or county of the head office. The Board's suggestion precipitated a lengthy debate at the 1916 ABA convention, and during the sessions a resolution opposing branch banking in any form was adopted. The president of the Association thereupon remarked: "I wish to place myself on record as saying that

National Bank Act, as now in force, by the Supreme Court precludes the establishment of branch banks." Comptroller of the Currency, 34th *Annual Report,* 1896, p. 103. He may have been referring to the United States Supreme Court opinion in *McCormick* v. *Market Bank* [165 U.S. 538, 549 (1896).].

[112] 27 Stat. 33 (1892) and 31 Stat. 1344 (1901). This legislation and the question of branching by national banks is reviewed briefly in the Comptroller of the Currency, 40th *Annual Report,* 1902, pp. 45–47.

[113] 29 Ops. Atty. Gen. 81 (1911).

[114] Collins, *The Branch Banking Question,* p. 51.

I expect to attend a meeting of the American Bankers Association when they reverse the action taken today . . . you are going directly contrary to sound, tried, proved banking experience."[115]

*Consolidation Act of 1918.* In 1918 some modest branching powers were indirectly granted to federally chartered banks under the National Bank Consolidation Act.[116] This statute permitted a national bank which had acquired branches at a time when it was under state charter to consolidate with another national bank and to retain such branches as were involved in the consolidation. Under this legislation, where state laws permitted branching, a national bank could acquire branches by organizing a state bank with branch offices, converting it into a national bank, and then merging it with the "parent" institution. This procedure was followed by a number of banks,[117] and by the mid-1920s 130 national associations maintained 318 branches, in contrast to 12 national banks with 26 branches in 1915.[118] This growth occurred despite the rather awkward procedure which had to be followed in such consolidations, since national banks were only permitted to acquire other national banks. It was not until 1927 [§ 7(b) of the McFadden Act] that a national bank was permitted to merge with a state bank directly under a federal charter, and one might add that it was not until 1950 that a state bank, under the so-called "two-way street" law, could directly consolidate with a national bank under a state charter.[119]

*Comptroller Crissinger's limited offices.* In 1921 Daniel R. Crissinger became Comptroller of the Currency. He feared the inroads state banking might make upon the national system unless some branching by federally chartered banks was permitted; therefore, in his first *Annual Report,* he recommended that the National Banking

[115] Chapman and Westerfield, *Branch Banking,* pp. 94–95.

[116] 40 Stat. 1043 (1918). It has been reported that the Comptroller of the Currency construed this to mean the consolidated bank could continue to operate the branches of both banks but not the head-office locations of both as branches. For a well-written review of developments from 1919–1938 see Raymond P. Kent, "Dual Banking between the Two World Wars," in Carson, ed., *Banking and Monetary Studies,* pp. 43–53.

[117] See Chapman and Westerfield, *Branch Banking,* p. 95; or Collins, *Rural Banking Reform,* p. 88.

[118] *Historical Statistics of the U. S.: Colonial Times to 1957,* p. 635.

[119] 12 U.S.C. 214–214C; 64 Stat. 455 (1950).

Act be amended to permit limited branching, but Congress did not act on his proposal.[120] As a result, Crissinger found what appeared to be another solution to this problem. He reversed the policy of his predecessors by allowing additional intracity tellers windows or offices for national banks (for the purpose of receiving deposits or checks—not to make loans) in areas where state bank branching was permitted. In his *Annual Report* for 1922, he again asked that the branch powers of national banks be expanded, and particularly emphasized the merits of a bill (H. R. 12415) then before Congress which would have granted these institutions the same branch privileges enjoyed in each state by state banks.[121] Nevertheless, this bill apparently died in committee.

At the annual meeting of the American Bankers Association in 1922, a resolution was adopted which stated:[122]

We regard branch banking or the establishment of additional offices by banks as detrimental to the best interest of the people of the United States. Branch banking is contrary to public policy, violates the basic principles of our Government and concentrates the credits of the Nation and the power of money in the hands of a few.

This antibranch attitude was shared in part by Crissinger's successor, Henry M. Dawes, who opposed widespread branching, and when he took office Dawes asked the Attorney General to render an opinion regarding the legality of the additional offices for national banks which had been authorized by his predecessor. The Attorney General in October 1923 replied that national banks had the power to open such limited-service offices within the boundaries of the place (city) specified in their organization certificate.[123] In the five year period

[120] Comptroller of the Currency, 59th *Annual Report*, 1921, p. 9.

[121] Comptroller of the Currency, 60th *Annual Report*, 1922, p. 4.

[122] U. S. Congress, Senate, Hearings on S. 1782 and H. R. 2, *Consolidation of National Banking Associations*, 1926, pp. 194–95. In 1923 there was a basic policy shift regarding branching on the part of the Federal Reserve. Instead of permitting state law to determine the branch powers of state members banks as it had generally done in the past, these banks were prohibited from establishing additional branches outside their head-office city. However, this seems to have resulted from a change in the composition of the Board, not from the ABA action. Chapman and Westerfield, *Branch Banking*, p. 100.

[123] 34 Ops. Atty. Gen. 1 (1923). The opinion and the Comptroller's regulations relating to these offices appear in Comptroller of the Currency 61st *Annual Report*, 1923, pp. 151–55.

1922–1926 the Comptrollers of the Currency issued permits for over 200 of these offices; and after the passage of the McFadden Act in 1927 these offices were authorized to become full-service branches.[124]

*The St. Louis case.* During this period the First National Bank in St. Louis established a branch office in a separate building several blocks from its main banking house, and its officers indicated that they planned to open additional branch banks at various other locations. Since branch banking was prohibited in Missouri by state law, the State Attorney General brought suit against the First National Bank on the grounds that the bank was acting in contravention of its national charter and of the act of Congress under which it was incorporated and that the establishment of a branch office by the bank was in violation of state statutes outlawing branching. The Lower Court found in favor of the State, and the Supreme Court of the United States upheld the decision in 1924.[125]

Although the specific question of the power of national banks to establish branches was more or less a secondary issue in the case, the Supreme Court did note the National Bank Act's reference in Section 8 to the business of the bank being transacted at "an office" located in "the place" specified. The opinion of the court stated: "Strictly the latter provision employing, as it does, the article 'an' to qualify words in the singular number, would confine the association to one office or banking house." The Court also concluded from an analysis of the 1865 amendment to the Act, which permitted conversions of some state banks with branches to national charters, that the wording of this change in the law ". . . goes far in the direction of confirming the conclusion that the general rule does not contemplate the establishment of branches." The Supreme Court described as "well-considered" the 1911 Opinion of Attorney General Wickersham which concluded national banks were not authorized to establish branches for the transaction of general banking business. In addition, the Justices noted that to the extent that there was disagreement between the 1911 and 1923 Opinions of the Attorney General: "We accept the view of the earlier opinion."

The *St. Louis case* left little doubt that the Supreme Court in 1924

---

[124] Comptroller of the Currency, 65th *Annual Report,* 1927, p. 3.
[125] *First National Bank in St. Louis* v. *Missouri,* 263 U.S. 640 (1924).

interpreted the wording of the National Bank Act as requiring banks chartered under this statute (with the exception of certain converted state banks) to maintain no more than one full-service office. This interpretation of the law was opposed by Solicitor General Beck in his brief in this action filed for the United States as *amicus curiae,* for he observed: "In the light of modern banking practice a narrow and literal construction of this section (§ 8 of the National Bank Act) is unworkable. The construction must be made with the practical situation in mind." But this argument was not accepted by the Court.

However, the Supreme Court's finding in the *St. Louis case* did not stop national banks from setting up at least some additional offices. In the 1911 Opinion of the Attorney General cited above, the view was taken that a national bank might legally maintain agencies restricted to special types of business (for example, dealing in bills of exchange). And the 1923 Opinion discussed in this chapter suggested the powers of national associations to organize limited-service offices were somewhat broader than had been indicated in 1911. As a result, the immediate effect of this decision upon the establishment of additional limited-service offices by national banks was negligible, for the Comptroller of the Currency interpreted this decision as being applicable only to full-service branches.

*McFadden Act.* Even before the St. Louis case was decided, the Comptroller of the Currency's staff had begun a review of national bank legislation to determine what modifications, if any, should be made in these statutes. Recommendations were obtained from bank examiners and bankers throughout the nation, and from these suggestions a bill was formulated for presentation to Congress. The legislation proposed was given extensive study by both the House and Senate Banking and Currency Committees, and almost identical bills embodying many of the Comptroller's ideas were reported out of committee in 1924.[126]

The resulting legislation, the McFadden Act,[127] was considered by

[126] See Comptroller of the Currency, 62nd *Annual Report,* 1924, pp. 2–3.

[127] 44 Stat. 1224 (1927). The background of this legislation is reviewed in Comptroller of the Currency, 65th *Annual Report,* 1927, pp. 1–2; and for a detailed discussion of Federal Reserve activity in this period and the evolution of the McFadden Act, see Chapman and Westerfield, *Branch Banking,* pp. 95–108.

many as a limited victory for the advocates of branch banking, for it did permit national banks to establish full-service branches,[128] which they could not do directly before that time. Yet, Congressman McFadden, in his remarks before the House prior to the passage of the bill, observed: "This resolution contains the fundamental anti-branch-banking policy of the House bill. It is an anti-branch-banking measure severely restricting the further spread of branch banking in the United States."[129] McFadden's conclusion apparently was based primarily on Section 7 of the Act which permitted both present and future members of the Federal Reserve System to establish new branches only within the limits of the "city, town or village in which said association is situated if such establishment and operation are at the time permitted to State Banks by the law of the State in question."

Thus, while this section did permit national banks to establish branches in many states, this was considered to be a minor concession on the part of the antibranch forces, since the law also provided that no national or state member bank could establish a branch outside of its home city, and no state bank with branches established outside its home city after February 25, 1927 could be admitted to Federal Reserve membership except upon relinquishment of such branches. As a result, many authorities viewed this statute as a compromise under which a limited amount of branching was to be permitted at the time but permitted at the possible expense of any widespread expansion of multiple-office banking in the future.

Almost immediately after the McFadden Act became law new proposals were made to expand the branch powers of member banks. Comptroller of the Currency Pole in 1928 proposed trade-area branch banking. President Hoover in his *Annual Message to Congress*

---

[128] This legislation also defined a branch, apparently for the first time in federal law, as follows: "The term 'branch' as used in this section shall be held to include any branch bank, branch office, branch agency, additional office, or any branch place of business located in any state or territory of the United States or in the District of Columbia at which deposits are received, or checks paid, or money lent."

[129] *Congressional Record,* 69th Cong., 2d Sess., January 24, 1927, p. 2166. The ABA in 1924 had supported the McFadden Act with the "Hull Amendments," which were designed to stop permanently the growth of branch banking in those states which at the time did not permit branching. In 1926 the ABA dropped its support of the "Hull Amendments."

in 1929 expressed his concern with bank failures and the growth of group and chain banking, and he noted that Congress might investigate the recommendations which had been made to permit national banks to branch within limited areas.[130] The Secretary of the Treasury echoed the President's remarks, calling for a thorough study of the banking organization problem.

In the years immediately following the passage of the McFadden Act, the general attitude toward bank structure was gradually changing. One writer described it as the "greatest transition in the history of banking psychology in our own and any other country."[131] The American Bankers Association, which had strongly attacked branching during its 1916 and 1922 conventions and supported the McFadden bill in 1926, in 1930 passed the following resolution:[132]

The American system of unit banking, as contrasted with the banking systems of other countries, has been peculiarly adapted to the highly diversified community life of the United States. The future demands the continued growth and service of the unit bank in areas economically able to support sound, independent banking of this type, especially as a protection against undue centralization of banking power. Modern transportation and other economic changes both in the large centres and the country districts make necessary some readjustment of banking facilities.

In view of these facts, this association, while reaffirming its belief in the unit bank, recognizes that a modification of its former resolutions condemning branch banking in any form is advisable. The association believes in the economic desirability of community-wide branch banking in metropolitan areas and county-wide branch banking in rural districts where economically justifiable.

The association supports in every respect the autonomy of the laws of the separate States in respect to banking. No class of banks in the several States should enjoy greater rights in respect to the establishment of branches than banks chartered under the State laws.

If this mood continued, branch bank powers would inevitably be broadened; and, with the introduction of a series of banking bills by Carter Glass in the early 1930s, the question merely seemed to be when branch banking would be expanded and by how much.

[130] *Ibid.*, 71st Cong., 2d Sess., December 3, 1929, p. 25.
[131] This was a quote by Chapman and Westerfield [*Branch Banking*, p. 113] of a remark by Melvin A. Traylor.
[132] *Ibid.*, p. 115.

*1930s—branch banking v. deposit insurance.*[133]   The McFadden
Act did not settle the branch banking question. With the vast number
of small bank suspensions in the late 1920s, the rapid growth of bank
holding companies in this same period, and the numerous methods
member banks had developed to circumvent the branch restrictions in
the federal law (for example, by establishing nonmember affiliates),
there was considerable interest in passing new branch bank legislation. As a result, hearings on "Branch, Group, and Chain Banking"[134]
were held by the House Banking and Currency Committee in 1930,
and branching was also examined in the hearings which were conducted by the Senate Banking and Currency Committee on the broader
topic of the "Operation of the National and Federal Reserve Banking
Systems" in 1931 and 1932.[135]

While there was much opposition to the expansion of the branching
authority of member banks, the general tone of the testimony in these
hearings seemed to be much more favorable toward multiple-office
banking than that which was heard a few years earlier. Comptroller of
the Currency John W. Pole, testifying in each of the above hearings,
endorsed branch banking, and he advocated not limited but trade-
area branching.[136] The Comptroller opposed establishing branch lines
according to political boundaries which had provided the standard
limitations in the past. Instead he argued in favor of relating the area
in which a bank could branch to a territory sufficiently large to
support a sizable bank (a minimum figure of 1 million dollars capital
and higher was frequently mentioned).

The Comptroller's ideas found expression in some of the banking
legislation introduced in the early 1930s. For example, the branch
provision in one of Carter Glass's bills incorporated a form of trade-

[133] I am indebted to Carter H. Golembe of the American Bankers Association, who noted that this topic had not been included in the review of the 1933
legislation in an earlier draft of this chapter. Much of the following was drawn
from his excellent article concerning "The Deposit Insurance Legislation of
1933," in the *Political Science Quarterly* (June 1960), pp. 181–200.

[134] U. S. Congress, House, Hearings, on *Branch, Chain, and Group Banking,*
1930. (Hereafter, House Hearings, 1930.)

[135] U. S. Congress, Senate, Hearings, on *Operation of the National and
Federal Reserve Banking Systems,* 1931.

[136] House Hearings, 1930, p. 6. This question is discussed in some detail in
Collins, *Rural Banking Reform,* Chapter XIII.

area concept permitting national banks to branch not only statewide regardless of state law but interstate so long as the branch was not more than fifty miles from the place where the parent was located.[137] Radical as this legislation may seem today, a shift in American banking organization of this magnitude or even greater would probably have been acceptable to the general public (if not to some legislators) at the time, for people were thoroughly disillusioned with the banking system.

But, as had happened on numerous occasions in the past in this country on the state level, when unit banking was threatened deposit insurance schemes were developed to overcome one of the most serious shortcomings of a system composed of thousands of relatively small banks—"its proneness to bank suspensions, in good times and bad."[138] Thus, as might have been expected, as the bills from which the Banking Act of 1933 was to evolve advanced through the legislative process, the importance of deposit insurance as a bulwark of the unit banking system became increasingly apparent in the debates.[139] Nevertheless, when the Banking Act of 1933 came out of a House-Senate Conference, it contained both a deposit insurance section and a provision permitting some expansion of national bank branch powers. One of the House conferees, Representative Goldsborough, justified the branch action on the grounds that if the House conference members who generally opposed branching failed to agree to some expansion of national bank branch powers it would have endangered the deposit insurance provisions of the Act. He stated:[140]

We decided that if we had a bank-deposit insurance bill it would not only tend to restore the confidence of the American people in the banks and in the business integrity of the country, but if bank deposits were insured and all the people knew that a reservoir of the assets of every bank in the United States was supporting the deposits in their bank, it would tend to restrain the tendency to branch banking. Therefore, we felt we should yield to the Senate provision.

[137] For a discussion of the provisions of this bill see U. S. Congress, Senate, *Operations of the National and Federal Reserve Banking Systems*, Report No. 584, 1932.

[138] Golembe, "The Deposit Insurance Legislation of 1933," *Political Science Quarterly* (June 1960), p. 195.

[139] Quoted *ibid.*, p. 197.

[140] Quoted *ibid.*, p. 198.

Considering the changes in American banking organization, especially during the last fifteen years, it is obvious that deposit insurance did not fix for all time the type of banking system this nation will have. Nevertheless, as Carter Golembe noted in a study of the antecedents and purposes of the 1933 legislation:[141]

At one of those rare moments in history when almost anything is possible, deposit insurance was advanced and accepted as a method of controlling the economic consequences of bank failures without altering the basic structure of the banking system; it thus provided a rallying point for men formerly in disagreement and confounded in equal measure those who did not admit a need for government action and those who sought fundamental reorganization of the banking structure.

There appears to be some disagreement among authorities regarding the specific role that deposit insurance played in stopping the branch movement,[142] although all would probably concede some major action, such as the initiation of an insurance program, was required to reopen the banks and to increase their stability. However, insurance was not the only possibility for there were a number of other alternatives, including nationalization of the banks and widespread branching. But, in any event, it was deposit insurance which was selected and this choice made continuation of the existing structure feasible.

The branch provision which was finally incorporated in the Glass Bill, when the law was enacted on June 16, 1933, permitted intrastate branch banking by national banks in those states where state banks were allowed to branch. However, national banks were to be subject to restrictions as to location imposed by state law on state banks.[143] This section of the law remains in essentially the same form today, although minor additions to it were made by the Banking Act of 1935. The 1935 legislation included provisions which authorized the establishment of a seasonal agency in a resort community by national banks and which required state member banks to obtain Federal Reserve Board approval of new branches.[144]

[141] *Ibid.*, p. 200.

[142] Chapman and Westerfield, *Branch Banking*, p. 120.

[143] 48 Stat. 162 § 23 (1933).

[144] 49 Stat. 684, 708 (1935); amending 12 U.S.C. 36(c). Banks applying for membership which had "outside branches" established after February 25, 1927 also had to obtain Board approval to retain them.

*1952 legislation.*   The Banking Act of 1933 also prescribed minimum capital requirements for national and state[145] member banks which acquired branches outside their head-office communities. These standards were designed by the legislators to restrict the number of branches and to retard the development of branch banking,[146] and they were considerably higher than the corresponding requirements for nonmember banks in many states. As a result, a sizable number of national and state banks were practically precluded and others refrained from locating branches outside their head-office cities even though they were authorized to do so.[147]

In 1952 these requirements were changed so that a member bank would be expected to have only the same capital and surplus required under state law for its branches. Comptroller of the Currency Ray M. Gidney in his *Annual Report* that year noted that this legislation placed national banks on a parity, for all practical purposes, with state chartered banks. And Gidney concluded: "The provisions of the new law are proving to be eminently satisfactory. They are, in part, responsible for the increased activity in the field of branch banking."[148]

*1962 amendment.*   In 1962 legislation was passed permitting a bank already operating branches to continue to operate such branches if it was a state bank and converted to a national bank, or if it was a national bank which took over another bank, or banks, in a merger or consolidation.[149] In either case, except for branches which were opened prior to 1927, the continued operation of existing branches was to be subject to the approval of the Comptroller of the Currency. The 1962 act specifically provided that this approval had to be withheld if, in an exactly similar situation, state law prohibited continued operation of branches by a state bank. Originally the provisions found in the 1962 legislation were included in the Financial Institu-

---

[145] Under Section 9 of the Federal Reserve Act. 12 U.S.C. 321.

[146] Chapman and Westerfield, *Branch Banking*, p. 121.

[147] Federal Reserve Board, *Banking Studies*, p. 117.

[148] 66 Stat. 633 (1952). Again, the legislation refers only to national banks, but state member banks must meet national requirements. The quotation is taken from Comptroller of the Currency, 90th *Annual Report*, 1952, pp. 5–6.

[149] American Bankers Association, *Banking Legislation in the Second Session, 87th Congress*, p. 9. The Act is 76 Stat. 667 (1962).

tions Act of 1957 which was not passed, and they had considerable industry support, for they merely eliminated some technical roadblocks to unimpeded movement between state and national charters.

*1966 Supreme Court decision.*[150] On December 12, 1966, the Supreme Court handed down a decision in regard to the branching powers of national banks which had been anxiously awaited by the banking industry. This litigation developed as a result of actions taken by former Comptroller of the Currency James Saxon during his term in office. Saxon had maintained that he had the authority to permit national banks to branch in at least some instances where state banks were precluded from doing so, and on a number of occasions he authorized national banks to establish additional offices when this same action if taken by a state bank would have been clearly in violation of state branch banking law.

The controversy centered around the meaning of the section of the National Bank Act [44 stat. 1228, 12 U.S.C. §§ 36(c)(1) and (2)] which reads as follows:

A national banking association may, with the approval of the Comptroller of the Currency, establish and operate new branches: (1) Within the limits of the city, town or village in which said association is situated, if such establishment and operation are at the time expressly authorized to state banks by the law of the state in question; and (2) at any point within the state in which said association is situated, if such establishment and operation are at the time authorized to state banks by the statute law of the state in question by language specifically granting such authority affirmatively and not merely by implication or recognition, and subject to the restrictions as to location imposed by the law of the state on state banks.

In very general terms, under the Comptroller's interpretation of this statute state law would decide "whether" and "where" branches may be located, but it would not determine the "method" by which the branching, if allowed, was effected. Therefore, since at least sixteen states included limitations in their branching statutes which seemed to fall in the third (method) category, in about one-third of the nation

---

[150] *First National Bank of Logan* v. *Walker Bank and Trust Company; First Security Bank of Utah* v. *Commercial Security Bank;* and *James J. Saxon, Comptroller of the Currency* v. *Commercial Security Bank,* 385 U.S. 252 (1966). The three cases were earlier granted certiorari and consolidated for argument before the Supreme Court. 384 U.S. 925 (1966).

federally chartered banks would have enjoyed a competitive advantage over state chartered institutions in the branching area if the Saxon ruling were allowed to stand.

Mr. Saxon's position in regard to national bank branching powers was challenged in the courts by banks and bank supervisory officials in separate actions initiated in about ten different states during his five-year term as "Administrator of National Banks." The first of these cases to be considered by the Supreme Court involved branches in the State of Utah, which has some very unusual branching provisions in its statutes. Under Utah law, with certain exceptions relating to large cities, no branch bank can be established in any city or town in which any bank regularly transacting customary banking business is located, unless the bank seeking to establish the branch takes over an existing bank which has been in operation at least five years. Despite this restriction in the state law, the Comptroller permitted two national banks to set up new branches, one in Logan and the other in Ogden, Utah, without taking over an established bank. In each instance the new branch was to be located in the same city in which its home office was situated.

The District Court approved the action by the Logan bank but this decision was reversed by the Court of Appeals. The Ogden bank, on the other hand, lost in both the District and Appeals Courts. The Supreme Court consolidated the Ogden and Logan cases for argument, and it affirmed the judgments of the appellate courts which had held that the state law had to be complied with in these actions.

Mr. Justice Clark delivered the unanimous opinion of the Supreme Court, which very briefly reviewed the background of the National Bank Act, the branch provisions in the McFadden Act of 1927, and the Banking Act of 1933, and then concluded:[151]

It appears clear from the résumé of the legislative history of §§36(c)(1) and (2) that Congress intended to place national and state banks on a basis of "competitive equality" insofar as branch banking was concerned. Both sponsors of the applicable banking Acts, Representative McFadden and Senator Glass, so characterized the legislation. It is not for us to so

[151] 385 U.S. 252, 261 (1966). While this writer considers this decision to be sound from the point of view of both the "letter" and "spirit" of the law, I have much less confidence that it is necessarily the best for the general public since the advantage of a dual banking system in part stems from the differences between the laws.

construe the Acts as to frustrate this clear-cut purpose so forcefully expressed by both friend and foe of the legislation at the time of its adoption. To us it appears beyond question that the Congress was continuing its policy of equalization first adopted in the National Banking Act of 1864.

Thus, with this decision competitive equality in branching between national and state banks appears to have been maintained.

The Utah decision is sound from the point of view of the intentions of Congress at the time the McFadden Act and Banking Act of 1933 were passed. The federal legislation *at most* was designed to give national banks branching powers comparable to those of state banks, and this would appear to be the position of the Supreme Court. Furthermore, although cases relating to the branching authority of national associations turn on a variety of factual and technical points, and the Comptroller's position might be upheld in one or more of these actions, the basic philosophy of the Supreme Court with its emphasis upon branching equality under state and federal law is unlikely to change in the foreseeable future.

STATE ACTION

Unfortunately, it is very difficult to classify states into very neat categories which are determined by the legal status of branch banking—statewide, limited, or prohibited. Many of the statutes are vague and their terminology is sometimes ambiguous, and it is perfectly reasonable for two investigators to reach different conclusions regarding whether or not a given state's law permits branching by commercial banks. This point is well-illustrated here by the decision to include in the limited branching classification only two of eight states which prohibit all full-service branching but which allow some limited-service offices.[152] This was done because both of these states, Arkansas and North Dakota, have been fairly liberal in terms of the

---

[152] Six other states permitted the establishment of limited service offices yet they were listed as prohibiting branching: Kansas, Missouri, Nebraska, Oklahoma, Texas, and Wisconsin. In the five states other than Wisconsin, there were 217 banks with additional offices and only 218 offices—all but one located in the head-office city—at the end of 1966. In Wisconsin, which currently allows limited branch banking, the former law permitted only new paying and receiving windows within 300 feet of the main office and the transactions had to be processed in the head office. Texas had a provision which resembled this.

location and the number of additional tellers windows or stations which they allow, while the other six states by law or administrative decision typically permit each bank to have only one additional office in the head-office city.

Since the division of states according to their branch legislation involves many admittedly arbitrary decisions, the classification of a given state at a particular time may be affected by the questions an investigator is trying to answer. In this study, for example, the review of state branching legislation was compiled to try to determine within rather narrow limits the time periods in which a considerable amount of major branch legislation was passed and the general pattern of the changes which occurred (if any) in these intervals. This information, in turn, is very useful in tracing the evolution of this country's branching statutes, for with a knowledge of when laws were revised it is much easier to try to develop a logical explanation regarding why these statutes may have been enacted.

On the other hand, the branching categories in which some of the states were placed would be far different if the objective of this research had been to test statistically the relationship between bank structure and other variables (see Chapter 8). For this purpose, it would usually be much more logical to use one of the many available publications containing numbers of branches and banks by state for the years being analyzed.[153] This would customarily be a much more meaningful source for statistical work, for the wording of the current law may have little relationship to the actual status of branch banking in a state. This is determined by many things, including past legislation, tradition, and the attitude of the bank supervisor toward branching, not merely by the language of the present statute.

*1896–1930.* The first survey of state branch banking legislation appears to have been made by the Comptroller of the Currency in 1896. It was developed from a fairly comprehensive questionnaire distributed to the state bank supervisors. The Comptroller summarized the results as follows:[154]

---

[153] For example, detailed data concerning the number of banks and branches by state may be obtained from the Banking Markets Unit, Federal Reserve Board, in mimeographed form for the years 1935–1966.

[154] Comptroller of the Currency, 33d *Annual Report*, 1895, p. 40.

Thirteen states do not allow branch banks. Ten states report no law prohibiting them nor providing for their establishment. In twenty states branches are permitted and to some extent encouraged by favorable legislation. [Two of the 45 states provided no information.]

Of the thirteen states which prohibited branching, it is doubtful that many actually had legislation to this effect. In fact, in most states, whether branches were permitted or prohibited, it was typically by implication or by custom, not by law.

A second survey of state branch bank laws was made by the Comptroller in 1902.[155] This investigation revealed essentially the same findings as were presented in the earlier survey. Among the few states which appear to have passed legislation in this interval were Louisiana, Massachusetts (for savings banks only), New York, which had enacted specific authorizations, and Missouri, which had enacted a prohibition of branching. The state officials were asked to indicate on the Comptroller's questionnaire the number and location of branch banks in their states, and the data provided, while noticeably incomplete, indicated there were few branch banks and those that existed had only a very small number of branches in operation.

Much more detailed analyses of state branch bank statutes were prepared by the National Monetary Commission in 1909.[156] By that time eight states by specific enactment had forbidden branching: Colorado, Connecticut, Mississippi, Missouri, Nevada, Pennsylvania, Texas, and Wisconsin. In addition, there were about a dozen states which apparently permitted branches of state banks and trust companies, according to the Commission's report. These branch banking states included: California, Delaware, Florida, Georgia, Maryland, New York, North Carolina, Oregon, Rhode Island, South Carolina, Virginia, and Washington. Several of these states placed restrictions on the location of additional offices; in nearly all of the "branch states," additional capital was required for each branch, and the establishment of a branch often had to be specifically authorized by a state official or officials.

Apparently no other detailed surveys of state branch banking laws

---

[155] The findings are summarized in the Comptroller of the Currency, 40th *Annual Report,* 1902, pp. 47–51.

[156] Barnett, *State Banks and Trust Companies since the Passage of the National Bank Act,* pp. 135–43; and Welldon, *Digest of State Banking Statutes.*

TABLE 2.3. LEGAL STATUS OF BRANCH BANKING, 1925–1967[a]

| Year | Branch Banking Allowed | | | Branches Prohibited | No Statute | No. of Changes[b] |
|------|------------|---------|-------|---------------------|------------|-------------------|
| | Statewide | Limited | Total | | | |
| 1910 | 9 | 3 | 12 | 8 | 31 | — |
| 1925 | 9 | 9 | 18 | 18 | 15 | 12[c] |
| 1930 | 11 | 10 | 21 | 23 | 7 | 10 |
| 1935 | 19 | 16 | 35 | 11 | 5 | 15 |
| 1940 | 21 | 16 | 37 | 10 | 4 | 3 |
| 1945 | 20 | 17 | 37 | 10 | 4 | 1 |
| 1950 | 19 | 17 | 36 | 11 | 4 | 2 |
| 1955 | 19 | 19 | 38 | 10 | 3 | 2 |
| 1960 | 20 | 18 | 38 | 11 | 2 | 2 |
| 1965 | 21 | 18 | 39 | 11 | 1 | 2 |
| 1967[d] | 21 | 19 | 40 | 10 | 1 | 1 |

[a] Includes Alaska and Hawaii. The District of Columbia is under statewide 1925–1965; districtwide branching has been authorized there since the passage of the Millspaugh Act [42 Stat. 500 (1922), ch. 147] on April 26, 1922.

[b] Number of times there were changes in the legal status of branch banking—not the number of states which changed their law—since the previous data were compiled.

[c] Changes from 1920 to 1925 only; this figure has been estimated.

[d] To December 31.

*Source:* Welldon, *Digest of State Banking Statutes,* and the laws of each state were examined to develop these data

were made from 1910 until the Federal Reserve System began to prepare its periodic compilations in the mid-1920's.[157] During this fifteen-year span, a great number of states passed legislation for the first time in this field, and most of the laws enacted either prohibited branch banking or restricted the location of branches to very limited areas.[158] (See Table 2.3) Researchers who have studied developments in this period have almost invariably concluded that an important

[157] The Comptroller of the Currency in his annual reports in the early twenties noted the number of states which permitted branching (e.g., 22 in 1922, 17 in 1923) but no details of possible surveys were found. Chapman and Westerfield, *Branch Banking,* [p. 85] contains a list of states divided by legal status of branch banking in 1910.

[158] The balance of the discussion in this review of state legislation is based upon this writer's evaluation of the status of branching in a given state. At times it disagrees with the opinions of some of the federal banking agencies, but when this occurs the alternative choice has been carefully considered.

stimulant to this branch legislation (and to multiple-office banking) was the enactment of a liberal branch banking statute in California in 1909. This law was to have far-reaching effects upon branch banking during the next two decades.[159]

At the time the California legislation was enacted, branching was of so little importance that three-fifths of the states had no branching statute. However, between 1910 and 1920 the best information available would seem to indicate that about ten states passed branch legislation and nearly all of these acts prohibited branch banking. These laws were very evenly distributed over the decade with no particular concentration in any given year or group of years. In fact, about the only unusual characteristic of these laws (apart from their negative nature) was that most of the states involved were located in the Deep South or the Mountain States, and the states in each region which enacted branch statutes were contiguous to each other or to other states which had previously prohibited branch banking.

The number of branches in operation more than doubled between 1910 and 1920, increasing from 548 to 1,281. However, the branching activity was dominated by state institutions, and only 21 of the 530 banks maintaining branches in 1920 had national charters. And from 1915 to 1920 both the Federal Reserve Board and the Comptroller of the Currency in nearly every *Annual Report* made some reference to the national banks' need for at least limited branching authority. In states where branches were permitted, national banks rarely offered any important opposition, except in California where both small state banks and national banks resisted the movement.[160] The national banks in branch states usually argued not for the elimination of state branch powers but for the expansion of their authority in this field. Thus, the development of branch banking by state banks put great pressure upon federal authorities to relax national bank branch prohibitions.

The efforts by the national bankers to obtain branch powers set off a counter reaction on the part of bankers who opposed branching in states where branches did not exist. The latter group feared that a federal branch law would apply to all national or Federal Reserve

[159] Chapman and Westerfield, *Branch Banking*, p. 84.
[160] Federal Reserve Board, Committee Reports, "Branch Banking," p. 112.

member banks regardless of state law and that this would not only place nonmember state banks at a distinct competitive disadvantage but would probably lead in time to a relaxation of state branch restrictions. As a result, a substantial antibranch bank movement began to develop with the primary goal of not only preventing the enactment of a federal branch banking statute but, so far as possible, stopping the expansion of branch banking everywhere.

While the efforts of these opposition groups were not sufficient to get branch banking banned by federal law, they were able to convince the legislatures in many states that laws prohibiting branch banking should be enacted. Between 1919 and 1929 over a dozen states passed such legislation, and in most of these states there was either no branch banking or it existed only on a very small scale.[161] Thus, the opponents of branching were most successful in those states where branch banking had really never presented a significant intrastate problem, and their antagonism was clearly aimed at proposed changes in federal legislation. (See Table 2.4)

About one-half of the states which prohibited branching in 1930 passed this legislation in one of two periods during the previous decade—1921–1923 or 1927–1929. The first interval was one of the major turning points in the history of branch banking in this country, for the number of branches rose from less than 1,300 to over 2,000 and the number of national banks maintaining branches increased substantially. It was during this same three years, 1921 to 1923, that the Joint Commission of Agricultural Inquiry investigating the causes of the collapse of the farm economy considered the difficulties of rural credit. The Commission indicated a "system of limited branch banking might furnish a possible solution to this problem," and the Federal Reserve Board in commenting upon this suggestion in its Ninth *Annual Report* noted that in some sections of the country branch systems already "appear to have gone far toward solving the problem."[162]

In this three-year span, as was noted earlier, Comptroller of the Currency Crissinger requested that Congress pass a limited branch bill for national banks, and when this was not done he began to authorize some of the institutions under his jurisdiction to establish

[161] *Ibid.,* p. 113.
[162] Quoted "Branch Banking in the United States," *Federal Reserve Bulletin* (December 1924), p. 927.

TABLE 2.4.   MAJOR CHANGES IN STATE BRANCH LEGISLATION, 1924–1967

| State or District | Status of Branching, 1924 | New Legislation and Date of Change | Status of Branching, 1967* |
|---|---|---|---|
| Alabama | P | 1935-L | L |
| Alaska | P | 1951-L; 1959-S | S |
| Arizona | S | — | S |
| Arkansas | P | 1935-L | L |
| California | S | — | S |
| Colorado | P | — | P |
| Connecticut | P | 1935-S | S |
| Delaware | S | — | S |
| District of Columbia | S | — | S |
| Florida | P | — | P |
| Georgia | S | 1927-P; 1929-L | L |
| Hawaii | S | — | S |
| Idaho | P | 1935-S | S |
| Illinois | P | — | P |
| Indiana | P | 1931-L | L |
| Iowa | NP | 1927-P; 1931-L | L |
| Kansas | NP | 1929-P | P |
| Kentucky | NP | 1954-L | L |
| Louisiana | L | 1938-S | S |
| Maine | L | 1935-S | S |
| Maryland | S | — | S |
| Massachusetts | L | — | L |
| Michigan | NL | 1933-S; 1945-L | L |
| Minnesota | P | — | P |
| Mississippi | L | — | L |
| Missouri | P | — | P |
| Montana | NP | 1927-P; 1931-L | L** |
| Nebraska | NP | 1927-P | P |
| Nevada | P | 1933-S | S |
| New Hampshire | NP | 1963-L | L |
| New Jersey | NL | 1925-L | L |
| New Mexico | P | 1935-L | L |
| New York | L | — | L |
| North Carolina | NS | 1928-S | S |
| North Dakota | NP | 1937-L | L |
| Ohio | L | — | L |
| Oklahoma | NP | 1957-P | P |
| Oregon | P | 1933-S | S |
| Pennsylvania | L | — | L |
| Rhode Island | S | — | S |

TABLE 2.4 (*continued*).

| State or District | Status of Branching, 1924 | New Legislation and Date of Change | Status of Branching, 1967* |
|---|---|---|---|
| South Carolina | NS | 1928-S | S |
| South Dakota | NP | 1933-S | S |
| Tennessee | NS | 1925-L | L |
| Texas | P | — | P |
| Utah | P | 1938-S | S |
| Vermont | NP | 1929-S | S |
| Virginia | S | 1948-L; 1962-S | S |
| Washington | P | 1933-S | S |
| West Virginia | NP | 1929-P | P |
| Wisconsin | P | 1931-L; 1947-P; 1967-L | L |
| Wyoming | NP | — | NP |

P, prohibited; L, limited; S, statewide; N, no legislation. N followed by P, L, or S indicates type of branching in a given state prior to the time legislation was enacted. A revision was not classified as "major" unless the state in question moved to a *new* classification (P, L, S, or N). This omits some important changes within categories but this does not affect the conclusions in the study.

\* To December 31. The Wisconsin law is not effective until March 1968.

\*\* Montana law is now being tested in the courts. The state Attorney General ruled in October 1966 that banks could not legally branch under the 1931 law. However, in September 1967 a federal judge found that limited branching was permitted, but the decision will be appealed.

*Source:* State banking statutes.

limited service branches in their head-office cities. The impetus these and other actions gave to the antibranch movement in the early 1920s was quite apparent by 1923 in the trial of the St. Louis case. This was the first clear test of the branching power of national banks, and the opponents of branching were so effective in convincing their state officials of the importance of this litigation that eleven state attorneys general filed briefs as *amici curiae,* supporting the position of those opposed to national bank branching.

The second interval in which a large number of states prohibited branch banking began with the passage of the McFadden Act in 1927 and terminated in 1929. In the 1927 legislation the antibranch forces had won a considerable but not a complete victory. Branching by national banks was limited to the head-office city (town, village) and it was allowed only if the relevant state law also permitted state banks to establish and operate such branches.[163] Within a few months after the new federal law was passed four states enacted legislation prohibiting branching and two other states approved similar statutes in 1929.

This was to be the last major expansion of this severe form of antibranch legislation. In the 1920s there were thousands of bank failures in rural areas, and by the last half of the decade chain and group banking were expanding rapidly, both particularly important factors in those states where the opponents of branching had their greatest strength. The bank suspensions (and weakness of banks in general throughout the country) tended to diminish the opposition to multiple-office (branch) banking, while the rise of multiple-unit (group) banking presented a new threat to the independent banker. As a result, much of the stimulus behind the antibranch movement was lost before 1930; and, after Kansas and West Virginia passed laws prohibiting branch banking in 1929, no additional legislation of this type was enacted until after World War II.

*1930–1967.* Since 1930 all but four of the twenty-eight major changes in state legislation resulted in an easing of branch restrictions. The only exceptions were Michigan, which switched from statewide to limited branching in 1945; Oklahoma, which in 1957 enacted its first branch statute continuing its de facto policy of prohibiting branches; and Virginia, which shifted from statewide branching to limited in 1948. Wisconsin had always prohibited branching, although there was a period beginning in 1931 when stations were permitted, and it reconfirmed its branch prohibitions in 1947.

Over one-half of the changes in branch legislation in this period were concentrated between 1931 and 1935. In these five years, fifteen states revised their branch laws or enacted such legislation for the first time. Twelve states shifted from prohibiting branches by statute to statewide (five) and limited branching (seven); and one state which

---

[163] National banks were permitted to continue to operate branches they controlled prior to the passage of the McFadden Act under certain conditions regardless of their location. As a result two national banks have interstate offices even today—The Bank of California National Association, with two offices in Washington and one in Oregon, and The First Camden National Bank and Trust Company (New Jersey), with one office in Philadelphia, Pennsylvania.

had limited branching and two states which had no previous branch legislation enacted laws permitting statewide branching. In most of these states the change in attitude toward multiple-office banking can be traced to the suspension of operations by many banks and the apparent weakness of numerous others. The objective appeared to be to merge the weak with the relatively strong banks, converting the acquired bank to a branch office. In this way it was hoped the number of failures could be reduced and the number of communities which would have no banking service would be held to a minimum.

In addition to the major branch banking statute amendments included in this study, which were defined as those law revisions involving a shift from one status of branching to another (such as, from limited to prohibited), there were many important "intra-status" changes. For example, the Stephens Branch Banking Bill enacted in New York in May 1934 divided the state into nine districts and permitted branching within these districts, while prior to that time banks could branch only within the head-office city.[164] But, although this new legislation involved a substantial broadening of the branching powers of banks in New York State, it was excluded from the data in Table 2.4 in this chapter since the state was classified as authorizing limited branching both before and after the new law was passed.

An effort was made to record these "intra-status" changes in branch laws in separate categories, but this involved a series of value judgments (such as, at what point does a "minor" change become a "major" change?) which could not be logically supported on a theoretical or on an empirical basis. Furthermore, this approach tended to make one lose sight of the basic objective of this compilation of state laws, which was to determine the time periods in which a considerable amount of major branch legislation was passed and to note any general pattern in these new laws. In any event the findings using the "intra-status" revisions appeared merely to reinforce the results achieved by employing the far less complicated (but still significantly judgmental) "inter-status" approach. Therefore, the more cumbersome procedure was discontinued and the results included in this chapter were limited to major changes as defined above.

From 1935 through 1967 there were only thirteen major changes in

[164] A population provision, a "home office protection rule," and other conditions were included in one or both of these laws.

commercial bank branch legislation involving ten different states. In this period the general pattern of easing branch restrictions which had been followed since about 1930 continued but at a much slower pace. However, for the first time since 1929 a state passed a statute which prohibited branching. As was noted above, both Wisconsin and Oklahoma enacted prohibitory laws in 1947 and 1957, respectively, but for all practical purposes these states had never allowed the establishment of full-service branches.[165]

Six states moved from prohibiting multiple-office banking by statute or policy to statewide (two) or limited branching (four) in this thirty-year span, and one other state changed from limited to statewide branching. (See Table 2.4) Virginia ended the period as it began, with statewide branching via merger permitted. Thus, in these three decades only Michigan substantially tightened its branch legislation, switching from statewide to limited branching.

THE PRESENT AND THE FUTURE

*Current status of branch banking.* It is sometimes suggested that "branch banking in the United States has been shaped to a large extent by federal and state laws."[166] While this observation would certainly appear to be valid, the previous review of the evolution of legislation at both governmental levels would also lead to the conclusion that there are many instances where the opposite is true—the type of statute which was enacted was determined by the form of bank structure which already existed.

Furthermore, the banking system in a given state, and in the nation today, has been influenced by many factors that are not directly related to legislation, including[167] the enormous size of the country and the physical characteristics of many of the states, the diversity and changing nature of the American economy, the general public's long-standing opposition to bigness and fear of concentration of financial power in the hands of a few, the question of states' rights and the

---

[165] Wisconsin did permit the establishment of receiving and disbursing stations in the early 1930s with limited functions, and these were later converted to full-service branches in many cases under the 1947 legislation.

[166] "Branch Banking in the U. S., 1939 and 1949," *Federal Reserve Bulletin* (July 1950), p. 818.

[167] Some of these factors are discussed in "Changes in Banking Structure, 1953–62," *ibid.,* (Sept. 1963) pp. 1191–95.

opposition to centralization of authority in the federal government, the incredible number of bank suspensions in the United States, particularly during the twentieth century, and the districting of the states for election purposes which gave the rural districts vast power in the House of Representatives and in many state legislatures.

Despite these many different elements which have influenced the development of the American banking structure, in certain parts of the country their effects were very similar, and as a result the present-day bank organization in large areas of the nation is surprisingly homogeneous. Widespread branching is predominantly a western phenomenon; unit banking is largely concentrated between the Mississippi and the Rockies, and the eastern third of the United States is primarily a limited branching area, although statewide branching and unit banking are also represented. (See Table 2.5 and Figure 2.1)

*The years ahead.* In recent years, the American financial system has been subjected to a number of investigations emanating from both the public and the private sectors of the economy. The first major study in this area, running from 1958 through 1961, was conducted by the Commission on Money and Credit which was organized "in response to widespread concern as to the adequacy of the nation's monetary and financial structure and its regulation and control."[168] In 1962 Comptroller Saxon appointed an advisory committee "to conduct a comprehensive study of the functioning of our National Banking System."[169] And, shortly after the Comptroller's committee was formed, President Kennedy announced that he had established an interagency committee on financial institutions to be headed by Walter Heller, the Chairman of his Council of Economic Advisers.[170] The President suggested the point of departure for this group was to be the recommendations of the Commission on Money and Credit, but the inquiry need not limit itself to this area.

Unfortunately, these investigations are of limited assistance in set-

[168] *Money and Credit—Their Influence on Jobs, Prices, and Growth,* p. 1. (Hereafter, CMC Report)

[169] *National Banks and the Future,* Report of the Advisory Committee on Banking to the Comptroller of the Currency, 1962, p. ix. (Hereafter, Saxon Report)

[170] *Report of the Committee on Financial Institutions to the President of the United States,* 1963. (Hereafter, Heller Report)

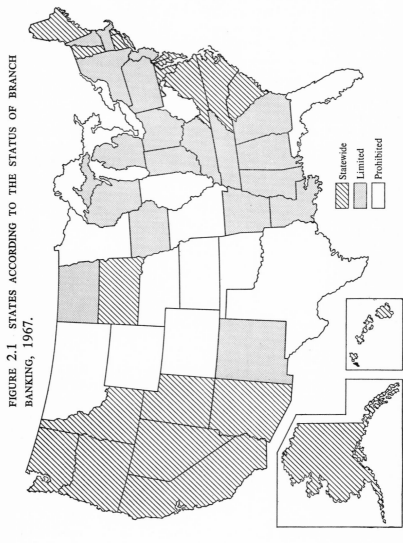

FIGURE 2.1 STATES ACCORDING TO THE STATUS OF BRANCH BANKING, 1967.

Statewide
Limited
Prohibited

*Source:* Table 2.5, using the status as determined by actual branches rather than by statute.

TABLE 2.5.   STATUS OF BRANCH BANKING BY STATE,* December 31, 1967

| States Permitting Statewide Branch Banking | States Permitting Branch bank- ing within Limited Areas | States Prohibiting Branch Banking | States with No Legislation regarding Branch Banking |
|---|---|---|---|
| Alaska | Alabama[1] | Colorado | P-Wyoming |
| Arizona | Arkansas[4] | Florida | |
| California | Georgia[3] | Illinois[4] | |
| Connecticut | Indiana[1] | Kansas[4] | |
| Delaware | Iowa | Minnesota | |
| District of Columbia | Kentucky | Missouri[4] | |
| Hawaii[9] | Massachusetts[1] | Nebraska[4] | |
| Idaho | Michigan[2] | Oklahoma[4] | |
| L-Louisiana | Mississippi[5] | Texas[4] | |
| Maine | P-Montana[8] | West Virginia | |
| Maryland | New Hampshire[2] | | |
| Nevada | New Jersey[1] | | |
| North Carolina | New Mexico[6] | | |
| Oregon | New York[7] | | |
| Rhode Island | North Dakota[4] | | |
| South Carolina | Ohio[2] | | |
| South Dakota | Pennsylvania[2] | | |
| Utah[10] | Tennessee[1] | | |
| Vermont | Wisconsin | | |
| Virginia[11] | | | |
| Washington | | | |

* If the status of branch banking in any given state [as measured by the relationship between number of banks and branches or the actual location of branches] appears to differ from the status as determined from the statutory provisions, this has been indicated by the P (prohibited), L (limited), or S (statewide) designations before the state in question.

[1] Permits branches within the city and county of head office.   [2] Permits branches within city, county, or county contiguous to county of head office.   [3] Permits banks in certain classes of cities to establish branches within limits of city of head office.   [4] Permits only an office (or in some cases offices) such as a drive-in facility for limited purposes, as distinguished from branches.   [5] Permits branches within 100-mile radius of head office.   [6] Permits banks to establish branches within the county or county contiguous to the county in which the parent bank is located, or within a certain distance of the parent bank.   [7] Permits banks to establish branches within the limits of the banking district in which the parent bank is situated.   [8] Banks in same county or adjoining counties may consolidate and maintain and operate offices in the locations of the consolidating banks. In all other cases branching prohibited except for a detached drive-up or walk-up teller facility. In October 1966 state Attorney General ruled branching not legal (see Table 2.4).   [9] Limited in Honolulu only.   [10] Except in first-class cities or counties containing first-class cities, no branch may be established in a city or town where a bank (or banks) regularly transacts business, unless the branching bank takes over an existing bank.   [11] *De novo* branches limited to parent bank's city, town, or county, but statewide branching via merger with existing banks.

*Source:* Statutes of the respective states.

tling the controversy regarding branch banking, for there was a wide divergence of opinion in their recommendations. The Commission on Money and Credit Report suggested that the best approach would be to permit trade-area branching for all banks and savings and loan associations. The trade area in some cases could be less than state-wide; yet, in others it could cross state boundaries.[171] As was noted earlier in this chapter, this concept is far from new. It was considered in setting up the twelve Federal Reserve Districts; it was recommended for national banks by Comptroller of the Currency John W. Pole in 1928; and it was included in many early versions of the Banking Act of 1933.

The Saxon Report, on the other hand, noted that the trade-area idea had much to commend it, but this committee felt that initially branching within twenty-five miles from the principal office, but not across state lines, would be appropriate for national banks even though state laws might be more restrictive.[172] In no case, however, would a national bank's branch powers be reduced below those of state banks in the state in which it was located. The Heller Report was far more general in its observations. It suggested that the statutory standards applicable to granting charters and approving branches should explicitly include "the effect on competition." It also observed that "federal and state governments, within their respective authorities, should review present restrictions on branching with a view to developing a more rational pattern, subject to safeguards to avoid excessive concentration and preserve competition."[173]

The future of these legislative recommendations is very unclear at this time. Nevertheless, there appears to be a willingness on the part of most groups to at least consider change in banking statutes, including branch laws.[174] And, with the many projects which have been initiated by federal and state government agencies and private groups to learn more about bank structure and bank performance,[175] the

---

[171] CMC Report, pp. 166–67.

[172] Saxon Report, p. 51.

[173] Heller Report, pp. 49–52.

[174] National Association of Supervisors of State Banks, *Report of the Committee to Evaluate Responses,* 1963, p. 10; and U. S. Congress, House, *Conflict of Federal and State Banking Laws,* 1963, p. 4.

[175] "ABA Grants $210,000 to NBER for 3-Year Study of Banking Structure, Performance," *American Banker,* March 11, 1966.

legislator will certainly have far better information available to him in reaching his decisions in this vital area than he has had in the past. Yet, few major revisions in branch banking legislation can be expected in the near future, for as Charls Walker of the American Bankers Association has remarked—changes in the pattern of commercial banking will be effected in an evolutionary rather than a revolutionary manner.

Although changes in bank structure legislation may come slowly, they will come and there can be little doubt that many laws will be amended to permit a further expansion of branch banking. However, this should not be interpreted as a forecast of the end of the small bank. In a nation as large as the United States and as diverse in terms of its geography, its population, and its economic development, both single-office (or local) and multiple-office banking can play a significant role, and it is very unlikely that either will be eliminated. But, on the other hand, it would be shortsighted indeed for even the stanchest critic of branching not to realize that in the longer run it is also very unlikely that any significant market area in this country will be without the services of both forms of bank organization.

# CHAPTER 3

---◄◆►---

# Chain, Group, and Correspondent Banking

## INTRODUCTION

THE GROWTH of branch banking within the United States has been inhibited by numerous legal restrictions which permit at most intra-state branching and which prohibit branching completely in some states. Many authorities conclude that it is largely[1] as a result of these legislative barriers that various hybrid forms of bank organization have become quite common in this country. In very general terms these firms would fall into one of two classifications—chains or groups. (The latter term will be used interchangeably with bank holding companies.)

In contrast to branch banking (often referred to as multiple-office banking), which involves only one bank but more than one banking office, chains or holding companies, as they are usually defined,

---

[1] One may point out numerous other factors which contributed to the growth of chain and group banking in the United States. Such things as the size of this country, a great concern with local autonomy, speculation on the part of investors, and others which also influenced the development of these systems will be discussed later in this chapter.

include at least two affiliated but separately chartered banks.[2] Branching by the individual banks, of course, is governed by state laws; therefore, in those states which permit branching, members of chain and group systems may be either single-office or multiple-office institutions. Hence, the title multiple-unit banking which is frequently employed in place of the expressions chain or group could be somewhat misleading.

It is common practice to discuss chains and groups individually. Nevertheless, it should be noted that in terms of the actual operations of these two forms of bank organization the differences may sometimes be minute, and these multiple-unit systems are often reviewed separately largely as a matter of convenience. In this book, for example, if the interest in two or more banks is held by a corporation, business trust, association, or similar organization, the arrangement has been designated as group banking; all other systems have been classified as chains. This procedure was followed merely to ensure that the terminology employed was reasonably consistent with existing federal legislation in this field and with most published statistics.

## MULTIPLE-UNIT BANKING[3]

### EARLY DEVELOPMENT

Although little information regarding the management and the ownership of banking institutions in the distant past is available, there is considerable evidence that individuals have served as officers and/or have held the controlling interest in two or more banks in the United States for nearly 150 years.[4] Initially, it would seem, American

---

[2] Obviously if they are banks and not merely banking offices they would in all probability be separately chartered, but this point could be overlooked. The choice of systems with only two or more members as chains or groups is admittedly arbitrary.

[3] The historical development of multiple-unit banking is discussed in Fischer, *Bank Holding Companies,* and Lamb, *Group Banking.* Many other references are included in these books.

[4] Multiple-unit banking also played a role in the development of some foreign banking systems. For a discussion of the use of this form of organization in British banking during the first half of the nineteenth century, see Crick and Wadsworth, *A Hundred Years of Joint Stock Banking.* Today, affiliates are

banks were combined in a rather informal manner through common ownership by a single person or by a small group of investors, but as the use of the holding company became more common (*circa* 1900) corporations were also formed for the purpose of purchasing and holding bank stock.

Most of the references to multiple-unit banking which are found in the financial literature appeared after 1880. Nevertheless, it is clear that chain systems had been formed in New York State by the 1820s and 1830s,[5] and a careful examination of the bank records in other states would probably reveal such arrangements also existed elsewhere in the nation at that time. In addition, some of the earliest banks chartered in this country had many of the attributes of bank holding companies. Both the First and the Second Banks of the United States operated their branches almost as if they were unit banks. Each branch had its own president and directors and these officials enjoyed considerable authority in managing their institutions.

A number of the state "branch" banks in the Midwest mentioned in Chapter 2, including the State Bank of Indiana, the State Bank of Iowa, and the State Bank of Ohio, had at least some of the characteristics of bank holding companies. The Board of Control, which supervised each of these systems, was described earlier as comparable in many ways to a state banking superintendent, but its operations also resembled those of some headquarters units of bank holding companies. It was this similarity which led a prominent banking scholar to remark in discussing the Bank of Indiana: "There is question whether it should be called a branch bank system or a group bank system."[6]

Although chain banking existed in America during the first half of the nineteenth century, banking structure studies have tended to draw their illustrations from works which emphasized multiple-unit systems formed after the mid-1880s. For example, an investigation of the economic growth of the "Twin Cities," Minneapolis–St. Paul, reported a small chain of banks was in operation in North Dakota in

---

still used by most United Kingdom banks to handle their overseas and even their Scottish and Irish operations. Auburn, ed., *Comparative Banking*, p. 8.

[5] Several chain systems in New York State which were in operation before 1835 are briefly discussed in Wilburn, *Biddle's Bank*, pp. 95, 101–103, 111–19.

[6] Chapman and Westerfield, *Branch Banking*, p. 43.

1887.[7] Shortly thereafter (1889) William S. Witham began what was eventually to be the largest chain in terms of number of affiliated banks in this country. Although Witham held no stock interest whatsoever in some of the banks associated with the chain, he exerted considerable influence over their operations by serving as their fiscal agent, auditing their books, borrowing money for them, aiding them in obtaining deposits, and assisting them in investing surplus funds.[8]

Other chains were reported to have been in operation in Chicago in 1893, and in various sections of the West North Central states and even the Pacific Northwest before the turn of the century.[9] In some instances the commercial banking functions of these systems were secondary to their operations in farm mortgages, for a number of chains were formed in rural areas to obtain agricultural paper which would, in turn, be sold by an investment affiliate located in a large city.[10] While these arrangements in some cases included as many as twenty affiliates, both the "farm mortgage oriented" systems and the more conventional chains in existence before 1900 were typically limited to a few banks.

During this early period of multiple-unit banking development, there was little concern with group systems, for no state amended its general incorporating law to permit one corporation to own stock in another corporation until New Jersey passed legislation permitting such action in 1888.[11] A few years later, an article appeared in the *Banking Law Journal* proposing the establishment of a "holding company for banks."[12] The author visualized a firm whose financial structure closely resembled some of today's group systems. His plan was submitted to bankers all over the country for criticism, and a

[7] Hartsough, *The Twin Cities as a Metropolitan Market* contains probably the most complete study of early chain banking in the Northwest. Another fine work in this area is Popple's, *Development of Two Group Banks in the Northwest.*

[8] Fischer, *Bank Holding Companies,* pp. 152–54.

[9] Cartinhour, *Branch, Group, and Chain Banking,* pp. 83–84. Thomas, "Concentration in Banking Controls through Interlocking Directorates as Typified by Chicago Banks," *Journal of Business* (January 1933), p. 9.

[10] Eckardt, *A Rational Banking System,* pp. 194–95.

[11] Donaldson, *Corporate Finance,* p. 715.

[12] Hayes, "A Plan for Bank Consolidation," *The Banking Law Journal* (July 15, 1892), pp. 56–60.

number of the responses were assembled in a booklet entitled *An Argument in Favor of the Organization of a Financial Corporation and Union of Banks.* The replies indicated there was a general feeling among the respondents that multiple-unit banking of this type would have been actively opposed because of the growing antitrust spirit at the time.

## 1900–1930

Shortly after the turn of the century, interest in multiple-unit banking grew quite rapidly. In fact, in the Northwest so many systems were organized that companies were formed whose business consisted largely of acting as agents in the purchase and sale of country bank stock. A number of bank holding companies were formed at this time, and several of these systems, such as the Union Investment Company which is now a division of the Northwest Bancorporation, remain as active participants in group banking today. These firms were not only the forerunners in the bank holding company movement, but their basic form of organization and policies provided a pattern which was followed by many multiple-unit bankers in succeeding decades.

At about the same time these early group systems were being established in the Northwest, interest in multiple-unit banking was also growing in Chicago. In 1903 James B. Forgan of the First National Bank devised the so-called Chicago Plan—a method whereby a national bank, which by law could not provide fiduciary services, could acquire a trust company.[13] Thereafter, through a trustee arrangement, it was made certain that the shareholders of both institutions remained identical. At present a variation of this method is still used by a few bank holding companies which are affiliated with but which do not own a large bank.

Multiple-unit banking was employed in Chicago not only because of limitations placed upon a bank's trust operations but also because branch banking was prohibited. To obtain representation in various sections of the city and the suburbs, numerous chains were established, and although over a half century has passed since these systems were organized, the reasons cited for their formation could well apply not only to Chicago but to many other areas in the 1960s.

[13] James, *The Growth of the Chicago Banks,* pp. 693–94.

To quote from an article in the *Journal of Business* which described the origin of these chains many years ago:[14]

The growth of population and increasing congestion of traffic made for rapid development of banking in the outlying districts. The downtown banks could hardly but look with envy at the lucrative savings bank business that thus developed. With branch banking prohibited, the only solution was to buy into established banks in the new territory or establish new ones.

By 1909 there were at least four small chains in operation in Chicago, and by 1917 the number had risen to nine.[15] In the later year, one authority indicated these systems included 27 banks and they held over one-half of the city's banking resources.[16]

Unlike Chicago institutions, which were limited to a single office, banks in the City of New York were allowed to establish branches under the provisions of legislation passed in 1898. (Laws of New York, 1898, Ch. 410.) Nevertheless, a substantial number of chain systems were also formed in Manhattan. National banks in New York, like their counterparts in Chicago, organized affiliates under state banking laws (in addition to security affiliates formed under general business incorporation statutes) to enable them to participate, at least indirectly, in activities (such as the trust business) which they could not engage in directly as national banks. In addition, the J. P. Morgan, George F. Baker, and the James Stillman interests controlled a large number of Gotham banks with vast assets, which were acquired during the period of general centralization of control of financial resources and industry in the late 1890s and early 1900s. Finally, there were some chain systems which were formed by speculators who acquired a number of banks by using the stock of one bank as collateral to buy others. Probably the best known of these systems was the Morse-Heinze chain, which is often credited with precipitating the Panic of 1907.[17]

---

[14] Thomas, "Concentration in Banking Controls," *Journal of Business* (January 1933), p. 9.

[15] *Ibid.*, pp. 3–4, 9. Also see James, *The Growth of the Chicago Banks*, pp. 956–58.

[16] Two of the large "Loop" banks were affiliated with chains at this time, and they accounted for three-fourths of the resources of all chain banks in the city.

[17] Corey, *The House of Morgan*, pp. 254–62, 350–59; and Noyes, *Forty Years of American Finance*, pp. 365 ff.

Since there was virtually no geographic restriction upon the expansion of multiple-unit banking, it is sometimes asked why the large New York City or Chicago banks with their tremendous resources did not develop trade-area or even nationwide bank holding company systems. These institutions did establish various types of affiliates as noted above,[18] and the Morgan-Stillman-Baker combination, the Pujo Committee money-trust investigation in 1912 revealed,[19] held 118 directorships in 34 banks and trust companies located in a number of cities. But these arrangements appeared to be related primarily to the quest for financial power and stock speculation of the times, and not to the long-run improvement of conventional banking operations through coordinated management of a group of affiliated banks. The less formal chain system, held together through interlocking directorates, was apparently most often employed by institutions in the nation's two major financial centers, and when the holding company device was used the organizations typically functioned much more as investment companies than management service holding companies.

The lack of interest New York and Chicago banks showed in forming widespread holding company systems is frequently explained by the fact that both the Loop and Wall Street bankers feared the group banking movement nearly as much as the possibility that federal legislation would authorize regional branch banking. The major institutions in these two financial centers had become important bankers' banks and had a vast correspondent business; therefore, their officers generally opposed group banking on at least two grounds. First, if the New York or Chicago banks formed holding companies and began to acquire banks in various parts of the nation, this action could have brought them into conflict with some of their major correspondents presently serving the banks in these areas. Second, if the large regional banks rather than firms in New York or Chicago formed group systems, these banks might have found that they could

[18] See "The Holding Company in Banking," *American Bankers Association Journal* (October 1927), pp. 255 ff; and "Investment Affiliates Thrive," *Ibid.* (May 1930), pp. 1027 ff. Peach, *The Security Affiliates of National Banks* is the best general study of this question.

[19] U. S. Congress, House, *Report of the Committee Appointed Pursuant to House Resolution 429 and 504 to Investigate the Concentration of Control of Money and Credit*, 1913, pp. 55–106. (Hereafter called Pujo Committee Report)

provide most of the services previously supplied only by the institutions in the established money centers.[20] Hence, instead of being leaders in the bank holding company movement, many "central reserve city" bankers joined forces with those individuals who advocated maintaining the status quo in banking structure.[21]

In addition to the bankers in New York and Chicago, their colleagues in other major cities also showed little interest in employing the holding company device to obtain affiliates throughout the nation. As a result the early group systems were usually quite small, with only a few members serving a very limited area.[22] However, at least one banker, Amadeo P. Giannini, felt that the growth of branch banking would not always be limited to a single city or state and that nationwide branch banking was inevitable. He fully appreciated the role that a bank holding company might play in developing a multiple-office system, having used the Stockholders Auxiliary Corporation and the Bancitaly Corporation to acquire banks in California and New York, respectively, before 1920. The former corporation was used in establishing a branch system in California, while the latter was expected to perform essentially the same role in the national market.[23] By the mid-1920s companies with which Giannini was associated owned all or at least a substantial part of the stock of the Bank of Italy (California), the Liberty Bank of San Francisco, and the Bank of America (Los Angeles), and they held stock in 67 other domestic banks and 59 foreign banks in sixteen countries.[24]

*Statistics.*[25] Prior to the late 1920s, bank supervisory authorities only rarely differentiated between chain and group banking. As a result, on those few occasions when multiple-unit banking statistics were gathered only aggregate data for these two forms of bank

[20] James, *The Growth of the Chicago Banks,* p. 956; Palyi, *The Chicago Credit Market,* pp. 209, 220–21; Collins, *Rural Banking Reform,* pp. 129, 162; and Curtis, "The Turning Financial Worm," *The Nation* (April 23, 1930), p. 490.

[21] House Hearings, 1930, especially Part XIV.

[22] Barnett, *State Banks and Trust Companies since the Passage of the National Bank Act,* p. 143.

[23] James and James, *Biography of a Bank,* pp. 76, 108–109, 270.

[24] Cartinhour, *Branch, Group, and Chain Banking,* pp. 137–38.

[25] Background information concerning the development of these statistics may be found in *Banking and Monetary Statistics,* section 8, pp. 294–96.

organization were compiled. Furthermore, even these composite statistics are of limited value to the researcher today, for the reports from which the figures were taken were fragmentary, and only systems comprised of three or more banks (rather than two or more banks as in the current definition) were included. These data are so poor that they should not be used in any type of time series analysis. They are cited below merely to indicate that surveys were made and to note some of their findings.

The earliest federal agency survey of chains and groups was made by the Federal Reserve Board's Division of Research and Statistics in 1922. This effort revealed there were approximately 800 multiple-unit banks in the United States. Later investigations showed 1,000 banks in chains and groups in 1926 and more than 1,400 in 1928.[26] No assets or liabilities figures are available for these years since the "Fed" did not compile any substantial amount of data beyond mere numbers of affiliate banks until the Congressional hearings on branch, group, and chain banking were held in 1930. Statistics gathered at that time for the House Banking and Currency Committee showed that at the end of 1929 some 332 multiple-unit systems controlled 9 percent of the banks (2,165) and 25 percent of the loans and investments (12 billion dollars) of all commercial banks in this country.[27]

To provide at least some indication of the individual market shares of group (bank holding company) systems, this writer gathered data as of December 31, 1929 for those firms which later registered as bank holding companies under the provisions of the Banking Act of 1933 and for those organizations which from the available literature could definitely be identified as bank holding companies.[28] These statistics revealed that bank holding companies controlled roughly one-fourth of the number and over one-half of the loans and invest-

[26] *Ibid.*, p. 296. For a detailed summary of these chain banking statistics see Darnell, "Chain Banking," *National Banking Review* (March 1966), pp. 307–32.

[27] *Ibid.*, p. 312. A survey of multiple-unit banking was also made by John Chapman in 1925. The results of this investigation are reported in his *Concentration of Banking*, pp. 327–29.

[28] A few small companies under 25 million dollars in resources were omitted. Compiled from "Roll Call of Leading Bank Groups in the United States," *American Banker*, February 20, 1930; House Hearings 1930, pp. 162–84, 454–55, 464–66; and various bank directories.

ments of all multiple-unit (chain and group) systems reported. Thus, bank holding companies, it would appear, had become the dominant element in the field of multiple-unit banking before 1930.

*State legislation and regulation.*   Many years before there was a federal multiple-unit banking statute, several states had enacted legislation to control chains and groups. One of the first of these state laws to be passed was in New York in 1908 following the collapse of the "Morse-Heinz chain" in Manhattan the previous year. The New York Law limited the holding by a trust company of the stock of another monied corporation to 10 percent of the amount of such stock outstanding.[29] Similar laws were enacted by California, New Hampshire, Texas, and Wisconsin. In addition, Wisconsin law required group-system directors to be residents of the state[30] and declared any organization authorized to do business in Wisconsin which had control of a state bank or trust company to be in the business of banking and subject to the supervision of the state banking department.[31]

In Missouri, a ruling of the state attorney general denied the right of a bank holding company to sell its stock in that state on the grounds that group banking was branch banking under a different guise.[32] Similarly, New Jersey and West Virginia passed laws which in effect prohibited group banking.[33] Other states, such as Michigan, were much more lenient and merely required bank holding companies to qualify with the state security commission before selling their stock.[34] In most states, however, except for the rule that one state bank could not own the shares of another state bank, there were no legal provisions whatsoever regarding the ownership of bank stock.[35]

*Federal legislation and regulation.*   Although a number of states passed laws to restrict the operations of multiple-unit banking institu-

[29] New York Superintendent of Banks, *Annual Report,* 1907–1908 fiscal year, p. XXII.

[30] Palyi, *The Chicago Credit Market,* pp. 193–94.

[31] "Status of Group, Chain, and Branch Banking in the United States," *American Bankers Association Journal* (July 1930), p. 67.

[32] Federal Reserve Board, Committee Reports, "Branch Banking," p. 205.

[33] *Ibid.*

[34] House Hearings, 1930, p. 1627.

[35] In some states bank stock could be owned but the maximum amount was specified (for example, 10 percent of the outstanding shares). Chapman, *Concentration of Banking,* p. 336.

tions, this legislation was sometimes difficult to enforce,[36] and its effect upon large multi-state firms was very limited. If adequate controls over these organizations were to be obtained, they had to come through Congressional action. Of course, some federal laws in this area had been passed, for Sections 7 and 8 of the Clayton Act[37] both contained provisions designed to eliminate many of the undesirable practices the Pujo Committee uncovered in its 1912 "money trust" investigations,[38] and this legislation appeared to apply to a few of the operations of chains and groups. But the antitrust laws were largely restricted to questions of interbank competition, and they were of little help to the bank supervisor who was concerned with such things as "upstream lending," loans secured by holding company shares, relations with nonbank subsidiaries, excessive dividends, and numerous other potential operating problems which might have developed within a multiple-unit system.

With the rapid expansion of group banking in the 1920s and the failure of several large multiple-unit systems in the 1920s and early 1930s, interest in obtaining further federal regulation of these firms was stimulated. Finally, the Federal Reserve was given some control over bank holding companies by the Banking Act of 1933, and its powers were increased substantially by the Bank Holding Company Act of 1956. This legislation and the recent efforts to grant the banking authorities similar powers in the field of chain banking will be considered in the analysis of chain banking and of group banking since 1930 which follows.

## CHAIN BANKING

INTRODUCTION

From the available literature one would have to conclude that the most rapid development of chain banking probably took place before 1925. But, since the early chain banking statistics which were gath-

[36] O'Connor, *The Banking Crises and Recovery under the Roosevelt Administration,* p. 6.

[37] Section 8 of the Clayton Act is discussed in Chapter 6 and Section 7 in Chapters 7 and 8.

[38] U. S. Congress, Pujo Committee Report, 1913. Especially see the Committee's recommendations, pp. 163–65.

ered may have been extremely inaccurate and since no data for both Federal Reserve member and nonmember systems were compiled after December 31, 1945,[39] any estimates regarding the growth of this form of multiple-unit banking would have to be classified at best as merely "educated guesses." However, bank structure articles published in recent years would seem to suggest that chain banking has increased substantially of late, especially in Colorado, Florida, Illinois, Missouri, and Texas.

Although the relationships between the associated banks in chain systems continue to be based upon the ownership of several banks by an individual or a small group of individuals, a variety of other methods are used to maintain a community of interest among a number of banks. For example, satellite and affiliate banking resemble this "classic" form of chain organization, although under these arrangements common ownership is not always a factor. In very broad terms, an affiliate bank is one organized by the directors of another bank, which may provide executive officers for the new institution and in some instances even assist in the original financing. While a satellite bank also has an affiliate relationship, this expression is most often applied when a new bank is located in the outlying trade area of its "parent" bank and it makes extensive use of the facilities provided by that bank.[40]

Numerous illustrations of affiliate and/or satellite banking could be drawn from government reports, the financial press,[41] and the findings in court actions[42] in recent years. From the statements in these publications it is apparent that these systems vary considerably from one area to another, depending upon the technical provisions of state law, the size of the banks involved, the philosophy of the banking community, and a variety of other factors; therefore, it is virtually impossible

[39] Federal Reserve Board, *Recent Developments in the Structure of Banking,* 1962, p. 10.

[40] These definitions were taken from Carter Golembe, "Present Structure of the U. S. Commercial Banking System," *The Bankers' Handbook,* p. 1003.

[41] See, for example, "Affiliates Grow in Colorado," *American Banker,* December 3, 1964; and "Howell Will Consider N. J. Affiliate Banking," *ibid.,* June 30, 1965.

[42] See "Branch Case Will Go to Oklahoma High Court," *ibid.,* June 3, 1966; *Northtown Bank of Decatur* v. *Becker,* 31 Illinois 2d 529, 202 N.E. 2d 540 (1964), and *Whitney National Bank* v. *Bank of New Orleans,* 323 F. 2d 290 (D.C. Cir. 1963); 379 U.S. 411 (1965).

to make any broad general statements concerning their organization. A few comments regarding some of the Texas and Illinois systems may lend some support to this conclusion.

In Texas, where both branch and group banking are prohibited, "shell corporations" are frequently employed to permit one bank to indirectly acquire a substantial stock interest in another bank. For example, in Dallas trustees hold in trust for the stockholders of the Republic National Bank all of the shares of the Howard Corporation, Republic National Company, and numerous other corporations. These companies in turn own stock in fourteen banks doing business in the Dallas area with total resources of over 250 million dollars. Despite the large number of banks and corporations involved, this organization and a number of others in Texas which are very similar have not been required to register with the Federal Reserve under the provisions of the Bank Holding Company Act of 1956 since they do not have 25 percent interest in two or more banks. Republic National and its associated companies, for instance, have combined holdings amounting to 20.0 percent of seven institutions and 24.9 percent of seven others.

In Illinois, affiliate relationships are often maintained through interlocking directorates and common officers as they are elsewhere; but in some cases bankers have made little or no effort to obtain working control over other institutions via stock acquisition. Instead, they have been satisfied merely to obtain the goodwill of individuals attempting to establish new banks by assisting them in their organizational efforts. Of course, there are many reasons not directly related to branching for performing this function, including the possibility that this may be the first step in establishing a long and profitable correspondent business; however, it was apparent from discussions with bankers in Illinois that they also hoped the close ties developed with these banks as a result of this service might make at least some of them likely candidates for membership in a future branch system.

The very informal relationship which may arise between a number of small banks and a large Chicago bank merely because the latter aids investors in their efforts to establish a new institution could not technically be termed chain banking. But, if one defines chain banking in terms of goals rather than by using as a criterion the degree of ownership or control, these arrangements would not differ significantly from many chain systems. Furthermore, not only counsel but financial assistance has occasionally been extended to the organizers of new banks, who use the *de novo* bank's stock as collateral for loans. Naturally, this type of lending, whether the security for the loan is shares in a *de novo* bank or an existing bank, could result in one bank achieving indirect control over another. Therefore, it is not surprising that Representative Wright Patman, in his study of chains a few years ago, indicated that such arrangements should be included in any analysis of chain banking.

PATMAN'S CHAIN BANKING REPORT[43]

In January 1963 Congressman Wright Patman submitted a report on chain banking to the House Select Committee on Small Business. This document was to be only the first of a number of studies prepared by the Committee's staff relating to "stockholder and loan links" among Federal Reserve member banks. The Board of Governors provided invaluable assistance in gathering the basic data for this work by sending questionnaires to the 6,100 banks under its jurisdiction. It requested statistics concerning the twenty largest stockholders of record, stockholdings of each director and principal officer, and any loans made by member banks secured by 10 percent or more of the stock of any other bank. But, although the Board of Governors cooperated in securing the desired information, its staff did not participate in the analysis of this material. The resulting studies were prepared by Mr. Patman's staff or by outside experts retained by the Committee.

*Definition of a chain.* Certainly one of the most difficult tasks faced in trying to determine the extent of chain banking in the United States is defining the term "chain." It has been suggested that a simple definition[44] similar to the one found in the Bank Holding Company Act might be adequate; yet, this standard would omit many organizations which should definitely be included in any compilation of chains.

---

[43] *Chain Banking: Stockholder and Loan Links of 200 Largest Member Banks,* Report by Wright Patman to the Select Committee on Small Business, House of Representatives, 1963. (Hereafter referred to as Patman's Chain Banking Report.)

[44] In actual practice, even this "simple" definition may be very difficult to use.

Repesentative Patman considered this problem in a letter written to Chairman William McChesney Martin, Jr., of the Board of Governors. In this note he observed:[45]

To determine the extent of chain banking it would apparently be necessary to know both (1) direct controls, and (2) indirect controls. Direct controls would be shown by stockholdings by the same individual or group of individuals in two or more banks. Indirect controls would not be indicated by such stockownership records, but might come about by a large bank supplying funds to individuals for the purpose of purchasing stock in a bank, taking back as collateral the stock of the smaller bank. In this way the large bank might have effective control over the small bank.

The definition of a chain system found in the Patman Report largely reflected these views. It was very broad, including even overlapping interests among the twenty largest stockholders of record in any two or more banks, and any bank loans secured by 10 percent or more of the stock in any other bank.

*Findings.*   Using the above-mentioned standard, Patman found "a whole network of links among the top stockholders of the largest member banks." Some of these links were centered in nominee[46] holdings of the large commercial banks, but, in addition, the study revealed that some 1,242 bank loans totaling 191 million dollars were secured by 10 percent or more of the stock in other banks. The report suggested that it was of particular importance that the preponderance of this lending occurred in states which prohibited branch banking or bank holding companies, and much of this loan activity was carried out across state lines.

*Criticism.*   M. A. Schapiro & Company's *Bank Stock Quarterly* (March 1963) strongly criticized the findings in the Patman report. It argued that ordinarily a chain is defined as an individual or group of individuals controlling two or more banks, and it suggested that the

[45] Patman's Chain Banking Report, p. III.

[46] In performance of their fiduciary functions, banks commonly employ the partnership form of nominee registration of securities held in such capacity, particularly corporate stocks, to take advantage of operating efficiencies associated with this practice, especially those related to collection of income and transfer of ownership. The bank's authority may vary from full power to buy, sell, and vote the stock to virtually no power whatsoever, with the beneficial owners able to exercise all prerogatives of ownership.

ordinary sense of control was ownership of 25 percent or more of the outstanding stock.[47] Using this definition, the *Quarterly* indicated that "the report provides conclusive evidence that there is not a single banking chain among the 200 largest member banks."[48] While this publication conceded that the customary definition of chain banking may be too narrow, it also noted that Congressman Patman's terminology may be too broad, for he found 400 chains among only 200 banks.[49]

Any definition of chain banking would have to be somewhat arbitrary. Nevertheless, Representative Patman's use of stockholder rank (within the top twenty) as a measure of control would not seem to be justified, for under this procedure individuals with only a small fraction of 1 percent interest in each of two or more banks are classified as chain bankers. When a stockholder's investment is this small, and he can control several banks, it would seem likely that his power stems from something other than the size of his equity investment in the institutions in question. In fact, his authority might be virtually unchanged if he held only directors' qualifying shares or even no shares at all.[50]

It would seem that before any measure of the magnitude of chain banking was established it might be asked why this information was needed. In the case of the Patman report, for example, data regarding direct and indirect control of banking institutions was desired "to round out the picture of banking concentration in the United States." Hence, the crucial element in the definition of a chain for the Patman study was the designation of what constituted control (or potential control).[51] To avoid studying individual banks, a proxy (or proxies) whose correlation with "control" was sufficiently high to satisfy the researcher had to be chosen. But, as noted above, how Patman's staff

[47] "The Patman Report," *Bank Stock Quarterly,* M. A. Schapiro & Co., Inc. (March 1963), p. 5.

[48] *Ibid.,* p. 6.

[49] *Ibid.*

[50] While this writer has no statistical evidence to support this conclusion, it would seem to be a fair statement based upon interviews with bankers in virtually all regions of this country and upon my experience as a bank employee.

[51] Since the typical chain definition refers to control of two or more banks by an individual or small group of individuals, one must also determine the meaning of "small group," which may be very difficult.

could have selected stockholder rank in preference to some minimum percentage of share ownership as this proxy is difficult to understand, although both admittedly have numerous weaknesses.

*Bank nominees.* Like brokers and dealers, many commercial banks when acting in a fiduciary capacity register securities in the name of a nominee,[52] and the possible role of these nominees in chain banking was considered in the Patman report. This study revealed that bank nominees comprised 18 percent of the twenty top stockholders in the 200 largest member banks.[53] But unfortunately without further information the authors of the report could find no way to judge the precise significance of this relationship. Nevertheless, the Patman study quite properly raised a number of important questions regarding the independence of action of a given bank if its competitors have important stock positions in it through nominee holdings.[54] While there is little available evidence concerning this problem, a survey of bank trust department operations made by this writer for the American Bankers Association[55] several years ago would lead to the general conclusion that the effect of such holdings of bank shares upon interbank competition would probably be minimal. Nevertheless, additional investigation of this question is needed.

*Loans on bank stock.* Another area examined in the Patman study was bank loans secured by the stock of another bank. In transmitting the survey data on this question to the Congressman, Chairman Martin of the Federal Reserve Board cautioned:[56]

The information regarding loans on bank stock requires careful interpretation, since these loans are made for a variety of purposes and, therefore, their existence does not in itself indicate any particular measure of management influence or control over the smaller bank.

[52] A nominee is a person (or persons) designated to represent or take the place in name only of another person, bank, company, or corporation.

[53] Patman's Chain Banking Report, p. 13.

[54] *Ibid.,* p. 17.

[55] This survey was carried out in connection with the writing of the "Trust Function" chapter of the American Bankers Association volume, *The Commercial Banking Industry,* a monograph submitted to the Commission on Money and Credit.

[56] Patman's Chain Banking Report, p. 79.

While the Patman report acknowledged that "management influence or control" was not prima facie revealed by the mere existence of loans of this type, it observed such a technique could be a means to this end.[57]

Patman found that of the 200 largest member banks included in the Federal Reserve survey some 111 held loans secured by 10 percent or more of the outstanding stock of a bank. Shares in a total of 1,161 banks were pledged as security in these transactions.[58] Nearly one-half of the bank stock loans both in terms of number of banks whose stock was used as collateral (537) and in terms of dollar amount (88 million dollars) were held by only eleven banks. The report indicated over 90 percent of the banks whose stock was pledged as security at these eleven institutions were located in thirteen states, twelve of which prohibited branch banking. It concluded that: "The evidence presented in this study on bank stock loans suggests that many have been made for the clear purpose of evading federal and state laws restricting branch, holding company, and chain banking."[59] Perhaps this statement is true, but it clearly could not be substantiated by the material in the Patman report.

Despite the questionable conclusions in this section of the report, the discovery that bank stock loans were concentrated in a small number of banks in a few states, at least to date, appears to be the most significant finding developed by Patman's staff from the Federal Reserve survey material submitted by the 200 largest member banks. Of course, one could devise numerous explanations for this phenomenon. For instance, it could be argued that on the average banks tend to be considerably smaller in the states which prohibit branch banking;[60] and, therefore, it is much more likely that 10 percent or more of the stock of a bank of this size would be held by one party (who

---

[57] *Ibid.*

[58] *Ibid.,* pp. 486 ff.

[59] *Ibid.,* p. 92.

[60] At the time the loan survey was made the median-sized bank in states which prohibited branching had deposits of 8 million dollars; in those states which had limited branching and statewide branching, the corresponding figures were 13 million dollars and 28 million dollars respectively. Computed from data in FDIC, *Annual Report* for the year ended December 31, 1962, pp. 116–17.

could use it as security for a loan) than would be the case if the institution were substantially larger. This thesis was given considerable support by the data in a subsequent analysis of all 6,100 banks which completed the Board's questionnaire.[61] But this study also expressed concern regarding the predominance of such a small number of banks in this market, noting: ". . . a great deal more must be learned about the forces motivating both lenders and borrowers before an adequate explanation of this observed concentration may be advanced."[62] This writer could only echo these remarks.[63]

GROWTH OF CHAIN BANKING

Although the multiple-unit banking statistics which were obtained during the 1920s did not distinguish between chain and group banking, five surveys were carried out by the Board of Governors in the 1930s and 1940s which did show chains and groups separately. In these studies a chain system was defined as a type of multiple-unit banking institution "in which the operations or policies of at least *three* independently incorporated banks [were] controlled by one or more individuals." (italics added)

The first of these more recent surveys reported 176 chains with 908 affiliates and 900 million dollars of deposits (this amount was estimated by this writer from loan and investment data) were in operation at the end of 1931. The corresponding figures for 1939 and 1945, respectively, were 96 and 115 chains, 424 and 522 affiliates, and 883 million dollars and 4,628 million dollars in deposits. Unfortunately, these studies, like those conducted in the twenties, cannot legitimately be employed in an effort to describe trends in chain banking (although this is often done, even by federal agencies), for

[61] *The Structure of Ownership of Member Banks and the Pattern of Loans Made on Hypothecated Bank Stock,* Staff Analysis to the Subcommittee on Domestic Finance, Committee on Banking and Currency, House of Representatives, 1964, Chapter 2.

[62] *Ibid.* This study expressed particular concern regarding the possible use of correspondent balances to obtain favorable terms on bank stock loans.

[63] Late in December, 1966, Representative Patman released a report which included a study of data provided (in many cases very reluctantly) by 3,200 banks and other financial institutions. The main elements in the report were the analyses of bank shares owned by other financial institutions and the discussion of the huge resources held by bank trust departments. U. S. Congress, House, *Bank Stock Ownership and Control,* 1966.

individuals who have used and developed these data state quite emphatically these compilations are of little real value.

*Current dimensions of chain banking.*[64]   As was noted earlier, the apparent significance of chain banking in the American financial system may differ tremendously depending upon the definition of this form of bank organization employed. To emphasize this point, the 6,100 member banks included in the questionnaire survey made by the Board of Governors were analyzed using two very different measures of chain banking. The first followed some of the standards suggested by Representative Patman in his *Chain Banking Report,* and the second used criteria which closely resembled the provisions in the Bank Holding Company Act of 1956.

The definition based largely upon Patman's legislative recommendations in this area would classify as chains two or more banks which had stockholders in common from among the top twenty in each bank (excluding registered bank holding companies), provided that the stockholder was a director, an officer, or an owner of 5 percent or more of the stock in each bank. Using this criterion, at least one-fifth of all member bank assets (45 billion dollars) and of all member banks (1,146) would have been listed as controlled by chains in 1962.[65]

The definition developed from the terminology in the Bank Holding Company Act, on the other hand, would include only those cases in which 25 percent of the shares of two or more banks were owned by an individual or the same group of individuals, ranking among the twenty largest stockholders.[66] Using this standard, only 175 chain

[64] Much of the data in this section was compiled or obtained directly from the unpublished doctoral dissertation on "Chain Banking as a Form of Banking Organization" by Jerome C. Darnell at Indiana University. Part of his thesis has been published under the title "Chain Banking," in the *National Banking Review* (March 1966), pp. 307–32.

[65] Selected characteristics of 45,000 stockholders of 5,600 member banks were placed on punch cards by Darnell and then sorted by computer. Identical stockholder names and addresses on the lists of more than one bank were then noted. This procedure has many faults, but it was the only method of determining whether a community of interest existed. Of course this would not uncover a great many chain systems; hence, these data might be viewed as a minimum.

[66] Only data for the "top twenty" stockholders are available. That is why this cutoff point was selected.

banks with approximately 1.5 billion dollars of deposits were recorded. If, in addition to the investments of individuals, the holdings
of corporate entities which were not subject to regulation under the
Bank Holding Company Act were included, the above totals would
increase slightly to 204 chain banks and 2.3 billion dollars of deposits. Most of these chains were very small, only one-fifth had more than
two affiliates, and the vast majority (85 percent) were located in
states that prohibited branch banking.

The above statistics were obtained by matching stockholders'
names and addresses with an electronic computer.[67] Obviously, this
procedure has numerous weaknesses and it surely would not have
discovered many interrelationships among member banks. Also, this
research could not consider nonmember banks since data concerning
them was unavailable. In regard to this point, in the 1939 through
1945 surveys member banks comprised on the average about one-half
of the chain banks in number and they held 85 percent of the chain
deposits. [68]

OPERATIONS

Since the multiple-unit banking definitions employed in this book
relegate chain banks to the "all other" category, it is very difficult to
generalize regarding their operations. Some very large chains are
essentially bank holding companies which for some reason have not
been required to register with the Federal Reserve. Others, especially
the smaller systems, are often the personal investments of one individual or a few individuals, and the role of the owner(s) in the management of the chain may vary enormously depending upon his talents
and interests. As a result, it is virtually impossible to select a list of
characteristics which purport to describe the operations of the "typical chain."

Nevertheless, questionnaires were distributed to a sample of chain
bankers by one investigator to try to learn something more about how

[67] U. S. Congress, House, *Twenty Largest Stockholders of Record in Member
Banks of the Federal Reserve System,* 1964.
[68] Also, no account is taken of chains which might consist of only one
member and one nonmember bank.

their organizations function.[69] The respondents indicated there was a much closer relationship among chain affiliates than this writer would have expected. For example, the replies emphasized that in actual practice these banks had numerous advantages over their independent competitors as a result of a better exchange of credit information, joint participation in large loans, cooperative solution of operating problems, a sharing of specialized equipment and personnel, and the establishment of common loan and investment policies. Since the owners of chain banks often serve as officers in a number of affiliates, this cooperation probably should have been expected to exist, but such action may be rather disturbing to the Department of Justice when these affiliates serve the same market area. Moreover, critics of chain banking point out that such arrangements are particularly undesirable, for in some cases the general public may not even be aware that common ownership exists among the supposedly competing banks.[70]

LEGISLATION AND REGULATION

There is still little effective state or federal regulation of chain banking. Section 8 of the Clayton Act, which restricts interlocking directorates among banks, has been amended several times but each of the revisions appears to have weakened rather than strengthened this legislation. Of course the supervisory authorities have been given considerable control over bank holding company operations by congressional action in 1933 and 1956. However, both of these acts referred to ownership of shares by a corporation, business trust, association, or other similar organization, and they apparently do not cover control of banks by individuals.

*1964 and 1966 statutes.* On September 12, 1964 Congress passed a bill under which insured banks were required to inform the appropriate federal banking agency of any changes of management

[69] These questionnaires were distributed by Jerome Darnell while he was a doctoral candidate at Indiana University. Some of the findings of Darnell's research appear in "Chain Bank Ownership and Operation," *National Banking Review* (December 1966), pp. 193–98.

[70] This writer has some doubt regarding this point, but it was suggested by several bank supervisors.

control and of any loans secured by 25 percent or more of the voting stock of such banks.[71] This legislation had been introduced because on five occasions in 1964 a new group had taken over a bank, and this action was followed by a rather sudden deterioration in the character of its assets. The FDIC therefore felt that existing law had to be revised so that the supervisory authority would be immediately aware of any change in control of an insured bank. Thereafter, it could keep the institution under observation if there appeared to be any possibility of fraud.[72]

The legislation relating to notice of change in management control of insured banks was only one of a series of actions which many people felt were necessary to strengthen the powers of the bank regulatory agencies. In his January 1966 *Economic Report,* President Johnson stated that appropriate regulations were required to protect the safety of deposits and savings of the public and to insure the most efficient and equitable regulation of financial institutions. Among other measures, he requested congressional action on financial legislation to "arm regulatory agencies with a wider range of effective enforcement remedies." The Financial Institutions Supervisory Act of 1966 which became law October 16, 1966 apparently met the recommendation of the President.[73]

This statute provides the federal banking agencies with intermediate-type powers short of their authority to take over or terminate the insurance of banks and savings and loan associations to stop undesirable actions by a bank's management. The new law authorizes the banking agencies to issue cease and desist orders under certain conditions if an insured bank has engaged or is about to engage in unsound or unsafe practices or to violate a law, rule, or agency regulation. Such violations or failure to comply with a cease and desist order could under specified circumstances result in the removal of an officer or director of an offending bank. While these laws were not specifi-

[71] 12 U.S.C. § 1817. 78 Stat. 940.

[72] U. S. Congress, House, Staff Report on *Acquisitions, Changes in Control, and Bank Stock Loans of Insured Banks,* 1967, analyzes the first two years' reports.

[73] 80 Stat. 1028 (1966), Title I (savings and loan associations) and Title II (commercial banks). These provisions are effective until June 30, 1972. Also see the House Report on the bill, Report No. 2077, (U. S. Congress, House, *Financial Institutions Supervisory and Insurance Act of 1966,* 1966).

cally aimed at multiple-unit banking, the question of the misuse of the assets of affiliate banks has usually been presented as a potential evil of chain banking, and to some extent this legislation may reduce this danger.

## BANK HOLDING COMPANIES

### INTRODUCTION

Most of the major bank holding companies in operation in the United States today were organized between 1925 and 1930. This development cannot be explained by any single variable, but rather a whole series of interrelated factors contributed to the expansion of group banking in this period. For instance, one would have to consider: the farm depression and the failure of small rural banks; the general consolidation movement in many other industries; the "snowball effect" as one holding company was formed and banks organized others to maintain their competitive position, correspondent business, and prestige; the restrictions on branch banking and the belief that the laws would soon change; and the investors' eagerness to purchase stock, including bank holding company shares.

While each of the above contributed to the interest in group banking which became so pronounced between 1925 and 1930, a careful study of the available evidence reveals that two of these factors were apparently much more significant than the others—the desperate condition of thousands of banks in this country and the "great bull market" in common stock. The weakness of banks made many of them anxious to join a group system, and the booming stock market made it possible for the holding companies to easily obtain the funds necessary to acquire new affiliates.[74] In some sections of the country the speculative element was dominant; while in others the sincere desire to prevent further bank failures prevailed. But, regardless of the importance of each of these causes in a particular area, it was the combination of the two which made the group banking movement of the late 1920s possible.

[74] Or the holding company could exchange shares with the banks desired on very favorable terms.

GROWTH OF GROUP BANKING

*1930–1948.* The early 1930s constituted a period of retrenchment rather than growth for bank holding companies. The need for banking reform spread from the agricultural areas to the cities, and the securities markets experienced a precipitous decline. Failures substantially reduced the number of banks in the nation, and several sizable group systems suspended operations. In addition, a number of bills were introduced in Congress which made the future of bank holding companies very uncertain, and little interest was shown in forming new systems. This may be noted from the statistics compiled by the Federal Reserve Board which reported that 97 groups with 978 banks were in operation in 1931, and only 52 groups with 479 banks in operation in 1936.

Another factor which contributed to the marked decline in the ranks of bank holding companies between 1931 and 1936 was the relaxation of legislation restricting branch banking. The number of states which permitted statewide branching doubled (nine to eighteen) during these few years, while the number of states which prohibited branch banking declined by 50 percent.[75] Furthermore, the Banking Act of 1933 permitted national banks to establish branches to the extent permitted state institutions, and as these branch laws were revised a number of groups became branch systems.

Although the Banking Acts of 1933 and 1935 would have to be described as favorable from the viewpoint of bank holding companies, still few new groups were organized. The depressed economy, the antagonism toward holding companies in general (as evidenced by the passage of the Public Utility Holding Company Act of 1935), and the fact that most groups had expanded too zealously in the 1920s continued to restrain any possible interest in multiple-unit banking. As a result, the position of groups in the American banking system showed relatively little change between the mid-1930s and 1948. In 1937, according to Federal Reserve data, these firms controlled approximately 7 percent of the commercial banking offices and 11 percent of the commercial bank deposits of all United States banks. In 1948 the respective percentages were almost unchanged. (See Table 3.1)

The development of group banking during this period, as reflected

[75] Chapman and Westerfield, *Branch Banking,* p. 5.

TABLE 3.1. OFFICES AND DEPOSITS OF BANK HOLDING COMPANIES FOR SELECTED YEARS, 1931–1966, AS REPORTED BY THE BOARD OF GOVERNORS OF THE FEDERAL RESERVE SYSTEM

| Year End | Number of Companies | Total Offices | Deposits (in $ million) | Percent of All U.S. Commercial Banks | |
|---|---|---|---|---|---|
| | | | | Offices | Deposits |
| 1931 | 97 | n.a. | n.a. | n.a. | n.a. |
| 1936 | 52 | n.a. | 6,841 | n.a. | 14 |
| 1937 | 47 | 1,344 | 6,453 | 7 | 11 |
| 1938 | 43 | 1,319 | 6,672 | 7 | 11 |
| 1939 | 41 | 1,296 | 7,173 | 7 | 13 |
| 1940 | 38 | 1,265 | 7,606 | 7 | 11 |
| 1941 | 37 | 1,246 | 8,175 | 7 | 12 |
| 1942 | 35 | 1,242 | 10,532 | 7 | 13 |
| 1943 | 31 | 1,201 | 12,407 | 7 | 11 |
| 1945 | 33 | 1,248 | 18,142 | 7 | 12 |
| 1948 | 20 | 1,231 | 15,290 | 7 | 11 |
| 1950 | 28 | 1,386 | 18,525 | 7 | 12 |
| 1951 | 31 | 1,458 | 20,496 | 8 | 12 |
| 1952 | 34 | 1,472 | 20,820 | 8 | 12 |
| 1954 | 46 | 1,018 | 14,277 | 5 | 8 |
| 1957 | 44 | 1,268 | 15,139 | 6 | 8 |
| 1958 | 43 | 1,266 | 15,998 | 6 | 7 |
| 1959 | 43 | 1,380 | 17,311 | 6 | 8 |
| 1960 | 42 | 1,463 | 18,274 | 6 | 8 |
| 1961 | 41 | 1,534 | 19,836 | 6 | 8 |
| 1962 | 44 | 1,657 | 21,203 | 6 | 8 |
| 1963 | 47 | 1,732 | 22,528 | 6 | 8 |
| 1964 | 48 | 1,839 | 24,959 | 6 | 8 |
| 1965 | 48 | 1,954 | 27,560 | 7 | 8 |
| 1966 | 58 | 2,363 | 41,081 | 8 | 12 |

n.a.: not available.

*Note:* The figures for 1931–1945 cover known groups controlling three or more banks; 1948 includes the twenty companies then registered under the Banking Act of 1933; 1950–1952 figures include known groups controlling two or more banks; 1954 includes known groups controlling 25 percent or more of two or more banks; and the 1957–1966 figures include companies registered under the Bank Holding Company Act of 1956, but no group is counted in the 1957–1966 data more than once even though some groups technically include more than one holding company. The First National Bank of Boston and Bank of America were not reported in the Board's data after 1952 and 1954 respectively.

*Source:* Fischer, *Bank Holding Companies,* p. 34; *Federal Reserve Bulletin,* 1962–1965; and Board of Governors of the Federal Reserve System.

in the data compiled by this writer for fifteen leading bank holding companies,[76] closely parallels the picture presented by Federal Reserve statistics. Following the contraction in holding company operations between 1930 and 1933, these firms increased the total number of banking offices which they controlled by only 5 percent during the next fifteen years. The most significant change was in the composition of the banking offices, for a substantial amount of switching from unit to branch banks occurred within the multiple-unit systems. Deposits of the leading groups rose by 300 percent between 1933 and the end of 1948, but this was somewhat less than the 320 percent growth achieved by all commercial banks.

*1949–1966.* Since 1949 a considerable expansion of bank holding companies has taken place. In many ways this interval has closely resembled the late 1920s, when group banking experienced its greatest development. In both periods there was substantial merger activity in other fields, an excellent market for the shares of well-known financial institutions, a movement of both population and industry, and a number of other conditions which encouraged the formation of groups.

As Congress considered bank holding company legislation from 1949 through mid-1956, the deposits of fifteen leading groups rose at approximately twice the rate achieved by all commercial banks. This great expansion of holding companies, much of it accomplished by acquisitions, was heavily concentrated in the 2½ year period between January 1954 and June 1956. There were two major forces behind the rapid increase of group acquisitions at that time. First, there was a fear that an extremely restrictive federal law would be passed by Congress following the hearings devoted to bank holding company legislation then in progress. Second, there was a desire on the part of

---

[76] The term "leading groups" as used in this chapter refers to the following 15 bank holding companies which have been in operation at least since 1933: Atlantic Trust Company, BancOhio Corporation; Barnett National Securities Corporation (including Barnett National Bank of Jacksonville); Baystate Corporation; Citizens and Southern Holding Company; First Bank Stock Corporation; First Security Corporation; First Wisconsin Bankshares; Marine Midland; Northwest Bancorporation; Old National Corporation; Shawmut Association; Trust Company of Georgia, Trustees First National Bank of Louisville; and Western Bancorporation. These firms hold about two-thirds of the deposits of all registered bank holding companies.

the officials of the Transamerica Corporation to rebuild their firm's bank stock portfolio after it had divested its interest in Bank of America N. T. & S. A., and the courts had ruled in its favor in the Federal Reserve Board Clayton Act suit in the early 1950s.

For nearly a decade after the Bank Holding Company Act of 1956 was passed, the growth of groups closely resembled the general expansion in the banking system. There was little change in the ratio of bank holding company deposits and offices to all commercial bank deposits and offices, and there certainly was no vast expansion of group banking as many had expected. But there was a substantial change in the deposits and offices of registered bank holding companies in the twelve month period from April 1, 1966 through March 30, 1967. In this interval, as a result of the July 1, 1966 amendment to the Bank Holding Company Act and pursuant to Section 5(a) of the Act, five bank holding companies registered with the Federal Reserve Board prior to the year-end 1966.[77] And, in this same twelve-month span, eight new groups with approximately nine billion dollars of deposits and 250 offices were formed. The deposits and offices of these eight systems respectively equalled one-third and one-eighth of the corresponding totals for all registered bank holding companies at the end of 1965. Although this increase is significant, its importance as an indicator of a major move toward group banking is tempered considerably by the fact that all but one of the eight new holding companies was located in either Florida or New York, and over 90 percent of the deposits were held by three of the Empire State systems.

OPERATIONS

Since bank holding companies range in size from a few million dollars to billions of dollars in deposits, it is nearly as difficult to develop an organization chart depicting the "typical" group system as it is the "typical" chain. Some of these firms control banks only in a single city or in a single state, but others are represented throughout large sections of the nation. A few of the firms have almost no staff in the holding company and their affiliate banks operate much as they would if the group did not exist, while others have centralized func-

[77] Federal Reserve Board, 53rd *Annual Report,* 1966, pp. 302–303.

tions to the point where their operations closely resemble branch systems.

From data compiled during visits to communities served by most leading bank holding companies and to their affiliates and headquarters units and from the replies to a rather lengthy questionnaire distributed to all major group systems, this writer prepared a fairly detailed description of the operation of these firms. Additional questionnaire surveys conducted in 1964 and 1966 revealed few major changes in the functioning of these firms; therefore, since most of these findings are already available in other publications,[78] the following discussion will be limited to the loan and interest rate policies of bank holding companies, for these elements are of primary importance to this study.

*Loans.* Probably the least centralized of all activities in group systems is the lending function. Only three of the leading holding companies maintain credit files. Of these three, only one reviews loans before they are made, as is often done in a branch system. The others follow the lending activity of their affiliates through occasional audits of their loan portfolios or by obtaining information concerning all (or a sample of) loans over a specified amount, which is submitted to the group or the credit department of one of the large affiliates for review after the loan is made. Frequently one affiliate may participate in a loan with another member of the system, but nearly all groups report that this type of activity is as common or more common with correspondents.

Most holding companies try to avoid becoming too involved in the lending function of their affiliates, since even a hint of "absentee" authority over loan approvals could often be very damaging to a group. Furthermore, this writer has noted in discussions with senior officers of these firms in recent years they have great fear that they might violate the antitrust laws very easily in this area. However, in consumer credit and in special fields such as leasing, the group headquarters is frequently very active, encouraging and promoting consumer credit and providing advice and consultation not only to the affiliate bank but to the customer in the case of leasing.

---

[78] Fischer, *Bank Holding Companies,* and my chapter in *The Bankers' Handbook.* (Chapter 81)

*Customer service charges and interest rates.* The service charges set by affiliates of a group vary considerably. These levies, as well as interest rates paid by the banks on time and savings deposits and interest rates charged on loans, are determined individually by each affiliate. The holding company may develop a more accurate analysis of costs for its members than would be found in many competitor banks, but ultimately local conditions will determine the rates paid and the rates charged. On occasion some smaller affiliates have displayed little interest in time money, and in such cases a group may suggest that the local banker become more competitive. But today any trend toward uniformity of rates within a group will probably be the result of federal regulation (such as Regulation Q) or money market conditions rather than group action.

### LEGISLATION AND REGULATION

If the definition of a bank holding company employed in present-day federal legislation (corporate ownership of 25 percent of the shares of two or more banks) were used, this form of bank organization would be found to exist in many nations, including those which have widespread branch banking. In the United Kingdom, for example, late in 1962 it was reported that the Provincial Bank acquired the share capital of the District Bank, and both institutions continued to function as separate entities. In addition, most of the major British banks have affiliates which handle their overseas and even their Scottish and Irish operations.

Bank holding companies exist in West Germany, too, for data submitted under the provisions of a new corporate disclosure law revealed that the "Big Three" nationwide branch banks' holdings of the shares of other financial institutions were substantial. The Deutsche Bank had interests of 25 percent or more in at least 23 other German banks; the Dresdner Bank reported like interests in 16 other banks; and the Commerzbank in 10.[79] Disclosure laws are being proposed or enacted in other European nations, and it would not be surprising, assuming this legislation is passed, to find similar interrelationships among banks in many other countries.

[79] Auburn, ed., *Comparative Banking*, p. 7, for the British data; and the German statistics may be found in "The Inside Dope," *Wall Street Journal,* November 30, 1966.

Although bank holding companies as defined above exist abroad, frequently they function much more like "pure" investment companies than do their counterparts in the United States. This may be explained in part by the limitations in this country upon bank investment in equity securities, including bank stock. But another factor which has affected the mode of operation of domestic bank holding companies has been the relatively severe statutory restrictions upon branch banking here in contrast to the more liberal branch provisions found in the laws of most other nations. Overseas, bank holding companies typically serve as a complement to widespread branch banking, but in America they act largely as a substitute for it.

Since bank holding companies appeared to permit banks to engage in quasi branch banking, even in areas where branching was prohibited, the same forces which have attacked branch banking in this country for much of this century also have endeavored to secure laws which would restrict the operations of the holding company form of bank organization. Their efforts met with some success when a few of the Pujo Committee's recommendations were included in the Clayton Act; however, it was not until 1933 that bank holding companies were subjected to some direct regulation under federal banking law, and comprehensive banking legislation relating to the operations of these firms was not enacted until 1956. The relevant sections of the two banking acts are briefly reviewed below, but the Clayton Act provisions will not be discussed until Chapter 7.

*The Banking Act of 1933.* With the vast expansion of holding company banking in the 1920s and the subsequent failure of several leading groups in the early 1930s, Congress considered enacting laws that would establish some degree of federal control over these firms.[80] As a result, a number of group banking provisions were inserted in the Banking Act of 1933, but this law covered only those bank

[80] From April 1924 through January 1928 the Federal Reserve Board prescribed as a condition of membership for every state bank which joined the system that such bank obtain permission even if an interest in another bank was acquired through an affiliated corporation. However, as a result of the passage of the McFadden Act some doubt arose with regard to the authority of the Board to prescribe this broad condition. For further details, see House Hearings, 1930, pp. 442–43.

holding companies which included a bank which was a member of the Federal Reserve System. These firms had to register with the Federal Reserve Board in order to obtain a permit to vote their stock interest in affiliated banks, and the Board had the power to grant or withhold this voting permit.

In acting upon each application for a voting permit, the Board was expected to consider the financial condition of the applicant, the general character of its management, and the probable effect of granting such permit upon the affairs of each subsidiary member bank. Voting permits could be granted a holding company affiliate if it would: agree to submit itself and its affiliated banks to examination by the Federal Reserve Board and to publish individual or consolidated statements of condition as may be required; show that it had no direct or indirect connection with organizations that underwrite and sell securities, except "governments" and selected other issues; and accumulate a reserve of readily marketable assets, other than bank stocks, as directed in the statute. In addition to these voting permit requirements, the Banking Act of 1933 also placed restrictions on lending by affiliated banks to the holding company or investing in its securities, and this law required that in the election of Federal Reserve Bank directors only one bank of a group could vote.[81]

Both the opponents of group banking and the regulatory authorities deemed the 1933 legislation inadequate. There were three obvious weaknesses in the provisions of this Act. First, registration was not mandatory for systems composed only of nonmember state banks; moreover, it was possible for some groups to control their banks without obtaining a voting permit. Second, except for the federal antitrust laws (which until the 1960s had not been employed with any

[81] The main holding company affiliate provisions of the Banking Act of 1933 [48 Stat. 162 (1933)] were §§ 2(c), 3(b), 5(c), 13, 16, and 21 [bank securities underwriting], 19, and 27. Some were amended by the Banking Act of 1935 [49 Stat. 684 (1935)] in §§ 301, 303(a) [securities underwriting], 311, 325, and 327. The restriction in the 1933 Act upon holding company affiliate voting in the election of Federal Reserve directors [§ 3(b)] was amended by § 13(e) of the 1966 amendment of the Bank Holding Company Act [80 Stat. 236 (1966)] which deleted any reference to "holding company affiliates" and instead limited the vote in any Federal Reserve District to one for all member banks in a holding company (as defined in the 1956 Act).

degree of success in the banking area), there was little or no control over bank holding company expansion. Third, group systems were permitted to continue investing in nonbanking enterprises.[82]

*The Bank Holding Company Act of 1956.* On several occasions in the late 1930s President Franklin D. Roosevelt publicly criticized group systems; and in a message to Congress in April 1938 he urged the gradual separation of banks from holding companies. The previous month several bills were introduced which, while they would not have eliminated these firms, would have prevented the establishment of new companies and the further expansion of existing firms. However, no action was taken upon them.

Little additional group banking legislation was submitted during World War II, but the federal banking agencies became more active in attacking these systems. In 1940 the Comptroller of the Currency called for the outright prohibition of bank holding companies; in 1943 the Federal Reserve Board asked for legislation to curb the further expansion or formation of groups; and in 1944 the FDIC recommended passage of a statute to outlaw multiple-unit banking. As a result, a number of additional bills were introduced but, as occurred in the case of the earlier legislation, they were not considered by Congress.

The concern of the regulatory agencies in Washington stemmed primarily from the growth of the Transamerica Corporation, a giant West Coast holding company whose interests included the Bank of America in California. Senator Tobey stated in regard to the group banking legislation he introduced in 1947 that it was aimed at this firm's extension of power and evolved because of the apprehension he and others had that "they would keep on." However, the "Tobey bill" failed to even come to a vote. Thereafter, a steady stream of multiple-unit banking legislation was introduced in the Congress. Finally, a compromise bill was approved by both the House and Senate and was

[82] Some very limited additional control over bank holding companies was achieved through the Securities Acts of 1933 and 1934, and minor amendments to the group banking provisions of the Banking Act of 1933 were included in the Banking Act of 1935. The Investment Company Act of 1940 exempted a bank holding company if it held a general voting permit from the Federal Reserve Board.

signed by President Eisenhower. Thus, on May 9, 1956, the Bank Holding Company Act became law.

The 1956 law was not a freeze or a death-sentence act, which many group bankers had feared it might be. Instead, it was a compromise bill containing at least some provisions that were probably unsatisfactory even to its most ardent supporters. The purpose of the bill was (1) to define bank holding companies, (2) to require divestment of their nonbanking interests, and (3) to control their future expansion.

(1) The law defines a bank holding company as any company (a) which directly or indirectly owns, controls, or holds with power to vote 25 percent or more of the voting shares of two or more banks, or (b) which controls in any manner the election of a majority of the directors of two or more banks. In the 1966 legislation amending the Bank Holding Company Act, a small change in this definition was made. The term bank was defined to include only institutions that accept deposits that the customer has a legal right to withdraw on demand; thus nondeposit trust companies would seemingly no longer be covered although they were in the original law.

(2) The Act with numerous exemptions makes it unlawful for a bank to engage in any nonbanking business or to retain direct or indirect ownership or control of shares of any company that is not a bank holding company.

(3) To regulate the expansion of group banking, the Act requires among other things that prior approval of the Board of Governors be obtained for a registered bank holding company to acquire directly or indirectly more than 5 percent in total of the voting stock of any bank, or for a company to become a bank holding company. (See Chapter 4 for a more detailed discussion of this provision.)

The Bank Holding Company Act of 1956 contained numerous other provisions, including such things as reporting requirements, details regarding the administration of the Act, rules concerning borrowing by a group or its subsidiaries, and judicial review of the Board's orders. The only important revision in the law prior to 1966 came through an amendment to the Small Business Investment Act of 1958.[83] This change permitted affiliates of a bank holding company to

[83] There was also a technical change in § 9 of the Bank Holding Company Act made August 28, 1958. [72 Stat. 951 (1958)]

invest in a small business investment company (SBIC) which is a subsidiary of a bank holding company. [74 stat. 196 (1960), § 5.]

*Changes in the law needed.* In the Board's report to Congress in which it reviewed its first two years' experience under this Act[84] and in its *Annual Report* each year thereafter,[85] the Governors made a series of suggestions regarding possible changes in this statute. The Board particularly emphasized the desirability of amending the Act in the following respects: To subject an organization to regulation as a bank holding company if it controlled 25 percent or more of the stock of a single bank; to include not only corporations, business trusts, and the like but also long-term trusts whether testamentary or inter vivos; and to include a variety of forms of organization (for example, certain registered investment companies, and firms operated for religious, charitable, or educational purposes) which had been granted specific exemption from this legislation. Except for the coverage of "one-bank" holding companies (about 550 companies with over 13 billion dollars of deposits in 1965), all of the above revisions were included in the 1966 amendments to the Bank Holding Company Act.[86]

The Board of Governors had further suggested that Section 6 of the Act, which had been interpreted as prohibiting intrasystem investments and the extension of credit by banks in a group, should be repealed, which it was in the 1966 legislation. However, cognate with this was a revision in Section 23A of the Federal Reserve Act which retained some of the provisions in Section 6 which the Board felt were desirable. The Board also indicated that the holding company affiliate provisions of the Banking Act of 1933 should be repealed to remove

[84] The Board's administration of this act is discussed in Backman, *The Bank Holding Company Act;* and Hall, "Bank Holding Company Regulation," *The Southern Economic Journal* (April 1965), pp. 342–55. For a detailed discussion of this topic see Hugon, "Federal Regulation of Bank Holding Companies," unpublished doctoral dissertation, University of Washington, 1964.

[85] *Bank Holding Company Act,* Report of the Board of Governors Federal Reserve System Pursuant to the Bank Holding Company Act of 1956. For more recent comments, see Federal Reserve Board, *52d Annual Report,* 1965, pp. 236–37.

[86] The 1966 amendments to the Bank Holding Company Act were enacted July 1, 1966. [80 Stat. 236 (1966)] Data for "one-bank" companies was compiled from U. S. Congress, Senate, *Amendments to the Bank Holding Company Act of 1956* (Lists of Bank Holding Companies and of Organizations that Would Apparently be Covered by the Bank Holding Company Act Incorporated in S. 2353), 1966.

the confusion and administrative burden resulting from the existence of two sets of laws relating to the same general subject but based upon different definitions of what constitutes a holding company, and this too was done in the 1966 statute.

It had long been predicted that amendments to the Bank Holding Company Act would be passed, for criticism of its provisions had come from many sources. President Eisenhower signed the bill with its special provisions and exemptions with some reluctance; state officials had often termed it inadequate; the Independent Bankers Association had voiced serious objections to some of its sections; and the Board of Governors had been rather rigid in its enforcement of some of the provisions of the law, apparently feeling that if there were inequities in it they should be removed by legislative action rather than by administrative interpretation.

The extensive changes in this legislation which were made in July, 1966 came only after lengthy hearings[87] and resulted in large part from the efforts of a rather unusual group of forces—the Railway Executives Association; a very large union involved in a struggle with the du Pont-owned Florida East Coast Railway (the thirty banks owned by the du Pont estate would have to be separated from its other interests under the law); the Association of Registered Bank Holding Companies, which hoped that through this legislation some long-desired amendments to the Bank Holding Company Act would be secured; Representative Wright Patman, Chairman of the House Banking and Currency Committee, who for many years had wanted to strengthen the 1956 law; and the Federal Reserve Board, which for eight years had been asking Congress to pass many of the provisions included in this statute. It may be some time before such a diverse and influential group interested in multiple-unit banking will find their interests generally coincide once again.[88]

[87] U. S. Congress, House, Hearings on H. R. 10668 and H. R. 10872, *Bank Holding Company Legislation,* 1964; House, Hearings on H. R. 7371, *To Amend the Bank Holding Company Act,* 1965; House, Hearings on H. R. 7372, *Amending the Bank Holding Company Act with Respect to Registered Investment Companies,* 1965; Senate, *Amendments to the Bank Holding Company Act of 1956,* Analyses of S. 2353, S. 2418, and H. R. 7371, 1965; and Senate, Hearings on S. 2353, S. 2418, and H. R. 7371, *Amend the Bank Holding Company Act of 1956,* 1966.

[88] In addition to federal legislation directly relating to bank holding companies, numerous state statutes also apply to these firms. Some of the more

## THE FUTURE OF MULTIPLE-UNIT BANKING

It is very likely that in the short run, if the bank supervisors and legislators are cooperative, there could be a sizable increase of multiple-unit banking in this country. This expansion has already begun in New York State, where four new group systems with about 8 billion dollars in deposits and 200 offices were formed in 1966 and early 1967. In time a substantial growth of bank holding companies also could occur in other states, particularly those which are currently weighing the merits of removing some of their restrictions upon the formation of bank holding companies.

Multiple-unit banking development has not been limited to group systems, for chain banking too seems to have expanded significantly in recent years. Moreover, while the terms chain and holding company may refer to two different types of bank organization from the viewpoint of the law, this difference is often of no importance from the standpoint of economic analysis, for many so-called chain systems still exist which would appear to be akin to bank holding companies but which do not have to register as such under federal law. These "chains" are held together through a variety of arrangements, including outright stock ownership by officers and directors or by employee profit-sharing trust funds, through holdings developed as a part of bank nominee operations, and through joint organization of new banks under limited partnerships.[89]

It would seem that in many cases the current interest in groups and chains stems from the possibility that branch banking restrictions will be relaxed. This would follow the pattern established in the past when multiple-unit systems were sometimes employed to acquire outlets at desired locations, which (if the expected change in legislation developed) later could be converted to branches. Some people argue that this is the reason for the great interest in forming group systems in New York State today and for the growth of chain banking in other

---

important legislation is outlined in Fischer, *Bank Holding Companies, pp.* 167–72.

[89] See the various Patman Committee studies; and Lanzillotti, *Banking Structure in Michigan,* Chapter III.

states where there is even a remote chance that the branch lines will be redrawn.[90]

While multiple-unit banking frequently serves as an intermediate step between unit banking and branch banking or between various shades of branch banking, it would seem that this hybrid form of bank organization should play a significant role in the American financial system regardless of the status of branch regulations. Perhaps this may not be true many years hence, as the function of the commercial bank continues to change. But, at least for the foreseeable future, given the size of the United States, its many social as well as geographic divisions, and the strong sentiment which still appears to exist in favor of "local autonomy" in this country, one can visualize numerous situations in which multiple-unit banking may be preferable to branch banking, for it provides many of the advantages which can accrue through functional specialization while it retains a high degree of independence in each affiliate. But, unfortunately, these differences between multiple-office and multiple-unit banking are usually ignored, and in the years ahead as in the past the development of chain and group banking will no doubt continue to be determined in large part by both actual and potential changes in branch banking legislation, not by the merits or weaknesses of multiple-unit banking.[91]

[90] In Indiana, for example, possible changes in the state branch lines had not even been considered by the legislature and yet numerous banks in the state through their "representatives" were actively bidding for institutions which were regarded as excellent branch prospects.

[91] Two organizations which received considerable publicity and which had many (if not all) of the characteristics of bank holding companies were the Whitney National Bank group and the Chase Manhattan-Liberty National Bank combination. The first organization, Whitney Holding Corporation, using the holding company device, attempted to acquire an affiliate in an adjoining county in a state which prohibited branching into another county and in a state which passed a law that was clearly designed to stop the acquisition in question. Following a series of legal actions [211 F. Supp. 576 (1962); 323 F. 2d 290 (1963); 376 U.S. 948 (1964); 379 U.S. 411 (1965)], a Lower Court (State) ruled the Louisiana antibank holding company statute applicable to Whitney. The decision was affirmed by the State Circuit Court of Appeals, and the Louisiana Supreme Court denied a petition for review (November 7, 1966). The counsel for Whitney filed a motion with the Federal Reserve Board to withdraw the Whitney Application. The Board granted the motion on December 30, 1966, concluding the administrative proceeding. See Federal Reserve Board, 53d *Annual Report,* 1966, p. 314.

The second unusual multiple-unit organization noted above resulted from the

## CORRESPONDENT BANKING

In addition to institutions which serve rather limited areas, most leading countries have at least a few nationwide branch banks operating within their borders. Yet, in the United States even the largest banks cannot establish branches beyond the confines of a single state, with the exception of offices abroad.[92] As a result this nation's banking system is composed primarily of very small institutions serving

---

planned acquisition in October 1965 of the stock of Liberty National Bank in Buffalo by Chase Manhattan Bank in New York, following a ruling by Comptroller Saxon in July 1965 that a national bank could lawfully acquire the stock of another domestic bank. However, Chase was obliged to file an application with the New York banking authorities under the State's Bank Holding Company Act [N. Y. Banking Law § 142(1)(b)], and, in order to vote the stock of Liberty, Chase filed with the Federal Reserve Board to obtain a voting permit as required under the Banking Act of 1933 [12 U.S.C. § 61]. The proposal was "killed" in February 1966 when the New York State Banking Board, following a recommendation made by the Banking Superintendent, denied Chase's application, primarily on the ground of the conflicting views of the Comptroller and the Fed regarding the authority of member banks to purchase the stock of other banks. Subsequently, the Federal Reserve Board indicated that in its opinion the Chase proposal would have violated not only the stock purchasing prohibition of 12 U.S.C. § 24 but also at least the spirit of the branch banking provisions of 12 U.S.C. § 36. In April 1966 the Board published a ruling making clear its position that a member bank had no authority to purchase the stock of another bank. And in May 1967 Comptroller Camp, who succeeded Saxon, cancelled the controversial ruling permitting national banks to acquire the stock of other banks. See Hackley, "Our Baffling Banking System," 52 *Virginia Law Review* 1966, 565, 612–15; "Camp Drops Four Controversial Saxon Rulings," *American Banker,* May 17, 1967; Saxon, "National Bank Ownership of a Subsidiary Bank," *The National Banking Review* (June 1966), pp. 547–48; and "Law Department," *Federal Reserve Bulletin* (May 1966), p. 655.

[92] However, banks chartered outside New York can establish facilities in New York City or other cities for the conduct of foreign business. This can be done through the use of an Edge Act or an "agreement" corporation organized pursuant to Section 25 of the Federal Reserve Act. These corporations can maintain offices in the United States, and they are not confined to the state of incorporation of their parent bank. Domestic employment of their funds is severely restricted, but they do have some of the characteristics of branches. Occasionally, one also hears stories of American banks indirectly securing outlets in New York or other cities through offices set up by foreign banks in which they have a substantial interest, but this writer has no evidence of this practice.

extremely limited areas. While advocates of "local banking" can cite numerous advantages of this form of bank organization, even its stanchest supporters would have to concede that its parochialism also creates numerous problems, and to overcome some of these weaknesses an intricate network of domestic correspondent arrangements has developed in this country.[93]

Despite the significance of correspondent banking in the American financial system, no extensive review of its evolution has been included in this study. The information needed was compiled, but it was omitted from this chapter because correspondent activity in this country has been traced in considerable detail in a number of works,[94] and much of the material gathered was found to be rather indirectly related to bank structure as defined earlier in this book. Therefore, the following discussion includes only a short historical note on interbank deposit data and concentrates almost entirely upon correspondent banking in the 1960s.

CORRESPONDENT BANK OPERATIONS[95]

*Reserves.* Interbank deposits are maintained by many banks because of services rendered to them by the depository. However, bankers' balances in many cases play a dual role, for, in addition to compensating a correspondent for its assistance, "due-from-banks" may also serve as a part of a state bank's required reserve. In 1966 all states, with the exception of Illinois, which had no statutory reserve requirements, permitted "country banks" to hold at least a part of their reserve against demand deposits in the form of balances with

[93] As early as 1784, the Bank of North America (later merged with the First Pennsylvania Banking and Trust Company) opened an account with The Bank of New York, and this account is still active under the latter's present corporate name (First Pennsylvania).

[94] Detailed accounts of the role of interbank deposits prior to the Great Depression may be found in Watkins, *Bankers Balances;* and Beckhart, ed., *The New York Money Market,* Vol. II. For more recent studies of this topic, see Finney, *Interbank Deposits,* and Scott's studies for the House Banking and Currency Committee—Correspondent Relations: A Survey of Banker Opinion (October 21, 1964); and A Report on the Correspondent Banking System (December 10, 1964).

[95] Scott, "Correspondent Banking in the USA," *The Banker* (August 1965), pp. 521–27. This article provides a very brief summary of the major findings of his studies, and it has been drawn upon heavily in writing these sections on correspondent bank services.

acceptable depository banks. Similarly, all states which had established a reserve which must be held against time deposits, except Missouri, allowed interbank deposits to meet all or part of this requirement.

*Check clearing.* One of the oldest and still the most important of all correspondent functions is to facilitate the clearing of checks and other cash items. Despite the existence of twelve Federal Reserve Banks and twenty-four branches, American commercial banks continue to rely very heavily upon their correspondents as clearing agents. Banks with deposits of 100 million dollars and over process over 40 percent of their out-of-town checks through correspondents, while the smallest banks (under 10 million dollars of deposits) handle over 90 percent of such items in this manner. (See Table 3.2) The reasons banks prefer this procedure rather than clearing directly through the "Fed" are numerous. They include less strict sorting requirements, later close-off time, acceptance of non-cash items and items on non-par banks, handling of foreign items, frequent granting of immediate credit for all cash items, microfilming out-of-town clearings, and policies in regard to carrying checks and currency over short distances.[96]

*Credit accommodation.* Another area in which the correspondent is frequently of considerable assistance is in credit accommodation. Roughly one-tenth of the smaller banks surveyed by the House Banking and Currency Committee's staff in their recent studies of correspondent banking reported they had established credit lines with their correspondents. These arrangements were usually made with one or two city banks; they varied from 100 thousand dollars to 8 million dollars; they were for both short and intermediate term; and the loans customarily involved collateral in the form of United States government securities. Sometimes funds were also secured by selling an asset such as mortgages, municipal bonds, or even consumer loans to city correspondents, and many country banks acquired federal funds provided or obtained by their city correspondents.

Because of legal limitations upon loans to a single borrower (often 10 percent of a bank's capital and surplus) the city bank may also be

[96] *Ibid.,* and "Correspondent Banking," *Monthly Review,* Federal Reserve Bank of Kansas City (March–April 1965), p. 10.

called upon to participate in a loan with a country bank. Such arrangements are also entered into when the country bank is short of funds or on occasion when it merely desires a particularly careful analysis of a given loan by the specialists in a larger bank. It should be added in considering loan participations that funds also flow from the rural area to the city, as country banks share in loans originated by their city correspondents. In terms of number of loans, the movement from the outlying areas to the cities appears to be dominant, but it is not clear from available evidence whether this is also true in terms of dollar volume.

*Other services.* In a brief analysis of his research concerning correspondent banking for the "Patman Committee," Professor Ira Scott presented the following list, admittedly incomplete, of other services offered by the city correspondent and used by the country bank:[97]

(1) Provision of new lending opportunities and deposits through the referral of new customers; (2) Investments advice; (3) Management advice on accounting systems, operational procedures, data processing and trust administration (in some cases with a co-fiduciary relationship); (4) Assistance in the recruitment and training of personnel; (5) Facilitation, as agent or dealer, of transactions in Federal Funds, US Government securities, municipal securities, commercial paper, bankers' acceptances and negotiable time certificates of deposit; (6) Safe keeping of securities; (7) Assistance in setting up group insurance and retirement plans for bank employees; (8) Bank wire (teletype) services; (9) Collections; (10) Provision of credit information as well as forecasts of economic activity and trends in the money and capital markets; (11) Absorption of the cost of wrapping and shipping currency and coin; (12) International banking services, including the provision of letters of credit, purchase and sale of foreign exchange, handling foreign collections and remittances, arranging for export-import credits and supplying foreign credit information and forecasts of business conditions abroad.

The extent to which some of these services are utilized is indicated in Table 3.2.

*Charges.* As has been noted, the primary means of compensating the city banks for their services is through the maintenance of deposit

---

[97] Scott, "Correspondent Banking in the USA," *The Banker* (August 1965), p. 524.

TABLE 3.2. CORRESPONDENT BANKING—SELECTED DATA FROM A SURVEY OF BANKS HOLDING DEMAND BALANCES IN OTHER BANKS[a]

| | Bank Deposit Size (million dollars) | | | | | | | | | |
|---|---|---|---|---|---|---|---|---|---|---|
| | 100 and over | | 50–100 | | 25–50 | | 10–25 | | Under 10 | |
| | Unit | Br.[b] | Unit | Br.[b] | Unit | Br.[b] | Unit | Br.[b] | Unit | Br.[b] |
| *Deposits with correspondents* | | | | | | | | | | |
| Average amount of demand balances (million dollars) | 12.2 | 10.1 | 4.8 | 3.9 | 2.7 | 2.2 | 1.3 | 1.2 | 0.4 | 0.6 |
| Average number of correspondents | 32 | 30 | 18 | 12 | 13 | 10 | 8 | 7 | 5 | 6 |
| Percent of banks also holding time deposits with correspondents | 9 | 7 | 13 | 6 | 3 | 2 | 1 | 1 | 1 | 7 |
| Percent of time deposits in form of negotiable certificates | 100 | 91 | 72 | 94 | 93 | 99 | 98 | 88 | 87 | 58 |
| *Credit and related services* | | | | | | | | | | |
| Percent of surveyed banks which reported: | | | | | | | | | | |
| Credit lines with correspondents | 3 | 8 | 5 | 13 | 8 | 11 | 8 | 12 | 9 | 10 |
| [*Average number of credit lines* | 1 | 2 | 2 | 2 | 2 | 2 | 1 | 1 | 1 | 2] |
| Borrowed from correspondent for short- or intermediate-term purposes[c] | 2 | 5 | 5 | 15 | 11 | 12 | 8 | 16 | 7 | 7 |
| Obtained funds from correspondent through sale of | 2 | | | 4 | 1 | | 1 | 8 | 1 | 3 |

| | | | | | | | | | | |
|---|---|---|---|---|---|---|---|---|---|---|
| through correspondent[c] | 78 | 75 | 68 | 58 | 35 | 46 | 19 | 31 | 23 | 28 |
| Participated in correspondent loans | 92 | 89 | 74 | 75 | 59 | 55 | 52 | 37 | 24 | 28 |
| [Average amount outstanding (million dollars)] | *11.9* | *12.0* | *1.5* | *1.2* | *1.1* | *0.6* | *0.4* | *0.3* | *0.2* | *0.3]* |
| Correspondent participated in loans of depositor bank | 88 | 85 | 80 | 63 | 65 | 64 | 55 | 60 | 35 | 55 |
| [Percent of dollar amount held by correspondent] | *53* | *50* | *55* | *62* | *54* | *78* | *61* | *61* | *60* | *69]* |
| *Other services*[c] | | | | | | | | | | |
| Average percent of out-of-town checks cleared through correspondents | 43 | 45 | 50 | 73 | 79 | 79 | 87 | 87 | 93 | 92 |
| Percent of banks using correspondents' services for: | | | | | | | | | | |
| Safekeeping of securities | 97 | 85 | 91 | 94 | 93 | 87 | 91 | 84 | 77 | 77 |
| Foreign exchange | 98 | 90 | 92 | 92 | 94 | 87 | 74 | 78 | 41 | 47 |
| Bank wire service | 87 | 79 | 80 | 90 | 86 | 83 | 80 | 86 | 47 | 53 |
| Data processing | 58 | 58 | 48 | 50 | 38 | 28 | 24 | 16 | 9 | 18 |
| Accounting advice | 44 | 38 | 35 | 41 | 32 | 33 | 34 | 35 | 19 | 28 |
| Investment advice | 45 | 51 | 68 | 67 | 68 | 67 | 68 | 61 | 68 | 72 |
| Transactions in U. S. Government ments | 71 | 61 | 73 | 67 | 78 | 63 | 81 | 75 | 75 | 84 |
| Transactions in municipals | 44 | 39 | 51 | 38 | 51 | 36 | 47 | 44 | 39 | 43 |
| Transactions in commercial paper | 16 | 9 | 18 | 22 | 18 | 15 | 19 | 15 | 20 | 15 |

a *Business Conditions*, Federal Reserve Bank of Chicago, March 1965. These data were compiled from a survey made by Subcommittee on Domestic Finance, Committee on Banking and Currency, during September and October of 1963 through a questionnaire sent to a sample of 2,650 banks. For details see U. S. Congress, House, Committee on Banking and Currency, *A Report on the Correspondent Banking System*, Committee Print, 1964.

b Banks having one or more branches.

c During preceding 12 months.

balances with them by country banks. Yet, on the average, less than 1 percent of the banks participating in the "Patman Committee" survey of correspondent banking stated that an actual estimate of the dollar value of these services had been made. This is surprising when one considers that less than 10 percent of the surveyed banks noted they maintained some minimum average balance which had been suggested by their correspondent, and a majority indicated that to the contrary the size of their demand balances was based on their estimate of the value of the services rendered by the city bank.[98]

In addition to the minimum balance system of remuneration, or "payment in kind," specific fees are now being increasingly adopted for some correspondent functions.[99] Services particularly suitable for the assessment of specific charges include: domestic and foreign collections, non-par check clearance, numerous international department transactions, safekeeping of securities, data processing, operations advice, and many others. To learn the customers' attitudes toward this development, the questionnaire distributed by the staff of the "Patman Committee" included an inquiry regarding the possible expansion of the use of such explicit fees in lieu of payment through the maintenance of a demand deposit. This proposition was soundly defeated—outright rejection of the idea ranging from 58 to 78 percent in various bank-size categories, with a tendency for the proportion of disapprovals to decrease as bank size increased.[100] This itself should raise some serious questions regarding the profitability of the present system to the large bank.

A sampling of banker opinion by *Banking,* the Journal of the American Bankers Association (ABA), several years ago revealed that officers of the larger institutions felt that about 90 percent of their correspondent accounts were profitable.[101] But, at about the same time the ABA survey was made, Howard Crosse, then a Vice President of the Federal Reserve Bank of New York, wrote:[102]

[98] U. S. Congress, House, Committee on Banking and Currency, *A Report on the Correspondent Banking System,* 1964, p. 7.

[99] Scott, "Correspondent Banking in the USA," *The Banker* (August 1965), p. 527.

[100] U. S. Congress, House, *Correspondent Relations: A Survey of Banker Opinion,* 1964, pp. 10–11.

[101] Waller, "Our Unique Correspondent Banking System," *Banking* (August 1961).

[102] Crosse, *Management Policies for Commercial Banks,* p. 18.

Correspondent banking, like dual banking, enjoys a measure of emotional as well as logical support. Correspondent relationships are frequently justified on the grounds of loyalty or appreciation for past services with little or no close analysis by either party of the present-day economics of the relationship. The large banks, seeking to maintain or enlarge their correspondent balances, have aggressively sought account activity often without regard to careful cost studies. In so doing they have encouraged some clearly uneconomic practices, such as the centralization of check sorting in the larger centers. This practice has resulted not only in higher overall costs to the banking system for check collection but in some delay in presentation of items as well.

Crosse concluded that it was probable that many correspondent relationships were unprofitable to one or both of the participants. More recent studies shed little light on this question, but they do seem to suggest that the larger depository banks are becoming much more thorough in their analysis of the costs and revenues of the correspondent function.[103]

STATISTICS

The aggregate value of correspondent banking operations is difficult to measure with any high degree of precision since the income from this function is usually earned indirectly.[104] While a bank sometimes may be reimbursed for certain out-of-pocket expenses, only a relatively small percentage of commercial banks report the payment of explicit fees or charges for correspondent services. Instead, in exchange for the facilities provided, as is well-known, the country bank maintains a deposit with the city bank, which the latter may in large part employ to acquire earning assets. Fortunately, data concerning interbank balances are shown in Reports of Condition, although generally interbank payments are not identified in Income and Dividend Reports. Thus, despite their many limitations, bankers' balances may be employed to provide at least a very rough measure of the economic importance of correspondent banking.

Although the items included in the interbank deposit category in published statistics have changed somewhat since the early 1900s, a general pattern is apparent in most time series relating to bankers'

---

[103] Some interesting analyses of the measurement of the value of correspondent banking appears in "More on Correspondent Banking," *Monthly Review,* Federal Reserve Bank of Kansas City (July–August 1965).

[104] *Ibid.* (March–April 1965), pp. 12–15.

balances. During the formative years of Federal Reserve operation, 1914–1920, interbank deposits as a percentage of total deposits declined by roughly one-half. (16 to 10 percent). Throughout the 1920s the ratio was relatively stable, varying between 8 and 10 percent. In the 1930s it increased substantially, rising to pre-Federal Reserve levels by the closing years of the decade.[105] (15 to 17 percent). There was only a modest growth of interbank deposits during the Second World War (1941–1945), while total deposits more than doubled, and once again the ratio fell to about 9 percent. Since 1945 it has varied within a limited range but has been slowly declining, reaching the 5 percent level in the early 1960s, and it has experienced little change since that time. (See Table 3.3)

Since (commercial) interbank time deposit data were first published separately in the early 1940s, these deposits have totaled under 250 million dollars in all but the last few years. Therefore, considering the tremendous growth of total time deposits in commercial banks, especially during the past decade, the ratio of interbank demand deposits to total demand deposits may have more relevance than a ratio computed using total deposits. Statistics compiled in this manner move in essentially the same direction as those discussed above, but the magnitude of the change during the last ten years is reduced by nearly one-half. Explanations for the interbank deposit decline usually include some reference to lower state bank reserve requirements, the growing importance of time and savings deposit functions which require less correspondent service, increasing interest rates which may raise the opportunity cost of holding interbank balances, the efforts by bankers and bond dealers to instruct and to assist the "local banks" in the use of their excess reserves (such as small federal funds transactions), the growth of small banks which may themselves produce the services formerly supplied by a correspondent, and the expansion of branch banking.[106]

At the end of 1966 the *American Banker* indicated 534 American commercial banks held interbank deposits (including both domestic

---

[105] *All Bank Statistics United States,* 1896–1955, p. 36, and *Banking and Monetary Statistics,* Federal Reserve Board, 1943 for data before 1935.

[106] "More on Correspondent Banking," *Monthly Review,* Federal Reserve Bank of Kansas City (July–August 1965), pp. 17–19; and Nadler, "The Coming Change in Correspondent Relationships," *Banking* (April 1966), pp. 45–46.

TABLE 3.3.   INTERBANK DEPOSITS HELD BY INSURED COMMERCIAL BANKS
1935–1966  (INCLUDES ALL DOMESTIC INTERBANK DEMAND DEPOSITS)

| Year End or Final Call Date | Interbank Demand Deposits ($ billions)ᵃ | Deposits ($ billions) | | Interbank as Percent of | |
|---|---|---|---|---|---|
| | | Demand | Total | Demand Deposits | Total Deposits |
| 1935 | 5.9 | 30.9 | 44.1 | 19.1 | 13.4 |
| 1936 | 6.7 | 35.3 | 49.3 | 19.0 | 13.6 |
| 1937 | 5.7 | 32.4 | 47.2 | 17.6 | 12.1 |
| 1938 | 6.7 | 34.9 | 49.8 | 19.2 | 13.5 |
| 1939 | 8.8 | 40.8 | 56.1 | 21.6 | 15.7 |
| 1940 | 9.8 | 47.7 | 63.5 | 20.5 | 15.4 |
| 1941 | 10.0 | 53.6 | 69.4 | 18.6 | 14.4 |
| 1942 | 10.2 | 71.6 | 87.8 | 14.2 | 11.6 |
| 1943 | 9.7 | 85.0 | 104.1 | 11.4 | 9.3 |
| 1944 | 11.1 | 101.8 | 125.8 | 10.9 | 8.8 |
| 1945 | 12.6 | 117.8 | 147.8 | 10.7 | 8.5 |
| 1946 | 10.9 | 103.4 | 137.0 | 10.5 | 8.0 |
| 1947 | 11.2 | 106.9 | 141.9 | 10.5 | 7.9 |
| 1948 | 10.3 | 105.2 | 140.7 | 9.8 | 7.3 |
| 1949 | 10.9 | 107.1 | 143.2 | 10.2 | 7.6 |
| 1950 | 12.0 | 117.0 | 153.5 | 10.3 | 7.8 |
| 1951 | 13.0 | 124.9 | 163.2 | 10.4 | 8.0 |
| 1952 | 13.0 | 130.0 | 171.4 | 10.0 | 7.6 |
| 1953 | 13.2 | 130.3 | 175.1 | 10.1 | 7.5 |
| 1954 | 13.4 | 134.8 | 183.3 | 9.9 | 7.3 |
| 1955 | 13.4 | 141.0 | 191.0 | 9.5 | 7.0 |
| 1956 | 14.2 | 144.4 | 196.5 | 9.8 | 7.2 |
| 1957 | 13.8 | 142.8 | 200.5 | 9.7 | 6.9 |
| 1958 | 14.0 | 149.5 | 215.2 | 9.4 | 6.5 |
| 1959 | 13.8 | 151.5 | 219.0 | 9.1 | 6.3 |
| 1960 | 15.4 | 155.7 | 229.0 | 9.9 | 6.7 |
| 1961 | 16.5 | 165.1 | 247.9 | 10.0 | 6.7 |
| 1962 | 14.6 | 163.2 | 261.4 | 8.9 | 5.6 |
| 1963 | 13.9 | 163.0 | 274.6 | 8.5 | 5.1 |
| 1964 | 16.2 | 178.7 | 306.2 | 9.1 | 5.3 |
| 1965 | 16.6 | 183.8 | 331.5 | 9.0 | 5.0 |
| 1966 | 17.7 | 191.7 | 352.8 | 9.2 | 5.0 |

ᵃ An estimated $100 million of time deposits is included in the data for 1935–1941.
Data include deposits of Mutual Savings Banks since they were not reported separately until 1961.

*Source: Call Reports of Insured Banks*, FDIC, Annually, 1935–1966.

and foreign accounts in the United States) of 500 thousand dollars or more.[107] At that time these balances totaled nearly 17 billion dollars. A large part of these deposits as in the past continued to be held by a handful of New York City banks, with Chase Manhattan the perennial leader in this field. It held correspondent balances of over 1.3 billion dollars or 12 percent of its total deposits,[108] and the second and third largest depository banks—First National City Bank of New York and Manufacturers Hanover—each reported roughly 800 million dollars in interbank balances.

As in other *American Banker* compilations of correspondent statistics in recent years, banks in the New York (2d) Federal Reserve District held well over one-third of the deposits due-to-banks shown in the survey. In addition, institutions in the Chicago (7th) District held approximately one-eighth of the nearly 17 billion dollars in correspondent accounts. Therefore, over fifty years after the Federal Reserve System was established, which many thought would virtually eliminate New York and Chicago balances, nearly one-half of the interbank deposits in major correspondent banks continued to be concentrated in the 2d and 7th Districts, and in reality the vast majority of the bankers' balances in these Districts (probably about four-fifths) were held in the two money market centers, New York City and Chicago.

Although no detailed evidence of the sources of these balances is included in the *American Banker* surveys or the published data of the banking agencies, some conclusions on this point may be drawn from research which has been done by this author and by others.[109] It would appear that nonmember and country-member banks tend to maintain their primary correspondent accounts with a reserve city bank in their trade area, with only minimum balances allocated to

[107] "Interbank Balances at U. S. Commercials," *American Banker,* December 20, 1966. The data were for September 20–30, 1966. It would have been desirable to have only domestic data for this study, but some banks did not provide the desired breakdown.

[108] Although the largest balances in absolute terms are found in New York, Chicago, and Boston, the highest ratio of interbank deposits to total deposits continues to be held by the National Stock Yards N. B., Illinois, 84 percent.

[109] See, for example, Finney, *Interbank Deposits,* pp. 24, 78; Fischer, *Bank Holding Companies,* pp. 108–10; and "How the Banker Chooses His Correspondent Bank," *Northwestern Banker,* reprint, recent but n.d.

New York City or Chicago banks. In turn, the reserve city banks tend to place their main balances with New York banks. No doubt, most observers would expect this deposit pattern to exist, and it would appear to be in line with the periodic surveys of correspondent banking made by the *Northwestern Banker,* which invariably disclose that the first consideration in choosing a correspondent is its location.

## THE ROLE OF CORRESPONDENT BANKING

Correspondent banking has often been termed the cornerstone of the unit bank system in the United States, and without these interbank relationships it would seem doubtful that the high degree of "local banking" which exists in this country would have remained long beyond 1900. But, with a well-developed correspondent system, unit banks have been able to provide for these many decades an accepta-ble[110] alternative to widespread multiple-office and multiple-unit banking. However, with the increasing branch banking and bank mergers, the growing cost consciousness of depository banks, the expanding use of computers (including the development of highly sophisticated bank credit card plans), and the generally changing role of a commercial bank as a financial intermediary, (particularly in the time and savings area), the next few decades should bring a major re-evaluation of the correspondent function. Ultimately, it would seem that correspondent banking will drastically change and, follow-ing the pattern of recent years, its relative importance will no doubt continue to diminish.

[110] This does not imply that it has (or has not) been the most satisfactory from the viewpoint of the public interest.

# CHAPTER 4

———◄◆►———

# Mergers and Acquisitions

IN ANY ANALYSIS of industry structure inevitably two questions will arise: how many competitors are there and how difficult is it to establish new firms in the market. Chapters 4 and 5 try to provide some general answers to these queries from the viewpoint of commercial banking.

In this chapter, intra-industry mergers and acquisitions which have had a substantial impact upon the number of operating commercial banks, are analyzed. The first section provides a short review of both bank and nonbank merger movements in the American economy. Next, the few federal banking statutes which directly affected bank amalgamations in the past are mentioned, and the primary legislation in this area today,[1] the Bank Holding Company Act of 1956[2] and the Bank Merger Act of 1960,[3] are examined in some detail. The origin, relevant provisions, amendments, and enforcement of these two statutes are discussed. And, in the third and final section of this chapter, some of the implications of bank mergers and acquisitions are considered.

---

[1] 15 U.S.C. § 21(a) gives the Federal Reserve Board concurrent authority with the Department of Justice to enforce Section 7 of the Clayton Act in cases involving bank stock acquisitions, but antitrust questions of this type are reviewed in Chapter 7.

[2] 12 U.S.C. §§ 1841–1848 (1956).

[3] 12 U.S.C. § 1828(c).

TERMINOLOGY

Although there are technical differences among these expressions, the terms absorption, combination, merger, consolidation, amalgamation, and acquisition, unless otherwise noted, will be used interchangeably in this chapter to describe any form of fusion or integration of independent companies which brings them under unified control. Therefore, to avoid any possible confusion, it should be mentioned at this point that the 1956 group banking legislation deals only with the acquisition of bank shares or assets by a bank holding company; it does not control the acquisition of the assets of one bank by another (even though the acquiring bank is a holding company affiliate). However, the latter transaction would be covered by the Bank Merger Act, which requires federal approval for a merger, a consolidation, an acquisition of the assets, or an assumption of the liabilities of one insured bank by another.

## MERGER MOVEMENTS

NONBANKING ENTERPRISES

*Merger waves.*[4] Students of industrial organization generally conclude that there have been three major merger movements in recent American history. The first took place in the 1890s and early 1900s; the second in the late 1920s; and the third occurred in two cycles from 1940 through 1947, and from 1950 apparently to the present time.[5] During the first series of mergers, which in many ways was perhaps the most important, many fields formerly composed of a large number of small- and medium-sized firms were transformed into industries dominated by a few large enterprises. This, of course, laid the basic foundation for the structure that has characterized much of the industry in this country in the twentieth century.[6]

The second significant merger movement took place between 1926 and 1930. To some extent this reflected the emergence of new leading

[4] This question is discussed in Nelson, *Merger Movements in American Industry, 1895–1956;* Federal Trade Commission, *The Merger Movement;* and U. S. Congress, House, *Mergers and Superconcentration,* 1962, pp. 9–21.

[5] Weston, *The Role of Mergers in the Growth of Large Firms,* p. 9.

[6] Nelson, *Merger Movements in American Industry,* p. 5.

industries in the years since the first merger wave. But Ralph Nelson in his detailed investigation of merger movements in the United States also suggested that the acquisitions in the late 1920s "represented attempts to restore industrial concentration achieved by the first merger wave, a concentration which had become diluted over the years."[7]

A third large-scale merger movement has been in progress since the beginning of World War II. A peak in consolidations was reached in 1947. After a brief decline the acquisitions rapidly increased once again in the early 1950s, and this expansion has continued in the 1960s. This wave of mergers differs substantially from those discussed earlier, for the greatest activity was not concentrated in a very few years. Instead this reorganization of business has been spread over two decades. Furthermore, the emphasis in the postwar period has been upon the acquisition of small firms through outright purchase by large firms, and a substantial proportion of these combinations has been of the conglomerate (diversification) variety rather than the horizontal or vertical arrangements which were most common in the earlier merger movements.[8]

*Mergers-quantitative aspects.*[9] For the seven-year period 1897–1903 Nelson recorded 2,864 mergers. Moreover, he observed that in five of these years, 1898–1902, there was a burst of merger activity never exceeded in importance in American industrial history. This turn-of-the-century merger wave produced such firms as U. S. Steel, American Tobacco, International Harvester, Du Pont, Corn Products, Anaconda Copper, and American Smelting and Refining, and its effect was both widespread and enduring.

The second merger movement,[10] which began after World War I

[7] *Ibid.*

[8] *Ibid.*, pp. 5–6. Recent developments are discussed in U. S. Congress, Senate, *Economic Concentration*, Hearings, 1964–1965; particularly Part I, "Overall and Conglomerate Aspects."

[9] *Ibid.* Part 2, "Mergers and Other Factors Affecting Industry Concentration," contains a summary table of mergers and acquisitions in mining and manufacturing from 1895 to 1964 drawn from Nelson, *Merger Movements in American Industry*; Thorp and Crowder, *The Structure of American Industry*; and the Federal Trade Commission's records.

[10] Collins and Preston, "The Size Structure of the Largest Industrial Firms, 1909–1958," [*American Economic Review* (December 1961)] includes an interesting analysis of this period.

and reached what Willard Thorp described as the "hysteria stage"[11] during the late 1920s, produced a tremendous number of acquisitions. In the six-year span from 1925 to 1930, 4,682 mergers were recorded. The movement culminated in 1929 with an all time high of 1,245 consolidations. In the decade from 1919 through 1929 it has been estimated that this activity resulted in the disappearance of 7,000 manufacturing and mining concerns.[12]

During the third merger movement, which has been in progress virtually the entire period since the early years of World War II, as was mentioned above two distinct cycles are apparent in the data. The Federal Trade Commission's (FTC) statistics for manufacturing and mining mergers reveal that about 2,100 firms were absorbed between 1940 and 1947, inclusive. The amalgamation activity subsided in 1948, reaching a postwar low in 1949, but resumed again in 1950 and it still seems to be in progress. In the last decade (1957–1966) alone, approximately 8,400 mergers and acquisitions of manufacturing and mining concerns were recorded by the FTC.[13]

*Merger cycles and their causes.*[14]  The rate of merger activity seems to be rather closely associated with the level of business activity, or so-called business cycles. In other words, there is a rather high positive correlation between mergers and major economic time series. For example, the merger movement of the 1920s ceased with the

[11] Noted in U. S. Congress, Senate, *Economic Concentration,* Hearings, 1964–1965, p. 502.

[12] *Ibid.,* p. 847. For a brief but informative survey of this and the other merger waves, see Pegrum, *Public Regulation of Business,* pp. 103–110.

[13] In 1966 total recorded mergers in the FTC's most comprehensive series (no bank mergers included) were 1,746 in contrast to the 995 reported in its Manufacturing and Mining series. [Federal Trade Commission, *News Release,* "Merger Activity" (February 24, 1967). This *News Release* containing detailed summaries of merger activity for the year and earlier data is typically distributed in February.] The coefficient of correlation between the FTC manufacturing and mining series and commercial bank mergers is only .29 (using data from 1936–1965), which suggests that the two series are largely affected by different factors and/or the same factors but in different ways. Assuming no correlation between the two series, a "T" test at the .05 level of significance would *not* "reject" the null hypothesis.

[14] The material in this section is drawn from U. S. Congress, Senate, *Economic Concentration,* Hearings, 1964–1965, pp. 505–508. This is part of the statement before the committee by Dr. Willard F. Mueller, Director, Bureau of Economics, FTC.

advent of the Great Depression and the first phase of the current movement ended with the 1948–1949 recession. On the other hand, the 13 percent increase in industrial production and 33 percent increase in industrial stock prices between 1954 and 1955 were associated with a rapid rise in merger activity. The large number of consolidations was maintained as industrial production rose in 1956, but with the slackening of business activity in 1957 and 1958 the total number of manufacturing and mining mergers recorded by the FTC declined slightly and the FTC's "large" merger series fell off sharply. Total merger activity revived again in 1959 and has since been maintained at a relatively high level.

The above observations would appear to be consistent with the findings of a number of investigators of industrial mergers. Researchers have revealed that although there may be a variety of reasons underlying a specific consolidation, the overall rate of acquisition is associated with general economic conditions.[15] Furthermore, there appears to be a particularly close relationship between merger activity and stock prices. Therefore, one might conclude that in periods when the economy is advancing and there is a good market for equities, it will be reasonably safe to predict that the pressure for mergers will also be intense.

COMMERCIAL BANKING

*1890–1919.* The consolidation movements in commercial banking usually paralleled those in the industrial sector of the economy. As larger units were formed in other industries, bankers also attempted to amass greater resources, and they logically turned to mergers as a source of rapid growth. Concentration in New York City banking, as measured by the share of total deposits held by the twenty largest incorporated banks and trust companies, rose from 35 percent in 1901 to 38 percent in 1906, and to 43 percent in 1911.[16] In the last year mentioned these twenty institutions represented over one-fifth of

[15] One study found the following were the principal factors behind mergers in industry and trade during the postwar period: the increasing cost of doing business, technological developments, the growing power of unions, the desire to diversify, and the overall expansion of the economy. See *Bank Mergers,* The Bulletin of the C. J. Devine Institute of Finance, No. 18.

[16] Corey, *The House of Morgan,* pp. 136–37, 191, 254–61, 295; and U. S. Congress, Pujo Committee Report, 1913, p. 56.

the nation's banking resources, and this figure would have been substantially higher if the great private banking houses were included.

Concentration in the banking industry increased in the late 1890s and early 1900s not only as a result of bank consolidations but through the same powerful interests securing substantial stock holdings in a number of banks and trust companies, and through interlocking directorates. In some cases this type of arrangement was made necessary by branch banking restrictions. For example, in New York State, which was one of the centers of this activity, from 1898 through 1919 only banks headquartered in New York City could establish branch offices.[17] As a result, during the first two decades of this century it was common in other metropolitan areas in the state for individuals to organize or acquire a number of banks and to serve as directors and/or senior officers of each of these institutions. This permitted bankers and investors to form quasi branch systems in communities where branching was prohibited by law.

Besides branch banking restrictions, other factors encouraged individuals to secure an interest in two or more banks. Frequently, state banks had powers (such as trust, mortgage lending) which were greater than those of national associations, but bankers desired the prestige of a federal charter. Therefore, affiliate banks were organized, often with similar titles, so that the maximum benefits of both state and federal charters could accrue to the shareholders of the parent bank. In some instances the institutions involved were both state chartered, for there were considerable differences at the turn of the century in the powers of state banks as opposed to state trust companies (the latter had much broader authority in the securities area and greater branching privileges in some states).

In this period identical large shareholders, interlocking directorates, and affiliate relationships were used by the Morgan-Baker-Stillman combination mentioned in Chapter 3. Similar arrangements, though on a smaller scale, developed in a number of cities outside New York (particularly in Chicago) in the early 1900s. However, neither these broadly based systems nor the more localized chains of banks discussed above were included in the very limited data compiled concerning bank mergers at that time and, with the

---

[17] *Laws of the State of New York,* 1898, Chap. 410; *ibid.* 1919, Chap. 37.

exception of the Pujo Committee hearings, only occasional references to them are found in banking literature. Thus this early consolidation movement in commercial banking is often ignored, although it would appear to have been very substantial in terms of the bank assets involved.[18]

*1920–1932.* A second major consolidation movement in banking appears to have begun in the early twenties, reaching a very high level about the same time as the second series of mergers in the industrial sector began (1925–1926) and continuing until 1932. (See Table 5.2) In the twelve years from the end of 1920 through the end of 1932 nearly 6,000 consolidations, mergers, and absorptions of commercial banks took place. In addition, it was in this same interval that most of the leading bank holding companies in operation today were formed through the acquisition of hundreds of formerly independent banks.

Many researchers have attempted to explain why this merger movement in banking occurred at that particular time. Certainly this development was influenced by a variety of things, including the amalgamations in other industries, the movement of population to the cities, the desire on the part of many banks to obtain a share of an expanding trust business, the relaxation of some federal branch banking restrictions in the 1920s and the easing of some state laws in the early 1930s, the generally prosperous economy of the 1920s, and the booming stock market. However, if a single factor had to be selected as the most important contributor to the wave of mergers in the 1920s and early 1930s, it would have to be the weakness of thousands of banks, for "many if not most of the absorption transactions of that period appear to have been alternatives to either failure or to voluntary liquidation."[19]

[18] For evidence of this early bank consolidation movement (in addition to the works cited in note 16), see Burr, *The Portrait of A Banker: James Stillman,* pp. 180–81, 186, and 219–22; Smith, *Trust Companies in the United States,* pp. 354–56; New York State Superintendent of Banks, *Annual Report* for the fiscal year 1897–1898, pp. viii–ix; 1899–1900, pp. viii–xi; 1906–1907, xl–xli; 1911–1912, pp. 14–15; and 1912–1913, pp. 30–32; also Peach, *The Security Affiliates of National Banks,* pp. 61–70.

[19] FDIC, *Annual Report* for the year ended December 31, 1960, p. 34. Additional comments from this FDIC report are included in Chapter 2 of the

*1933–1940.* The number of mergers continued at a fairly high level from 1933 through 1940. In this eight-year span there were approximately 1,600 consolidations of commercial banks, or 200 a year, as contrasted with an average of 500 a year from 1921–1932 inclusive. (See Table 4.1 and 5.2) Many of these acquisitions, available information would seem to indicate, involved a continuation of the pattern established in the earlier period in which stronger banks acquired weaker institutions. In fact this activity was encouraged and facilitated at the time by the FDIC, which began its insurance operations on January 1, 1934, and by the Office of the Comptroller of the Currency.[20]

*1941–1953.* The number of mergers declined substantially in the 1940s and early 1950s. Between 1941 and the end of 1953 there were roughly 1,100 amalgamations of commercial banks, or an average of slightly under ninety each year. (See Table 4.1) In this interval consolidations in smaller communities were reported in many cases to have been due to the unavailability of suitable personnel to carry on the management of the banks in question upon retirement of their senior officers.[21] In larger cities, such as New York, on the other hand, some mergers were reported to have also resulted from the relatively high ratio of capital to total assets of the city banks, which was reflected in common share prices which were less than book value. This in turn encouraged amalgamations, for through merger the stockholders of the acquired bank were sometimes able to realize the full book value of their shares in cash in contrast to their discounted value in the over-the-counter market. In addition, the need for larger

present study. The staff report of the Federal Reserve Board to the Subcommittee on Monopoly of the Senate on the *Concentration of Banking in the United States* (1952) noted: "Many of the mergers and absorptions through the twenties and early thirties were forced lifesaving jobs—cases where stronger institutions took over the weaker to prevent the failure of the latter or where two or more institutions combined to create a stronger one." (p. 6) Also see American Bankers Association, *The Commercial Banking Industry*, p. 46.

[20] From Lamb, *Group Banking*, pp. 36–37; and from comments in the Comptroller of the Currency's *Annual Reports* in this period.

[21] Federal Reserve Board, *Concentration of Banking in the United States,* 1952, p. 6.

TABLE 4.1. CHANGES IN THE NUMBER OF COMMERCIAL BANKS IN OPERATION IN THE UNITED STATES AND OTHER AREAS, 1936–1966*

| Year | Banks in Operation at Beginning of Year | Beginning Operations | | Ceasing Operations | | Net Changes during Year | Banks in Operation at End of Year |
|---|---|---|---|---|---|---|---|
| | | New Banks | Other | Mergers Absorptions Consolidations | Other | | |
| 1936 | 15,374 | 65 | 1 | 224 | 65 | −223 | 15,151 |
| 1937 | 15,151 | 63 | 1 | 252 | 81 | −269 | 14,882 |
| 1938 | 14,882 | 37 | – | 157 | 59 | −179 | 14,703 |
| 1939 | 14,703 | 35 | 2 | 158 | 48 | −169 | 14,534 |
| 1940 | 14,534 | 37 | 6 | 126 | 52 | −135 | 14,399 |
| 1941 | 14,399 | 45 | – | 67 | 48 | − 70 | 14,329 |
| 1942 | 14,329 | 18 | 5 | 100 | 68 | − 22* | 14,307 |
| 1943 | 14,307 | 48 | – | 87 | 62 | −101 | 14,206 |
| 1944 | 14,206 | 65 | 5 | 74 | 35 | − 39 | 14,167 |
| 1945 | 14,167 | 115 | 4 | 76 | 27 | + 16 | 14,183 |
| 1946 | 14,183 | 145 | 3 | 94 | 19 | + 35 | 14,218 |
| 1947 | 14,218 | 112 | 1 | 86 | 11 | + 16 | 14,234 |
| 1948 | 14,234 | 78 | 2 | 78 | 15 | − 13 | 14,221 |
| 1949 | 14,221 | 67 | 12 | 83 | 12 | − 16 | 14,205 |
| 1950 | 14,205 | 68 | 2 | 94 | 17 | − 41 | 14,164 |
| 1951 | 14,164 | 60 | 4 | 83 | 13 | − 32 | 14,132 |
| 1952 | 14,132 | 67 | 4 | 102 | 13 | − 44 | 14,088 |
| 1953 | 14,088 | 64 | 1 | 115 | 14 | − 64 | 14,024 |
| 1954 | 14,024 | 72 | – | 209 | 6 | −143 | 13,881 |
| 1955 | 13,881 | 115 | – | 235 | 5 | −125 | 13,756 |
| 1956 | 13,756 | 122 | – | 191 | 7 | − 76 | 13,680 |
| 1957 | 13,680 | 84 | 4 | 158 | 3 | − 73 | 13,607 |
| 1958 | 13,607 | 92 | 4 | 158 | 5 | − 67 | 13,540 |
| 1959 | 13,540 | 117 | – | 169 | 2 | − 54 | 13,486 |
| 1960 | 13,486 | 132 | – | 130 | 4 | − 2 | 13,484 |
| 1961 | 13,484 | 113 | – | 147 | 6 | − 40 | 13,444 |
| 1962 | 13,444 | 183 | – | 183 | 5 | − 5 | 13,439 |
| 1963 | 13,439 | 300 | – | 155 | 2 | +143 | 13,582 |
| 1964 | 13,582 | 335 | 2 | 133 | 11 | +193 | 13,775 |
| 1965 | 13,775 | 198 | 1 | 149 | 7 | + 43 | 13,818 |
| 1966 | 13,818 | 122 | 1 | 137 | 19 | − 33 | 13,785 |

* Only total includes increase in number of banks due to inclusion of 94 noninsured trust companies and 29 noninsured banks not previously included as banks in FDIC records. These data differ slightly from those in Tables 2.1 and 2.2 primarily because the Board of Governors obtains these statistics from the FDIC, and the latter includes the U. S. Possessions and Trust Territories in the Pacific and the Panama Canal Zone which are omitted from the Board's data used in the earlier tables. However, some of the differences stem from agency definitions, etc. particularly for the earlier years.

Sources: "Number of Banks and Branches 1936–1963," Banking Markets Unit, Board of Governors of the Federal Reserve System (mimeographed); and 1965, 1966 and 1967 Supplements to this release.

lending limits and the desire to reduce operating costs have been suggested as other important motives behind mergers at that time.[22]

*1954–1966.* From 1954 through the end of 1966 there were approximately 2,150 bank mergers, or an average of about 165 a year. This was very close to the level achieved in the late 1930s, but it was only about one-third of the corresponding figure for the years from 1920 through 1933.[23] Moreover, there were so many other dissimilarities between the first series of bank acquisitions reviewed in this chapter and the current amalgamations that two leading students of this subject decided "the analysis of bank mergers during the late twenties and early thirties is not very useful in understanding the present merger movement."[24]

Fortunately, there have been a number of investigations of amalgamations in banking in recent years, and they provide valuable insight into current trends. For example, a study by the staff of the C. J. Devine Institute of Finance at New York University's Graduate School of Business Administration concluded:[25]

The principal motives in most of the postwar bank mergers have been: (a) the desire to diversify and to improve banking services such as development of consumer loans and saving deposits, to increase the line of credit that can be extended to a single customer, and to enlarge trust and international business in order to remain in competition and grow; (b) to strengthen management and to acquire qualified management succession personnel in order to assure continued efficient operations. This has been an important factor in many mergers involving both small and large

[22] *Ibid.,* pp. 6–7. Also see Comptroller of the Currency, 89th *Annual Report,* 1951, p. 2 for factors influencing mergers. The research of David and Charlotte Alhadeff discussed later in this chapter raises some serious questions regarding the significance of many of the factors usually credited with initiating the merger movement at that time, including management succession problems.

[23] However, one study has noted that if one considers the ratio of population or dollars of gross national product to the number of banks at the beginning and end of these respective periods, the percentage decline in the 1950s and early 1960s much more closely resembles the decline in the 1920s. Shull, "Competition in Banking: A New Old Problem," *Business Review,* Federal Reserve Bank of Philadelphia (January 1963), pp. 12–13.

[24] Alhadeff and Alhadeff, "Recent Bank Mergers," *Quarterly Journal of Economics* (November 1955), p. 503.

[25] *Bank Mergers,* C. J. Devine Institute of Finance, Bulletin No. 18, pp. 21–22. This study presents an additional list of factors relating specifically to mergers in New York City.

banks; (c) the desire of banks to follow their customers to the suburbs and to reach the rapidly rising middle class in need of banking services. . . .

Other motives could no doubt be added to this group and there may be some reservations concerning the importance of some of the items included, but most would appear on any "standard list" of the leading causes of bank mergers in the past ten to fifteen years. However, it should be mentioned that the Alhadeffs, in their research done approximately a decade ago, found that in 1953 and 1954 two basic factors seemed to have motivated the sharp acceleration of bank mergers: pressures resulting from uneven rates of growth by different banks during the rapid over-all expansion at that time and the desire to establish or expand branch systems.[26] They considered most of the other items in the "standard list" cited above and concluded that they were more likely to have facilitated the amalgamation movement in that brief span than to have initiated it.

If (as in the case of the first period analyzed in this section, 1921–1932) a single factor was selected as the major contributor to the bank mergers of the 1950s and 1960s it would have to be the desire to expand branch systems.[27] (See Table 4.2) Between 85 and 90 percent of the institutions taken over by other banks in this interval were converted into branches of the surviving bank.[28] Furthermore, approximately three-fourths of the banks acquired by major bank holding companies in this period were absorbed by other affiliate banks (or vice versa).[29] In all fairness to the banks involved, however, it should also be noted that while the number of merged banks was substantial in this recent consolidation movement, *de novo* branches accounted for about 75 percent of the additional offices added to branch systems in the 1950s and 85 percent in the 1960s.[30]

[26] Alhadeff and Alhadeff, "Recent Bank Mergers," *Quarterly Journal of Economics* (November 1955), p. 531.

[27] This, in effect, would be a composite of many of the factors mentioned earlier.

[28] Federal Reserve Board, *Recent Developments in the Structure of Banking,* 1962, p. 8; and Federal Reserve Board, "Developments in the Structure of Banking in the Early 1960s," 1965, p. 9. (mimeographed)

[29] Fischer, *Bank Holding Companies,* p. 43; and data since 1960 compiled by this writer.

[30] The corresponding figure for the period between 1933 and 1950 was 70 percent. Federal Reserve Board, "Developments in the Structure of Banking in the Early 1960s," 1965, p. 5. (mimeographed)

| Year | Branches in Operation at Beginning of Year | Beginning Operations | | Ceasing Operations | | Net Changes during Year | Banks in Operation at End of Year |
|---|---|---|---|---|---|---|---|
| | | Facilities Conversions Replacements | New Branches | Branches | Other | | |
| 1936 | 3,248 | 73 | 100 | 56 | — | + 117 | 3,365 |
| 1937 | 3,365 | 90 | 93 | 66 | — | + 117 | 3,482 |
| 1938 | 3,482 | 50 | 37 | 52 | — | + 35 | 3,517 |
| 1939 | 3,517 | 53 | 41 | 50 | — | + 44 | 3,561 |
| 1940 | 3,561 | 47 | 42 | 57 | — | + 32 | 3,593 |
| 1941 | 3,593 | 24 | 53 | 38 | — | + 39 | 3,632 |
| 1942 | 3,632 | 54 | 39 | 50 | — | + 43 | 3,675 |
| 1943 | 3,675 | 215 | 18 | 44 | — | + 189 | 3,864 |
| 1944 | 3,864 | 131 | 39 | 17 | 16 | + 137 | 4,001 |
| 1945 | 4,001 | 109 | 61 | 15 | 131 | + 24 | 4,025 |
| 1946 | 4,025 | 68 | 143 | 22 | 151 | + 38 | 4,063 |
| 1947 | 4,063 | 58 | 148 | 23 | 9 | + 174 | 4,237 |
| 1948 | 4,237 | 61 | 153 | 19 | 1 | + 194 | 4,431 |
| 1949 | 4,431 | 90 | 156 | 12 | — | + 234 | 4,665 |
| 1950 | 4,665 | 112 | 192 | 17 | 7 | + 280 | 4,945 |
| 1951 | 4,945 | 102 | 240 | 23 | — | + 319 | 5,264 |
| 1952 | 5,264 | 121 | 221 | 19 | — | + 323 | 5,587 |
| 1953 | 5,587 | 118 | 280 | 18 | 10 | + 370 | 5,957 |
| 1954 | 5,957 | 192 | 337 | 29 | 8 | + 486[b] | 6,443 |
| 1955 | 6,443 | 229 | 439 | 45 | 4 | + 619 | 7,062 |
| 1956 | 7,062 | 195 | 521 | 33 | 5 | + 678 | 7,740 |
| 1957 | 7,740 | 160 | 503 | 27 | 4 | + 632 | 8,372 |
| 1958 | 8,372 | 154 | 569 | 33 | 3 | + 696[b] | 9,068 |
| 1959 | 9,068 | 178 | 602 | 49 | 9 | + 722 | 9,790 |
| 1960 | 9,790 | 132 | 755 | 52 | 8 | + 829[b] | 10,619 |
| 1961 | 10,619 | 149 | 790 | 54 | 5 | + 880 | 11,499 |
| 1962 | 11,499 | 183 | 856 | 41 | 6 | + 992 | 12,491 |
| 1963 | 12,491 | 163 | 1,054 | 48 | 8 | +1,161 | 13,652 |
| 1964 | 13,652 | 138 | 1,028 | 46 | 1 | +1,119 | 14,771 |
| 1965 | 14,771 | 144 | 1,064 | 54 | 7 | +1,147 | 15,918 |
| 1966 | 15,918 | 135 | 1,098 | 57 | 7 | +1,169 | 17,087 |

[a] Not all these data correspond with those found in Tables 2.1 and 2.2. For an explanation see Table 4.1. [b] Net change includes 6, 9, and 2 branches transferred as result of absorption or succession in 1954, 1958, and 1960 respectively.

Sources: "Number of Banks and Branches 1936–1963," Banking Markets Unit, Board of Governors of the Federal Reserve System (mimeographed); and 1965, 1966 and 1967 Supplements to this release.

*Why banks merge: survey results.* The previous discussion of bank amalgamations included frequent references to the opinions of researchers and government agencies regarding the reasons banks merge. The factors bank management feels led to the consolidation of a given institution with another or to the acquisition of a bank by a holding company may also be of some interest, despite the fact that the dangers associated with drawing conclusions from questionnaire responses are legion.[31]

A survey was conducted by the Comptroller of the Currency to learn more about the factors which led to the sale of 101 national banks to other national banks and 68 national banks to state-chartered banks from 1950 through May 1, 1955. The reasons the banks were sold according to the survey responses were as follows (more than one reason prompted many of the sales):

| | | | |
|---|---|---|---|
| Management problems | 68 | To achieve a more competitive status | 7 |
| Attractive prices | 65 | Bank located in overbanked community | 5 |
| Identical owners' desire to combine bank | 33 | Uneconomic banking units | 4 |
| Weak earning capacity of selling bank | 21 | Embezzlement | 4 |
| Closely held bank's owners desired to retire | 9 | To obtain fringe benefits for officers and employees | 4 |
| Larger bank needed in community | 7 | Miscellaneous | 12 |

This writer conducted a survey of a somewhat different type of amalgamation—banks acquired by holding companies. The universe consisted of the nearly 150 banks which joined fifteen leading group systems between 1949 and the end of 1965. Nearly 80 percent of the banks completed the questionnaire distributed. With this rather high rate of response, combined with the fact that about one-fourth of the replies were obtained during lengthy personal interviews with senior officers of the banks involved, somewhat more significance may be attached to these findings than would usually be the case, but nevertheless the limitations of these data are still very severe.

This last point can be illustrated by the pattern noted in about one-fifth of the responses. While a majority of the replies in the survey contained some additional explanation regarding the situation at the

---

[31] See for example the comments of Alhadeff and Alhadeff in "Recent Bank Mergers," *Quarterly Journal of Economics* (November 1955), p. 504, n. 3.

time of the merger, most of these questionnaires merely listed three items: the need for more capital, the need for more specialized or diversified services, and the need for accommodating larger lines of credit. The frequency with which this trio of answers occurred combined with almost a complete lack of discussion might suggest that these replies were the "good reasons" rather than the "real reasons" behind a given acquisition to which the Alhadeffs referred in their study of bank mergers.[32]

Another factor which was mentioned very frequently in the responses, especially in the 1961–1965 period,[33] was the problem of management succession. This is one of the most difficult problems faced by the owners of small banks. Two enlightening studies of the personnel question which have been made in the Midwest and the South clearly show a tremendous shortage of younger executives in many rural institutions.[34] In a large number of banks a shortsighted executive reaches the age of retirement and finds that he has not employed an adequate successor. Frequently this has resulted from the owner's or operating officer's reluctance to pay a salary adequate to attract a capable young executive. A bank cannot operate without management, and when it seems that considerable effort may be required to find a replacement the possibility of a merger becomes very attractive.

Although the above factors have been significant, the most important element in the affiliation with holding companies appears to have been the stockholders' interest in either obtaining a more liquid security or achieving a profitable gain in an exchange of stock. These stockholder goals were designated collectively as the primary reason for the merger in 40 of the 115 replies. One or the other of these benefits to the shareholders was placed among the first three factors by about 80 percent of the respondents. Even more impressive, nineteen of the questionnaires (one-sixth of all responses) listed one of these two factors as the only reason these banks joined a holding company. (See Table 4.3)

[32] *Ibid.*

[33] This study was originally prepared for this writer's book on *Bank Holding Companies* and has been updated for this work. Much more detail appears in the earlier book, pp. 114–19.

[34] Arrington, "A Factual Study of the Deficiency of Rural Bank Management in Georgia and the Problem of Managerial Succession"; and Isbell, "Management Succession in Smaller Banks."

TABLE 4.3. REASONS FOR JOINING GROUP SYSTEMS AS RANKED BY 115
BANKS ACQUIRED, 1949–1965

| | Rank Given | | | | | Only |
| Reason | 1st | 2d | 3d | 1st or 2d* | 1st, 2d, or 3d* | Reason Given |
|---|---|---|---|---|---|---|
| Lack of management succession | 18 | 6 | 3 | 27 | 35 | 6 |
| Desire of major stockholder for more liquid holdings | 23 | 10 | 7 | 40 | 58 | 6 |
| Need for more capital | 4 | 9 | 6 | 16 | 24 | — |
| Need for more specialized or more diversified services | 13 | 6 | 11 | 20 | 37 | — |
| Need for accommodating larger lines of credit | 8 | 14 | 14 | 26 | 48 | — |
| Lack of fair profit on capital invested with costs too high or earnings insufficient | 2 | 2 | — | 4 | 5 | 1 |
| Opportunity to gain a profitable premium through an exchange of stock with a group | 17 | 11 | 8 | 38 | 54 | 13 |
| Other | 2 | 1 | 1 | 3 | 4 | — |

* Some persons rated a given reason equally with another; therefore, columns 4
and 5 do not equal the respective totals for columns 1, 2, and 3.

Source: Questionnaire replies from 115 banks which merged with 15 leading bank
holding companies.

In this survey of banks which joined major group systems during
the past sixteen years, no factors other than the above were frequently
mentioned as the reason a sale had been negotiated. Several executives stated (in confidence) that extremely favorable pension arrangements and fringe benefits had influenced their decision to support affiliating with a group. A few respondents mentioned that they
had joined a multiple-unit system because of a fear of large, non-
holding company competitors moving into their area. Only one or two
replies discussed benefits to be gained from additional specialization
of executive personnel and the opportunity to use more modern
equipment. The problem of inadequate earnings was mentioned only

five times; other than this the profits question apparently was not considered of great importance in any of the mergers.

But, while profits and costs are rarely mentioned in questionnaire responses such as those cited in the two surveys above, and while few researchers conclude these elements are of much significance in initiating mergers and acquisitions, they may be much more important than most people have found them to be. Howard Crosse, in his book on bank management, drawing upon many years experience as a senior officer at the Federal Reserve Bank of New York, observed:[35]

The failure to recognize [the importance of costs] results from the fact that the costs which bring about bank mergers are not revealed in the statistics because they are prospective costs. Prospective costs are the costs which the small bank faces but has not actually met. They include the salary cost of a suitable replacement for top management, the cost of fringe benefits that have never actually been provided for employees, the cost of meeting the competition in savings interest rates, the cost of mechanization and modernization which have never been undertaken. These are costs which a successful bank must pay in a competitive situation if it is to provide the services offered by other banks, but they are costs which dismay the stockholders and directors of many small banks who have not faced up to the obsolescence of their management practices and physical plant.

Yet, Crosse feels the most important initiating factor in the current merger trend lies much deeper than most of the banking problems mentioned. It is "part and parcel of the economic development of the nation," including the changing character of communities, improved transportation and increased customer mobility, growth in shopping centers and chain stores, and the general merger movement in progress in the United States.

## REGULATION[36]

### FEDERAL CONTROLS BEFORE THE 1956 AND 1960 LEGISLATION[37]

Prior to the passage of the Bank Holding Company Act of 1956 and the Bank Merger Act of 1960, the federal bank supervisory

[35] Crosse, *Management Policies for Commercial Banks*, pp. 22–23.

[36] This discussion is limited to banking statutes; the merger and stock acquisition provisions of the antitrust laws are reviewed in Chapter 7.

[37] The federal laws concerning bank mergers in the mid-1950s are summarized in Senate Report No. 2583, 84th Cong., pp. 2–4.

authorities had very little control over commercial bank consolidations or acquisitions. Of course, the Federal Reserve Board had enjoyed concurrent jurisdiction with the Department of Justice in the enforcement of Section 7 of the Clayton Act since 1914,[38] but the Board was unsuccessful in the only action it initiated under this authority.[39] Thus, until the past decade, bank amalgamations could usually be accomplished with limited (and, in some cases, no) danger of "interference" on the part of the federal banking agencies.[40]

*Comptroller of the Currency.* The Comptroller's office as a chartering authority appeared to have the most extensive powers of any of the federal bank supervisors in the bank merger area. The Comptroller of the Currency's approval had to be obtained in all bank consolidations or mergers (in the technical sense) where the resulting or continuing institution was to be a national bank.[41]

*Federal Deposit Insurance Corporation.* Without prior written consent by the FDIC, no insured bank was permitted (1) to merge or consolidate with any noninsured bank or institution, (2) to assume the liabilities of any noninsured bank or institution, or (3) to transfer assets to any noninsured bank or institution in consideration for the assumption of liabilities of the insured bank.[42]

*Federal Reserve Board.* The modest controls the Board was granted over bank holding companies under the Banking Act of 1933

[38] 38 Stat. 730, 734 (1914), § 11; as amended, 15 U.S.C. § 21(a).

[39] The *Transamerica case,* see Chapter 7.

[40] Comptroller Ray M. Gidney in testifying before Congress in 1960 stated one of the principal reasons for the passage of bank merger legislation was the fact "that many bank mergers are not now subject to federal jurisdiction and may take place without the approval of any federal authority." U. S. Congress, House, *Regulation of Bank Mergers,* Hearings, 1960, p. 5.

[41] 12 U.S.C. § 33, 34(a); 34(b). Prior approval did not appear to be necessary in the case of assumption of liabilities or the purchase assets, however, if no diminution of aggregate capital or surplus resulted. But even in such circumstances the Comptroller did not seem to be powerless, for he had to approve the necessary increase in capital of a national bank, and if one of the banks was to continue as a branch he had to authorize this as well. U. S. Congress, House, *Regulation of Bank Mergers,* Hearings, 1960, p. 6.

[42] 12 U.S.C. § 1828(c). The FDIC had a form of indirect control over nonmember insured bank acquisitions since the Corporation's approval was required before a new branch could be established. 12 U.S.C. § 1828(d).

placed no significant restrictions on acquisitions by group systems.[43] However, the Federal Reserve did have some authority over bank mergers, at least indirectly, for state member banks at that time appeared to be subject to essentially the same restrictions in the establishment of branches as national banks except that approval had to be obtained from the Federal Reserve Board instead of from the Comptroller of the Currency.[44]

*All agencies.* Section 18(c) of the Federal Deposit Insurance Act required federal approval of a merger, a consolidation, or an assumption of liabilities involving insured banks when as a result of the action a diminution of aggregate capital stock or surplus occurred. The relevant section of the law read in part:[45]

No insured bank shall (i) merge or consolidate with an insured state bank under the charter of a state bank or (ii) assume liability to pay any deposits made in another insured bank, *if the capital stock or surplus of the resulting or assuming bank will be less than the aggregate capital stock or aggregate surplus, respectively, of all the merging or consolidating banks* or of all the parties to the assumption of liabilities, at the time of the shareholders' meetings which authorized the merger or consolidation or at the time of the assumption of liabilities, unless the Comptroller of the Currency shall give prior written consent if the assuming bank is to be a national bank or the assuming or resulting bank is to be a District bank; or unless the Board of Governors of the Federal Reserve System gives prior written consent if the assuming or resulting bank is to be a state member bank (except a District bank); or unless the [FDIC] gives prior written consent if the assuming or resulting bank is to be a nonmember insured bank (except a District bank). . . . [Emphasis added]

There were many instances in which this legislation did not effectively restrict mergers because the aggregate capital stock or aggregate surplus of the participating banks was not reduced. For example, from 1955 through 1958 inclusive the following mergers or assumptions of liabilities did not require approval by the Federal Reserve, the FDIC, or the Comptroller of the Currency respectively:[46]

[43] See Chapter 3.
[44] 12 U.S.C. § 321.
[45] 12 U.S.C. § 1828(c), enacted September 21, 1950.
[46] Computed from data included in U. S. Congress, Senate, *Regulation of Bank Mergers*, Report No. 196, 1959, pp. 14–15.

| Continuing Bank | Number | Percentage of All Such Amalgamations | Resources of Banks Not Requiring Approval ($ million) |
|---|---|---|---|
| A State Federal Reserve System member | 97 | 47 | 7,445[b] |
| An insured, nonmember state bank | 49 | 40 | 438 |
| A national bank or District of Columbia bank | 7 | 2[a] | 52 |

[a] Percentage of all merger, consolidation, and assumption cases, although only the last would possibly not require Comptroller approval.

[b] The size of this figure in large part reflects the inclusion of the Chase Manhattan Bank merger, which was one of the largest bank amalgamations in American history; yet, it did not require federal approval.

Thus, a relatively small percentage of the transactions in which the continuing bank was a national bank escaped federal control under Section 18(c) of the Federal Deposit Insurance Act, but a very large percentage of the cases in which the continuing bank was a state institution was not covered.

Although the above summary of merger regulation could leave a person with the impression that at least national bank consolidations probably were strictly controlled, this conclusion would appear to be quite false. For example, an item of particular importance for the analysis in this chapter is the weight given to competitive factors in considering applications to combine two or more banks. Yet the Comptroller was no doubt hesitant to reject an application on competitive grounds, for this may merely have resulted in the surrender of a national bank charter and reincorporation as a state bank. Furthermore, the statute under which the Comptroller operated contained no explicit reference to weighing competition in considering whether the fusion of two banks should be permitted. For these and numerous other reasons, in practice the Comptroller's supposed authority to disapprove amalgamations was of little importance. In fact, only 22 of 731 merger applications were denied by the Office of the Comptroller of the Currency between 1950 and the end of 1958 on the basis of competitive considerations.[47]

[47] U. S. Congress, Senate, *Amend the Bank Merger Act of 1960*, Hearings, 1965, p. 44.

*Old Kent case.*[48] A very large number of the mergers which took place prior to 1960 in which the continuing bank was state chartered were often beyond federal control as mergers. But, if the banks were located in states which permitted branch banking, in most instances the resulting institution found it necessary to apply to one of the federal banking agencies as well as to state officials to obtain permission to operate the acquired bank as a branch. It is apparent that the banking authorities made at least a limited effort to use these branch powers to ensure that amalgamations were subjected to competitive tests. This is evident from the following remarks of Jerome Shay, Assistant General Counsel of the Federal Reserve Board in the 1966 hearings to *Amend the Bank Merger Act:*[49]

Through the Board's authority to pass on branches of state member banks, it tried to consider the competitive aspects of these things and look at the merger not from the standpoint of the merger, as such, where we wouldn't be able to under the merger law, but rather from the standpoint of passing on the branch application. Because so often the absorbed bank is operated, as you know, as a branch of the resulting bank.

And Comptroller of the Currency Gidney observed in his 1955 *Annual Report* that he made a practice of studying the geographic location and distribution of the branch offices of merging banks to determine ". . . the extent of existing competition between those branches and the competition that would be provided by other banks if the merger were to be approved."[50]

The use of this competitive test by the federal agencies seemed to be of doubtful legality after the decision by the United States Court of Appeals for the District of Columbia in *Old Kent Bank and Trust Company* v. *Martin* in 1960.[51] This action arose after the Board denied the application of the Old Kent Bank and Trust Company of Grand Rapids, Michigan, a state member bank, to operate the seven

[48] Much of the material in this section was drawn from Thiemann, "The Bank Merger Act of 1960," pp. 9–17.

[49] U. S. Congress, Senate, *Amend the Bank Merger Act of 1960*, Hearings, 1965, p. 29. Similar comments by Governor William McC. Martin, Jr. appear in U. S. Congress, Senate, *Legislation Affecting Corporate Mergers*, Hearings, 1956, p. 50.

[50] Comptroller of the Currency, 93d *Annual Report*, 1955, p. 18. This report (pp. 17–19) contains a detailed discussion of factors considered by the Comptroller of the Currency in approving mergers and consolidations.

[51] 281 F. 2d 62 (1960).

offices of the Peoples National Bank as branches after their merger. Since the continuing bank was a state member bank, the Comptroller had no role in this activity and the Board could review the merger only in the case of a reduction in aggregate capital stock or surplus, but this had not occurred.

In this case, the Board attempted to prevent the merger by rejecting the branch request. It did so because ". . . of the adverse effect the proposed transaction would seem likely to have on competition in the area."[52] The bank offered several alternative plans but these too were denied by the "Fed." In the meantime, the Michigan Banking Commission acted favorably on the bank's merger application and the consolidation was accomplished as of the close of business July 31, 1958.

Despite the Board's negative decision, the new bank began operating the seven former offices of Peoples National Bank as its own branches on August 1, 1958. On the same date, the bank filed a suit for declaratory judgment against the Board of Governors, challenging the right of the Board to (1) approve or disapprove mergers or consolidations of national banks into or with state member banks, (2) approve or disapprove the retention and operation by a resulting state member bank of branches which were in lawful operation by constituent national and state member banks as of the date of a consolidation or merger, and (3) disapprove an application for the retention and operation of such branches on the ground of an adverse effect on competition. Old Kent began the action in order to forestall any attempt by the Board to initiate proceedings to remove it from membership in the System, since the Board has the authority to require any member bank to surrender its membership if it finds that the bank has failed to comply with the Federal Reserve Act or with one of the Board's regulations.

In April 1959 the District Court granted a motion for summary judgment in favor of the Board and denied a cross-motion for summary judgment filed by Old Kent. The District Court held that the statute governing the establishment and operation of branches by state member banks included branches acquired as a result of a merger.[53] Old Kent's attorneys had contended that the effect on

[52] Quoted in Thiemann, "The Bank Merger Act," p. 11.
[53] *Ibid.*, p. 16.

competition should not be considered when passing on a branch application, and to this the court responded that when[54]

Congress empowers an agency to "approve" an action, it normally requires the agency to consider the probable effects of the actions within the area of agency responsibility. The existence of too much or too little competition may cause serious harm in banking as it may in other areas of business. Thus, it is important for the Board to consider whether an applicant may be seeking to establish a large number of branches in order to give it an undue competitive advantage over other member or nonmember banks in a given locality.

Old Kent appealed the District Court's ruling and obtained a reversal from the Court of Appeals in 1960. By a vote of 2 to 1 the court held that[55]

the statutory word "establish" does not include "operate after acquiring by merger," and the statutory phase "any new branch" of a state member does not include "any existing branch of a national bank that merges with a state member bank." In short, we think a state bank does not "establish any new branch" when it retains the branches it has acquired by merger.

This decision was not appealed to the Supreme Court by the "Fed," for less than two weeks after it was handed down the Bank Merger Act of 1960 was approved by Congress. This legislation substantially broadened the scope of federal supervisory jurisdiction in the area of bank mergers, and it was thought by the Board's counsel that appeal would probably serve no useful purpose.[56]

THE BANK HOLDING COMPANY ACT OF 1956.[57]

*Acquisition provisions.*[58]   The 1956 statute made it unlawful except with the prior approval of the Board for any action to be taken

[54] *Old Kent Bank and Trust Company* v. *Martin,* 172 F. Supp. 951, 952 (1959). The bank was joined by the National Association of Supervisors of State Banks in this action, which filed a brief amicus curiae.

[55] *Old Kent Bank and Trust Company* v. *Martin,* 281 F. 2d 61, 62 (1960). In a Pennsylvania case a denial by the state authorities of an application for permission to merge was reversed by the courts in part on the basis of the absence of specific statutory standards to this effect. *Dauphin Deposit Trust Company* v. *Myers,* 130 A. 2d 686 (1957).

[56] Letter from Howard Hackley, Federal Reserve Board General Counsel, July 8, 1966.

[57] 70 Stat. 133 (1956).

[58] Other provisions are discussed in Chapter 3.

which resulted in a company becoming a bank holding company or for any bank holding company to acquire ownership or control of any voting shares or any bank if, after such acquisition, the company owned or controlled more than 5 percent of the voting shares of such bank. Any merger or consolidation of two bank holding companies required the Board's consent. No bank holding company or subsidiary thereof, other than a bank, could acquire all or substantially all assets of a bank without the approval of the Board.

While the Board was given the authority to grant or deny any bank's application to expand, it had to obtain the views of other bank authorities, the Comptroller of the Currency for national banks, or the appropriate state official. If the comptroller or state banking superintendent disapproved of the transaction, hearings had to be held. At the conclusion of the hearing the Board of Governors could accept or reject the application on the basis of the record made at the hearing.

In determining whether or not to approve any acquisition, merger, or consolidation the Board was required to consider the factors listed in Section 3(c) of the Act:

(1) the financial history and condition of the company or companies and the banks concerned; (2) their prospects; (3) the character of their management; (4) the convenience, needs and welfare of the communities and the area concerned; and (5) whether or not the effect of such acquisition or merger or consolidation would be to expand the size or extent of the bank holding company system involved beyond limits consistent with adequate and sound banking, the public interest, and the preservation of competition in the field of banking.

Items (1) to (3) are very similar to those included in Section 19 of the Banking Act of 1933,[59] and (1) to (4) follow very closely the standards set out for various purposes in the Banking Act of 1935.[60] However, (5), with its emphasis upon competition, seems much more akin to antitrust than to the usual banking legislation.

Throughout the hearings on the numerous bills considered, great concern about states' rights was expressed, and the Bank Holding Company Act made clear that it did not prevent any state from

[59] 48 Stat. 162 (1933). They were also similar to Section 322 of the Federal Reserve Act (12 U.S.C. § 322) which was added in 1917. 40 Stat. 232 (1917).
[60] 49 Stat. 684 (1935), § 101 amending § 12B(g) of the Federal Reserve Act.

exercising such powers and jurisdiction as it may have had (or later acquired) with respect to banks, group systems, or subsidiaries thereof. [§7] Furthermore, the so-called Douglas amendment [§3 (d)] included in the 1956 legislation required that an out-of-state bank holding company could not acquire shares or assets of any bank in a state which had not specifically authorized this type of acquisition by statute.

*Regulation of expansion under the Act.*[61] It would appear that the majority of the Federal Reserve Board in reviewing applications under Section 3 of the Bank Holding Company Act (the "bank acquisition" section) has been quite liberal, considering the general concern regarding an undesirable expansion of group systems expressed by the Congress in passing the 1956 legislation. Nevertheless, it can be argued that this might have been expected, for as George Hall concluded in his investigation of group system regulation: "It is unclear whether Congress wished to control the total amount of banking resources in the holding company sector, the absolute size of individual companies, the size of companies relative to their markets, or the ability of individual companies to influence the performance of their markets."[62]

Under Section 3(c) of the 1956 Act the Board, before approving an acquisition by a bank holding company, had to consider[63]

whether or not the effect of such acquisition or merger or consolidation would be to expand the size or extent of the bank holding company system involved beyond limits consistent with adequate and sound bank-

[61] There have been a number of fine studies of this topic. See, for example, Backman, *The Bank Holding Company Act,* Bulletin of the C. J. Devine Institute of Finance, Nos. 24–25, pp. 5–51; Dorset, "Bank Mergers and Holding Companies and the Public Interest," *The Banking Law Journal* (September 1963), pp. 759–79; Hall, "Bank Holding Company Regulation," *Southern Economic Journal* (April 1965), pp. 342–55; and Hugon, "Federal Regulation of Bank Holding Companies," particularly Chapter VII. Since the data in these studies are now several years old, some of the statistics in the Hugon study have been brought up to date.

[62] Hall, "Bank Holding Company Regulation," *Southern Economic Journal,* (April 1965), p. 346.

[63] J. L. Robertson, "Taking A Long View of the Holding Company Act," [*Commercial and Financial Chronicle,* November 1, 1956, p. 1855] contains some strong criticism of a few of these standards.

ing, the public interest, and the preservation of competition in the field of banking.

The terms "adequate and sound banking," "public interest," and "preservation of competition" are extremely difficult to define, and the law did not indicate the weight to be given to one of these elements as opposed to another.[64] Therefore, the detailed discussions of cases involving the acquisition of banks by holding companies which have appeared periodically in the *Federal Reserve Bulletin* were examined to reveal as much as possible about the factors evaluated by the Board in reaching its decisions. The reader should be warned that the compilation of the statistics from these reports necessarily involved many value judgments on the part of this writer; thus, these figures should be employed only to note general trends or tendencies, since it is doubtful that the findings of two researchers in this area would be the same for all of the cases.[65]

The premise underlying the Board's findings under the Bank Holding Company Act from 1956 through 1966 apparently was that multiple-unit systems were not evil per se and that each decision had to be reached independently after a careful analysis of the five factors cited in Section 3(c) of the Act. A review of each of approximately 90 cases involving bank acquisitions by previously existing groups considered by the Board during this ten-year span reveals the following. (See Table 4.4) Of the factors mentioned in the statute, the first three (financial history, prospects, and management) were not even included in this writer's summary table because the proposed acquisitions virtually always met the required standards in these categories. In addition, in over three-fourths of the cases the examination of the fourth factor (the convenience, needs, and welfare of the community) led the Board to conclude that the acquisition had prospective beneficial effects.

Therefore, it would seem that of paramount importance in deter-

[64] The Federal Reserve Board has sponsored two studies in this area. Robert J. Lawrence, *The Performance of Bank Holding Companies* was published by the Fed in June 1967, and Charles Phillips is currently preparing a monograph on bank holding company decisions.

[65] For more information concerning the individual cases, see "Law Department," *Federal Reserve Bulletin*, which presents the findings of the Board in each case. The Banking Markets Unit of the Board of Governors of the Federal Reserve System has also prepared some tabulations of the Board's decisions.

TABLE 4.4.  PRINCIPAL FACTORS CONSIDERED IN GRANTING OR DENYING APPLICATIONS UNDER SECTION 3 OF THE BANK HOLDING COMPANY ACT, 1956–1966*

| Competitive Factors | Percentage of All Competitive Factors Considered | | | When Considered— Percentage | | |
|---|---|---|---|---|---|---|
| | Total | Ad-verse | Not Ad-verse | Ad-verse | Not Ad-verse | Total |
| Competitive effect upon independent bank(s) | 29 | 8 | 21 | 27 | 73 | 100 |
| Change in number of competing banks in primary market | 13 | 1 | 12 | 27 | 73 | 100 |
| Applicant's increase in offices or deposits as % of total in the area | 18 | 6 | 12 | 33 | 67 | 100 |
| Competitive effect upon applicant's banks | 21 | 5 | 16 | 24 | 76 | 100 |
| Concentration of power among large bank holding companies in the area | 19 | 6 | 13 | 30 | 70 | 100 |
| Total or arithmetic mean | 100 | 26 | 74 | 28 | 72 | 100 |

| Banking Factors | Percentage of All Banking Factors Considered | | | When Considered— Percentage | | |
|---|---|---|---|---|---|---|
| | Total | Signifi-cant | Not signifi-cant | Signifi-cant | Not signifi-cant | Total |
| Benefit to convenience, needs, and welfare of community | 70 | 54 | 16 | 77 | 23 | 100 |
| Role in solving management or capital needs | 30 | 20 | 10 | 69 | 31 | 100 |

* Data for a few early cases were not published.
Source: Hugon, "Federal Regulation of Bank Holding Companies," pp. 164, 279–98 for data to May, 1960, and Federal Reserve Bulletins from 1960–1966.

mining whether an application would be approved or denied was the fifth factor, the potential effect the acquisition might have upon the competitive situation in the market. In many ways the findings of this writer's research are not new and only serve to lend support to those of another investigator, who concluded:[66]

> It would appear that the basic policy of the Board could be summed up in two sentences. Any holding company expansion which would not materially change the existing structure of a banking market will be approved. Any proposal which would significantly change the role of holding companies in a local area will be disapproved.

Despite the large number of decisions the Board has handed down, it is virtually impossible to develop a set of criteria from them which would be of much assistance in evaluating the prospects of an application that fell into what might best be described by the colloquialism the "gray area." Nevertheless, an applicant might get some solace from the fact that approximately 70 percent of the requests for permission to establish new holding companies in the last ten years and about 85 percent of the bank acquisitions were approved. (See Table 4.5) Hence, if an application could legitimately be classified as a "marginal case," the odds would be high in favor of approval.

The Board left little doubt that if a holding company had a very substantial share (one-third to one-half) of the business in a given market[67] or a very large company was entering an area previously served by "independent" banks of reasonably comparable size, unless the situation was very unusual the request would probably be rejected. But, on the other hand, if the concentration was not extremely high or the action would not clearly have adverse effects upon an "independent" bank it was highly probable that the application would be accepted. Naturally, this type of decision making may be expected in an industry in which the "convenience and needs" of communities were so often assumed to be satisfied best by maintaining essentially the status quo in banking markets. But this philosophy of the regula-

[66] Hall, "Bank Holding Company Regulation," *Southern Economic Journal* (April 1965), p. 352.

[67] Hugon, "Federal Regulation of Bank Holding Companies," p. 192; and Backman, *The Bank Holding Company Act,* p. 43. Backman notes "The significance of such a standard is limited because it is based on the experience in only a few decisions"; however, the hypothesis would still seem to be valid as tested using many more decisions.

TABLE 4.5.  FEDERAL RESERVE BOARD BANK HOLDING COMPANY DECISIONS,
MAY 9, 1956–DECEMBER 31, 1966

| | Applications Considered* | | | |
|---|---|---|---|---|
| | Formation of New Bank Holding Companies | | Acquisition of Banks by Existing Bank Holding Companies | |
| | Number Approved | Number Denied | Number Approved | Number Denied |
| 1956 (from May 9) | — | — | 1 | — |
| 1957 | — | — | 7 | 2 |
| 1958 | 1 | 1 | 3 | 1 |
| 1959 | 1 | — | 6 | — |
| 1960 | — | — | 10 | 1 |
| 1961 | 2 | — | 9 | 3 |
| 1962 | 5 | 2 | 13 | 3 |
| 1963 | 2 | 1 | 5 | 3 |
| 1964 | 3 | 1 | 6 | — |
| 1965 | 2 | 1 | 11 | 2 |
| 1966 | 6 | 2 | 15 | 2 |
| Total | 22 | 8 | 86 | 17 |

* Applications may involve more than one bank.
Source: Association of Registered Bank Holding Companies.

tory authorities, which may be traced in large part to the thousands of
bank failures nearly two generations ago, has changed in recent years,
for the "Fed" and the other federal banking agencies in weighing the
competitive effects of bank acquisitions have shown increasing concern regarding their impact upon the consumer as well as the pro-
ducer of banking services.

THE BANK MERGER ACT OF 1960[68]

Origin.   While bank holding company expansion (both actual and
potential) was being investigated by Congress between 1946 and
1956, the more basic question of bank mergers was not ignored,
although it received considerably less publicity. During World War II
bank amalgamations and competition were explored in a number of
articles in the press and in scholarly journals, and by the mid-1940s

[68] The antitrust aspects of this Act are discussed in greater detail in Chapter
7.

officials of the federal banking agencies had begun to request that banks be included if Congress revised the Clayton Act to cover asset acquisitions. However, when the "asset acquisition" provision of Section 7 of the Clayton Act was added through the Celler-Kefauver amendment, it appeared that the addition of banks to its coverage might have defeated the bill, and many people argue this was the reason that they were omitted.

In September 1952 a House Judiciary Committee Staff Report on "Bank Mergers and the Concentration of Banking Facilities" noted that since banks acquired other banks almost exclusively through the purchase of assets, bank mergers were for all practical purposes uncontrolled.[69] The report recommended the enactment of legislation to regulate these acquisitions. The following year, 1953, Congressman Celler introduced a bill (H.R. 2928) which, following suggestions in the Judiciary Committee Report, would have required that all banks obtain the approval of one of the federal banking authorities before either directly or indirectly acquiring the assets of another bank.[70] Under this legislation these agencies would have been instructed to determine whether the effect of the merger might be "to lessen competition unduly or to tend unduly to create a monopoly" in the field of banking. Although this bill died in committee it was nevertheless important, for it signaled the beginning of a substantial drive to bring all (or at least most) bank consolidations under federal banking agency control, and it explicitly recognized the need to include some form of competitive test to be employed by the authorities in considering a merger application.

A bill which was identical to the 1953 legislation was submitted by Representative Celler in January 1955 (H.R. 2115), and a similar bill (H.R. 6405) was introduced in May of that year. The most noteworthy difference between these proposed statutes was the competitive test included in the latter, which required the banking officials to deny a merger request if the effect "may be substantially to lessen competition or tend to create a monopoly"—the standard found in

[69] Mergers in this sentence referring to all ways in which a bank might be acquired—except by stock acquisition, which was already covered under Section 7 of the Clayton Act.

[70] Much of the material in this section was drawn from Thiemann, "The Bank Merger Act of 1960," Chapter 3.

Section 7 of the Clayton Act. Neither bill was reported out of committee.

Also in 1955, H.R. 5948 was introduced by Congressman Celler. It was significantly different from the above-mentioned bills for it would have placed bank mergers under the Clayton Act instead of amending banking law. This legislation would have expanded this statute by adding the statement:[71]

And no bank, banking association, or trust company shall acquire, directly or indirectly, the whole or any part of the assets of another corporation engaged also in commerce, where in any line of commerce in any section of the country, the effect of such acquisition may be substantially to lessen competition or to tend to create a monopoly.

This amendment was intended to prevent the ". . . circumvention of Section 7's prohibition on the purchase of bank stocks through the purchase of bank assets."[72] In opening the hearings on H.R. 5948, Congressman Celler remarked:[73]

The wording [in the "old" Section 7] left a widely exploited gap. Banks and corporations could acquire assets of other firms and thus avoid the provisions of Section 7. This gap insofar as it applies to industrial corporations, was closed by the Celler-Kefauver Antimerger Act of 1950. My bill, H.R. 5948, would close the gap insofar as banks are concerned and prohibit bank mergers achieved by asset as well as stock acquisitions.

The Chairman of the FDIC and the Comptroller of the Currency voiced objections to the Celler bill, indicating that the terminology of the Clayton Act was too restrictive and that jurisdiction over bank mergers should be placed exclusively with the bank supervisory agencies by amending Section 18(c) of the Federal Deposit Insurance Act.[74] The Federal Reserve was less critical of the bill, merely suggesting that the word "unduly" be substituted for "substantially," and requesting that the Board be excluded from any enforcement authority so that the exclusive authority for the enforcement of the Clayton Act as to banks would be the Attorney General through proceedings

[71] U. S. Congress, House, *Bank Mergers*, Hearings, 1955, p. 3.

[72] U. S. Congress, House, *Amending an Act Approved October 15, 1914*, House Report 1417 to accompany H.R. 5948, 1955, p. 4.

[73] U. S. Congress, House, *Bank Mergers*, Hearings, 1955, pp. 1–2. (Also, see the House Report to accompany H.R. 5948, p. 3.)

[74] *Ibid.*, pp. 56–78.

instituted by his direction.[75] H.R. 5948 passed the House early in 1956; however, a jurisdictional dispute developed in the Senate between the Banking and Currency Committee and the Judiciary Committee regarding the proper Senate body to consider this proposed legislation. It is not clear whether or not this affected the actions of the Judiciary Committee to which it had been referred, but in any event the bill was never reported out of committee.[76]

A second antitrust bill (S. 2075) was introduced in 1955 by Senator Sparkman. It too would have amended Section 7 of the Clayton Act to prohibit bank mergers which substantially lessened competition or tended to create a monopoly, and it would have required a ninety day waiting period after the Attorney General was notified of the merger plans before the transaction could be consummated. No action was taken on this bill.

In April 1956 the Treasury Department submitted a draft of a proposed banking bill to the Bureau of the Budget for approval. This legislation, which took the form of an amendment to Section 18(c) of the Federal Deposit Insurance Act, was designed "to provide safeguards against mergers and consolidations of banks which might lessen competition unduly or tend unduly to create a monopoly."[77] On May 16 the Budget Bureau advised the Treasury that it had no objection to presenting such a bill to Congress and that, if enacted, the legislation "would be in accord with the program of the President." The Treasury Department immediately transmitted a copy of the draft bill to both Houses of Congress.

One week later, on May 23, Senators Fulbright and Capehart introduced S. 3911 (hereafter termed the Fulbright bill), which was identical to the Treasury's draft bill;[78] and hearings on it were held in June of 1956. In general, the banking community agreed that if legislation was to be passed S. 3911 was the proper way to handle bank mergers. For example, the ABA adopted a resolution early in 1956 which stated:[79]

---

[75] *Ibid.*, p. 50.
[76] Thiemann, "The Bank Merger Act of 1960," p. 58.
[77] U. S. Congress, Senate, *Regulation of Bank Mergers,* Hearings on S. 3911, 1956, p. 5.
[78] *Ibid.*, p. 2.
[79] *Ibid.*, p. 91.

The American Bankers Association recommends to Congress that *if* legislation be enacted it should be by amendment to the Federal banking laws to place the final responsibility for approval or disapproval of bank mergers in the appropriate bank supervisory authorities as to the banks subject to their respective jurisdiction and supervision. [Emphasis added]

Thus, although the ABA did not appear to be fully convinced that the bank merger legislation was essential, if a statute had to be enacted S. 3911 seemed to be acceptable.

The three Federal banking agencies were unanimous in their support of the Fulbright bill. L. A. Jennings, Deputy Comptroller of the Currency, stated that he favored the preservation of a healthy, competitive climate within which sound banks might operate to service the needs of the public. According to Jennings, S. 3911 would best effectuate such an objective by insuring against any future eventualities that "might result in an undue lessening of competition in certain communities or sectors." However, he also testified to the importance of tempering competitive considerations with the various banking factors and was opposed to allowing the Justice Department to enjoin a bank merger solely on the basis of its effect on competition. In his words:[80]

We strongly believe that the important and vital banking considerations must be weighed in conjunction with purely competitive factors if sound decisions are to be made, and that the officials of the Federal bank supervisory agencies who are intimately familiar with banking in all its phases throughout the United States are the one best equipped to make such decisions.

The other federal banking authorities were of much the same opinion.[81]

Opposition to S. 3911 was centered primarily in the Department of Justice. Stanley Barnes, Assistant Attorney General in charge of the Antitrust Division, vigorously opposed the bill. He contended that it was a weak and ineffective solution to the bank merger problem, for its standard of illegality was less stringent than under Section 7 of the Clayton Act. He was also of the opinion that the passage of S. 3911 would seriously dissipate enforcement of the antitrust laws by decentralizing responsibility. Barnes favored applying the standards of Sec-

[80] *Ibid.*, p. 14.
[81] *Ibid.*, pp. 33, 49.

tion 7 to bank asset acquisitions. And, to those supporters of the bill who argued that this form of regulation would bring about many suspensions of weakened banks which could remain viable only through merger, he responded that the Justice Department had always refrained from prosecuting mergers where "because of either inadequate management, obsolete equipment, or a failing market, the acquired corporation's prospects for survival seemed dim."[82]

Despite the Assistant Attorney General's attack upon S. 3911, it was reported favorably by the Senate Banking and Currency Committee. In the Senate floor debate on the bill, attempts were made to amend it by inserting a Clayton Act test of the legality of a bank merger (substantially to lessen competition, etc.), by requiring the banking authorities to request the opinion of "Justice" concerning the competitive impact of a merger, and by giving the Attorney General virtual veto power over mergers which he felt would violate Section 7 of the Clayton Act unless one of the banks involved could present a "failing-company defense."[83] These amendments were rejected by the Senate, and on July 25, 1956 the bill was passed. But Congress adjourned almost immediately thereafter, and the House did not have time to consider the bill.

In 1956, in addition to the Fulbright bill, which would have amended banking law, four bills which would have revised the antitrust laws with respect to bank mergers were introduced. H.R. 9424 was similar in many respects to H.R. 5948 of the previous session, but the new bill also included a pre-merger notification requirement. Hearings were held on the bill, and it was passed by the House and sent to the Senate. The Senate Subcommittee on Antitrust and Monopoly held hearings to consider this bill and two others related to bank mergers—S. 3424, identical to H.R. 9424, and S. 3341.[84]

Opposition to the bills was centered in the three federal banking agencies and the American Bankers Association. All were in general agreement with the legislation's objectives, but they felt these goals

[82] *Ibid.*, p. 64.

[83] 102 *Congressional Record*, p. 14347, July 25, 1956. For a discussion of the "failing-company defense," see *International Shoe Company* v. *Federal Trade Commission*, 280 U.S. 291, 299–303 (1930).

[84] U. S. Congress, Senate, *Legislation Affecting Corporate Mergers*, Hearings, 1956. H.R. 9781, which had essentially the same goals, was also introduced in 1956 but it was not acted upon.

should be achieved through banking, not antitrust legislation. Bills S. 3341 and S. 3424 were never reported out of the Senate Judiciary Committee. Bill H.R. 9424 was reported but the bank asset acquisition provision had been struck and the provision of the Fulbright bill adopted in its place.[85] Nevertheless, the bill was not brought to the Senate floor until the final hours of the session, and the Senate adjourned before taking any action on it.

On March 4, 1957 Senator A. Willis Robertson introduced the Financial Institutions Act (S. 1451). Section 23 of Title III of this legislation incorporated the provisions of S. 3911, the bank merger bill which had passed the Senate the previous year. The American Bankers Association (ABA) and numerous other groups testified in support of this section of the proposed legislation, and once again the Justice Department voiced its opposition to it. Attorney General Brownell suggested that bank mergers be covered by the Clayton Act, but if Congress felt that these transactions should be handled at least initially under banking laws, the banking statute should include a competitive standard comparable to that of Section 7, a procedure for intervention by "Justice," and an antitrust saving provision[86] such as that included in the Bank Holding Company Act.[87]

Nevertheless, S. 1451 was reported out of committee on March 4, 1957 with the provisions of Section 23, Title 3 unchanged. The same series of "antitrust amendments" voted down in the case of S. 3911 in 1956 were submitted along with an antitrust saving provision and all were rejected, the last—saving clause—by a vote of 58 to 28. The bill was passed with the bank merger section intact and it was sent to the House, but Congress adjourned before hearings were completed. The House hearings were resumed in January, 1958, and were completed

[85] Thiemann, "The Bank Merger Act of 1960," p. 62. Some interesting comments regarding the reason this change was made and the role of the banking and antitrust laws appear in U. S. Congress, Senate, *Mergers and Price Discrimination*, Senate Report to accompany H.R. 9424, 1956, pp. 24–25.

[86] 70 Stat. 146 (1956), § 11. It reads as follows: "Nothing herein contained shall be interpreted or construed as approving any act, action, or conduct which is or has been or may be in violation of existing law, nor shall anything herein contained constitute a defense to any action, suit, or proceeding pending or hereafter instituted on account of any prohibited antitrust or monopolistic act, action, or conduct."

[87] U. S. Congress, Senate, *Financial Institutions Act of 1957*, Hearings on S. 1451, 1957, p. 132–34.

the following month, but the Committee failed to report the bill before the end of the 85th Congress.

In the 85th Congress (1957–1958) four bills were also introduced which would have amended Section 7 to cover bank asset acquisitions. Hearings were held by the House Antitrust Subcommittee on two of the bills, H.R. 264 and H.R. 2143, but neither was reported out of committee. The Senate Subcommittee on Antitrust and Monopoly also considered two bills, S. 198 and S. 722, but the banking provisions in both were struck before hearings on them began in April 1958.[88] Early in the 86th Congress two additional bills were introduced which had essentially the same objective as those noted above, S. 1004 and H.R. 4152, but no action was taken on either bill.[89]

At the beginning of the 86th Congress, Senators Robertson, Capehart, and Fulbright introduced a bill, S. 1062 to regulate bank mergers by amending the Federal Deposit Insurance Act. The bill contained the same provisions that were in S. 3911 and Section 23, Title III of S. 1451. The Comptroller of the Currency, the Board of Governors of the Federal Reserve System, the FDIC, and The American Bankers Association gave their support to the measure. In addition, the American Bar Association reversed a previous position in favor of extension of the asset acquisition provisions of the Clayton Act to banks, and it endorsed the bank merger section of S. 1451.[90] The Department of Justice indicated it still advocated the approach suggested by Attorney General Brownell in the hearings on the Financial Institutions Act of 1957.[91] A number of amendments to the bill were suggested,[92] including the addition of an antitrust saving clause and a requirement that public hearings concerning the mergers be held.[93] But, with the exception of one provision requiring, not merely

[88] U. S. Congress, Senate, *Legislation Affecting Sections 7, 11, and 15 of the Clayton Act*, Hearings, 1958, pp. 91–94.

[89] 105 *Congressional Record*, p. 1965 (February 5, 1959) and *ibid.*, p. 2078 (February 9, 1959). S. 1005 concerning premerger notification was also introduced along with S. 1004.

[90] Funk, "Antitrust Legislation Affecting Bank Mergers," *The Banking Law Journal* (May 1958), p. 378. This article contains a fine summary of the early legislation in this area.

[91] U. S. Congress, Senate, *Regulation of Bank Mergers*, Hearings on S. 1062, 1959, p. 9.

[92] *Ibid.*, p. 120.

[93] *Ibid.*, pp. 105–106.

authorizing, the banking authority approving a merger to request an opinion of the Attorney General regarding the competitive aspects of a given acquisition, and another provision calling for the submission of semiannual reports to the Congress on mergers approved by each agency, none was adopted.[94] The bill containing these two amendments was passed by the Senate in May of 1959.

It was not until February of 1960 that a subcommittee of the House Banking and Currency Committee began hearings on S. 1062.[95] The hearings were completed in a few days and the bill was reported out of committee not too long thereafter. However, the bill which was to be voted upon by the House differed considerably from the version passed by the Senate.

Of particular significance was a change which substituted terminology very similar to that of the Clayton Act in regard to "the effect of the transaction on competition (including any tendency toward monopoly)" in place of the "unduly lessen" or "unduly to create" phraseology in the Senate version. The House Banking and Currency Committee also made several other revisions in the Senate bill:[96]

First, the bank supervisory agency having jurisdiction over the transaction would be able to act to save a failing bank without first obtaining the views of the other two agencies. Second, the views of the other two agencies were to be confined to the competitive factors and the procedure for submitting such reports was made to conform to that used in obtaining a report from the Attorney General. Third, instead of semiannual reports to Congress, the banking agencies were to include the necessary information in their annual reports. Fourth, the summary of the Attorney General's advice on each merger was to be prepared by the Attorney General, rather than by the banking agencies themselves. Fifth, notice of a proposed merger was to be published in a newspaper of general circulation in the community or communities where the main offices of the banks involved were located.

On April 4, 1960, the substantially revised S. 1062 passed the House without further change. The Senate agreed to the House amendments on May 6, 1960, and the President signed the bill into

[94] U. S. Congress, Senate, *Regulation of Bank Mergers*, Report No. 196, 1959, p. 2.
[95] U. S. Congress, House, *Regulation of Bank Mergers*, Hearings on S. 1062, 1960.
[96] Thiemann, "The Bank Merger Act of 1960," p. 107.

law one week later.[97] The new legislation was schizophrenic to say the least, for it was part banking and part antitrust law, and it was accompanied by a Senate report and a House report which clearly indicated that both standards were to prevail.[98] This confusion was to lead to bitter controversy among federal government agencies, a series of bank antitrust suits, a major revision of the law within a few years, and ultimately further litigation to clarify the terminology in the amended statute.[99]

*Provisions.* Until 1960 Section 18(c) of the Federal Deposit Insurance Act[100] had been the primary source of federal control over bank mergers in which the continuing institution was not a national bank. As has been noted, the federal banking agencies' powers (except for insured bank mergers with noninsured banks) were limited under this provision to cases involving a reduction of the capital stock or surplus of the combined banks resulting from the transaction. The Bank Merger Act of 1960[101] substantially revised this section and considerably broadened its coverage.

The "new" Section 18(c) required that no merger, consolidation, acquisition of assets, or assumption of liabilities of one insured bank by another[102] was to be consummated without the prior written consent of the Comptroller of the Currency if the acquiring, assuming, or resulting bank was to be a national bank or a District of Columbia (D.C.) bank, or of the Board of Governors of the Federal Reserve System if the acquiring, assuming, or resulting bank was to be a state member bank (except a D.C. bank), or of the FDIC if the acquiring, assuming, or resulting bank was to be a nonmember insured bank (except a D.C. bank). Except in emergencies, notice of impending mergers had to be published in a local newspaper for a given period before an agency could act on the application; and the agencies were

[97] 74 Stat. 129 (1960).

[98] This is discussed in Chapter 7, "The Effect of the Bank Merger Act on the applicability of Section 7."

[99] *U. S.* v. *Philadelphia National Bank,* 374 U.S. 321 (1963); and the 1966 Amendment to the Bank Merger Act of 1960. [80 Stat. 7 (1966)]

[100] 12 U.S.C. 1828(c).

[101] 74 Stat. 129 (1960).

[102] Cases involving an insured and a noninsured bank were already covered by this section and this provision remained in the law, unchanged after the 1960 amendment.

ordered to include in their respective annual reports each year certain information concerning all mergers approved during the period covered by the report.

In evaluating merger applications, the appropriate agency was to consider:[103]

The financial history and condition of each of the banks involved, the adequacy of its capital structure, its future earnings prospects, the general character of its management, the convenience and needs of the community to be served, and whether or not its corporate powers are consistent with the purposes of this Act. [These are the so-called banking factors.] . . . [T]he appropriate agency [had to] also take into consideration the effect of the transaction on competition (including any tendency toward monopoly), and [it was not to] approve the transaction unless, after considering all of such factors, it finds the transaction to be in the public interest.

Unless the agency in question found that it had to act immediately in order to prevent the probable failure of one of the banks involved, it was to request an advisory opinion on the competitive factors in the case from the Attorney General and the other two federal banking authorities. Nevertheless, these opinions were to be only advisory in nature and the final decision was to rest with the agency which enjoyed primary jurisdiction as noted above.[104]

*Administration of the Bank Merger Act.* The "banking factors" which the designated federal agency was to consider were taken almost verbatim from Section 6 of the Federal Deposit Insurance Act.[105] One observer noted that since this was the insurability provision of the "FDIC" statute, it could be argued[106]

that by making these criteria applicable to bank mergers Congress directed the appropriate agency to evaluate the solvency of the absorbed banks. If failure of the merging bank were imminent, merger into a

---

[103] 12 U.S.C. 1828(c).

[104] However, the Supreme Court in *U. S.* v. *Philadelphia National Bank* [374 U.S. 321 (1963)] indicated that this action did not preclude later attack under the antitrust laws.

[105] 64 Stat. 873 (1950), § 6; 12 U.S.C. § 1816.

[106] "Bank Charter, Branching, Holding Company and Merger Laws: Competition Frustrated," *Banking Law Journal* (August 1962), p. 647. This is a fairly detailed analysis of the subjects noted in its title, and it should be read by those interested in this area.

solvent bank would be approved; but if all the merging banks were solvent, the agency would then have to ascertain any adverse effect on competition relying heavily on the opinion of the Attorney General.

But, as the above writer observed, the Congressional reports accompanying the Bank Merger Act[107] and the floor debate suggest that the legislature intended the test to be somewhat broader than this, with the general advantages (and disadvantages) of the merger being weighed against the competitive effects, even though both banks were considered to be solvent.[108]

Certainly the Federal banking agencies appear to have interpreted the Bank Merger Act in the broader sense, for between 1960 and 1966 the acquisitions in which failure of one of the banks was imminent were rare. In a great many cases, on the other hand, it was very clear that the bank supervisor was balancing what might be described as "increased solvency" versus decreased competition, since there was no indication that the suspension of one of the banks was even a remote possibility.

After a detailed analysis of the administration of the Bank Merger Act, two investigators concluded that all the federal agencies shared a common approach to their duties under this legislation, each regarding mergers as an appropriate way to improve the performance of banking markets.[109] However, these researchers found some variation in the agencies' basic policy toward mergers. They characterized the approaches followed by the supervisors as follows: Comptroller—the balanced banking structure doctrine stressing the need for a banking system composed of some small, some medium-sized, and some large banks; the FDIC—the strengthening of competition doctrine seeking improved market performance by making banks more homogeneous in size; and the Federal Reserve Board—the variety of banking

[107] U. S. Congress, Senate, *Regulation of Bank Mergers*, Report No. 196, 1959; and House, *Regulation of Bank Mergers*, Report No. 1416, 1960.

[108] Furthermore, this approach would appear to be in line with Section 18(d) of the Federal Deposit Insurance Act, which specifies the same "insurability" factors are to be considered by the FDIC in granting or withholding consent for a state noninsured bank to establish a new branch, and this would not necessarily involve either a merger or a failing bank. See 64 Stat. 873 (1950); 12 U.S.C. 1828(d).

[109] Hall and Phillips, *Bank Mergers and the Regulatory Agencies,* p. 156.

services doctrine emphasizing the need to provide existing customers with a broad range of banking facilities.[110]

Despite these differences all of the agencies appear to be in agreement that, although there is no question of solvency involved, the positive banking factors may outweigh the negative competitive factors, and "increases in concentration as a result of a merger are regarded as a necessary price to pay to increase the availability of local banking services."[111] This position of the federal banking officials was considerably different from that of the courts in antitrust cases, particularly in the banking area where concentration seemed to settle the issue in the Philadelphia-Clayton Act decision, and a merger between "major competitors" was treated as a virtual per se violation in the Lexington-Sherman Act case.[112]

In 1960, when the Bank Merger Act was signed into law, many people felt that its objective was not only to provide the federal banking authorities with a more complete set of controls over bank amalgamations but also to reduce substantially the number of mergers and ensure that greater emphasis would be given to competitive factors by the supervisory authorities in reviewing merger applications.[113] If this were the goal, the results are not impressive as measured by available statistics. Between May 13, 1960, the day the Merger Act became law, and December 31, 1966, 1001 merger applications (97 percent) were approved by the federal banking authorities and only 34 (3 percent) were denied. (See Table 4.6) The Federal Reserve had the highest rate of disapprovals, nearly 10 percent, and the FDIC the lowest, about 1 percent. In addition, in the 6½ years from 1954 through mid-1960 there was an average of 176 mergers per annum,[114] and in the 6½ years after the statute was

[110] *Ibid.*, pp. 156–57. These few paragraphs cannot begin to do justice to the Hall-Phillips study; it is especially valuable, for it considers bank mergers primarily from the viewpoint of the antitrust and industrial organization specialist. Similar conclusions to those in the above study may be found in Thiemann, "The Bank Merger Act of 1960," pp. 158–59.

[111] *Ibid.*, p. 158.

[112] These actions are discussed in Chapter 7.

[113] U. S. Congress, Senate, *Regulation of Bank Mergers*, Report No. 196, 1959, p. 1.

[114] U. S. Congress, Senate, *Amend the Bank Merger Act of 1960*, Hearings, 1965, p. 16; and the federal banking agencies.

TABLE 4.6. DISPOSITION OF MERGER APPLICATIONS UNDER SECTION 18(C) OF THE FDIC ACT TO THE FEDERAL BANKING AGENCIES, MAY 13, 1960–DECEMBER 31, 1966*

| Year | Comptroller Approved | Comptroller Denied | FDIC Approved | FDIC Denied | Federal Reserve Approved | Federal Reserve Denied | Total Approved | Total Denied |
|---|---|---|---|---|---|---|---|---|
| 1960 | 58 | 1 | 21 | 0 | 17 | 3 | 96 | 4 |
| 1961 | 72 | 2 | 31 | 0 | 32 | 4 | 135 | 6 |
| 1962 | 110 | 6 | 44 | 0 | 37 | 5 | 191 | 11 |
| 1963 | 89 | 2 | 31 | 2 | 31 | 3 | 151 | 7 |
| 1964 | 88 | 0 | 29 | 0 | 16 | 2 | 133 | 2 |
| 1965 | 81 | 1 | 47 | 0 | 21 | 0 | 149 | 1 |
| 1966 | 89 | 2 | 37 | 0 | 20 | 1 | 146 | 3 |
| Total | 587 | 14 | 240 | 2 | 174 | 18 | 1001 | 34 |

* These data are not necessarily identical with those in Table 4.7 because of differences involving multiple acquisitions in a single transaction and partial acquisitions.

*Source:* U. S. Congress, Senate, *Amend the Bank Merger Act of 1960*, Hearings on S. 1698, 1965, pp. 16–18, and the respective banking agencies.

enacted (mid-1960 through the end of 1966) the average declined by only 19 to 157. (See Table 4.7) In aggregate, in this interval, the three federal banking agencies under Section 18(c) of the Federal Deposit Insurance Act authorized the acquisition of 1,018 banks with resources of over 19 billion dollars.

JUSTICE VERSUS THE BANKING AGENCIES

The Department of Justice was extremely disturbed by the relative ease with which bank acquisitions and consolidations were accomplished both before and after the passage of the Bank Holding Company and Bank Merger Acts. Although there had long been some question regarding the applicability of Section 7 of the Clayton Act to bank mergers, there was little doubt that it applied to bank holding company acquisitions, and there was a distinct possibiilty that Sections 1 and 2 of the Sherman Act applied to both forms of amalgamation. Therefore, "Justice" considered that its powers under both Section 7 and Sections 1 and 2 should be tested to determine whether it could act to prevent mergers that appeared to be anticompetitive. Between February 1961 and February 1966, the Justice Department initiated ten separate actions against banks and/or bank holding

TABLE 4.7. MERGERS APPROVED UNDER BANK MERGER ACT, MAY 13, 1960–DECEMBER 31, 1966: NUMBER OF BANKS ACQUIRED AND THEIR TOTAL RESOURCES*

| Year | All Cases | | Comptroller Approval Required | | Federal Reserve Approval Required | | FDIC Approval Required | |
|---|---|---|---|---|---|---|---|---|
| | Total Number | Resources ($ million) | Number | ($ million) | Number | ($ million) | Number | ($ million) |
| 1960 | 99 | $ 1,734 | 61 | $1,138 | 17 | $ 456 | 21 | $ 140 |
| 1961 | 133 | 5,995 | 72 | 1,990 | 32 | 3,292 | 29 | 713 |
| 1962 | 193 | 2,207 | 112 | 1,166 | 37 | 311 | 44 | 730 |
| 1963 | 151 | 3,519 | 89 | 2,023 | 35 | 501 | 27 | 995 |
| 1964 | 139 | 2,238 | 93 | 1,390 | 18 | 286 | 28 | 562 |
| 1965 | 167 | 2,096 | 88 | 1,041 | 27 | 516 | 52 | 539 |
| 1966 | 136 | 1,641 | 78 | 781 | 22 | 614 | 36 | 246 |
| Grand Total | 1,018 | $19,430 | 593 | $9,529 | 188 | $5,976 | 237 | $3,925 |

* These figures were compiled from detailed tables included in the FDIC *Annual Reports*, and before the above data are employed for other analysis it is suggested that the footnotes in each of these tables be checked, for they contain some information which should be of value to the researcher who must work with very accurate statistics.

*Source*: FDIC, *Annual Reports* for the years ending December 31, 1960–1966.

companies charging these institutions with violation of the "merger provisions" of the antitrust laws. (See Table 7.1) Two of these cases were reviewed by the Supreme Court and both were decided in favor of "Justice."

As a result of the first two bank decisions by the High Court, *Philadelphia* and *Lexington,* there were no longer three but four banking agencies in Washington, for the final arbiter in merger applications would sometimes be the Attorney General (and the courts). Hence, the Bank Holding Company Act, which many people felt left the Fed in full control of holding company acquisitions, and the Bank Merger Act of 1960, which many bankers felt had settled the question of final authority over bank mergers (except for standard judicial review) had to some extent been superseded by the antitrust laws. But jurists, federal agencies, bankers, lawyers, and economists—not to mention leading members of Congress—arrived at diametrically opposed interpretations of the same statutory language, particularly in regard to the Merger Act,[115] and an internecine conflict among government agencies erupted which no administration could long endure. Clarification of the respective roles of the banking laws and antitrust laws was desperately needed. In February 1966 the Bank Merger Act was substantially revised, and in July 1966 the Bank Holding Company Act was amended. Unfortunately, instead of clarification the new statutes may only have introduced added confusion, for they included new, untested standards whose significance cannot even be estimated until a body of case law develops. (See Chapter 7 for a discussion of the 1966 Amendments and a review of actions instituted before and after they were enacted.)

STATE CONTROLS

State banking officials also have authority to regulate mergers under their jurisdiction. The latest survey of state bank supervision made by the American Bankers Association revealed that the power to authorize mergers was granted to the Supervisor in 38 states, to the Banking Board in 5 states, and to the Supervisor and the Board in 3 states.[116] Judging from the wording of the state statutes in this area,

[115] U. S. Congress, House, *Bank Merger Act Amendment,* Report No. 1221, 1966, p. 2.

[116] American Bankers Association, *State Bank Supervision: Ninth Quinquennial Survey, 1964,* p. 48. The remaining states had various other arrangements.

administrative approval of such transactions is usually provided for under state law to protect the stockholders, depositors, and other creditors.[117]

The standards employed in the statutes often vary considerably from one state to another; however, it is apparent that in most states the laws are designed to ensure that the various banking factors (capital structure, character of management, and others) will be reviewed in considering a merger application.[118] In a study made several years ago during the hearings on the Bank Merger Act of 1960, it was found that among the state laws only seven made explicit reference to the public convenience and nineteen to the public interest in evaluating a bank merger request.[119] At that time, apparently only two state statutes expressly considered the question of the possible impact of a merger upon competition;[120] but, no doubt at least partly because of the recent concern with bank antitrust litigation, all states reported in the 1964 ABA survey that they make studies of bank concentration and competition in connection with merger applications.[121]

## THE EFFECT OF BANK MERGERS
## AND ACQUISITIONS

The alleged advantages of the operation of local banks in contrast to widespread branch banks are[122]

That the bank will be better adapted to the wants and habits of the people—that a local feeling will be excited in its favour, hence the inhabitants of the district will take shares—that a better system of management may be expected, as it can more easily be governed and will be more under control—that a panic in the district will not affect all parts of the country . . . [and] that banks will be of a moderate size, and hence will be attended with the advantages arising from numerous banks acting

---

[117] "Bank Charter, Branching, Holding Company and Merger Laws: Competition Frustrated," *The Banking Law Journal* (August 1962), p. 651.

[118] Thiemann, "The Bank Merger Act of 1960," p. 19.

[119] U. S. Congress, Senate, *Regulation of Bank Mergers*, Hearings on S. 1062, 1959, pp. 183–200, contains a compilation of state bank merger statutes.

[120] And, in some cases, when they did refer to competition it was to warn against any adverse effects of competition upon existing banks.

[121] Some states have begun to enact statutes similar to the federal Bank Merger Act requiring administrative consideration of competition.

[122] Gilbart, *The History of Banking in America*, p. 82.

as checks upon each other, instead of a few large banks who may combine for objects injurious to the nation.

Many of these arguments in favor of the operation of local banks, with some small changes in terminology, could well have been taken directly from testimony before Congressional committees or from publications issued by those groups opposed to large branch banks today, and, yet, this statement was written by a British financier, James Gilbart, who studied banking in America 130 years ago. As one might expect, since his monograph was printed in 1837, the same year that the first free banking act was passed, Gilbart's comments regarding contemporary American banking did not include any reference to unit banks, for the two alternatives as he saw them in this country at the time were limited (county or statewide branching) or widespread (nationwide) branching.

Gilbart discussed the virtues of both limited branching and widespread branching. In regard to the benefits which were supposedly to accrue from the latter, he listed the standard items, among them: greater safety for the public, better credit standards, an improved flow of funds from surplus to deficit areas throughout the nation, better trained management, more banking offices in small places. In weighing the merits of local versus widespread branching Gilbart was forced to conclude that although there had been much discussion of this topic there was really very little evidence available concerning such basic problems as the best number of branches for a bank and where they should be located in relation to the head office, and no general rules had evolved which might have been applied in making such a decision.

It has been well over a century since Gilbart's work was published, but still very few guidelines have been developed to aid the bank supervisor or legislator who must make decisions regarding banking organization. For example, not long ago a contributor to the *National Banking Review* in evaluating a recent bank structure study noted, much as Gilbart might have done, that this book did not establish an unambiguous criterion for the correct number of banking offices. This, the critic remarked, was "not surprising or especially distressing [for] neither has any other study to date."[123] Thus, after 130 years

[123] Taken from Thomas Gies' book review of Robert Lanzillotti's *Banking Structure in Michigan* which appeared in the *National Banking Review* (December 1966).

Gilbart's query regarding the optimum branch system remains unanswered, and from the viewpoint of present-day knowledge of bank structure this illustration is certainly not atypical.

Until recent years few researchers devoted much effort to solving questions such as those mentioned above. As a result books on banking structure rarely contained much more than a description of the banking system at a point in time, and they included virtually no analysis of the possible relationship of bank size or form of organization to costs, pricing, the quality and quantity of services provided, and other relevant economic variables.

Since the 1950s, however, there have been numerous efforts to learn more about banking structure and performance. Unfortunately the results thus far have been something less than spectacular. A Federal Reserve Board economist in a report on the findings of research in this area concluded: "One major achievement relates not to the additions to existing knowledge but rather to what has been deducted."[124] Moreover, his remarks would seem to suggest that there is little chance of providing any "general rules" to be applied in making decisions in this field, at least in the near future. Nevertheless, this Federal Reserve official and most other students of banking structure would probably agree that an important step toward a better understanding of the operations of banks of various sizes and different forms of bank organization has been taken during the past ten or fifteen years, and this effort merits careful consideration if for no other reason but to learn what has been done and to build upon it.

THE FINDINGS OF BANKING STRUCTURE RESEARCH

The findings of banking structure research to date have already been presented in an excellent 200-page summary and appraisal of the literature prepared by Jack Guttentag and Edward Herman, which is now available to the general public. And the American Bankers Association has made a substantial grant to the National Bureau of Economic Research to carry out additional investigations in this area.[125] Therefore, the discussion of this topic in this book has been limited to a brief review of pricing, operating efficiency, and resource

---

[124] Holland, "Research into Banking Structure and Competition," *Federal Reserve Bulletin* (November 1964), p. 1397.

[125] National Bureau of Economic Research, 46th *Annual Report,* June 1966, "Anticipating the Nation's Needs for Economic Knowledge," pp. 4, 61–62.

168

allocation in Chapter 8, and the following comments regarding bank holding company acquisitions. Hence it is strongly recommended that any reader particularly concerned with the impact of bank structure, as well as its evolution and regulation, use this work in conjunction with one or more of the studies of bank performance now available,[126] especially the Guttentag-Herman study.[127]

*The meaning of bank acquisitions: an illustration.* Much of the research in the bank structure field has been severely hampered by a shortage of relevant statistics; by developments in markets that affect the investigator's findings but which are unrelated to structural characteristics; by the conversion of merged banks to branch offices, making "before and after" comparisons very complicated; and by numerous other factors. Therefore, to try to overcome some of the most obvious limitations in this type of inquiry, this writer has conducted numerous personal interviews and gathered detailed financial statement data concerning a very unusual group of banks.

The institutions chosen to be analyzed were banks that were acquired by holding companies between 1948 and 1962,[128] which were not merged with another bank, and which operated in localities where there was at least one other competing commercial bank. Group affiliates located in sixteen communities in about ten different states met the above standards. While it must be acknowledged that this is a relatively small sample not randomly selected (which places rather severe limitations upon any general conclusions which might be drawn from it), still it is hoped that these statistics may make a modest contribution toward the understanding of some of the possible effects of mergers and acquisitions.[129]

[126] Three useful short summaries of research in this field are also available: Holland, "Research into Banking Structure and Competition," *Federal Reserve Bulletin* (November 1964); Smith, "Research on Banking Structure and Performance," *ibid.* (April 1966); and Mote, "Competition in Banking: What Is Known? What Is the Evidence?" *Business Conditions,* Federal Reserve Bank of Chicago (February 1967).

[127] Jack M. Guttentag and Edward S. Herman, *Banking Structure and Performance* [New York University Graduate School of Business Administration, Institute of Finance, The Bulletin, No. 41/43, 1967 ($3.00)].

[128] More recent acquisitions were not used since they provide little or no time for the holding companies' influence upon bank operations to be reflected in the banks' statistics.

[129] There is always the possibility that considerable bias could be introduced

The structure of asset, liability, and capital accounts of new group affiliates changed substantially between the year-end before they merged with a holding company and December 31, 1965. The rate of growth of loans and discounts of the holding company banks was much lower than that of the "independents" in the pre-merger period, but in the post-merger period the trend was reversed as the new group banks raised their holdings of these assets by 50 percent while the "independents' " loan portfolios experienced only a 33 percent increase. (Each started with essentially the same loan to deposit ratio.) (See Table 4.8) Both the holding company affiliates and their competitors made sizable reductions in their United States government securities holdings, and each added to its portfolio of "other securities." However, the holding company affiliates reduced their governments somewhat less than the independents and increased their "other

TABLE 4.8.  SELECTED BALANCE SHEET ITEMS EXPRESSED AS A PERCENT OF TOTAL ASSETS FOR NEW GROUP AFFILIATES AND THEIR COMPETITORS (VARIOUS DATES, 1936–1965)

|  | Pre-Merger Year-End | | Year-End Before Merger[a] | | December 31, 1965 | |
|---|---|---|---|---|---|---|
|  | Holding Company | Other | Holding Company | Other | Holding Company | Other |
| Cash | 26.5 | 26.1 | 25.3 | 19.9 | 11.2 | 13.6 |
| Governments[b] | 46.5 | 48.5 | 30.9 | 36.0 | 21.9 | 25.0 |
| Other Securities | 5.2 | 6.7 | 9.2 | 8.5 | 13.0 | 10.9 |
| Loans and Discounts | 19.4 | 16.7 | 33.2 | 33.9 | 49.8 | 45.2 |
| Deposits | 93.8 | 94.6 | 93.1 | 92.5 | 89.2 | 90.8 |
| Capital | 5.5 | 5.1 | 6.0 | 6.2 | 8.0 | 7.9 |

[a] The year-end before merger divides the pre-merger through December 31, 1965 period in half.
[b] Federal government securities.
Source: Polk's Bank Directory, 1932–1966. Data include 16 group banks and 33 competitors.

if holding companies had consistently selected the most rapidly growing or least progressive bank in each area, therefore data were gathered covering approximately equal pre-merger and post-merger periods. In addition, because of the possibility that the time periods employed were atypical, statistics covering several different intervals for each community were analyzed.

securities" slightly more; thus the group banks' ratio of investments to total assets fell by only 5.1 percentage points as compared with an 8.6 percent reduction by their competitors.

The most drastic change among the new group affiliates was in their cash assets. These were reduced by about 55 percent in contrast to the 35 percent reduction by the "independents," once again reversing the pattern found in the pre-merger period. On the other hand, the ratios of deposits to total assets and capital to total assets of the holding company banks and their competitors changed at approximately the same rate in both the pre- and post-merger periods, although in the latter interval the group affiliates' deposit ratio declined and capital ratio advanced slightly more than their competitors', and the reverse was true in the earlier period.[130]

From the above data, and from discussions with bank officers of all of the institutions in many of the communities in which banks were acquired by holding companies since 1948, a few general observations can be made concerning the effects group acquisitions may have had upon the banks in this sample.[131] Officers of most of the acquired banks reported some improvement in gross operating earnings after affiliation with a group system, but added employee benefits and the bank's share of the cost of administering the holding company had in many instances largely offset these gains. Competing bankers reported their firm's earnings position had not noticeably weakened (and in a number of cases it had improved) after the entry of the group into their community. However, the market situation was described as more competitive after the change to group ownership, and a number

---

[130] A much more detailed statistical analysis of the findings of this investigation was being prepared by this writer for future publication. However, a similar study (*The Performance of Bank Holding Companies* by Robert Lawrence) was published by the Federal Reserve Board in June 1967. Since both Professor Lawrence's study and my own were inspired by my earlier efforts published in *Bank Holding Companies,* and since we both used before and after analysis of group banks and their local competitors, there seems to be little value in continuing my work in this area. This is particularly true because Professor Lawrence seems to have done a fine job, contributing many original ideas to the analysis, and his detailed study appears to support my preliminary findings in most cases.

[131] This is also an extension of an earlier study of group bank acquisitions made by this writer, and despite the passage of five years since the earlier investigation the findings were almost identical.

of independents revealed that "some increase in outlays had been required to meet and beat the innovations introduced by the group system."

No significant change in interest rates paid or received by the group banks or the "independents" could be traced directly to the entry of a holding company into the areas studied. This would seem to follow from the general policy of virtually all groups, which requires that such decisions be made by the individual banks depending upon local conditions. From the information supplied, a similar conclusion might be drawn regarding wages and salaries.

The most obvious change by the new holding company affiliates was in their emphasis upon loan expansion, particularly in the consumer credit field. This is reflected in the much higher loan-to-deposit ratios of these institutions after they were acquired, as contrasted with the "independents'." There was no evidence of "exploitation or denudation" of the rural communities by the group (such as using the affiliate as a source of funds to be employed in the financial center, thus making them unavailable for local economic development).[132] In fact, no substantial increase or decrease in loan participations or in loans extended outside the community was reported after the banks were acquired, and the investment portfolios of the group banks, which might be viewed as a form of "external" lending, both before and after the bank joined a group system comprised a smaller percentage of holding company affiliate than independent bank assets.[133]

Thus, it would seem fair to conclude from these sample data that on balance the communities' borrowing needs were better served after multiple-unit systems entered these areas.[134] Yet, some people could argue that the above discussion considers only one aspect of a bank's service to the individual who needs a loan. For example, it ignores the fact that some customers complained because they had been required to file a financial statement for the first time or because they had to

[132] Galbraith, *The Economics of Banking Operations*, pp. 199–205, contains some interesting comments regarding this general topic.

[133] Moreover, the municipal bond portfolios which are more likely to contain "local issues" than the U. S. government portfolios were substantially larger in the group banks.

[134] It could be argued that credit standards might have been weakened and loans were granted which should not have been extended, but this position gains little support from the loss experience of these banks to date.

supply collateral or obtain a cosigner, which they had not done in the past. Group bankers and many bank examiners might suggest that these actions by the new affiliate may merely reflect improved credit standards and the desire on the part of system banks to maintain good credit files (which are so often absent in smaller banks), but opponents of multiple-unit banking argue that this action by holding companies is indicative of the diminishing importance of "character lending" which is a direct result of "absentee ownership."

The "independents" suggest that this increased formality supposedly introduced by the holding company does much to destroy the close customer-banker relationship which they note is one of the greatest virtues of local banking in this country. They feel that their mode of operation is favored by the customer, and some support for this position could be drawn from the fact that despite the increased lending by the group affiliates, the additional services they frequently offered, and the power and expert management of the major holding companies, their share of total deposits decreased from 39 to 36 percent in the post-merger period in the sixteen communities studied in contrast to a 3 percentage point gain in the pre-merger period.

A much more detailed study somewhat along the lines of the above investigation has been made by Ernest Kohn of the New York State Banking Department, and the results are published in his *The Future of Small Banks* released in December 1966. Kohn found that ". . . merger expansion by large banks does not create insurmountable difficulties for their smaller competitors. The available evidence does not support the view that most small banks are incapable of rising successfully to the challenge of the entry of a large bank into their community."[135] Kohn, in the conclusions to his study, also raised some serious questions concerning certain types of home office protection rules and the relevance of some of the factors considered in merger cases when they are reviewed by banking agencies and the courts. In regard to the latter point he observed:[136]

Moreover, some merger or holding company proposals involve large banks seeking to acquire small banks in communities or areas where other

[135] Kohn, *The Future of Small Banks*, p. 18. This was a sequel to his *Branch Banking, Bank Mergers, and the Public Interest*, mentioned earlier.
[136] *Ibid.*, p. 19.

small banks are located. The results of this study indicate that in evaluating the competitive impact of such proposals, substantial weight need not be given by the bank supervisory agencies or by the courts to unsupported assertions or to *a priori* assumptions that most small banks will be unable to compete successfully if the larger institution is permitted to enter their community or area.

While this writer's conclusions would seem to support those of Dr. Kohn, for the independent bankers in the communities analyzed in the holding company study appeared to compete very successfully with the large group systems, both of these studies have numerous limitations and their results would have to be stamped as preliminary. Furthermore, even if these findings were indisputable, those responsible for banking policy decisions involving branching, mergers, and holding company acquisitions would still have to consider an array of other variables in addition to the above in weighing the effects of these actions and their possible long-run implications for the general public.

# CHAPTER 5

---◄◆►---

# Chartering

THE SUPREME COURT in the *Philadelphia Case* indicated: ". . . the so-called failing company defense . . . *might* have somewhat larger contours as applied to bank mergers because of the greater public impact of a bank failure compared with ordinary business failures."[1] [Emphasis added] Thus, although the justices of this nation's highest court in their decisions in recent years have shown a great concern for the preservation of competition in all industries, they suggested even before the 1966 Bank Merger Act amendment that bank mergers were *sui generis*—that banking was sufficiently different from other industries so that within limits competition in banking might be afforded special treatment under the antitrust laws.

This approach to bank competition is not new, for it has probably been the most important single factor affecting bank entry for about forty years. In fact the real significance of the Supreme Court's observation regarding the "larger contours" in bank merger cases involving institutions in financial difficulty is not that it was made but that it was relegated to a footnote. In recent decades public officials have been primarily concerned with preserving banks, not banking competition, and as a result entry into this field has been severely limited. However, several times in American banking history the pendulum has swung toward "monopolistic chartering" with very restricted entry only to return to "competitive chartering" with relatively free entry. Thus, the uncertainty in the Court's statement,

[1] 374 U.S. 321, 371–72 (1963), n. 46.

174

combined with numerous other developments in banking in the 1960s, may reflect at least a modest movement in the direction of competition once again.

## DEVELOPMENTS IN THE NINETEENTH CENTURY

### BEFORE 1838

For well over a half century, from the establishment of the Bank of North America in 1781 until the passage of the free banking acts in the late 1830s, bank charters in the United States were all granted under special legislative acts of incorporation. In those states where business was most active, applications to the legislature for permission to establish banks became a nuisance and often a scandal.[2] In New York, for example, charters were granted by Whig and Democratic governments only to their own partisans as part of the spoils system,[3] and even the purchasing of bank shares was controlled by political bosses.

The corruption of the lawmakers which could be traced to special chartering was well known, and bank reform movements gained numerous supporters. However, this was only one of many reasons people demanded a change in American banking at that time. In addition, some groups denounced the limited entry into banking as undemocratic;[4] the bullionists attacked the issuance of paper money by banks; numerous wildcatting schemes did much to destroy the public's confidence in bank notes; usurious interest rates were charged by many institutions; and, as the wave of speculation and spending[5] which characterized the 1830–1837 period came to an end, hundreds of banks failed[6] leaving the financial system of this nation "virtually a wreck" with the Panic of 1839 ahead.[7]

[2] Carson, ed., *Banking and Monetary Studies*, p. 7.

[3] Quoted in White, *Money and Banking*, p. 335.

[4] Helderman, *National and State Banks* (pp. 11–24) contains an interesting discussion of developments in this period.

[5] Lightner, *The History of Business Depressions*, pp. 124–38.

[6] *Ibid.*, p. 127. Lightner estimates 618 banks failed in 1837 and about 900 in the two years 1837–1838.

[7] Chapman and Westerfield, *Branch Banking*, pp. 50–51. It is often argued that the 1839 Panic was merely a continuation of the 1837 Panic. See Lightner, *History of Business Depressions*, p. 137.

1838–1863

Chapman and Westerfield in their *Branch Banking* described the situation in the mid-1830s as follows:[8]

In an era when capital was scarce, because the country was young and the period for the accumulation of capital had been short, but when the need for capital to finance the expanding territory and population was great, this waste through rotten banks was more than a democratic people, with the vote at hand, could patiently tolerate forever.

Hence, it seemed to be only a matter of time before the various anti-bank elements would solidify to try to secure bank reform through new legislation, and if they were successful the statutes passed would inevitably affect bank chartering. During the late 1830s and 1840s bills inspired by these groups were signed into law; but, strangely, the legislation enacted in one area was often the antithesis of that approved in another. Some statutes called for virtually unlimited bank chartering (free banking), while others outlawed this practice completely.[9]

*Free banking.* The bank reform laws which were to prove to be of most lasting significance were the free banking acts passed initially in Michigan in 1837 and New York in 1838. These were anti-monopoly (not anti-branch) statutes designed to "open the business of banking to a full and free competition," for free banking apparently took its name from the fact that anyone was permitted to engage in it if he met a set of prescribed conditions. In those parts of the nation, such as the South, where wealth was mainly agricultural and business enterprise was less important, banks were few in number but often extremely strong, and free banking made very little headway.[10] But, over much of the country, the free banking principle gained a wide acceptance.

In some sections the free banks were very successful; in others—especially in what are now the North Central states—they were ruinous. Not only did banks fail, but the practices engaged in by free bankers were almost unbelievable and would be humorous were it not

[8] Chapman and Westerfield, *Branch Banking*, pp. 49–51.
[9] Both free banking and banking prohibitions are discussed in greater detail in Chapter 2.
[10] Carson, ed., *Banking and Monetary Studies*, pp. 8–9.

for the fact that they were so disastrous. Bray Hammond has described the situation as follows:[11]

In Michigan the same [free banking] law was enacted while pending in New York and, within two years, more than 40 free banks had been established and had failed. Wisconsin and Indiana, carried away with the democratic ideal of free banking and the hope of making something out of nothing, followed Michigan's example. Speculators bought bonds, issued notes to pay for them, and eluded their debtors by taking to the woods among the wildcats. Notes were issued by banks with no known place of business, and no regular office hours; and kegs of nails with coin lying on top were moved overnight from "bank" to "bank" to show up as cash reserves just ahead of the bank examiners.

*Banking prohibited.* While the friends of banking argued for bank reform, the opponents of banking waged a vigorous campaign for the elimination of banks. In those states which had the worst experience with financial institutions, the opposing ("no-bank") group met with remarkable success. Several states established constitutional provisions which forbade corporate banking, and the lawmakers in some other states simply refused to grant corporate charters. Thus, individuals who decided to organize banks were not given the shield of limited liability. Nevertheless, private banks were organized to provide banking service in many areas where corporate banking was prohibited, and where individuals could still obtain state bank charters they did so in large numbers in the 1840s and 1850s. As a result, by 1863, when the National Currency Act was passed which permitted the chartering of national banking associations, the number of state banks in operation exceeded 1,400, more than twice the amount reported prior to the panic of 1837.[12]

## 1864–1900

*1865 federal legislation.* With investors given the opportunity to obtain federal charters for their banks following the enactment of the 1863 legislation, many members of Congress had assumed that state banks would quickly seek membership in the national banking system, but by mid-1864 less than one-third of the chartered commer-

---

[11] *Ibid.,* p. 9.
[12] The accuracy of these early bank data is always subject to question. See *Historical Statistics of the United States: Colonial Times to 1957,* pp. 615–16.

cial banks were operating under national authority. Therefore, in an attempt to force state banks to convert to national associations, Congress passed the Act of March 3, 1865, discussed earlier in this book. The act read in part:[13]

Every national banking association, state bank, or state banking association, shall pay a tax of 10 percentum on the amount of notes of any state bank or state banking association, paid out by them after the first day of July 1866.

Since most bankers considered currency issuance essential to bank operation, they rapidly switched to national charters. In January 1865 the number of national banks had risen to 1,294; and by October 1865 there were more than 1,500. Although apparently many private banks remained in operation after the mid-1860s, the number of state chartered banks declined from nearly 1,100 reported in mid-1864 to approximately 300 in the fall of 1865.[14]

*Revival of state banking.* There was little change in the number of state chartered banks from the end of 1865 to the late 1870s and early 1880s. But, in this interval deposit banking expanded rapidly and less reliance had to be placed on the circulation privilege. And, as more and more people realized a bank could operate profitably without issuing currency, the Comptroller of the Currency's virtual monopoly of bank chartering was broken, and state chartered banks once again began to assume an important role in the American financial system.

*Development of a dual banking system.* State and federal banking authorities began actively to compete for additional members in their systems by the 1880s. As a result, any effort by the Comptroller to make use of his seemingly limited discretionary authority in rejecting a national bank charter application was very likely to be followed by

---

[13] 13 Stat. 469, § 6. The goal of this legislation was to ensure that national banks would supersede state banks, for "both cannot exist together." *Congressional Globe,* 38th Cong., 2d Sess., February 27, 1865, p. 1139.

[14] The state bank figures exclude private banks which did not obtain corporate charters under state law. The first time data for private banks were reported (1877) they were nearly equal in number to the combined total of state and federally chartered banks. Unfortunately, no deposit or asset data were provided. Federal Reserve Board, Committee Reports, "The Dual Banking System," p. 135.

the granting of a charter to the same incorporators by state officials (and vice versa).[15] Both classes of bank supervisory agency were "solicitous for the relative importance in numbers and resources of banks under their respective jurisdictions," which "had an important bearing on the exercise of their discretionary powers," and charters were granted quite freely.[16]

With economic conditions generally favorable for the establishment of new banks between 1880 and 1900 and with little resistance on the part of the supervisory authorities to the formation of new institutions, the number of commercial banks grew rapidly. There were less than 3,000 commercial banks reported in operation in 1880; 7,000 in 1890; and well over 12,000 in 1900. While the federally chartered banks were dominant by far in 1880, ten years later there were as many state banks (excluding private banks) as national banks; and by the turn of the century, the state chartered institutions outnumbered the federal two to one and their assets were only slightly under those of national banks.[17] Thus, the dual banking system, in the most meaningful sense of two relatively large groups—one state and one federal—of private, chartered banks (in contrast to the monolithic, quasi-public Banks of the United States), had finally evolved.

## CHARTERING PHILOSOPHY

*State authorities.* With the decline in the number and importance of state chartered banks after the passage of the National Bank Act, there was apparently a cessation of state banking legislation in most areas. The approval of the Texas constitution of 1876, which declared: "No corporate body shall hereafter be created, renewed, or extended with banking or discounting privileges,"[18] was a rare exception to this pattern. In most instances, old laws designed to regulate state banks of issue simply remained obsolete and unchanged on the statute books or they were swept away by code revisions.

[15] Peltzman, "Entry in Commercial Banking," p. 5.

[16] Federal Reserve Board, Committee Reports, "Dual Banking System," p. 123.

[17] These data were all compiled from *Historical Statistics of the United States: Colonial Times to 1957,* pp. 626–31.

[18] Barnett, *State Banks and Trust Companies since the Passage of the National Bank Act,* p. 23. The Texas constitution was amended in 1904 to permit the chartering of banks, and a general banking law was passed in 1905.

As late as 1892, in a digest of state laws, it was remarked:[19]

It seems unnecessary to incorporate the state banking laws in this edition. Nearly all the States, except the newer States and Territories, have special chapters in their corporation acts concerning banks and moneyed institutions, but these chapters are usually of old date, and have practically been superseded for so long a time by the national banking laws that they have become obsolete in use and form.

Thus, as the number of state banks began to increase in the 1870s and 1880s, their operations were inhibited by out-of-date laws in some states and in others they were subjected to virtually no regulation whatsoever. If the state authorities had a "chartering philosophy" in this period it is almost impossible to describe except to note that in present-day terms it would appear to have been extremely liberal.

Although there was very little new banking legislation between 1865 and the early 1890s, there were a number of significant developments concerning bank chartering during the last half of the nineteenth century. These changes did not necessarily relate to a "philosophy" (the weight given various factors in considering the merits of a charter application), but they did substantially affect the way in which charters were obtained as the states moved gradually from incorporation by special acts to general incorporation laws. George Barnett, in his *State Banks and Trust Companies since the Passage of the National Bank Act,* traced the evolution of state bank chartering as follows: 1865 to 1875, probably a majority of the banks formed were incorporated under special acts; from 1875 to 1887, incorporation under the business incorporation law was most popular; and after 1887, the general banking law was the vehicle used almost universally to incorporate state banks and trust companies.[20]

*Comptrollers of the Currency.* The National Currency Act passed in 1863 [12 stat. 665] and its successor the National Bank Act approved in 1864 [13 stat. 99] are most closely associated with efforts on the part of federal government officials to secure a currency with "uniformity of style, uniformity of goodness, and a larger demand for government securities."[21] However, this legislation had sev-

[19] *Ibid.,* p. 11.
[20] *Ibid.,* p. 34.
[21] White, *Money and Banking,* p. 372.

eral other goals relating to the strengthening of the American banking system. For example, it has often been argued that a major cause of bank failures in the free banking era was the shortage of paid-in capital in many state banks;[22] therefore, particular care was exercised in framing the national bank statutes to guard against the establishment of banks without sufficient stockholders' equity. To prevent the formation of undercapitalized institutions, the 1864 Act provided that a national association could not obtain a charter unless it met minimum capital requirements as determined by the size of the city in which it was located, and the law also established rules regarding the timing of the initial (50 percent) and subsequent payments.[23]

At that time, the capital requirement provisions of the National Bank Act were probably the major restriction upon entry into this industry,[24] for while this legislation in part reflected the government's concern with the soundness of banks, it appeared to grant only limited discretionary authority to the Comptroller of the Currency in considering charter applications. The National Bank Act (§ 17) merely stated:

Before such association shall be authorized to commence the business of banking, the comptroller shall examine into the condition of such association, ascertain especially the amount of money paid in on account of each of the directors of such association, and the amount of capital stock of which each is the bona fide owner, and generally whether such association has complied with all the requirements of this act to entitle it to engage in the business of banking; and shall cause to be made and attested by the oaths of a majority of the directors and by the president or cashier of such association, a statement of all the facts necessary to enable the comptroller to determine whether such association is lawfully entitled to commence the business of banking under this act.

Since the National Bank Act followed free banking principles, ease of entry was to be expected. But "ease" should not be confused with

[22] Laibly, "Supervisory Control of Commercial Banks," p. 20; and Knox, *A History of Banking in the United States,* p. 315. For discussion of early bank failures, see *ibid.,* pp. 319–28.

[23] 13 Stat. 99 (1864), §§ 7, 14. Fifty percent of the capital stock had to be paid in before an association could commence business.

[24] Peltzman, "Entry in Commercial Banking," pp. 3–4. And in the 1880s, as deposit banking made state charters with their typically less stringent capital requirements a meaningful alternative to national charters, even this restriction was of limited importance.

"unlimited" entry. The decision to approve a given application was not automatic even though all of the requirements clearly spelled out in the law were met. The Comptrollers of the Currency considered such things as the state in which a bank was to be established; the location of the community in the state and possible alternative locations for the national bank(s) to serve a particular area (which clearly forecloses any possibility of unlimited entry); the economic situation; the individuals applying for the charter; and numerous other criteria.[25] Nevertheless, in general, it would be correct to state that entry remained quite free during the early years of the National Banking System.

Within a relatively short time after the National Banking System began operation a major impediment to free chartering arose. Under the 1864 federal legislation (§ 22) national banks were authorized to issue no more than 300 million dollars of notes for circulation in total. And, under an act passed March 3, 1865, this sum was to be apportioned among the states and territories—150 million dollars according to "representative population" and the remainder "having due regard to the existing banking capital, resources, and business of such states, districts, and territories."[26] But, on the same day the "distribution rule" was enacted, a second law was signed which required the Comptroller to give preference to existing state banks as opposed to new associations in granting charters until July 1, 1865.[27]

These two federal statutes appeared to be somewhat contradictory, for if the preference were given to state bank conversions it would prevent a strict enforcement of the apportionment provision, since most of the banks in a position to avail themselves of the law were located in the New England and Middle Atlantic states. The Comptroller of the Currency and Secretary of the Treasury therefore had to decide which of the two laws was to be followed, and they construed the act preferring conversion of state banks as taking precedence over

[25] This information was obtained from the letters and office memoranda of the Comptrollers of the Currency in this period which were being used by my colleague Ross Robertson in his research on "The First Hundred Years of the National Banking System." He has no responsibility for the observations included in the text, however.

[26] 13 Stat. 498 (1865). This act was passed the same day legislation was enacted which literally taxed state bank notes out of existence.

[27] 13 Stat. 469 (1865).

the apportionment statute, and permitted conversion to go on, although this inevitably led to the nullification of the currency distribution requirement. This procedure was followed even after July 1, 1865, when the preference for state conversions was to terminate. As a result, by July 1867 the entire amount of circulation had been issued to converted state banks, regardless of their location;[28] and banks in the Northeastern part of the United States, as might have been expected, received a circulation far in excess of the amounts to which they would have been entitled under the apportionment law.

With the authorized circulation allocated to national associations exhausted, this posed considerable problems for the chartering authority. Therefore, an additional 54 million dollars was authorized for banks in states having less than their planned proportion in 1870,[29] and in 1875, in the Specie Resumption Act, the limitation placed on the aggregate amount of circulating notes which could be issued by national banks was repealed.[30]

The effect the currency restrictions had upon the chartering of national banks between 1865 and 1875 was summarized by Comptroller of the Currency John Jay Knox in his *Annual Report* for 1875 (p. XV) as follows:

The national banking system was intended to be a free system, and from the beginning the organization of banks was open to all; but the amount of circulation originally authorized having subsequently become exhausted, the establishment of banks with circulation was, of necessity, for a time suspended. The act of January 14, 1875, however, removed all restrictions in this respect; and since that date every application which has conformed to the requirements of the law has been granted.

With this restriction removed, the Comptroller's office appeared to be playing only a passive role in the chartering of new banks. This finding is suggested by a comment in the 1881 *Annual Report* (p. 11): "The Comptroller has no discretionary power in the matter, but must necessarily sanction the organization or reorganization of such associations as shall have conformed in all respects to legal requirements." Thus, by the 1880s free banking had returned to the national banking

---

[28] Knox, *History of Banking in the United States*, p. 271.
[29] 16 Stat. 251 (1870).
[30] 18 Stat. 296 (1875).

system, and this philosophy was to dominate the chartering of both state and national banks for the balance of the nineteenth century.[31]

## DEVELOPMENTS 1900–1935

During the closing decades of the nineteenth century, many authorities argue, the Comptroller of the Currency and state banking superintendents were engaged in a "chartering race." Until about 1880, the Comptroller had two distinct advantages in this "competition," for only national banks enjoyed the privilege of note issue; and, in developing sections of the nation (particularly the South and West) which depended heavily upon outside capital, non-resident investors were often more willing to supply the equity for a new bank if it were chartered by federal rather than state authorities.[32] But, over the years, as deposit banking grew in importance and most states became reasonably self-sufficient in supplying needed bank capital, these virtues of national charters became far less significant.

On the other hand, the advantages of state banks seemed to grow in importance as those of national banks diminished. From 1880 at least until the establishment of the Federal Reserve System in 1913, state charters might have been preferred by bank incorporators for numerous reasons. Some of the more important factors favoring state charters (not all of these may have been of importance in a given state) were: lower capital requirements, more liberal lending and investing powers, ability to engage in fiduciary business, smaller legal reserve requirements, greater branching authority, right to purchase and deal in corporate stocks, and less strict supervision.[33] Therefore, it is not surprising that between 1880 and 1895 the number of state commercial banks increased much more rapidly than the number of national banks. State banks rose from 650 to over 6,000 in this interval, while national banks advanced only from about 2,100 to slightly over 3,700.[34]

[31] There was no significant change in the number of national or state banks, however, until the late 1880s.

[32] Federal Reserve Board, Committee Reports, "The Dual Banking System," p. 7.

[33] Ibid., pp. 11, 14.

[34] Historical Statistics of the United States: Colonial Times to 1957, pp. 626,

To make the national system's standards more competitive with those of state banks, Comptroller Eckels in 1896 urged that Congress amend the National Bank Act. He suggested that the minimum capital requirement in places with 2,000 inhabitants or less be reduced from 50 thousand to 25 thousand dollars, that national banks with the Comptroller's approval be permitted to establish branches in communities with less than 1,000 population, and that national banks be allowed to issue notes to the full par value of the bonds by which they were secured. These recommendations were repeated in subsequent reports of the Comptroller of the Currency, and they were supported by the President and the Secretary of the Treasury. Finally, in the Gold Standard Act of March 14, 1900,[35] the capital reduction (but in areas with 3,000 inhabitants or less not 2,000) and the note issue amendments were enacted;[36] yet, no action was taken on the branch banking suggestion.

One writer described the developments in this period as follows:[37]

The tremendous increase since 1880 in the number of state-chartered banks, and the stationary condition of the national system after 1894 had been watched with considerable uneasiness by those who had hoped or expected that the national-bank act would make the further chartering of state banks unnecessary. Since it was apparent that the increase in state banks was mainly due to their ability to satisfy the demand for banking facilities in the more sparsely inhabited districts, and since it did not appear feasible to legislate the state systems out of existence, Congress decided in 1900 to acknowledge the existing struggle between the two systems, and, by reducing the minimum capital requirements for a national charter from $50,000 to $25,000, bade the national system to accept the challenge.

Hence, while the number of national banks remained relatively constant at about 3,700 from 1896 to the turn of the century, after the passage of the 1900 legislation both applications and approvals rose substantially, and by 1907 there were over 6,400 federally chartered banks in operation. Nevertheless, state banks continued to enjoy

---

630. These early state data are of questionable accuracy. Thus the data should be viewed as suggesting the direction and magnitude of changes rather than exact numbers.

[35] 31 Stat. 45 (1900).

[36] Federal Reserve Board, Committee Reports, "The Dual Banking System," pp. 11–13.

[37] Bremer, *American Bank Failures*, p. 29.

many advantages, growing quite steadily despite the added competition from federal charters, and by 1907 they outnumbered the national banks by more than two to one.[38]

## PANIC OF 1907

The initial bank failure in the United States apparently was that of the Farmers Exchange Bank of Gloucester, Rhode Island in 1809.[39] During the next century and a half in this country, many thousands of other institutions were to meet a similar fate; runs on banks were to become common; and there was to be a general suspension of specie payments in 1814, 1837, 1857, and 1861–1879.[40] Yet, through much of this period banking officials retained essentially the free banking philosophy until the entire banking system collapsed in the Great Depression.

But, while bank entry remained relatively free until the 1930s, during the first three decades of the twentieth century, there was a gradual change in attitude on the part of both state and federal authorities in weighing charter applications following the Panic of 1907. This crisis, the fourth in less than four decades (1873, 1884, 1893, and 1907), was particularly important in showing the need for fundamental changes in the American financial system, "for it was a banking panic—a 'rich man's crisis'—rather than a general business collapse, inasmuch as the underlying economic condition of the country was sound."[41]

The Panic of 1907 was in many respects the most serious this nation had ever experienced. In the spring of that year there was a break in prices on the stock market, but both the banking and the business communities retained considerable optimism. There was some fear regarding the strength of the New York banks in an emergency, for their ratio of capital to liabilties had declined substantially during the previous decade, as had their percentage of cash to deposits. In addition, trust companies had shown a phenomenal

---

[38] For example, as late as 1909 only thirteen states had minimum capital requirements as high as those of national banks and it seems that in over one-half of the states banks could be organized with a capital of 10 thousand dollars or less. Welldon, *Digest of State Banking Statutes,* Table A.

[39] Carson, ed., *Banking and Monetary Studies,* p. 5.

[40] White, *Money and Banking,* p. 347.

[41] Kent, *Money and Banking,* p. 326. See also, Lightner, *History of Business Depressions,* ch. 23.

growth both in numbers and in the amount of strictly banking business which they were doing, and since they were inadequately controlled either by the government or the clearing houses, they represented a weak spot in the banking community.[42]

Therefore, Professor Sprague, in his *History of Crises Under the National Banking System*, was led to conclude that given the condition of the banks, the concentration of vast amounts of bankers' balances in a handful of interest-paying New York institutions, the substantial and increasing amount of loans made in New York by outside banks, the sizable government surpluses of the period, and the "grandfatherly attitude toward the banks" adopted by the government which tended to encourage unsound banking, the New York money market was far more subject to severe strain in 1907 than at any other time in the 35 years covered by his investigation.[43]

During the third week of October 1907, the mettle of the New York banks was to be tested, and many were found wanting. The immediate cause of their difficulties can be traced to the weakened condition of the Morse-Heinz chain, which had been built through a pyramiding of bank shares and used to finance the speculations of its owners and their associates.[44] One member of the chain applied to the Clearing House for assistance on October 16 and received it, but the necessary investigation by the Clearing House revealed the problems did not end with this single bank. The more closely the situation was examined, "the more alarming was the state of affairs disclosed; it became evident that the rottenness was not confined to the Mercantile Bank but extended to an even larger institution of the chain, the Knickerbocker Trust Company."[45]

Word of the weakness of the chain spread rapidly, and on October 22, 1907, a line stretched from the doors of the Knickerbocker Trust Company for more than a block—a panic-stricken queue. By noon the bank was closed, and by the following morning every trust company in New York faced a line of terrified depositors. By the end of the week[46]

[42] Mussey, ed., *The Reform of the Currency*, p. 243.
[43] Sprague, *History of Crises Under the National Banking System*, pp. 228–34.
[44] See Noyes, *Forty Years of American Finance*, pp. 365 ff; and Corey, *The House of Morgan*, pp. 338–48.
[45] Burr, *The Portrait of a Banker: James Stillman*, pp. 220–21, and 226.
[46] *Ibid.*, p. 231.

nine banking institutions in Greater New York had closed their doors besides those elsewhere, and men had died from the excitement or from the terror or by their own hand. While the stock exchange collapse was past the worst in a few days the captains were by no means relieved of strain, for the banking crisis lasted well into November. [And] runs on various trust companies in all parts of the nation continued for weeks.

This relatively brief but extremely severe panic thereby illustrated once again the weaknesses of the financial system in this country. Shortly thereafter, the National Monetary Commission's studies were initiated, and within a few years the Federal Reserve Act was passed. Naturally, the greatest concern was with the development of a strong central bank in this period, and the question of bank charters received only limited attention, but pressure was also beginning to build to end the "chartering race" between state and national banks. And, while thousands of new banks were to be established in the next two decades, the strength of free banking was to diminish each year as the discretionary powers of the supervisory authorities to reject charter applications were expanded.

DISCRETIONARY POWER

*State authorities.* In the early part of the present century supervisory officials in many states were allowed little discretion in the granting of charters to new banks. Usually no power of refusal was given to banking boards or commissioners.[47] In only a few states were these officials specifically empowered or required to consider the public convenience and necessity in granting charters or even to investigate the integrity or reliability of the proposed incorporators. Often where bank supervisors had this authority they called for its elimination.

In the early 1900s in New York State, for example, the State Attorney General notified the Superintendent of Banks that the banking law charged the latter "with a discretion and responsibility in [issuing a certificate of authorization for a new bank] contrary to the view hitherto held, and contrary to the practice followed since the creation of [the Banking] Department." While this power was apparently implied by the banking law, it was clearly and expressly conferred by the trust company statute, and it was the superintendent's

[47] Federal Reserve Board, Committee Reports, "The Dual Banking System," p. 51.

duty, not merely his privilege, to enforce it. The New York superintendent in 1905 found that this provision vested him with authority "that no official should possess in such cases." He recommended that the trust company statute "be changed to permit trust companies to be formed wherever capital chooses to so interest itself," and that the banking statute be amended to make clear "that the right to a bank charter is as free and absolute as it was under the Act of 1838 and under the Banking Act of 1882, and, as . . . it had been supposed to be under the Banking Law of 1892."[48]

However, within two years banks in the Empire State and across the nation were to face the disastrous Panic of 1907, and the New York banking superintendent was soon to be pleading not for a reduction but for an expansion of his discretionary authority in regard to both bank and trust company charters and branch applications.[49] The New York special commission on banks in 1907 supported the superintendent and strongly advocated that he be permitted to reject an application if he felt the banking facilities in a community were ample;[50] in 1908 a "public convenience and advantage" test for new banks and branches was added to the state's banking law.[51]

There was considerable difference of opinion in this country at the time regarding the desirability of conferring such powers on a bank supervisor.[52] This was apparent at the seventh annual session of the National Association of Supervisors of State Banks in 1908, for the committee on uniform laws recommended that supervisors should be given authority to decide whether the proposed incorporators of a bank are proper persons to conduct a banking business, and also to determine whether any need of such a bank exists in the locality in which it is proposed to establish it. But the recommendation was eliminated from the report as adopted, apparently because many of these state officials were opposed to having any power to determine

[48] New York State Superintendent of Banks, *Annual Report* for the fiscal year 1903–1904, xxxiii.

[49] New York State Superintendent of Banks, *Annual Report* for the fiscal year 1906–1907, p. xxviii.

[50] Mussey, ed., *The Reform of the Currency*, p. 281.

[51] New York State Superintendent of Banks, *Annual Report* for the fiscal year 1907–1908, pp. xxiv–xxv. Trust Company charters were already covered by a "convenience and advantage" provision [Chap. 546 of the laws of 1887]; the Laws of 1908 applied to banks [Chap. 125], bank branches [Chap. 156], and trust company branches [Chap. 194].

[52] Mussey, ed., *The Reform of the Currency*, p. 281.

the need of a community for additional banking facilities.[53] This might have been expected, for one of the goals of the states in ending special chartering was to eliminate (or at least substantially reduce) lobbying in connection with the granting of charters. Hence, one could surmise, the bank superintendents were willing to continue to follow the conditions laid down in most general banking laws which gave them very limited discretionary authority in issuing charters, for this in turn made them subject to somewhat less political pressure.

During the next quarter century this philosophy was to change considerably.[54] In 1909 only two state bank supervisory agencies in reviewing charter applications had the discretionary authority to approve or reject them on the basis of both the "legitimate purpose and integrity of the applicants" and the "public need and convenience" factors relating to the establishment of a given bank. However, by 1932 both of these powers were specified in the statutes of thirty states.

The Federal Reserve in 1932 provided the following breakdown of state agency discretionary authority in reviewing charter requests in these two bench-mark years:[55]

*Requirements of State Bank Supervisory Agencies Relative to the Organization of New Banks*

| Selected Criteria | Number of States 1909 | 1932 |
|---|---|---|
| Agency must only be assured of legitimate purpose and/or integrity of applicants | 12 | 4 |
| Agency must only take into consideration the public need and convenience for banking facilities | 4 | 8 |
| Agency must take into account both of the above | 2 | 30 |
| Total number of states in which some discretionary power is authorized | 18 | 42 |

[53] *Ibid.,* p. 282.

[54] A useful general summary of developments in this area is found in Stokes, "Public Convenience and Advantage in Applications for New Banks," *The Banking Law Journal* (November 1957), pp. 921–31.

[55] Federal Reserve Board, Committee Reports, "The Dual Banking System in the United States," p. 145.

Thus, by 1932 the banking board, commissioner, superintendent, or other chartering authority had almost complete discretionary power in most of the states to grant or refuse applications for bank charters, subject in a number of states to appeal or review by the courts or by special boards. Furthermore, in over three-fourths of the states these officials were specifically instructed by law to consider the public convenience or public necessity for the proposed bank.[56]

*Comptroller of the Currency.* The 1884 edition of *Instructions in Regard to the Organization, Extension, and Management of National Banks* required that an application for a bank charter be endorsed by a member of Congress from the district in which the bank was to be established, or be accompanied by letters from prominent individuals "vouching for the character and responsibilities of the parties, *and the necessities of the community* where the bank is to be located." [Emphasis added] In the 1891 edition the "character and responsibility" tests were included using almost identical wording; yet, the "necessities" criterion was omitted, as it was in a revised edition of this booklet in 1893 and a reissue of the 1893 pamphlet printed in 1900. Whether this was an intentional deletion (or reduction of emphasis) of the "convenience and needs" requirement, this writer was not able to ascertain; nevertheless, the tone of Comptroller Edward S. Lacey's and Comptroller James H. Eckels' *Annual Reports* in 1891 and 1893, respectively, would lead one to conclude that it would be much more likely national bank entry restrictions would have been tightened rather than eased at that time.[57]

The idea that the Comptroller's Office may have been more strict in its chartering actions in the 1890s than it was in the 1880s is given a modest amount of support from analysis of available data concerning the growth in the number of national banks in this period. The net change in the number of commercial banks at five year intervals from 1880 to 1920 was as follows:[58]

[56] *Ibid.,* p. 51.
[57] Comptroller of the Currency, 29th *Annual Report,* 1891, pp. 9–15; and 31st *Annual Report,* 1893, pp. 10–25.
[58] Compiled from data in *Historical Statistics of the United States: Colonial Times to 1957,* pp. 626, 630. The state data include commercial banks and private banks, and they are less accurate (particularly in the early years) than the national data. These figures do not represent the total number of new banks. If the data were adjusted to show all new banks instead of the net figure,

|  | National | (%) | State | (%) |
|---|---|---|---|---|
| 1881–1885 | 613 | ( 10) | 365 | ( 2) |
| 1886–1890 | 795 | ( 13) | 2,579 | ( 14) |
| 1891–1895 | 231 | ( 4) | 1,492 | ( 8) |
| 1896–1900 | 16 | ( 0) | 617 | ( 3) |
| 1901–1905 | 1,933 | ( 32) | 3,792 | ( 20) |
| 1906–1910 | 1,474 | ( 25) | 4,888 | ( 26) |
| 1911–1915 | 459 | ( 8) | 2,417 | ( 13) |
| 1916–1920 | 427 | ( 7) | 2,474 | ( 13) |
| Total | 5,948 | (100) | 18,624 | (100) |

From this brief summary, it would appear that free banking was clearly in vogue in the national system in the 1880s, when the "necessities" criterion was included in the Comptroller's "Instructions" pamphlet, and that the total number of national banks increased much more slowly from 1891 through 1900, after the discretionary provision was dropped. As a result, one might be tempted to conclude that chartering regulations were tightened, not eased, in this interval. However, this ignores the fact that there were about 1,000 bank failures during the 1890s (257 national) which may have discouraged those who might have submitted charter applications, and which certainly reduced the number of national banks. Moreover, the substantial increase in the number of both national and state banks in the 1880s may have slightly dampened the interest in obtaining new charters in the 1890s.

The chartering philosophy of the Comptroller of the Currency after the turn of the century is much more clearly defined. Within a relatively short time following the 1900 reduction of the capital requirement for national banks in smaller communities from 50 thousand to 25 thousand dollars, approximately 1,000 informal charter applications were filed with the Comptroller. In addition, between March 14 when the law was passed[59] and October 31, 1900, 509 formal applications were approved, three-fourths of them for banks with capital of less than 50 thousand dollars.[60]

---

the growth of state systems (in terms of number of banks) would be even greater than presented in this table, since there were over four state bank failures for every national bank failure in this interval.

[59] 31 Stat. 45 (1900).

[60] American Bankers Association, *The Bank Chartering History and Policies of the United States*, p. 18.

During the next decade, 1901–1910, over 3,500 new national banks were formed, or nearly one-half the total number of federally chartered banks in operation in 1910. (This vast increase in the number of charter applications in this decade, after the change in capital requirements, also raises some serious doubt regarding the importance of the role of the Comptroller's office in restricting new bank charters in the 1890s as compared with the lack of interest in obtaining national charters.) But, after the Panic of 1907–1908, the actions and statements of Comptroller Murray suggested that the attitude of his office toward applications to charter new banks was shifting from ease to "moderate ease," and that the period of free banking was gradually coming to a close.

In 1900 *Pratt's Digest* described the Comptroller's powers in approving charters as follows:[61]

This certificate [authorizing a national bank to commence business] the association is entitled to as a matter of right; and the Comptroller cannot withhold it, unless he has reason to believe that the association has been organized for objects other than those contemplated by the National banking laws.

But, by 1917, the same publication noted the increasing use of discretionary authority by the Comptroller of the Currency. The *Digest* stated:[62]

The Comptroller, as heretofore, publishes each application for authority to organize a National Bank, but prior to formal approval he [investigates] the standing of the applicants, the demand for a bank in the place, and the prospects of success if it is established and conservatively managed.

This new philosophy toward bank entry could be noted in the 1909–1911 *Annual Reports* of Comptroller of the Currency Lawrence O. Murray. From 1900 through 1908, in the section of the Comptroller's report which reviews the organization of new national banks each year, there was no reference to restrictions upon entry. However, in 1909 Comptroller Murray revealed that his office was being more careful than it had been before in the scrutiny to which it subjected proposed bank incorporations,[63] and the Comptroller spe-

[61] Peltzman, *Entry in Commercial Banking*, p. 4.
[62] *Ibid.*
[63] Mussey, ed., *The Reform of the Currency*, p. 279.

cifically mentioned that he was trying to prevent the formation of associations "in a place the population and business of which are insufficient to warrant the establishment of a national bank."[64]

In his 1910 report, Comptroller Murray noted:[65]

Applications for authority to convert state banks into national banking associations are made by the directors, and each case of this character is investigated for the purpose of determining whether the bank has been conducted in conformity with law, its measure of success, and also as to the character of its assets and general business.

In view of the fact that the bank stock is generally regarded as a very desirable investment the organization of banks, both national and state, has been very active during recent years, and it has been shown to be evident to both federal and state authorities that many banking institutions are organized, or organization attempted, without giving due consideration to their demand or their prospects of success. As far as possible the *state authorities are now acting in harmony with the Comptroller* in the upbuilding of banking conditions by preventing the organization of banks where the demand therefor is not apparent or where organization is attempted by those whose character and standing are questionable. [Emphasis added]

Thomas Kane, Deputy Comptroller of the Currency, in his history of the operations of the Comptroller's office, described Murray's actions as follows:

No Comptroller of the Currency before [him] ever assumed the right to determine the question of the business needs for a new bank, or an additional association, in any city, town, or place. That question was left to the organizers and the subscribers for the stock in the proposed institution. . . . [for] it was held that they had the same right to engage in the business of banking as those already in the business.[66]

The emphasis upon "convenience and needs" criteria in this period could also be observed in the application form which was included in the Comptroller of the Currency's booklet, *Instructions Relative to the Organization and Management of National Banks,* for 1909. In this edition the "three prominent public officials" (judge, postmaster,

---

[64] Comptroller of the Currency, 47th *Annual Report,* 1909, p. 18.

[65] Comptroller of the Currency, 48th *Annual Report,* 1910, p. 19. In the Comptroller's 1911 (p. 19) and 1912 (p. 25) reports, the existence of ample banking facilities is given as the first cause of charter application denials.

[66] Kane, *The Romance and Tragedy of Banking,* pp. 393–94. This book provides an excellent review of the operation of the Comptroller's office from 1864 to 1922.

mayor), who were to endorse the application for the federal charter, not only had to vouch for the character and responsibility of the applicants but each official also had to agree that he was "of the belief that the conditions locally are such as to insure success if the bank is organized and properly managed."[67]

Despite the growing use of discretionary authority on the part of the Comptroller of the Currency following the Panic of 1907–1908, the number of national banks rose substantially from 1909 through 1920, inclusive. During the early years of this interval, 1909–1912, approximately one application was rejected for every four approved, a "denial rate" which was not reached again for nearly a decade. (See Table 5.1) But, after 1912, relatively few federal charter requests were disapproved until 1921.

State officials were also very lenient in permitting the establishment of new banks in this period, and the number of commercial banks in the nation reached 30,000 in 1920. This may be contrasted with 24,500 commercial banks (including private banks) in operation in 1910, and 12,500 in 1900. In this same twenty-year span, the population per banking office declined by nearly one-half, from over 6,000 to 3,500, reflecting the much more rapid expansion in banks than in population.

Between 1920 and 1925, entry into the National Banking System remained comparatively free, but the rejection rate was far higher than it had been in the previous five years. In 1922 Comptroller of the Currency D. R. Crissinger in his *Annual Report* warned:[68]

If the Federal Reserve System is to be perpetuated and maintained in the strength and authority which are desirable, there must be national banks in sufficient number and strength. And if national banks are to be assured in such numbers, they must be given charters liberal enough to constitute inducement to remain in the system.

He strongly emphasized the need for a large national system, which may in part explain the decline in the rate of denials of charter requests in 1922 and 1923.[69]

[67] Comptroller of the Currency, *Instructions and Suggestions Relative to the Organization and Management of National Banks,* 1909, p. 4. This terminology was also used by the Comptroller in his 1909 *Annual Report,* pp. 18–19. It was not used in the 1906 "Instructions."

[68] Comptroller of the Currency, 60th *Annual Report,* 1922, p. 2.

[69] Crissinger's term in office ended in April 1923.

TABLE 5.1. NATIONAL BANK CHARTER APPLICATIONS, 1910–1966ᵃ (INCLUDING CONVERSIONS)

| Year Endᵇ | Applications Received | Applications Acted Upon in Periodᶜ | | | | | |
|---|---|---|---|---|---|---|---|
| | | Rejected | (%) | Approved | (%) | Total | (%) |
| 1910–15 | 1,385 | 123ᵈ | (11) | 993 | (89) | 1,116 | (100) |
| 1915–20 | 1,678 | 110 | (9) | 1,170 | (91) | 1,280 | (100) |
| 1920–25 | 1,359 | 294 | (24) | 944ᵉ | (76) | 1,238 | (100) |
| 1925–30 | 1,323 | 537 | (46) | 621 | (54) | 1,158 | (100) |
| 1930–35 | 1,200 | 154 | (15) | 892 | (85) | 1,046 | (100) |
| 1935–40 | 185 | 32 | (22) | 115 | (78) | 147 | (100) |
| 1940–45 | 158 | 31 | (24) | 99 | (76) | 130 | (100) |
| 1946–50 | 241 | 93 | (44) | 119 | (56) | 212 | (100) |
| 1951–55 | 271 | 80 | (36) | 141 | (64) | 221 | (100) |
| 1956–60 | 349 | 116 | (42) | 162 | (58) | 278 | (100) |
| 1961–65 | 1,370 | 581 | (46) | 671 | (54) | 1,252 | (100) |
| 1966 | 99 | 45 | (47) | 51 | (53) | 96 | (100) |

ᵃ Many things are not shown by these data, such as "informal" applications discouraged, and on the average about one-fifth of the applications was abandoned.

ᵇ Data were compiled as of fiscal year end October 31 until 1942, but as of calendar year end thereafter.

ᶜ These data include applications received both in the current period and remaining from the previous period.

ᵈ Comptroller's *Annual Report* states only "remainder held for more information or abandoned"; thus no rejections were listed in 1914 and 1915.

ᵉ 1925 approvals not listed in the Comptroller's *Annual Report*. The data were obtained from *The Bank Chartering History and Policies of the U. S.*, A.B.A., 1935, p. 26.

*Source:* Comptroller of the Currency, *Annual Reports*, 1910–1963; *National Banking Review* (March 1964), p. 449; *ibid.* (March 1965), p. 443; and *ibid.* (March 1966), p. 417. 1966 data from the Comptroller of the Currency.

From 1924 through 1930 the ratio of rejected applications to approvals for national charters was at a very high level. In fact from 1926 through 1930 nearly one-half of the applications considered were declined. (See Table 5.1) Thus, contrary to what is often suggested, the so-called "chartering race" between the federal and state authorities had ceased by the mid-1920s, and it did not continue into the 1930s. The restrictive attitude of the national system toward charter applications at that time could be noted in the 1927 report of Comptroller of the Currency J. W. McIntosh. In this report he observed.[70]

[70] Comptroller of the Currency, 65th *Annual Report, 1927*, pp. 13–14.

This bureau is subject at all times to the demand for charters for new national banking associations. One of its most difficult problems is to avoid a conflict between the interests of the applicants and the needs of the community for additional banking facilities. There is a strong tendency on the part of many of those interested in securing charters for new banks to believe and to urge that because they or their associates are willing to risk their personal funds in capitalizing an institution a charter should be granted. The chances of success based on local banking and business conditions and the responsibility of investing the money of potential depositors which would be attracted to them is given but scant consideration. An analysis of the applications which this office has received for the establishment of new banks shows that there is too often a desire to organize banks in localities where the communities are amply served and which would not support new institutions with a likelihood of any fair measure of success.

Extreme care should be exercised in granting charters, both for National and State banks. This has been my policy with respect to national bank charters. During the current year only 44 per cent of the number of applications received for the establishment of new national banks was approved, as compared with 52 per cent the previous like period and an average of 72.8 per cent over the eight prior years, with a high of 82.7 per cent just subsequent to the World War. In other words, despite the fact that the number of applications received remains about the same, the number approved by this office is constantly becoming fewer and in the current year a less number of applications was approved than has been approved any year during the past 10-year period.

In addition, the 1928 report of Comptroller John W. Pole reported that his office "continued to exercise a policy of extreme care in granting charters for national banks based primarily on needs of a community for additional banking facilities."[71]

Between 1931 and 1935 the percentage of applications to form new national banks which were rejected declined considerably, reaching a low point of 11 percent in 1934. Moreover, there was also an unusually high ratio of applications approved to total applications received. This has frequently led people to conclude that the Comptroller's office was extremely lax, permitting large numbers of new banks to be chartered in a period when thousands of institutions were failing. Nothing could be farther from the truth.

In reality, less than 100 of the nearly 800 national banks chartered

[71] *Ibid.,* p. 12. There were no additional comments in the 1929 or 1930 reports.

in this interval were new institutions. The other 700 banks were established with the cooperation of the Comptroller's office to take over banks in weakened condition or to acquire the assets and assume the liabilities of suspended national and state banks.[72] Thus, the "free banking era" in the national system had ended some years before the Great Depression began.[73]

SUSPENSIONS, 1921–1935

It has often been argued that the competition between federal and state bank chartering authorities to build or to maintain the numbers and resources of the systems which they supervised created an "over-banked" condition in this country in the twenties. For example, the summary of the American Bankers Association's investigation of bank chartering released in 1935 concluded: "The following study gives an impressive revelation of how great a part mistaken public policies in the chartering of banks in the United States played in creating the unsound banking structure which finally collapsed with the Bank Holiday in 1933."[74] This belief was shared by many individuals, including prominent economists and government officials as well as members of the banking industry,[75] and it provided more than adequate support for the shift by supervisory authorities to greater emphasis on the preservation of banks than on competition. This move away from relatively free banking began after the Panic of 1907 expanded greatly in the 1920s and 1930s and continued into the 1960s.

It is logical to conclude that the termination of free banking was due in large part to the thousands of bank failures in this country between the 1890s and 1935. In support of this thesis, changes in legislation can be cited and revisions in charter application forms can

[72] See Comptroller of the Currency, 69th *Annual Report*, 1931, p. 14; 70th *Annual Report*, 1932, p. 22; 71st *Annual Report*, 1934, p. 41; 72nd *Annual Report*, 1934, p. 50; and 73rd *Annual Report*, 1935, p. 47.

[73] This does not mean to suggest the chartering policies might not have been improved in this period.

[74] American Bankers Association, *The Bank Chartering History and Policies of the United States*, p. 5.

[75] Peltzman, "Entry in Commercial Banking," p. 7. For an excellent review of this question, see Alhadeff's, "A Reconsideration of Restrictions on Bank Entry," *The Quarterly Journal of Economics* (May 1962), and the many references therein.

be noted. But, on the other hand, it cannot be ignored that, as mentioned above, freedom of entry may in turn have been the cause of a great many of the bank suspensions. Therefore, although it may seem out of place to consider "exit" from an industry in a chapter devoted to entry, the bank suspensions[76] during the 1920s and early 1930s are briefly reviewed in this section.

*1921–1929.* The first two decades of the twentieth century were generally characterized by rising commodity and land prices, especially during the war years. Under these conditions, banking losses were limited and the number of new banks expanded rapidly. But, between 1920 and 1921 the nation's economy experienced a precipitous decline and the bankers' favorable position was swiftly reversed. Many institutions suddenly found themselves with large amounts of frozen assets; and, in at least one state (Iowa) it was estimated that if the banks had been required to liquidate, even within two years' time, 95 percent would have proved insolvent.[77]

Although business activity soon recovered, the prices of farm products, which had declined over one-third from their highs in 1919, persistently remained at this lower level throughout the 1920s. As a result, farmers suffered considerably and bankers serving agricultural areas faced tremendous pressures. To make the situation even worse, numerous single crop communities were bankrupted as one crop failure followed another.[78] The dilemma was made complete by the huge farm mortgage debt which had been built up during the war period. This impaired the farmer's ability to obtain bank loans for the planting and harvesting of crops,[79] and the land values in the agricul-

[76] Bank suspensions comprise all banks closed to the public either temporarily or permanently by supervisory authorities or by a bank's board of directors, except if closed only during a special holiday declared by civil authorities. Banks which were reopened or taken over by other institutions after suspension have been counted as bank suspensions. Statistical material for this section has been gathered largely from data in the *Federal Reserve Bulletin* (September 1937), pp. 866–910, which contains one of the most complete statistical summaries available of suspensions in this period, and pp. 1204–24 of the December 1937 *Federal Reserve Bulletin,* which provides some excellent analyses of these data.

[77] House Hearings 1930, pp. 191, 1779, 1803.

[78] Popple, *Development of Two Bank Groups in the Northwest,* pp. 60–61, 99–100.

[79] *The Banking Situation in the United States,* pp. 141–42.

tural communities collapsed.[80] As a result the country banks were faced with dwindling deposits, an increased demand for funds, inability to obtain repayment of existing borrowings, and a decline of value in the security for past loans.

Edmund Platt, vice governor of the Federal Reserve Board, summed up the situation facing the country banker as follows:[81]

Now, I ask you, how would you like to be a country banker? Years ago Mr. Mueller started his little country bank at Mueller's Corner. Slowly but surely his little bank grew, and in course of time by indefatigable efforts, and untiring devotion, his bank did show very fair earnings, was a credit to its village, and Mr. Mueller was respected, honored, and esteemed. Now one sad day for Mr. Mueller, the Federal Reserve Bank was grafted unto the financial world and the first thing they did to this little bank that all the villagers were so proud of, was to arbitrarily take away his exchange. Then along comes the Federal land bank, and they take away his farm mortgages. Scarcely has he recovered a part of his wind, when the city insurance men in fleet automobiles roll along the cement roads the farmer built with money out of his pockets and grab most of his insurance. Then the chain store drives out of business his best customer, the country general store. As if these locusts were not enough to make life scarcely bearable, it began to be rumored all over the village that Mueller's bank was losing its grip, and deposits began to fade away. Result? Mueller's bank failed. Mueller lost his money, his job, and all of his friends. To make his life still more burdensome, self-appointed critics cried out to the world at large that all country bankers were unscientific, unfit, incapable, and should never have been allowed to start a bank. I will propound this query to all fair minded men: Could Alexander Hamilton, George Reynolds, Charles E. Mitchell, A. W. Wiggins, or William Woodward with all their science, with all their skill, with all their ability have done any better than poor Mueller? Is it not ridiculous to say that the best banker in the largest city in all the world would have succeeded at Mueller's Corner any better than Mueller did?

While many of the rural bankers' difficulties can be traced to the problems cited by Governor Platt, to poor economic conditions, to the population exodus to the cities,[82] and to "high powered" stock salesmen offering 6 to 7 percent (nontaxable) utility preferred shares

[80] U. S. Congress, Senate, *Operation of the National and Federal Reserve Banking Systems,* Hearings on S. Res. 71, 1931, p. 510.

[81] House Hearings 1930, p. 2014. See also *The Automobile and the Village Merchant,* Bureau of Business Research, University of Illinois, Bulletin 19, 1928.

[82] American Bankers Association, *Present Day Banking,* 1958, pp. 18–19.

on the installment plan,[83] there was still another source of consternation to the country banker—too many other country bankers. Bank charters were obtained so readily that in some cases two or more banks were established in villages of less than 500 people.[84] Naturally, in situations such as these, even with exceptional management, a bank would have found it almost impossible to enjoy sufficient earnings to justify its existence.[85] It might be noted that those who promote the "over-banking thesis" gain considerable support from the available statistics, for bank suspensions were most prevalent in those states with the largest increase in the number of banks between 1900 and 1920 and in those states which had a low population per bank in 1920.[86] However, it could be argued that even if the number of banks had been substantially reduced, there may still have been far too few qualified individuals to run them.

Any analysis of small bank failures would be incomplete if no consideration were given to the managerial factor. It should be understood that there were and are thousands of well-managed banks in the rural areas of this country. Nevertheless, a number of investigations have found that weak administration has been a very important cause of bank suspensions. A Federal Reserve study of the period 1921–1927 reported slow or past-due paper was the most important factor leading to bank failures,[87] but poor management was also high on the list.[88] In addition, an investigation by the Comptroller of the Currency noted that of all national bank failures from 1865 to 1936 "local financial depression" was the first cause of failure and the second was "incompetent management."[89]

[83] "Critical Problems Concerning Country Bankers," *The Analyst,* September 23, 1929, pp. 492–93.

[84] O'Connor, *The Banking Crisis and Recovery under the Roosevelt Administration,* pp. 85–86.

[85] House Hearings 1930, p. 917.

[86] American Bankers Association, *The Bank Chartering History of the United States,* pp. 30–32.

[87] Naturally this accumulation of worthless or overdue paper may also be the result of bad management. It might also be noted the failures in this period were largely in rural areas as opposed to small urban areas.

[88] House Hearings 1930, p. 444.

[89] O'Connor, *The Banking Crisis and Recovery under the Roosevelt Administration,* p. 90. A smaller study of the 1921–1929 period showed 28 percent of the banks studied failed because of "incompetent management" and 54 percent because of "local depression." American Bankers Association, *The Bank Chartering History of the United States,* p. 37.

*1930–1935.* The collapse of the stock market in 1929 and the depression of the early 1930s forced still more banks to the point where failure was inevitable. The banks were faced with a rapid decline in the income of their customers and in the underlying values of their loans and investments. As prices and production fell and unemployment grew, bank failures spread to the larger cities, and a number of sizable metropolitan institutions suspended. As depositors noted the failure of vast numbers of banks, they sought to remove their funds from their own depositaries; thus "runs" developed and many banks which might otherwise have survived were forced to suspend operations. As a result, annual bank failures rose to the point where they had to be measured in thousands. (See Table 5.2)

There were numerous efforts to save the banking system in the early 1930s. The National Credit Corporation was formed in October 1931;[90] the Reconstruction Finance Corporation was created by Congress in January 1932; and some provisions of the Glass-Steagall Act of February 1932[91] were also aimed at assisting the beleaguered banks. Nevertheless, failures continued upward, reaching their peak in 1933, when nearly 4,000 banks suspended.

On March 6, 1933, President Roosevelt issued a proclamation declaring a nationwide bank holiday for four days.[92] During this interval the banks were not to pay out any coin, bullion, or currency, or to transact any other banking business whatever unless permitted by the Secretary of the Treasury.[93] This was followed on March 9 by the passage of the Emergency Banking Act,[94] and on the same day a proclamation was issued extending the bank holiday indefinitely. An additional major step to strengthen the banking system was taken in the Banking Act of 1933, when the Federal Deposit Insurance Corporation was established.[95] Thereafter, in 1934 and 1935 there were less

[90] Kent, *Money and Banking,* pp. 328–29.

[91] 47 Stat. 56 (1932), pp. 328–29.

[92] The year 1933 was not the first occasion a bank holiday was observed in the United States. Holidays occurred in emergencies, such as the Chicago fire of 1871, the Boston fire of 1872, the Baltimore fire of 1904, and the San Francisco earthquake of 1906.

[93] "Bank Suspensions, 1921–1936," *Federal Reserve Bulletin,* (December 1937), p. 1207.

[94] 48 Stat. 1 (1933).

[95] 48 Stat. 162 (1933), § 8. This was to be only temporary legislation; the "permanent" act was included in the Banking Act of 1935. 49 Stat. 684 (1935),

than 100 suspensions, fewer than fifty each year, and the greatest crisis in the history of American banking had passed.

*Statistical summary.*   In the nine years from 1921 through 1929 inclusive there were about 5,400 bank suspensions—an average of 600 a year as compared with approximately 100 per year during the previous three decades. And, between 1930 and the end of 1933 nearly 9,000 commercial banks suspended, or over 2,200 on an annual basis. Thus, in this brief thirteen-year span, over 14,000 banks closed, which was nearly one-half the number in operation at the beginning of the period.

Of the 14,000 banks which suspended in this interval, 11,300 were state chartered and 2,700 were national banks. Approximately one-half of the suspensions, both in terms of number and of total deposits, were reported in the North Central states, which were primarily agricultural. Between 1921 and 1929 some 95 percent of the failures were in communities with less than 25,000 population; and, despite the substantial increase in failures in larger metropolitan areas in the 1930s, nearly 90 percent of all suspensions in this later period also occurred in localities with under 25,000 inhabitants. About five-sixths of the suspended banks in this thirteen-year span had capital stock of less than 100 thousand dollars and over 90 percent had loans and investments of less than 2 million dollars.[96]

THE BANKING ACT OF 1935

*Over-banking.*   As was noted earlier in this chapter, the "excessive" chartering by both state and federal authorities through the first quarter of this century was commonly considered to be a major

---

Title I. Deposit Insurance schemes had been tried before by the states. In fact some states had used insurance as a selling point in their contest with federal authorities to secure member banks. Many of these plans are discussed in Robb, *The Guaranty of Bank Deposits.*

[96] Since it is often argued that although branch or group banking may increase concentration in some markets, this is more than offset by the strength of these systems in times of stress, fairly detailed data were compiled regarding failures by type of bank organization. The results showed branch and group banking performed very well in the twenties, but in the thirties the results were not significantly better than those of unit banks. Since the findings were inconclusive and their relevance to American banking in the 1960s was questionable, these pages were dropped from the text.

TABLE 5.2.  ANALYSIS OF CHANGES IN NUMBER OF INCORPORATED COMMERCIAL BANKS IN CONTINENTAL UNITED STATES, 1921–1935[a]

| Year | Net Change during Period | Began Operations | | | Ceased Operations | | | | Other Changes— Net[f] |
|---|---|---|---|---|---|---|---|---|---|
| | | Total | New Banks[b] | Reopenings of Suspended Banks[c] | Total | Absorbed[d] | Suspended[e] | Voluntary Liquidations | |
| Total 1921–1935 | −14,060 | 7,661 | 4,539 | 3,122 | 22,062 | 6,676 | 14,301 | 1,085 | +341 |
| 1921 | −188 | 565 | 472 | 93 | 814 | 305 | 461 | 48 | +61 |
| 1922 | −198 | 527 | 409 | 118 | 772 | 394 | 343 | 35 | +47 |
| 1923 | −424 | 526 | 458 | 68 | 1,003 | 329 | 623 | 51 | +53 |
| 1924 | −672 | 491 | 383 | 108 | 1,191 | 373 | 738 | 80 | +28 |
| 1925 | −501 | 484 | 403 | 81 | 1,001 | 363 | 579 | 59 | +16 |
| 1926 | −943 | 505 | 345 | 160 | 1,461 | 462 | 924 | 75 | +13 |
| 1927 | −812 | 423 | 296 | 127 | 1,260 | 567 | 636 | 57 | +25 |
| 1928 | −765 | 305 | 252 | 53 | 1,084 | 534 | 479 | 71 | +14 |
| 1929 | −1,008 | 304 | 235 | 69 | 1,321 | 636 | 628 | 57 | +9 |
| 1930 | −1,818 | 308 | 153 | 155 | 2,129 | 769 | 1,292 | 68 | +3 |
| 1931 | −2,728 | 380 | 105 | 275 | 3,110 | 798 | 2,213 | 99 | +2 |
| 1932 | −1,571 | 372 | 93 | 279 | 1,950 | 433 | 1,416 | 101 | +7 |
| 1933 | −3,226 | 1,020 | 323 | 697 | 4,302 | 322 | 3,891 | 89 | +56 |
| 1934[g] | +891 | 1,263 | 511 | 752 | 379 | 231 | 44 | 104 | +7 |
| 1935 | −97 | 188 | 101 | 87 | 285 | 160 | 34 | 91 | — |

[a] Excludes mutual savings banks and private banks. The reader should be warned that published data for this period vary tremendously, and the above statistics are at best a compromise.

[b] Excludes new banks organized to succeed operating banks, but for 1933 and 1934 includes new banks organized to succeed national and state banks unlicensed after the banking holiday.

[c] For 1921–1932 includes reopenings accompanied by a change of name and issuance of a new charter. For 1933–1934 includes banks closed during the banking holiday in March 1933 which were licensed subsequent to June 30, 1933. Banks licensed between March 15 and June 30, 1933, are not included in this table (either as suspensions or reopenings).

[d] Decrease in number resulting from consolidations, mergers, and absorptions of going banks. Does not include suspended banks that were taken over by other banks.

[e] Includes banks which reopened in the same or a subsequent year.

[f] Chiefly conversions from private banks, but including some unclassified changes, particularly in 1933.

[g] Changes in 1934 include banks that had been closed at the time of the banking holiday and were unlicensed as of December 30, 1933, but were approved for deposit insurance or licensed in time to reopen on January 2, 1934, and other changes between those dates. The data for 1934 were compiled on both the above (old basis) and a new basis employing revised definitions to make them comparable with the current statistics published by the FDIC. See FDIC, *Annual Report*, 1960, p. 33.

*Source:* Federal Deposit Insurance Corporation, *Annual Report*, December 31, 1960, p. 32; and U. S. Congress, Senate, *Monetary Policy and the Management of the Public Debt*, 1952, p. 556.

contributor to the bankruptcy of the American banking system in the 1930s. The Superintendent of Banks of South Dakota stated at a N.A.S.S.B. convention in 1929:[97]

I think perchance one of the greatest dangers that confronted the banking industry in South Dakota was a contest and conflict between the national and state systems some five years ago. Each system was fighting the other and, in an effort to win, each was granting charters beyond the interests of the communities. That fight was responsible for much of the failure of banks in the State of South Dakota.

Numerous illustrations of the "over-banked" condition of many sections of the country, which appeared to result from competitive chartering, could easily be provided.[98] For example, in Iowa a town with only 1,300 population had four banks in 1921, and a decade later only one remained in business. Bankers in a community in South Dakota with a population of only 300, which was already served by a state bank, were granted a charter by the Comptroller of the Currency to establish a national bank. The result was two crippled banks. Another South Dakota town of 600 inhabitants had three banks, and eventually all failed. A county in North Dakota with a population of 10,000 had eighteen banks about 1920, but by the end of 1931 only three were still in existence. In a single Montana county with 14,000 inhabitants there were twenty-one banks in operation in the early 1920s; however, only two remained in 1931. These instances are not merely isolated examples, for they typify the conditions in many agricultural states in the early 1920s, particularly in the Northwest and in the South.

By 1920 nineteen states had less than 3,100 people per bank, and in one-half of these states the figure was under 2,000. This latter group appears on a map as a solid block located in the Midwest and Northwest. In three of these states, North and South Dakota, and Nebraska, the population per bank was only about 1,000.[99] Thus, if an estimate were made that the average family included between three and four members, this would mean that there was one commercial

[97] Federal Reserve Board, Committee Reports, "Dual Banking System," p. 97.

[98] Much of the material in this section was drawn from *ibid.*, pp. 97–101.

[99] U. S. Congress, Senate, *Monetary Policy and the Management of the Public Debt,* 1952, p. 578.

bank for approximately every 250 to 300 family units in each of these states.

Expressions of fear regarding the growing number of banks appeared with some frequency in the annual reports of the state banking agencies between 1910 and 1920.[100] Also included in these publications were pleas for additional discretionary authority to reject charter applications. Nevertheless, most state officials enjoyed only limited powers in this area until the 1920s; and, with the tremendous pressures exerted upon the supervisors by the general public and the politician friends of those who wished to establish new institutions, bank chartering continued unabated.

Far too often charters were issued for the organization of banks in communities in which banking facilities were already more than ample. Moreover, these applications were approved even though the men who were to run the new institutions appeared to know little or nothing about the management of a commercial bank. Unfortunately such banks were probably doomed to failure before they began operation; yet, they were established, and with their collapse the existence of many other institutions was also imperiled. The situation in the state of Indiana in the 1920s, as summarized by the Study Commission for Indiana Financial Institutions, well illustrates the conditions which prevailed in much of the nation in this period:[101]

Authorities are unanimously agreed that the indiscriminate chartering of banks has been one of the major causes for the difficulties through which we have recently passed. Receivers, liquidating agents, and other persons familiar with the affairs of failed banks suggested, in 41 instances, that bank failures in Indiana have been due to improper chartering. . . . Intimate knowledge of individual failures, however, leads to the inescapable conclusion that many of the practices leading to bank failures were directly caused by 'cut-throat' competition which sprang up in various communities as a result of too many banks or of the chartering, often for direct or indirect political reasons, of 'spite' banks.

*The federal government's solution.* In discussing the licensing of banks and the power given to the F.D.I.C. under the provisions of the Banking Act of 1935, Leo T. Crowley, Chairman of the Corpora-

[100] Federal Reserve Board, Committee Reports, "Dual Banking System," p. 99.

[101] *Report of the Study Commission for Indiana Financial Institutions,* 1932, p. 87.

tion's Board of Directors, stated at the 1935 A.B.A. New Orleans convention:[102]

It should help to prevent a recurrence of the evil which is to be greatly feared, namely, the return of the over-banked condition of the early twenties. . . . For the eighteen months period from January 1, 1934, to June 30, 1935, over 1,400 new banks were licensed by supervisory authorities. Ninety were in communities with a population of 250 or less; 169 were in communities with a population from 250 to 500, and in some instances, there were already other banks in these very towns. I do not wish to infer that the granting of some of these licenses was not wholly justified. Yet these figures give a graphic picture of one of the most serious problems confronting the Corporation, and one in which everyone of you is vitally interested. Whether or not the uneconomic unit is insured, its influence on the general banking system can not be anything but destructive. The power given the Corporation to protect itself against the risks of insuring banks which it knows are bound to fail sooner or later only helps the Corporation. Unless state supervising authorities, your Association and the public discourage the organization of banks doomed to failure, the over-banked conditions and the consequent evils thereof are bound to return.

But, if the federal government was to provide a really lasting solution to the "over-banking problem,"[103] it had to do much more than secure the cooperation of state agencies and trade associations, for while an incumbent official may be most sympathetic toward the restriction of bank entry his successor remains an unknown quantity.

If free banking was to be terminated, the competition between state and federal chartering authorities had to be stopped. To some extent this could be accomplished through membership of state banks in the Federal Reserve System; however, it seemed very unlikely that the inability of an institution to become a member bank would prove sufficiently discouraging to enough incorporators to ensure that excessive chartering would not occur.[104] Thus, if control over the formation

[102] Quoted in American Bankers Association, *The Bank Chartering History and Policies of the United States*, p. 5.

[103] This writer is not thoroughly convinced that "over-banking" is really a meaningful expression; hence, the quotation marks. It may mean far different things to different people.

[104] Of course, the Banking Act of 1935 [49 Stat. 684 (1935), Title I, amending Section 12B of the Federal Reserve Act (y)(1)], stated in part: "No State bank which during the calendar year 1941 or any succeeding calendar year shall have average deposits of $1,000,000 or more shall be an insured

of new banks was to be achieved under the 1935 legislation, it had to come through the only other federal banking agency which maintained close relationships with large numbers of state banks—the Federal Deposit Insurance Corporation.

Fortunately, for those who advocated more limited entry into banking, the deposit insurance concept was welcomed by the general public and accepted by most of the commercial banks. By the end of 1935, a few months after the temporary federal deposit insurance plan was replaced by the permanent plan under the Banking Act of 1935, over 90 percent of the banks in the United States were admitted to insurance. Thus, since federal authorities could withhold the deposit insurance which bankers seemed to view as extremely important for successful operation at the time, they appeared to have the necessary power to control the chartering of new state banks within very narrow limits.

Under the Banking Act of 1935, the FDIC and the other federal banking agencies were given discretionary authority in the granting of nearly all bank charters. The formation of national banks, of course, was to be under the jurisdiction of the Comptroller of the Currency; the establishment of new state member banks was to be approved by the Federal Reserve Board; and the organization of nonmember insured banks was to be regulated by the FDIC.[105] In their administration of this law, the 1935 statute required the federal agencies to consider: "The financial history and condition of the bank, the adequacy of its capital structure, its future earnings prospects, the general character of its management, the convenience and needs of the community to be served by the bank, and whether or not its corporate powers [were] consistent with the purposes of this section."[106] (The same criteria had to also be employed by the FDIC in evaluating a nonmember insured bank's branch application; hence, this form of entry too was subject to the "convenience and needs test.")[107]

---

bank or continue to have any part of its deposits insured after July 1 of the year following any such calendar year during which it shall have had such amount of average deposits, unless such bank shall be a member of the Federal Reserve System." This provision, however, drew its strength from deposit insurance. The provision was repealed June 20, 1939. [53 Stat. 843 (1939)]

[105] 49 Stat. 684 (1935), Title I, (e)(2) and (f)(1).
[106] *Ibid.*, (g).
[107] *Ibid.*, (v)(5).

Thus, with the passage of the Banking Act of 1935 the standards so often employed under agency regulations were written into law; and, with the relative attractiveness of deposit insurance to commercial banks, the federal authorities could feel confident that few institutions would be organized which would not be required to meet the federal standards.[108] As a result, this statute virtually eliminated the threat of a new "chartering race" between the state and national systems unless it was acceptable to federal authorities, and this legislation left no doubt that free banking in the United States was at an end.[109]

## DEVELOPMENTS 1936–1966

### ENTRY UNDER THE NEW STANDARDS

Since 1936 the rate at which new banks were established in the United States has been below that of the 1920s and early 1930s. The number of new institutions formed averaged about 300 per year from 1921 to 1935, but only 80 per year from 1936 through 1960. However, between 1960 and 1967 the number of newly chartered banks rose tremendously to about 200 each year, approaching the pre-depression level (see Tables 5.2 and 5.3). There were also very wide fluctuations in the amount of bank failures from 1921 to 1966. The number of bank suspensions fell from a rate of nearly 1,000 a year in 1921–1935 to about 70 each year from 1936 to 1940, and during the last quarter century there have been only about five failures annually.

In the closing sections of this chapter, the actions, philosophies, and powers of the chartering authorities, both state and national, during the last three decades are considered, with particular emphasis upon Comptroller Saxon's administration. In addition, the bank suspensions in the postwar period are examined; and finally, some general observations are made regarding the need for free entry.

---

[108] Supervisors in 42 states make it a policy to insist that new state banks qualify for deposit insurance, and in at least three others it is required by statute. However, from 1960 through 1964 only two uninsured banks opened in the states which did not require deposit insurance by statute or by policy. In a few of the states which supposedly require insurance, several banks have opened without it since 1960, but virtually all were accepted for insurance shortly thereafter. See American Bankers Association, *State Bank Supervision, Ninth Quinquennial Survey 1964*, p. 45.

[109] Peltzman, "Entry in Commercial Banking," p. 9.

*State authorities.* There were very few state banks organized between 1936 and 1950. While this may in part be explained by a stricter policy in regard to bank entry by state officials, the primary reason the number of newly chartered banks declined so substantially in this period was that there was little interest in forming them. A survey made by the Joint Economic Committee of Congress and published in 1952 revealed that very few applications had been made for state bank charters during these fifteen years.[110] The State of Maine, for example, had no applications for charters in this interval; the State of Delaware had received none for ten years; and the State of Pennsylvania had three applications (all granted) in this period. The only important exceptions to this rule were the rapidly growing states of the Southwest. In Texas, for example, 298 state bank charters were applied for and 255 were approved between 1940 and 1950.

The reason most frequently cited for rejection of some of the small number of applications received was a lack of profit prospects. In explaining why there were so few requests for permission to organize new banks, a number of supervisors pointed out that their states were "economically mature" and their present network of banking institutions already complete. Other state banking officials cited the low level of banking profits relative to those in other industries as the primary cause of the lack of interest in forming additional commercial banks. In a few cases it was mentioned that bank stocks were generally selling below their "break-up values" and that this provided little inducement to form new institutions.

In more recent years, 1951–1966, the number of bank charter applications has increased substantially. This development may be traced to the high level of economic activity and larger bank profits between 1950 and 1960; but, in addition, during the last six years the actions by the office of the Comptroller of the Currency have certainly stimulated the interest in organizing new state as well as national banks. Throughout this fifteen-year span there has also been a major bank merger movement, and many of the arguments presented in Chapter 4 regarding this activity would also apply to the formation of new banks and *de novo* branches.

The average number of banks chartered each year between 1936 and 1945 was 48, while the corresponding figure for 1946–55 was 70.

[110] U. S. Congress, Senate, *Monetary Policy and the Management of the Public Debt,* 1952, p. 995.

TABLE 5.3. NEW BANKS AND DE NOVO BRANCHES ORGANIZED IN THE UNITED STATES, 1936–1966[a]

| Year | New Banks[b] | | | | | | De Novo Branches[c] | | | | | |
|---|---|---|---|---|---|---|---|---|---|---|---|---|
| | | | | State Banks | | | | | | State Bank Branches | | |
| | | | | | Nonmember | | | | | | Nonmember | |
| | All | Total Na-tional | Total State | Mem-ber | Insured | Non-insured | All | Total National | Total State | Member | Insured | Non-in-sured |
| 1966 | 118 | 25 | 93 | 5 | 70 | 18 | 1,096 | 546 | 550 | 227 | 307 | 16 |
| 1965 | 198 | 88 | 110 | 4 | 90 | 16 | 1,074 | 593 | 481 | 195 | 281 | 5 |
| 1964 | 336 | 200 | 136 | 3 | 120 | 13 | 1,025 | 585 | 440 | 176 | 261 | 3 |
| 1963 | 298 | 162 | 136 | 3 | 115 | 18 | 1,065 | 654 | 411 | 196 | 214 | 1 |
| 1962 | 183 | 63 | 120 | 4 | 103 | 13 | 874 | 486 | 388 | 155 | 225 | 8 |
| 1961 | 112 | 26 | 86 | 2 | 71 | 13 | 788 | 431 | 357 | 176 | 181 | – |
| 1960 | 135 | 32 | 103 | 5 | 77 | 21 | 771 | 429 | 342 | 148 | 188 | 6 |
| 1959 | 117 | 23 | 94 | 4 | 75 | 15 | 584 | 297 | 287 | 141 | 142 | 4 |
| 1958 | 97 | 19 | 78 | 2 | 63 | 13 | 540 | 306 | 234 | 113 | 120 | 1 |
| 1957 | 87 | 20 | 67 | 3 | 51 | 13 | 501 | 278 | 223 | 109 | 112 | 2 |
| 1956 | 123 | 30 | 93 | 6 | 72 | 15 | 522 | 307 | 215 | 112 | 100 | 3 |
| 1955 | 116 | 28 | 88 | 4 | 72 | 12 | 442 | 231 | 211 | 104 | 105 | 2 |
| 1954 | 73 | 18 | 55 | 6 | 43 | 6 | 341 | 172 | 169 | 88 | 79 | 2 |
| 1953 | 64 | 12 | 52 | 10 | 36 | 6 | 280 | 145 | 135 | 69 | 63 | 3 |
| 1952 | 73 | 15 | 58 | 4 | 45 | 9 | 217 | 101 | 116 | 59 | 56 | 1 |
| 1951 | 62 | 9 | 53 | 2 | 42 | 9 | 234 | 108 | 126 | 69 | 56 | 1 |
| 1950 | 68 | 7 | 61 | 8 | 44 | 9 | 179 | 74 | 105 | 50 | 52 | 3 |
| 1949 | 72 | 12 | 60 | 6 | 42 | 12 | 158 | 75 | 83 | 47 | 32 | 4 |

| | | | | | | | | | | | | |
|---|---|---|---|---|---|---|---|---|---|---|---|---|
| 1948 | 80 | 15 | 65 | 5 | 41 | 19 | 151 | 68 | 83 | 36 | 41 | 6 |
| 1947 | 111 | 19 | 92 | 14 | 65 | 13 | 145 | 64 | 81 | 31 | 47 | 3 |
| 1946 | 142 | 21 | 121 | 9 | 97 | 15 | 142 | 51 | 91 | 38 | 49 | 4 |
| 1945 | 117 | 17 | 100 | 8 | 82 | 10 | 65 | 29 | 36 | 11 | 21 | 4 |
| 1944 | 69 | 8 | 61 | 5 | 48 | 8 | 37 | 10 | 27 | 2 | 19 | 6 |
| 1943 | 49 | 3 | 46 | 4 | 31 | 11 | 19 | 3 | 16 | 3 | 13 | – |
| 1942 | 22 | – | 22 | 2 | 12 | 8 | 31 | 11 | 20 | 3 | 15 | 2 |
| 1941 | 53 | 7 | 46 | 1 | 32 | 13 | 50 | 15 | 35 | 7 | 22 | 6 |
| 1940 | 32 | 3 | 29 | – | 24 | 5 | 43 | 13 | 30 | 2 | 28 | – |
| 1939 | 30 | 3 | 27 | 1 | 24 | 2 | 48 | 6 | 42 | 6 | 34 | 2 |
| 1938 | 39 | 1 | 38 | – | 22 | 16 | 50 | 7 | 43 | 6 | 34 | 3 |
| 1937 | 62 | 7 | 55 | 3 | 38 | 14 | 95 | 29 | 66 | 3 | 62 | 1 |
| 1936 | 62 | 6 | 56 | – | 27 | 29 | 88 | 33 | 55 | 9 | 41 | 5 |
| 1936–45 | 535 | 55 | 480 | 24 | 340 | 116 | 526 | 156 | 370 | 52 | 289 | 29 |
| 1946–55 | 861 | 156 | 705 | 68 | 527 | 110 | 2,289 | 1,089 | 1,200 | 591 | 580 | 29 |
| 1956–65 | 1,686 | 663 | 1,023 | 36 | 837 | 150 | 7,744 | 4,366 | 3,378 | 1,521 | 1,824 | 33 |
| 1936–65 | 3,082 | 874 | 2,208 | 128 | 1,704 | 376 | 10,559 | 5,611 | 4,948 | 2,164 | 2,693 | 91 |

a These figures do not correspond to those in Tables 4.1 and 4.2 primarily because the above statistics do not include all of the "Other Areas" covered in the FDIC reports. See Table 2.1 for an explanation of the differences.

b Exclusive of (1) new banks organized to succeed operating banks and (2) reopenings of suspended banks.

c Excludes banks converted to branches and facilities reclassified as branches.

Source: Annual Reports of the Board of Governors of the Federal Reserve System and Federal Reserve Bulletin, May 1948, p. 508. Data for the current year usually appear in the February issue of the Federal Reserve Bulletin.

However, during the past eleven years (1956–1966) 1,116 new state chartered banks were organized, or approximately 100 per year. There was a very noticeable increase in the number of newly organized state banks from 1962 to 1964, following Mr. Saxon's appointment as Comptroller of the Currency and the introduction of his rather liberal chartering philosophy. But, with the shift of the Comptroller's office to a more restrictive policy in 1965 and 1966, it appears that the states have followed suit, for the number of new state chartered banks declined rather abruptly after 1964.

In 1964 a survey was made of state bank supervision by the American Bankers Association. This investigation revealed that approximately four-fifths of the states had some form of statute requiring bank charter applicants to furnish detailed information substantiating the existence of a public need for a bank in a proposed location. In addition, the bank supervisors in several other states requested this information from bank incorporators, despite the fact that it was not specifically required by statute.[112]

A more detailed examination of the wording of state chartering legislation carried out several years before the ABA study revealed that most of the state laws on this point had the same intent and effect as the statute passed in New York after the Panic of 1907, although the terminology was often quite different. Seventeen states used the "public convenience and advantage clause" found in the old New York law; ten states employed the terms "convenience and necessity," "necessity," or the equivalent; and the other state laws contained phrases such as the "public interest," "reasonable public demand," "public necessity, convenience and advantage," and "need of further banking facilities." The acts of five states made no reference to a standard such as those noted above but they did require findings on specific items which covered essentially the same ground as the public convenience and advantage criteria.[113]

[111] In a survey of over 13,000 banks made by the Franklin National Bank, Mineola, New York, in 1963, nearly all of the comments appended to the 2,800 responses noted that "open branching and new bank chartering are leading to a weakening of the nation's banking structure," and the blame for this development was laid at the door of Comptroller James J. Saxon.

[112] American Bankers Association, *State Bank Supervision, Ninth Quinquennial Survey, 1964,* p. 47.

[113] Stokes, "Public Convenience and Advantage in Applications for New Banks," *The Banking Law Journal* (November 1957), p. 924.

These state bank chartering statutes delegated to the supervisory agencies the responsibility for factual determinations concerning applications which required degrees of precision varying from such specific economic indicia of profitable operation as retail sales in the area to such general criteria as "good and sufficient reasons," the "general good," and that the bank is "justified."[114] Notwithstanding these verbal differences, the above-mentioned survey of bank supervisors by the Joint Economic Committee in 1952 revealed that the prospect of profitable operations was the key determinant; and, when this prospect existed, other factors were taken into account, such as public convenience, the quality of management, and the competitive situation. Competition, it should be noted, was used in the dual sense of avoiding too much competition (that is, enough to threaten the profitability of existing institutions) and of introducing some competition where little or none existed. It was apparent from the questionnaire responses that there was a general anxiety to avoid the "overbanked" condition which prevailed in the twenties,[115] which appears to have been the most significant single element affecting state bank chartering philosophy from 1936 to 1966.

*Federal authorities, 1936–1961.* The period from 1936 to 1961 might be characterized as one of relative stability in regard to the chartering of new national banks as well as state banks. In this interval, only a very small number of national bank applications was received each year—this figure declining from an average of about 300 annually from 1911 through 1935 to 50 each year between 1936 and the end of 1961. (See Table 5.1) To some extent this reduction was due to a lack of interest on the part of prospective bank incorporators; but, in the later years of this period (between 1946 and 1961), the large number of rejections (about 40 percent) also must have discouraged many individuals from even submitting an application.[116]

[114] "Bank Charter, Branching, Holding Company and Merger Laws: Competition Frustrated," *The Banking Law Journal* (July 1962), pp. 564–65. In some states there is a banking board which considers charter applications, but Oklahoma has gone a step further and has established a Court of Bank Review to consider disputed decisions of the board. The court's first case is discussed briefly in "Oklahoma Court of Review," *American Banker*, May 12, 1966.

[115] U. S. Congress, Senate, *Monetary Policy and the Management of the Public Debt*, 1952, p. 989.

[116] This argument would seem to draw considerable support from the fact that Comptroller Saxon made it clear that charter applications would be

While the number of charter requests received by supervisory authorities was small relative to the level achieved prior to 1935, it was still substantial in absolute terms, for during the quarter century following the Great Depression 1,955 new banks were organized. (See Table 5.3) Fewer of these institutions were federally chartered than might have been expected, since only 335, or 17 percent, were national banks, which was considerably below the 33 percent ratio of national to total commercial banks at the end of 1935. Thus, it would appear to be fair to assume that the federal standards or the chartering philosophy of the Comptrollers of the Currency, or both, was discouraging entry into the national system. It is not difficult to find numerous reasons why between 1935 and 1960 a bank would have preferred the state to the federal chartering standards (for example, membership in the Federal System was not necessary, the organization and operation requirements were often much more lenient, and so on). But, other than the increase in the rate of rejections after 1945, there is very little information available which would provide some measure of the effect the chartering philosophy of the Comptroller's office may have had upon the choice of a federal as opposed to a state charter in this 25-year period.

The Comptroller of the Currency's *Annual Reports* from 1935 to 1961, unlike those issued several decades earlier, contained almost no discussion of the chartering policies followed by the administrator of national banks. About the only reference to this question found in these publications was a check list of factors which were studied prior to acting upon an application for a new charter which was included in the 1959 report. The items in this list were divided into several subclassifications, including management, ownership, capital, earnings, convenience and needs, and other.[117] The convenience and needs section is of particular interest, for included among the things to be

---

welcomed in the 1960s, for the number of new applications rose from 446 in the 1956–1961 period to 1,273 between 1962 and the end of 1965. (See Table 5.1)

[117] Comptroller of the Currency, 97th *Annual Report*, 1959, pp. 16–17. However, one should be very careful not to place too much stock in such reasons for denying applications, since "the supervisory statement denying a charter may read in terms of needs and convenience, but more often than not, what will have been found lacking is management." Crosse, "Banking Structure and Competition," *Journal of Finance* (May 1965), p. 356.

considered in reviewing an application to establish a new bank was the "location of the proposed bank in relation to . . . the financial needs of the immediate trade areas to be served. (*Is area reasonably well or inadequately served by existing banks and branches?*)" [Emphasis added] From this statement it would appear that at the time a new bank could not be chartered in a community if in the opinion of the Comptroller the existing banks in the area were doing a fairly good job.

There is no information available which provides a detailed analysis of the weight given to factors such as those mentioned above by the Comptroller's office in 1959. Nevertheless, from data published in the early 1950s and 1960s, it would seem reasonable to assume that the "convenience and needs" criteria were extremely important in the evaluation of requests to establish new banks throughout the interval from 1936 to 1961. The 1952 Joint Economic Committee report discussed earlier in the review of state bank chartering, for example, included tabulations of the number of charter, branch, and conversion applications approved and rejected by the Comptroller, and it also noted the reasons requests were denied each year from 1941 to 1950. These data showed that insufficient need was listed as at least one of the reasons for rejection on 104 of 114 of the bank applications disapproved, and 181 of 283 branch requests were not accepted by the Comptroller during this period because of "insufficient need" or "unfavorable future prospects." In addition, the Joint Economic Committee Report revealed that from 1941 to 1950, 13 and 1 percent of the branch applications, respectively, were rejected because of the "priority of another bank's application" or the fact that the office might be "detrimental to another bank."[118] The criteria used at that time were also employed a decade later, for a study by the Comptroller's office revealed 69 of 72 branch application rejections during 1962 were based upon "insufficient need" or "priority of another bank's application."[119]

*Federal authority: the Saxon administration.* On November 16, 1961 James Saxon took office as Comptroller of the Currency.

[118] U. S. Congress, Senate, *Monetary Policy and the Management of the Public Debt*, 1952, pp. 929–31.
[119] Comptroller of the Currency, *Studies in Banking Competition and the Banking Structure*, 1966, p. 107.

Through frequent speeches by the Comptroller[120] and his staff and no doubt a fair amount of "word-of-mouth" advertising by "satisfied customers," the number of requests to establish new banks which were received by the Comptroller's office began to mount rapidly. During 1961, Comptroller Ray M. Gidney's last year in office, there were 97 applications received during the year. In 1962, Comptroller Saxon's first full year as Comptroller, there were 176 requests to establish new banks, and in succeeding years the number increased tremendously, with 490 in 1963 and 468 in 1964. Thus, in three years the Comptroller's office received 1,134 charter applications, which was more than had been submitted in the previous 20 years. (See Table 5.4)

During the 1965 Senate Investigation into Federally Insured Banks Comptroller Saxon was asked by Senator John L. McClellan to explain this phenomenal increase in charter requests. The Comptroller's response as it appears in the record of the hearings was as follows:[121]

MR. SAXON. I think probably a public understanding that the then closed industry image would be removed. . . .

SENATOR MCCLELLAN. In other words, was it due, in your judgment, to a liberalized policy with respect to issuing national bank charters?

MR. SAXON. Yes, sir; that is correct. I think we are overcoming an extreme on the other side.

SENATOR MCCLELLAN. I wanted to get those figures so we could see. You felt that there had been undue restrictions with respect to the issuing of national bank charters and, therefore, you ought to liberalize the policy and let that be known.

MR. SAXON. That is correct.

SENATOR MCCLELLAN. And that, you think, does account for the tremendous increase in the number of applications received?

MR. SAXON. I think this is a fair statement.

[120] James J. Saxon, *The Promise of Free Enterprise,* remarks before the symposium of The Survival of Free Enterprise, May 1, 1963 (p. 6), contains an excellent example of Saxon's promotion of chartering. In this talk he stated: "Decades of excessive controls have created the image of banking as a closed industry—an industry in which reliance upon governmental protection, and constricted scope for initiative have become ingrained. This image can be changed only by allowing the burgeoning forces of private enterprise to enter this industry with greater freedom.

[121] U. S. Congress, Senate, *Investigation into Federally Insured Banks,* Hearings, 1965, p. 93.

TABLE 5.4.   DISPOSITION OF APPLICATIONS FOR NATIONAL BANK CHARTERS
BY QUARTERS, 1962–1966

| Applications Considered | 1962 | 1963 | 1964 | 1965 | 1966 |
|---|---|---|---|---|---|
| 1st quarter: Approved | 18 | 53 | 51 | 10 | 22 |
| Rejected | 3 | 14 | 38 | 47 | 5 |
| 2d quarter: Approved | 31 | 66 | 57 | 16 | 5 |
| Rejected | 5 | 35 | 52 | 60 | 18 |
| 3d quarter: Approved | 35 | 76 | 47 | 13 | 14 |
| Rejected | 1 | 64 | 56 | 9 | 9 |
| 4th quarter: Approved | 48 | 63 | 30 | 13 | 10 |
| Rejected | 8 | 62 | 96 | 6 | 13 |
| Entire year: Approved | 132 | 258 | 185 | 52 | 51 |
| Rejected | 17 | 175 | 242 | 122 | 45 |
| *Applications Received** | | | | | |
| Conversions | 23 | 30 | 30 | 31 | 33 |
| Primary | 153 | 460 | 438 | 108 | 66 |
| Total | 176 | 490 | 468 | 139 | 99 |

* Not all applications are considered in the same year they are received and some
are abandoned.
Source: Motter, "Bank Formation and the Public Interest," National Banking Review (March 1965), p. 306; National Banking Review issues: (June 1965), p. 602; (Sept. 1965) p. 133; (Dec. 1965), p. 282; (Mar. 1966), p. 417; and the Comptroller of the Currency. Table includes state conversions to national charter.

Similar comments by James Saxon can also be found in his testimony in the 1963 House Banking and Currency Committee Meetings with Department and Agency Officials, and Trade Organizations.[122] Comptroller Saxon was not the first administrator of the National Banking System in recent years who felt that the efforts of existing banks to provide the best possible service for their customers would be stimulated considerably by the threat of potential new entrants into the banking industry. Comptroller Ray Gidney, for example, on a number of occasions chartered new institutions in areas where the existing banks did not appear to be meeting the needs of the community.[123] Therefore, the apparent conflict between the chartering philos-

[122] U. S. Congress, House, Meetings with Department and Agency Officials, and Trade Organizations, Hearings, 1963, pp. 135–36.
[123] Klebaner, "Bank Mergers, Business Loans, and the Structure of Banking

ophy of Mr. Saxon and that of many of his predecessors did not stem from a difference in basic objectives. Rather, the divergency may be traced to the methods employed to achieve these goals.

All Comptrollers of the Currency from the late 1930s through 1966 were surely dedicated to the protection of the public interest. However, their interpretations of the "public convenience and need" provisions of the law were not always the same. From the beginning of this period until the Saxon Administration, the Comptrollers could be characterzed in very general terms as primarily concerned with bank failures; hence, entry was very limited. On the other hand, Comptroller Saxon felt that this approach to chartering was proper for a public utility, but the banking industry, despite its extensive regulation, was not a utility.[124] Therefore, existing banks enjoyed no private right to be protected against competition;[125] and, although he did not advocate free entry,[126] Saxon suggested that the severe restrictions upon the formation of new banks which had existed in the past should be relaxed.

Under no Comptroller in this period could entry be described as completely closed or completely free. The differences among them involved relative freedom. Mr. Saxon, in contrast to his recent predecessors, placed somewhat greater emphasis upon bank competition than upon bank preservation. Nevertheless, he, like the other Comptrollers, retained a basic fear of "over-banking" both in the sense of causing a sizable increase in bank failures and preserving the opportunities for new banks to grow to efficient size.[127] And, even under his administration, after a brief flurry of chartering activity, entry remained far below free banking standards.

---

Markets," *The American Journal of Economics and Sociology* (October 1963), p. 502.

[124] See for example, James J. Saxon, Remarks at the 68th Annual Convention of the Kentucky Bankers Association, October 22, 1962, pp. 2–4. (mimeographed)

[125] Comptroller of the Currency, *Studies in Banking Competition and the Banking Structure*, 1966, p. 403.

[126] Naturally, there are numerous restrictions upon entry (such as capital, location, existence of "brand" products, and others), but this refers to freedom from discretionary authority on the part of government officials in the granting of a charter.

[127] Comptroller of the Currency, *Studies in Banking Competition and the Banking Structure*, 1966, p. 403.

Saxon noted the public authorities had been sluggish in their response to emerging requirements, and artificial shortages of needed banking services had appeared as a result of postwar changes in the size and location of population and industry.[128] Thus, when he took office new charter applications were encouraged not only by the comments of the Comptroller but by a rejection rate of approximately 11 percent, the lowest in four decades. (See Tables 5.1 and 5.4) But this liberal chartering policy did not continue very long, for by the fourth quarter of 1962 the rate of denials had begun to rise, and by the last half of 1963 nearly one-half of all charter applications were being rejected.

The Comptroller noted in "A Statement of Policy" in his 1964 *Annual Report* that "a temporary halt may occasionally be required in the chartering of new banks in some markets" to sustain the viability of the banking system. Apparently this situation had arisen in the District of Columbia, in Florida, and in California during 1963, for by November of that year either a complete ban or near-moratorium on new national banks had been put into effect in these areas. In addition, Saxon reported that similar action in Texas and in Westchester and Nassau Counties in New York was being considered.[129] But despite the Comptroller's more restrictive approach to chartering in some sections of the country, in 1963 the number of new national banks exceeded the number of new state banks for the first time in many decades.

The rate of rejections of charter requests for 1963 climbed to 40 percent from the 11 percent level of 1962, and it reached nearly 60 percent in 1964. Late in February 1965 the Comptroller announced that the District of Columbia and selected areas of 13 states had been closed to new entry of national banks,[130] and during the first half of

[128] *Ibid.*

[129] "Saxon Declares Near-Moratorium," *American Banker*, November 19, 1963.

[130] *California:* Los Angeles, Oakland, San Francisco and San Diego metropolitan areas, Orange County, "and a number of other areas in the state which are patently well banked at this time"; *Colorado:* Denver metropolitan area; *Connecticut:* All major banking markets; *Florida:* Dade, Broward, and Orange counties; *Hawaii:* Honolulu; *Illinois:* Chicago metropolitan area; *Maryland:* Montgomery and Prince Georges counties and the Baltimore metropolitan area; *Minnesota:* Minneapolis and St. Paul metropolitan areas; *New Jersey:* All major banking markets; *New York:* Long Island; *Oklahoma:* Oklahoma City

that year the rate of denials of new bank charter applications advanced to 80 percent, which on an annual basis would have been the highest by far in the 55 years for which data were compiled for this book. Only the very small number of applications considered and the very large proportion of them which involved conversions of state banks (nearly 40 percent), which are rarely denied, reduced the rate of application rejections to 70 percent for the entire year 1965.[131] In 1966 only 96 applications were considered as opposed to 174 in the previous year, and slightly over 50 percent were approved. But, once again, this figure includes a large number of conversions (23 of the 51 approvals) and primary application rejections remained at a very high level.

Thus, only a few years after Saxon became Comptroller and established a policy which permitted new firms to enter the banking industry at a rate not experienced since the free banking era of the first quarter of this century, entry appeared to be even more difficult than it was before he took office. However, this does not take into account the fact that *de novo* branches of both state and national banks continued to be approved at a record pace. (See Table 5.3) And, even more important, no statistic could adequately reflect the new attitudes toward bank expansion (and bank regulation in general) which had emerged since Comptroller Saxon was appointed in 1961.

In a press conference held a few weeks before Comptroller Saxon took office, Secretary of the Treasury Douglas Dillon emphasized the importance of the independence of the Comptroller of the Currency, and indicated that what Mr. Saxon would do as Comptroller, in Mr. Dillon's words, "was his responsibility and not mine."[132] How independently Mr. Saxon was to act and the controversy his decisions were to create no doubt few people could have predicted. Some of his

---

and Tulsa metropolitan areas; *Texas:* Austin, Dallas, Fort Worth, Houston, Lubbock, and San Antonio metropolitan areas; *Virginia:* Arlington and Fairfax counties, Alexandria, and the Norfolk, Richmond, and Roanoke metropolitan areas. Listed in *The Wall Street Journal,* February 23, 1965, p. 3.

[131] In terms of national charters actually granted, 25 of 190 in 1963, 27 of 203 in 1964, and 25 of 103 in 1965 involved conversions of state banks.

[132] "Independence of Saxon," *American Banker,* October 19, 1961.

policies were condemned by resolutions of the Independent Bankers Association (IBA),[133] and he was both praised and criticized by the National Association of Supervisors of State Banks (NASSB). The Executive Vice President of the NASSB, Hollis Burt, quite aptly described Saxon's term in office when he remarked:[134]

We are witnessing an extraordinary performance by the leader of the national banking system who in his zeal to get national banks moving, has gone slightly overboard in his disregard for state laws. Let's keep the record straight—he has done much which needed doing for years. But at the same time, he has bent and stretched some laws to the point that they are hardly recognizable. And, while this could be debated endlessly, the result has been an opening of the gates of opportunity for national banks as we have not seen before and they are surging ahead. Soundly? This is a good question that only time will tell.

But, while the long run implications of Comptroller Saxon's actions remain in doubt, he accomplished much during his five years in office from 1961 to 1966. To paraphrase the observations in an editorial in *The New York Times* published the day he was to testify in the Conflict of State and Federal Law hearings: Saxon may have been overzealous in his campaign and too sweeping in some of his proposals, but the shaking up he gave the banking industry was the best thing that could have happened to it.[135]

SUSPENSIONS, 1934–1966

*1934–1944.* During the period of adjustment following the Great Depression, the number of banks which were required to close because of financial difficulties remained relatively large, although far below the figure for the early 1930s. From 1934 through 1944, nearly

---

[133] "Resolutions," *The Independent Banker* (May 1963), p. 9. The 1963 House Hearings on *Conflict of Federal and State Banking Laws* were held to investigate "certain rulings and interpretations of law" by Mr. Saxon, probably as a result of a resolution of the IBA. See p. 1 of the hearings.

[134] Hollis W. Burt, "The Handwriting on the Wall," Speech before the Graduating Class of the Virginia-Maryland Bankers School, August 26, 1965, p. 4. (mimeographed)

[135] *Bank Stock Quarterly*, M. A. Schapiro & Co., June 1963, (p. 16) contains excerpts from this article. William B. Camp became Acting Comptroller in November 1966 and Comptroller of the Currency on February 1, 1967.

500 commercial banks with deposits of over 500 million dollars suspended operations,[136] which accounted for approximately three-fifths of the deposits and five-sixths of the number of banks that have failed since the early thirties. (See Table 5.5) In the majority of the cases prior to the end of World War II, the problems of these banks could be traced to poor asset condition and a consequent lack of capital. This weakness, in turn, was brought about by several factors, including mismanagement, deteriorating local economic conditions, and an inability to restore financial positions which had been seriously impaired during the 1930–1933 depression years.[137]

Under the temporary deposit insurance fund (January 1, 1934 to August 22, 1935) many banks in this relatively poor condition were admitted to insurance although they had only a negligible capital cushion. Fortunately, a large number were able to strengthen their financial position as the economic situation in the country improved, but many others could not. As a result, during the 1937–1938 recession, nearly 150 insured commercial banks with deposits of 93 million dollars failed, and in 1939–1940 an additional 102 insured commercial banks with 300 million dollars of deposits met a similar fate.

In 1941 and 1942 there was also a substantial number of failures; however, this was to be the last occasion in this thirty-three year span when more than ten suspensions would occur in a single calendar year. Furthermore, the era of the "classic" bank failure resulting from a depression or recession had virtually come to a close, for the suspensions during the next two decades were to be determined almost completely by internal thievery rather than external economic conditions.

*The postwar period, 1945–1966.* From 1945 through 1966, over 100 commercial banks were closed in the United States because of financial difficulties. About two-thirds were insured by the FDIC. Of the noninsured institutions, approximately one-half were unincorpo-

---

[136] To avoid repetition of the term "closed because of financial difficulties," the expressions "failed" and "suspended operation" will be used interchangeably with it, although there are technical differences between them.

[137] FDIC, *Annual Report*, 1958, pp. 28–29. The discussion of the 1935–1945 period is drawn primarily from this report.

TABLE 5.5.  NUMBER OF COMMERCIAL BANKS CLOSED BECAUSE OF FINANCIAL DIFFICULTIES, 1934-1966

| Year | Total | Non-Insured | Insured | Year | Total | Non-Insured | Insured | Year | Total | Non-Insured | Insured |
|---|---|---|---|---|---|---|---|---|---|---|---|
| 1934 | 61 | 52 | 9 | 1945 | 1 | – | 1 | 1956 | 3 | 1 | 2 |
| 1935 | 32 | 6 | 26 | 1946 | 2 | 1 | 1 | 1957 | 3 | 1 | 2 |
| 1936 | 72 | 3 | 69 | 1947 | 6 | 1 | 5 | 1958 | 9 | 5 | 4 |
| 1937 | 83 | 7 | 76 | 1948 | 3 | – | 3 | 1959 | 3 | – | 3 |
| 1938 | 79 | 7 | 72 | 1949 | 9 | 4 | 5 | 1960 | 2 | 1 | 1 |
| 1939 | 71 | 12 | 59 | 1950 | 5 | 1 | 4 | 1961 | 9 | 4 | 5 |
| 1940 | 48 | 5 | 43 | 1951 | 5 | 3 | 2 | 1962 | 3 | 2 | 1 |
| 1941 | 16 | 2 | 14 | 1952 | 4 | 1 | 3 | 1963 | 2 | – | 2 |
| 1942 | 23 | 3 | 20 | 1953 | 5 | 1 | 4 | 1964 | 8 | 1 | 7 |
| 1943 | 5 | – | 5 | 1954 | 4 | 2 | 2 | 1965 | 9 | 4 | 5 |
| 1944 | 2 | – | 2 | 1955 | 5 | – | 5 | 1966 | 8 | 1 | 7 |
| _Totals_ | | | | _Totals_ | | | | _Totals_ | | | |
| _Number and Deposits ($million)_ | | | | _Number and Deposits ($million)_ | | | | _Number and Deposits ($million)_ | | | |
| 1934–1944 | 492 | 97 | 395 | 1945–1955 | 49 | 14 | 35 | 1956–1966 | 59 | 20 | 39 |
| 1934–1944 | $525 | $41 | $484 | 1945–1955 | $108 | $8 | $100 | 1956–1966 | $258 | $12 | $246 |

_Source:_ Federal Deposit Insurance Corporation (FDIC) and FDIC, _Annual Report_, 1964, pp. 222–23. For detailed information regarding specific failures, see FDIC, _Annual Report_, 1963, pp. 36–41; 1958, pp. 48–83, 98–127; and 1959–1962 for tables regarding insurance disbursements.

rated private banks which were frequently operating with no supervision nor examination by a bank supervisory agency.[138]

It is very difficult to pinpoint the single problem in a financial institution which contributed most to its failure.[139] Nevertheless, the circumstances preceding the development of financial difficulties in each of the commercial banks which required disbursements by the FDIC from 1946 through 1965 inclusive were analyzed to determine if any general pattern in them could be noted. The findings, as would have been expected, clearly indicated the vast change which has occurred in the underlying causes of the 61 bank suspensions in the postwar period as compared with those in earlier decades.

In contrast to the 1920s and 1930s, when local financial conditions and poor management were leading causes of bank failure, from 1945 through 1965 over two-thirds (41) of the suspensions studied resulted from defalcation. And irresponsible management, usually resulting from a change in control of a bank, added 15 more failures in this interval. In three instances since 1945 poor (but not necessarily "irresponsible") practices and/or kiting involving relatively large sums were apparent at the time of the failure. In only 2 cases, both before 1955, was failure clearly associated with weak local economic conditions.

During the first decade after World War II (1946–1955), the factors contributing to the suspensions might be described as primarily internal—the failure not being preceded by a change in control of the bank in question. However, since 1955 new ownership of a bank (or what might be termed external factors) has become more and more important. This may be noted from the following summary of the findings in the analysis of the circumstances preceding financial difficulties in the 61 insured banks requiring FDIC disbursements from 1945 to 1965:[140]

[138] FDIC, *Annual Report,* 1963, p. 27.

[139] The number of banks is too small to carry out any meaningful analysis of failures by type of bank structure in a state.

[140] This writer is indebted to the staff of the FDIC who supplied the underlying data for this analysis of factors contributing to bank failures. In this discussion the total number of banks differs slightly from the total in Table 5.5 because some of the banks included in the table required no FDIC disbursements.

| Circumstance | 1946 to 1950 | 1951 to 1955 | 1956 to 1960 | 1961 to 1965 | 1946 to 1965 |
|---|---|---|---|---|---|
| Defalcation but not preceded by change in control | 15 | 9 | 6 | 7 | 37 |
| Defalcation preceded by change in control | 0 | 1 | 3 | 0 | 4 |
| Change in control but no defalcation occurred | 0 | 2 | 2 | 7 | 11 |
| Irresponsible management but no change in control | 0 | 0 | 0 | 4 | 4 |
| Other | 2 | 2 | 0 | 1 | 5 |
| | 17 | 14 | 11 | 19 | 61 |

Some of the factors contributing to bank suspensions were described by Joseph W. Barr, former Chairman of the FDIC, in his testimony during the Investigation into Federally Insured Banks. He reported that there were three elements which were nearly always present in these failures in the 1960s:[141]

First of all, dishonest activities; second, acquisition [of] bad assets financed by high-cost funds not received in the usual course of business and carried as certificates of deposit; and third, sudden unsavory shifts in bank control which preceded the failure.

The Federal Reserve Bank of Richmond *Monthly Review* was even more succinct in its appraisal of the most recent suspensions, for it reported that virtually all of these failures had a single characteristic in common: they were the result of efforts on the part of one or more individuals to use the assets or in some cases the money-raising potential of commercial banks for personal gain.[142] The insolvency of

[141] U. S. Congress, Senate, *Investigation into Federally Insured Banks,* Hearings, 1965, p. 141. The circumstances surrounding many of the recent suspensions is spelled out in considerable detail in *ibid.,* Parts 1–4, and in U. S. Congress, Senate, *Investigation into Federally Insured Banks,* Report No. 1103, 1966.

[142] "Recent Bank Failures—Why," Federal Reserve Bank of Richmond, *Monthly Review* (September 1965), p. 4. K. A. Randall of the FDIC in discussing the eight failures from late 1962 through the fall of 1964 said all of "the banks were looted by promoters through evasions of the law." "Failed Banks Raided," *American Banker,* October 22, 1964. In 1963 hearings were held by the House, Government Operations Committee on *Crimes Against Banking Institutions* and a report was issued (House Report No. 1147, 1964)

the 93 million dollar Public Bank of Detroit in the fall of 1966 may have been an exception to this rule; but even this failure, one of the largest which has ever occurred in this country, appears to have resulted from poor lending policy, not from poor economic conditions.[143]

Probably the most significant of the postwar failures were the fourteen banks which closed because of financial difficulties in a two-year period from 1963 through early 1965. The suspension of these institutions stimulated an interest in bank failures, which had been dormant for three decades, on the part of the legislators, the press, and the general public. Lengthy hearings were held by both Houses of Congress concerning bank and banking agency operations, and an act was passed in September 1964 requiring notice of change in control of the management of insured banks.[144] In addition, as was mentioned in Chapter 3, the Financial Institutions Supervisory Act became law in October 1966, giving the regulatory agencies broad new powers to curb unsafe and unsound practices by both banks and savings and loan associations.[145]

---

which contains some interesting discussion of both internal and external crimes against banks.

[143] "FDIC Kept Watch," *American Banker,* November 3, 1966. Only five of the banks which suspended between 1921 and 1936 had loans and investments of over 100 million dollars. ["Bank suspensions," 1921–1936, *Federal Reserve Bulletin* (September 1937), p. 1218.] Public Bank appears to be the largest failure since that time.

[144] Public Law 88–593 (September 12, 1964); 78 Stat. 940, 941 (1964). This legislation requires prompt disclosure by the chief executive officer of any insured bank of any change in control of the bank or of any loan or loans secured by 25 percent or more of the voting shares of any insured bank. There are exceptions to this rule, including a borrower who has been an owner of record for one year or transactions involving stock of a newly organized bank before it is opened. This legislation is reviewed briefly in Chapter 3.

[145] 80 Stat. 1028 (1966). This legislation, as it applies to commercial banks, permits the "appropriate federal banking agency," if it feels an insured bank is about to engage in unsafe or unsound practices or is already so engaged, to order a hearing to determine if a cease and desist order should be issued. If the questionable action by the bank may threaten its solvency or otherwise seriously prejudice the interest of depositors, a temporary cease and desist order may be issued by the agency. Other provisions provide judicial review of the order; removal of a director or officer (they may also be suspended or prohibited from further participating in the conduct of the affairs of the bank); and other controls.

*Effect upon bank chartering.*   Surprisingly, the relatively few commercial banks which closed because of financial difficulty in recent years may have had a substantial impact upon the chartering of new banks at both the state and federal levels. Earlier it was noted that the increasing rate of charter application rejections by the Comptroller appeared to discourage many individuals who otherwise would have been interested in establishing new banks, and his stricter standards seemed to result in a less lenient attitude toward charter applications on the part of state officials. At least some of this change in philosophy and decline in charter requests must also be credited to the bank failures early in 1965, for published statements of banking officials suggest that these suspensions resulted not only in a slowdown in charter applications but also in greater reluctance on the part of some bank supervisors to approve those requests that were submitted.

The aversion of banking agency officials to granting new bank charters following the failures in 1963 through 1965 is understandable, for they were subjected to a greal deal of criticism because of the relative ease with which charters were obtained in this period. Some of the strongest attacks came from the members of the Senate Committee on Government Operations which conducted the Investigation into Federally Insured Banks early in 1965. The Committee was greatly disturbed by what it considered to be "inadequate investigation of the honesty, integrity, and financial ability and reputation of the owners and officials of newly chartered banks," and its report issued in April 1966 voiced particular concern regarding the chartering activities of the Comptroller of the Currency. Mr. Saxon was reproached because his liberalized chartering policy supposedly had attracted applicants for national bank charters who were "persons of highly questionable character and who [lacked] adequate financial resources and responsibility for conducting legitimate banking ventures."[146]

While the Comptroller defended his actions most effectively before the Committee and in subsequent exchanges in the press, there can be little doubt that these attacks have made his office more cautious in granting charter requests. Moreover, the controversy which developed regarding national bank charters and the extensive publicity given to

[146] U. S. Congress, Senate, *Investigation into Federally Insured Banks*, Report No. 1103, 1966, pp. 3–4.

the bank failures during the last few years has definitely made some state officials much more cautious in approving charter applications. Thus, as has happened so often in the past, an increasing number of bank failures apparently has inspired a growing public concern about bank suspensions,[147] which in turn has led to more limited entry into this industry.[148] Ironically, in the current situation the classic over-banking arguments have little relevance, for failures have been few and the primary cause of the suspensions has been weakness of character rather than weakness in the economy. Yet, this handful of suspensions appears to have at least temporarily removed the modest threat of freer entry into this industry which existed for a brief span in the early 1960s.

*Condition of entry.* Economists often discuss the condition of entry in an industry, which in very general terms means the advantages that established firms have over the potential entrant in cost or price.[149] In effect "it is a measure of the height of barriers to new competition in the industry" and "the degree of threat of new competition as a force potentially regulating the conduct and performance of sellers who are already producing in the industry."[150] The barriers to entry appear to take three forms in the "unregulated" industries: namely, advantages related to product differentiation and buyer preference; advantages enjoyed because of absolute superiority of existing firms (for example, lower costs at any level of production); and advantages gained through the existence of economies of scale in an industry. However, in addition to the above possible barriers to entry, banking has one other often insurmountable obstacle which the potential entrant must overcome—the bank supervisor's discretionary authority (convenience and need test) in granting charter applications. This aspect of entry is examined in the closing pages of this chapter.[151]

[147] For example, it affected the sale of new bank stock in some areas, and incorporators were forced to withdraw their applications. See "Slowdown in New Bank Charters," *American Banker,* November 30, 1965.

[148] This does not mean to imply that under such circumstances this is not the logical thing for an elected official or political appointee to do.

[149] Bain, *Industrial Organization,* p. 33.

[150] *Ibid.,* p. 237.

[151] Free entry in the sense the term is sometimes employed in economic theory, with firms able to enter and produce a homogeneous good at the same

*Is banking really different?* The New York free banking act of 1838, reflecting the antipathy toward the monopolistic practice of special chartering, apparently gave the administrative authorities no power to prevent the formation of a bank, even though they felt that its organization was not needed and could not be justified on economic grounds.[152] How different the views were a century later can be noted from a comment in Adolf Berle's classic article on "Banking under the Antitrust Laws:"[153]

Operations in deposit banking not only affect the commercial field, but also determine in great measure the supply of credit, the volume of money, the value of the dollar, and even, perhaps, the stability of the currency system. Within this area considerations differing from and far more powerful than mere preservation of competition may be operating under direct sanction of law. It is the theory, in ordinary commercial fields, that competition is the desirable check on price levels, the process by which the efficient are rewarded by survival, and the inefficient eliminated by failure. The price of business failures is not regarded as too high for the community to pay in view of advantages to consumers, stimulus towards greater efficiency, and freedom of enterprise. But it is doubtful (to say the least) whether any such assumption is indulged in respect to deposit banks; certainly the theory is not there accepted to the full extent of its logic. A bank failure is a community disaster, however, wherever, and whenever it occurs. While competition may be desirable up to a point in deposit banking, there is a clear bottom limit to its desirability.

The president of the National Association of Supervisors of State Banks, Charles R. Howell, testified in the 1965 Bank Merger Act hearings that banks have never been treated as ordinary business corporations by the states or by the federal government, for these authorities have recognized "that certain industries are so charged

---

cost as existing firms, clearly does not exist in most banking markets, for product differentiation is usually present as is some variation of costs even if one ignores the fact that new charters are granted only sparingly. For an excellent discussion of the question of entry in banking (which does not necessarily agree with all the statements above) see Alhadeff, *Monopoly and Competition in Banking,* Chapter 11.

[152] Stokes, "Public Convenience and Advantage in Applications for New Banks and Branches," *The Banking Law Journal* (November 1957), pp. 922–23, n. 4.

[153] Berle, "Banking under the Antitrust Laws," 49 *Columbia Law Review* 589, 592 (1949).

with the public interest that their success or failure cannot be left entirely to the principles of competitive survival."[154]

It is argued that "the failure of a construction firm or grocery store, while regretable, does not necessarily damage the economic fiber of a community."[155] On the other hand, a bank suspension is presumed to be much more likely to have this undesirable effect. Therefore, since it is assumed that after some point is reached in establishing banks in a market there is a positive correlation between the number of additional banks formed and bank failures, the "needs" test is applied before a charter is granted.

But what constitutes sufficient need? In many cases this standard is met only if demand is adequate to support comfortably the existing banks plus a new bank.[156] Thus, the sort of gentleman's competition (you compete but not so much that the other fellow gets hurt) which has developed in many banking markets should not be surprising to investigators, for it is instilled in these institutions at "birth." Moreover, the friendly competitor approach is encouraged by supervisory authorities who often hold that bank failures are so disastrous that they should at all costs be held at an absolute minimum.

Such comments as those made by state bank supervisors before the Joint Economic Committee in 1952 typify the thinking of individuals who support the restricted entry philosophy. For example, the Oregon supervisor stated: "I do not believe that . . . I should approve a second bank . . . where it seems evident that the existing bank would be weakened by the loss of a portion of the existing business." The California superintendent remarked: "competition is not a reasonable public necessity in banking." And the Connecticut commissioner observed: "sound and ethical competition is . . . a healthy thing but, of course, not to the extent of hazard to existing independent banking institutions."[157]

As a result of the type of thinking regarding bank entry which has

[154] U. S. Congress, Senate, *Amend the Bank Merger Act* of 1960, Hearings on S. 1698, 1965, p. 199. The president of the ABA testified in a similar vein, see *ibid.,* p. 63.

[155] *Ibid.,* p. 199.

[156] Horvitz, "Stimulating Bank Competition through Regulatory Action," *Journal of Finance* (March 1965), p. 2.

[157] Quoted in *ibid.* See Chapter 6 of the present study for additional discussion of this question.

prevailed in this industry, many bankers have reached the point where they believe their institutions have a private right to be protected against competition.[158] But, if this right exists, how is the public interest to be protected with even the limited threat of potential entry by a new competitor removed? It is sometimes suggested that the unusual amount of governmental supervision to which the banks are subjected makes them somewhat different from firms in less regulated industries; therefore, the public interest will be served despite the elimination of potential competitors. However, banks are not public utilities; and, if a bank desires the same protection from competition usually enjoyed by a utility, it would seem reasonable to require that banks also accept controls similar to those found in the regulated industries[159] (including the fixing of charges for banking services by the authorities). Naturally, this would not be acceptable to the banking community, and in a "free enterprise society" where public controls are supposedly to be held to a minimum, this added regulation would not seem to be warranted.

While bank entry should not be closed as with a public utility, most observers would probably concede that it also cannot be as free as in the "unregulated industries." This point of view draws considerable support from the fiduciary nature of banks, the role of banking in the nation's monetary mechanism, and the desirability of maintaining public confidence in banking institutions.[160] Thus, as one might expect, a compromise between completely closed and completely free entry has quite naturally evolved in the banking industry.[161]

---

[158] James J. Saxon, *The Promise of Free Enterprise,* Speech before the Symposium on the Survival of Free Enterprise, May 1, 1963, pp. 4–5.

[159] Regulated industries is used here in the technical sense usually employed by the courts in antitrust cases. See Chapter 7 in the discussion "Banking as a Regulated Industry."

[160] Numerous other arguments could also be presented. Nevertheless, this writer is far from convinced that the impact of a bank failure upon a community is much more of a disaster than the closing of the one industry in a town. Moreover, there is often an alternative to failure—merger in the same community with another bank which would often not be the case if another type of firm was involved. In addition, of course, deposit insurance may soften the blow.

[161] See Donald Jacobs' interesting discussion of this question in "The Framework of Commercial Bank Regulation: An Appraisal," *The National Banking Review* (March 1964), pp. 343–52.

*Time for a reconsideration of bank entry.*[162] The present procedures which permit banking agencies to determine whether or not additional firms should enter this field have considerable merit. Nevertheless, it would seem that a review of the standards employed by the bank supervisors is long overdue. With the exception of a limited period during the first few years of James Saxon's administration as Comptroller of the Currency, the dominant element in the consideration of requests to establish new banks was the impression that in the absence of entry barriers, "over-banking" and bank failures would be widespread. However, this outcome is far from certain; and, while it is unlikely that even the most stanch advocate of free enterprise would support the removal of all bank entry restrictions if this meant failures would occur on a grand scale,[163] many people would agree that there are occasions when some additional failures may in fact be desirable.[164]

In his book *Industrial Organization,* Professor Bain notes: "There is a maximum likelihood of monopolistic output restriction and excess profits in highly concentrated oligopolies with blockaded entry. . . ." [165] While Bain does not deal with financial institutions in this work, the market situation mentioned in many ways quite aptly describes commercial banking in most communities. Furthermore, there is very little possibility that this condition will change barring a vast expansion of branch banking, and this seems highly unlikely.[166]

[162] A person interested in this question should read Alhadeff's article "A Reconsideration of Restrictions on Bank Entry," *The Quarterly Journal of Economics* (May 1962), pp. 246–63.

[163] See *ibid.,* pp. 260–63; and Jacobs, "The Framework of Commercial Bank Regulation: An Appraisal," *The National Banking Review* (March 1964), p. 351.

[164] Horvitz in his study "Stimulating Bank Competition through Regulatory Action" [*Journal of Finance* (March 1965), p. 3] observed: "Obviously bank failures are not desirable, but failures may be symptomatic of vigorous competition, and vigorous competition *is* desirable."

[165] Bain, *Industrial Organization,* p. 35. Bain in his *Barriers to New Competition* on page 216 notes: "Perhaps the most surprising finding of our study . . . is that the most important barrier to entry discovered by detailed study is probably product differentiation." This condition is also present in banking markets.

[166] This discussion relates only to the entry of a number of new competitors into the thousands of communities now served by only one or two banks; in states or trade areas this might lead to greater not less concentration of banking resources.

It might be argued that a strong antitrust policy is the answer, for this will tend to maintain the number of firms at least at their present level and minimize collusive action. But this may do little to ensure an economically satisfactory operation by the banks in question. The regulatory authorities might stimulate some institutions to provide better service, but the greatest safeguard to excellent bank performance (assuming in this economy an effective but minimum amount of regulation is desired) remains the threat of entry of a new institution.[167]

Deane Carson and Paul Cootner in their excellent "The Structure of Competition of Commercial Banking in the United States" concluded: [168]

The parsimony with which chartering authorities now approach the creation of new banks is a direct consequence of the experience with free banking and lax chartering in the nineteenth and early twentieth centuries. The resulting fiasco, generated by overbanked communities in many sections of the country, provided a lesson to regulatory authorities which has not been forgotten by their successors.

But the small number and type of bank failures which have occurred since 1936; the relative ease with which the Federal Reserve could provide funds to commercial banks if needed, unlike the 1920s and early 1930s; the changed structure of American banking with thousands of weak banks eliminated; the existence of deposit insurance which should discourage runs on banks and minimize any loss to depositors; and the enlarged role of government in maintaining economic stability should call for at least some change in the protectionist view which has dominated bank entry for decades. However, it should be emphasized that this is not a plea for free banking but only for a reduction of the weight given to survival criteria by the supervisory agencies in considering charter applications.[169]

Several years ago the Franklin National Bank of Long Island canvassed thousands of commercial bankers across the nation to learn their views on bank entry. For nearly two years prior to the time the

[167] Phillips, "Competition, Confusion and Commercial Banking," *The Journal of Finance* (March 1964), p. 44.

[168] In *Private Financial Institutions*, p. 132.

[169] See *ibid.*, p. 134; and George W. Mitchell's, "Mergers Among Commercial Banks" in Phillips, ed., *Perspectives on Antitrust Policy*.

survey was conducted, there was relative ease both in approving *de novo* branches and granting charters, and the effect this had upon the thinking of the respondents was very apparent in the replies, for[170]

over and over again [they] warned that the proliferation of new banks and branches would result in a wave of bank failures similar to the 1920s and 1930s caused by over-banking, cut price competition to obtain accounts, and the destruction of good sound banking.

These survey results could have been predicted, for inevitably, when bankers at large are questioned regarding bank structure, the collapse of banking in the past or the danger of a "money monopoly"—a handful of giant, nationwide branch banks—is raised to counter the threat of even a modest relaxation of entry restrictions.

This is not to criticize the respondents, for they quite logically have a local view of a national economic question. Certainly, few firms welcome another competitor into "their" market (unless they are threatened with antitrust prosecution), and it is reasonable for them to present any seemingly legitimate defense available to forestall the entry of a new firm. However, the banking supervisor must go beyond a given community in reaching his decision, deciding in favor of the local interest only if it and the public interest coincide.

The banking agency should base its decisions upon reasonable probabilities, and judge arguments in the light of conditions in the American economy in the second half of the twentieth century, learning from the past but not hamstrung by it. If this were done, at most it would call for a change in the agency's emphasis in using its discretionary powers, not the elimination of them. As a result, a greater emphasis would be given to the managerial element, and no doubt somewhat less to the "convenience and needs" factor. This would bring bank entry a little closer to entry in the "unregulated industries," with the wisdom of a bank's incorporators (who are risking their capital) given greater consideration.

In this way a promising bank management and an adequately capitalized institution would not find entry foreclosed because it made the competitive situation less comfortable for existing firms. On the other hand, since bank capital and managerial talent are both in relatively short supply, this would not mean a vast increase in bank

[170] *News from Franklin National Bank,* release, September 26, 1963, p. 2.

charters, and it should result in better banking service for the general public and a more efficient banking system for the nation.[171]

[171] The above analysis has given little attention to the question of entry via branching. As a general rule it may be stated that the same principles of public convenience and advantage apply to an application for a branch as to a request to establish a bank. [See Stokes, "Public Convenience and Advantage in Applications for New Banks and Branches," *The Banking Law Journal* (November 1957), pp. 926–27.] However, questions of "home office protection" and in some states even branch office protection often apply. Entry by branching is considered in Motter and Carson, "Bank Entry and the Public Interest: A Case Study," *National Banking Review* (June 1964); Horvitz, "Stimulating Bank Competition through Regulatory Action," *The Journal of Finance* (March 1965); Jacobs, "The Framework of Commercial Bank Regulation," *National Banking Review* (March 1964).

CHAPTER 6

————◄◆►————

# Commercial Banking and the Federal Antitrust Laws: Interbank Cooperation

## INTRODUCTION

"THE ANTITRUST LAWS of the United States of America are unique in scope of content and rigour of enforcement," [1] commented a British scholar in a recent publication. There can be little doubt that this observation is correct, despite the fact that many other nations have enacted at least some form of antitrust statute, [2] and new laws or efforts to strengthen existing laws are occasionally reported in the foreign press. [3] In England, for example, despite its recent antitrust legislation and the courts' apparent expansion of common-law doctrine to cover new forms of restraint of trade, there is still much less

[1] Neale, *The Antitrust Laws of the United States of America*, p. 1.

[2] See Iinkai, *Antitrust Legislation of the World as of 1960*. For a comparative study of the antitrust laws and international antitrust cases, respectively, see U. S. Congress, Senate, *Foreign Trade and the Antitrust Laws*, Part 2, 1965; and——, Senate, *International Aspects of Antitrust*, Part 2, 1967.

[3] See, for example, "Will Mergers Pass Scrutiny," *The Economist* (England), March 6, 1965; and "How New Combines Law May Affect 'Little Guys,'" *The Financial Post* (Canada), February 6, 1965. Also see Rostow, "British and American Experience with Legislation Against Restraints of Competition," 23 *Modern Law Review* 477 (1960).

emphasis upon regulation to promote competition for its own sake than is found in this country; and in Germany the 1957 Law Against Restraints of Competition, as amended in 1965, distinguishes between "good" cartels and "bad" cartels—a practice which the antitrust advocate in this country would undoubtedly find repugnant.[4] However, these differences between trade regulation in the United States and abroad should be expected, for in America the concept of "antitrust" is much more than a body of law—it is, as Mr. Justice Fortas of the U. S. Supreme Court observed, "a remarkable compound of law, economic philosophy, cultural commitment, and social religion."

Since the interpretation of the wording in the antitrust statutes may vary substantially depending upon an individual's (or a nation's) social and economic ideology, it is possible for different courts or the same court at different times to reach completely opposite conclusions in cases which involve essentially the same set of facts.[5] This may be traced in part at least to the flexibility in the antitrust law, which many feel is a virtue of this legislation. Attorney General Katzenbach has stated: "One of the great strengths of the antitrust laws, like the Constitution, is that they are broad statements, adaptable to changing conditions. And conditions—both with respect to business activity and court decisions—are changing with both considerable force and considerable speed."[6] Certainly there are few industries whose experience with the antitrust laws provides a better illustration of the type of change described by the Attorney General than commercial banking, but many leading bankers would probably be reluctant to concede that there was much virtue in this particular development.

IMMUNITY FROM ANTITRUST PROSECUTION

Until recent years it was quite generally assumed that the Clayton Act and perhaps even the Sherman Act did not apply to commercial

---

[4] "Petrol Solus Agreements: British Common Law of Restraint of Trade in A New Context," 52 *Virginia Law Review* 690 (1966); and *BNA's Antitrust and Trade Regulation Reports,* October 4, 1966, B-1.

[5] The author recognizes that the wording of these laws may not be atypical, but the importance of the social and economic questions which are raised by them surely sets these statutes apart from much of our other legislation.

[6] Remarks by Attorney General Nicholas deB. Katzenbach, prepared for delivery before the Business Council, May 8, 1965. (mimeographed) It should be emphasized that he referred to "conditions," not to "ideology."

banks. The arguments presented in support of this position typically took one of two forms: either commercial banking was not subject to antitrust prosecution because the business of banking was not commerce; or, banking was regulated by specific statutes passed by the Congress, and it was therefore exempted from the application of the antitrust laws.

Since the federal antitrust statutes were enacted pursuant to Congress' power to regulate commerce among the several states, many people thought that these laws could not apply to commercial banks. This contention was based on a number of Supreme Court decisions in the mid-1800s which held that the business of insurance (traditionally considered to be closely related to banking) was not commerce and that transactions in money were not part of commerce. One of the most noteworthy of these cases was *Nathan* v. *Louisiana,* in which the Court held that an individual who uses his money and credit in buying and selling bills of exchange". . . was not engaged in commerce, but in supplying an instrument of commerce."[7] Although on occasion some criticism of the "commerce immunity thesis" was voiced, this belief held fast for almost a century.[8]

It was not until 1944 when the Supreme Court handed down its decision in *United States* v. *South-Eastern Underwriters*[9] that those who doubted that the banking industry really enjoyed immunity from antitrust prosecution were provided with significant judicial support for their position. In *South-Eastern Underwriters* the court rejected the long-standing argument that the business of insurance was not commerce in finding that the defendants' anticompetitive acts violated the provisions of the Sherman Act. The opinion read in part:[10] "No

[7] *Nathan* v. *Louisiana,* 49 U.S. 73, 81 (1850).

[8] Williams, "Banking and the Antitrust Laws," *The Banking Law Journal* (May 1964), pp. 377–92. This article contains an excellent discussion of developments in this area prior to the "Philadelphia case," and this writer has drawn much from Williams' work in preparing this section of the chapter.

[9] *U. S.* v. *South-Eastern Underwriters Association,* 322 U.S. 533 (1944). In an earlier case, *National Labor Relations Board* v. *Bank of America N.T. & S.A.* (9th Cir., 1942) operations of this large, national bank were considered to have "affected commerce" within the meaning of the National Labor Relations Act. [130 F. 2d 624 (1942)] For numerous other references concerning banking as "commerce," see *Lorenzetti* v. *American Trust Company,* 45 F. Supp. 128 (1942).

[10] *U. S.* v. *South-Eastern Underwriters Association,* 322 U.S. 533, 553 (1944).

commercial enterprise of any kind which conducts its activities across state lines has been held to be wholly beyond the regulatory power of Congress under the Commerce Clause." Thus, since the businesses of banking and of insurance were so closely related, serious doubt was also cast upon the "exempt status" of commercial banks.[11]

The Antitrust Division of the Department of Justice, convinced that the *South-Eastern Underwriters* decision supported its efforts to prevent anticompetitive practices in banking as well as in most other fields, in 1946 brought its first action against a segment of the banking industry. In *United States* v. *Mortgage Conference of New York*,[12] the Government filed suit against the 38 members of a trade association, which included 17 savings banks, 8 trust companies, and 1 commercial bank. It was charged that these firms, through their association, violated Section 1 of the Sherman Act by setting minimum amortizing rates and terms, by following standard appraisal procedures and valuations, and by not lending to builders for new construction in areas where the members already had substantial investments. All but five of the defendants consented to the entry of final judgment,[13] which required the dissolution of their association and enjoined each of them from participating in the challenged conduct either by agreement or through another association.[14]

Several other cases which provided fairly convincing evidence that commercial banks were not exempt from antitrust prosecution were tried in the late 1940s and early 1950s. Two of the most important of these actions were *United States* v. *Morgan* and *Transamerica* v. *Board of Governors of the Federal Reserve System*. In the former case the defendants stated that their business was regulated by the Securities Act of 1933 and the Securities Exchange Act of 1934, and the provisions of these acts amounted to an implied exemption from the Sherman Antitrust Act. The District Court did not accept this argument and tried the case, but when the trial was completed the

[11] An outstanding article concerning this question is Berle's, "Banking Under the Antitrust Law," *Columbia Law Review* (May 1949), pp. 589–606.

[12] *U. S.* v. *The Mortgage Conference of New York*, Civ. 37–247 (S.D.N.Y.).

[13] Williams, "Banking and the Antitrust Laws," *The Banking Law Journal* (May 1964), pp. 383–84. Williams notes the other 5 defendants were ultimately dismissed by stipulation.

[14] 1948–1949 *Trade Cases* ¶62273. In a somewhat similar case, *U. S.* v. *Chicago Mortgage Bankers Association*, [123 F. Supp. 251 (1954)], the District Court dismissed the complaint after the trial was concluded.

circuit judge held that evidence was insufficient to establish the existence of a conspiracy or combination among the defendants and he
dismissed the complaint.[15]

The second case, involving Transamerica Corporation, a West
Coast holding company, was most unusual, for it was the only time
the Board of Governors ever brought suit to enforce Section 7 of the
Clayton Act.[16] Although the holding company did not employ the
argument that banking was not commerce, the court, nevertheless,
considered this question, and it concluded that the commercial banks
involved were engaged in interstate commerce.[17] Instead of attempting
to use this defense, Transamerica's attorneys argued that banking was
regulated by specific statutes, such as the provisions found in Section
8 of the Clayton Act, and Congress did not intend to cover banking
under more general legislation. Thus, Transamerica held that since
the only authority given to the Board was to enforce those sections of
the Clayton Act applicable to banks, and Section 7 did not specifically
apply to banking, the "Fed's" suit should be dismissed. This thesis
was rejected by the court.[18]

Therefore, by the mid-1950s it was reasonably clear that the business of commercial banking was "commerce," and banks enjoyed no
special immunity from antitrust prosecution. However, with the passage of the Bank Merger Act of 1960, it would probably be safe to
say that most commercial bankers and their attorneys (not to mention
a great many members of Congress) were once again thoroughly
convinced that at least bank mergers were not subject to prosecution
under the Clayton Act. But, in 1963, in the *Philadelphia National
Bank case,* and in 1964 in the *Lexington case,*[19] the United States
Supreme Court clearly indicated that the immunity assumption was
unfounded, that banking is commerce, and that banks are not exempt
from the Clayton Act or the Sherman Act. Both of these cases and the
*Transamerica case* will be discussed at greater length in the next
chapter.

[15] *U. S.* v. *Morgan,* Civ. 43–757 (S.D.N.Y.), 118 F. Supp. 612, 623 (1953).
[16] *Transamerica Corporation* v. *Board of Governors of the Federal Reserve
System,* 206 F. 2d 163 (1953).
[17] *Ibid.,* at 165 and note 3.
[18] *Ibid.,* at 165–66.
[19] *U. S.* v. *Philadelphia National Bank,* 374 U.S. 321 (1963), and *U. S.* v.
*First National Bank and Trust Company of Lexington;* 376 U.S. 665 (1964).

## THE ROLE OF THE ANTITRUST LAWS

The balance of this chapter will be primarily devoted to an analysis of commercial bank clearinghouse agreements, price-fixing and related nonmerger antitrust problems, and interlocking directorates. However, since many individuals who are interested in banking operations may not be overly familiar with the antitrust field, it may be helpful to digress briefly at this point to consider the aims of antitrust policy and some of the provisions of the Sherman Act and of the Clayton Act.

It was noted earlier that no other nation has a body of antitrust law which is at all comparable to ours. In fact, while numerous restrictive practices (such as cartels) have not only been permitted but have been encouraged by many foreign governments, in the United States combinations, pools, and the practices of the natural monopolies, especially the railroads, were the focus of early criticism, for while the common law made some agreements, such as output restriction and price fixing, unenforceable, no action could be taken against the parties to such contracts.[20] To obtain greater control over these and numerous other undesirable practices, by the turn of the century nearly two-thirds of the states had approved some form of antitrust statute[21]—over twenty of these laws being passed before federal legislation was enacted in 1890.

The same social and economic forces that impelled the states to act against industrial combinations were also felt by the federal government. Antitrust became a political issue significant enough by 1888 that the two principal presidential parties each carried an antitrust plank in its platform. Within two years the Sherman Antitrust Act

[20] Wernette, *Government and Business,* p. 247.

[21] This book does not consider the question of state antitrust laws. This topic is reviewed in Hanson and von Kalinowski, "Status of State Antitrust Laws with Federal Analysis," 15 *Western Reserve Law Review* 9 (1963); and some discussion of their application to banks may be found in *American Law Reports Annotated* [83 A.L.R. 2d 374, 376–77]. The reader interested in the general area of state antitrust laws should examine the proceedings of an American Bar Association symposium on this topic held in 1965. See 29 *American Bar Association Antitrust Section* 255–300 (1965). A recent bank case involving a test of state antitrust laws which contains valuable references in this area is *Kelley* v. *Michigan National Bank,* 141 N.W. 2d 73 (1966). The decision was filed by the Supreme Court of Michigan, April 5, 1965.

was passed by the Senate with only one dissenting vote and by the House of Representatives without any. But weakness in the Sherman Act, combined with judicial interpretation of the law, including the adoption of the "rule of reason,"[22] once again made antitrust an issue in the presidential election of 1912, and two new pieces of antitrust legislation, the Clayton Act and the Federal Trade Commission Act,[23] were passed in 1914.

Important additions to the Clayton Act were made in 1936 and in 1950. In the former year the Robinson-Patman Act, directed against price discrimination, was enacted, and in 1950 the Celler-Kefauver Act amended Section 7 to remove any doubt that corporate acquisitions effected through the purchase of assets were covered. In addition the 1950 legislation included significant changes in the definition of the "relevant market." It might be added that revisions were also made in Section 8 concerning interlocking bank directorates by the Banking Act of 1935 and by earlier commercial banking legislation.

The philosophy which underlies the above antitrust statutes and their amendments was described by Earl Kintner, the former head of the Federal Trade Commission, as follows: [24]

Considerations larger than self-interest and concern for the future welfare of a given enterprise also dictate a regard for the antitrust and trade regulation laws. For these laws are principal guardians of the free enterprise system. An article of faith lies at the very roots of American political and economic philosophy: that undue concentrations of power are inherently destructive of the aims of a free society, whether those concentrations be in private hands, as in a monopoly, or in governmental agencies. This country has never ceased to doubt the myriad claims of those who urge that a multitude of "benefits" flow from cartelization or statism. The American answer to man's age-old problem of how best to distribute power can be summarized in one word: pluralism. The doctrine of pluralism asserts that the needs of men are best served when power is

[22] The rule of reason under the Sherman Act, at least between 1911 and the *Alcoa* decision in 1945, has been described as follows: ". . . Large firms, whatever their control of the market, were to be judged primarily by one criterion: did the circumstances of their formation and the characteristic pattern of their market behavior evince an intent to monopolize?" Dirlam and Kahn, *Fair Competition,* p. 45.

[23] The Federal Trade Commission lacks jurisdiction over banks. See *U. S.* v. *Philadelphia National Bank,* 374 U.S. 321, 336, n. 11 (1963).

[24] Kintner, *An Antitrust Primer,* pp. xii–xiii. Quoted with the permission of the Macmillan Company.

distributed among many; that the goals of the nation are best implemented by a combination of many individual decisions rather than by a single decision imposed and enforced by a single power source. Both our polity and our economy are premised on the belief that the individual citizen should exercise maximum control over his own development.

In a similar vein a former chief of the Antitrust Division of the Department of Justice stated: "I am personally convinced, as I think each of you should be, that without the antitrust laws, America could not possibly have become the great, free, and prosperous country that it is." [25] And the late Senator Estes Kefauver, in a speech while Chairman of the Senate Antitrust and Monopoly Subcommittee, observed: [26]

Some segments of the business world look on any increase in government activity against monopoly or concentration as "business harassment." It represents nothing of the kind; rather, it is the American way of demonstrating that we intend to preserve our charters of economic freedom. Without these charters—the antitrust laws—we would not be the world's strongest economic nation.

Of course, a number of the bankers and bank researchers who read this work may not share the views of these government officials. In fact, it would be surprising if many students of banking did not strongly disagree with the above conclusions regarding the role of antitrust in the preservation of our free enterprise system, for, as Senator Kefauver noted, individuals often consider the active enforcement of these laws as merely another illustration of the centralization of power in the federal government. However, regardless of the reader's opinion of the ideas expressed in these quotations, it is hoped that he will keep in mind the fundamental philosophy that they expound, for this is vital if one is to understand the formulation of antitrust policy by the government and the interpretation of the antitrust statutes by the Supreme Court in recent years.

## PROVISIONS OF THE SHERMAN ACT AND CLAYTON ACT

The Sherman Act (15 U.S.C. §§ 1–7, as amended) contains two main prohibitions:

[25] William Orrick, Jr., "Antitrust: Past and Future," speech before the Town Hall, Los Angeles, California, May 19, 1964, p. 1. (mimeographed)

[26] Kefauver, "Affront to Free Enterprise," The Independent Banker (March 1963), p. 30.

*Section 1.* Every contract, combination in the form of trust or otherwise, or conspiracy, in restraint of trade or commerce among the several States, or with foreign nations, is hereby declared to be illegal. . . .

*Section 2.* Every person who shall monopolize, or attempt to monopolize, or combine or conspire with any other person or persons, to monopolize any part of the trade or commerce among the several States, or with foreign nations, shall be deemed guilty of a misdemeanor. . . .

The Clayton Act (15 U.S.C. §§ 12 ff., as amended) attacks the antitrust problem in much more specific terms than does the Sherman Act. It declares four types of restrictive or monopolistic practice to be illegal. They are in brief: price discrimination (Section 2), exclusive dealing and tying contracts (Section 3), acquisition of competing companies (Section 7), and interlocking directorates (Section 8). The provisions include numerous qualifications and exceptions which will be noted in the sections of this chapter devoted to the problems in question.

The provisions of the Clayton Act were designed to reach in their incipiency acts or practices which might eventually lead to adverse competitive effects. Except in instances where per se violations are involved, many authorities feel the Sherman Act is not violated unless actual and substantial adverse competitive effects have resulted. Under the Clayton Act, however, illegality can be found in conduct which has the probable result of substantially lessening competition.[27] But today the difference may be minute.

## PRICE FIXING: BACKGROUND

In an earlier section of this chapter, some of the court decisions which convinced many individuals that banks enjoyed immunity from antitrust prosecution were considered. However, it would be misleading not to note that in addition to these judicial opinions certain activities by the bank regulatory agencies, especially in regard to clearinghouse agreements, also contributed substantially to the confusion concerning the status of commercial banks under the federal antitrust laws. The following section will consider some of the actions by supervisory authorities which made price fixing agreements among

[27] Kintner, *An Antitrust Primer,* p. 23.

commercial banks virtually standard operating procedure. This analysis has been included to provide some background information for those who are not familiar with this area of banking history, for many people are shocked when they discover that in the past it was not only common for banks to discuss pricing policies with other banks serving the same general area, but this was done with the permission of and often at the insistence of governmental agencies.

## CLEARINGHOUSE AGREEMENTS

Historically, the soundness of the banking system has been of greater legislative and supervisory concern than the fostering of competition in this industry. In fact, following each of our major financial panics there was a flurry of criticism regarding the overzealous competition of some banks and a plea for more cooperation among these financial institutions. Of course, occasionally in the literature one uncovers comments such as the criticism of the activities of clearinghouses by the Pujo Committee in 1913. The Committee recommended:[28]

Such [clearinghouse] associations should be further prohibited from prescribing rates of interest or discount, rates of interest allowed on deposits, rates of exchange, or any other regulation not appropriate to its function of instrumentality for the collection of checks by banks of the same community one from another, that interferes with competition.

Far more typical than the above comments by the "money trust" investigators were remarks such as the following made shortly after the Panic of 1873 by Comptroller of the Currency John Jay Knox: ". . . Unity of action among the leading banks of the great cities will do more to reform abuses than any congressional enactment. . . ."[29] He went on to praise the activities of the New York Clearinghouse which were designed to prevent the payment of interest on deposits.[30] After the Panic of 1884, Comptroller of the Currency Henry W. Cannon stressed the benefits to be derived from the united action of clearinghouse associations in abolishing interest on deposits.[31] Thus, by the turn of the century when a work was published

[28] U. S. Congress, Pujo Committee Report, 1913, p. 162.
[29] Comptroller of the Currency, 11th *Annual Report,* 1873, p. xxix.
[30] *Ibid.,* p. xxxi.
[31] Comptroller of the Currency, 22nd *Annual Report,* 1884, pp. 57–59.

which was devoted exclusively to these institutions it was probably to be expected that fixing uniform rates of interest on deposits and fixing uniform rates of exchange and of charges on collections would be included in the list of "important special functions" of clearing-houses.[32]

During this period the element which was of prime importance to bank supervisory authorities was the payment of interest on bankers' balances. These balances were not only associated with the money panics mentioned above but also with earlier panics as well, and instances of condemnation of the payment of interest on bankers' deposits may be found even in the 1830s and 1840s.[33] But, while much of the criticism was directed only toward bankers' balances, especially those held in New York City, in some respects the problem was conceived as applying to all commercial bank demand deposits.

Under the caption "Dangerous Competition," the New York State Superintendent of Banks in his *Annual Report* in 1905 warned of the dangers inherent in the payment of "undue rates of interest upon deposits," and he called for interbank cooperation to stop this practice. He stated:[34]

I can but look with fear and misgiving upon the competition for deposits which has arisen in the last few years among and between the banks and trust companies of the State. This competition is so great that unusual, and, in my opinion, unwarranted rates of interest are paid to depositors. Competition in banking is not like competition in mercantile and other branches of business. The banks and trust companies are dealing with the people's money. Their first duty is to so manage their institutions as to keep this money safe beyond question, and it is far more important to the depositors that their principal be safely invested, and that the bank or trust company be at all times ready and able to pay them back upon demand, than that they should get a little more interest upon it. As I have frequently pointed out before, the payment of undue rates of interest upon deposits is necessarily followed, and naturally so, by a desire on the part of an institution to obtain the greatest possible rate upon its loans and investments. This in turn strongly tends to loans and investments which in other circumstances ordinary prudence would reject. I regard this compe-

[32] Cannon, *Clearing-Houses*, p. 12. See also Spahr, *The Clearing and Collection of Checks*, Chapter V.

[33] Watkins, *Commercial Banking Reform in the United States*, pp. 73–77.

[34] New York State Superintendent of Banks, *Annual Report*, Fiscal year 1904–1905, pp. xxvi–xxvii; and 1907–1908, p. xxxv.

tition, and its attendant results, as the greatest menace to banking in this State to-day. The task of abating the evil lies with the officers and directors of our banks and trust companies. There is nothing in the law which will prevent the payment of interest at such rates as they may determine, but common prudence counsels that it is time to call a halt, and *that all should get together for the purpose of putting these matters upon a more conservative basis, and adjusting them so as to eliminate so far as possible the element of danger to which I have referred.* I can not too strongly impress this upon the bankers of the State. [Emphasis added]

The Superintendent noted that the danger in this practice had been recognized by the bankers in Albany, and an understanding was arrived at by which the banks and trust companies there agreed not to pay interest upon active accounts having balances of less than 10 thousand dollars. This arrangement he suggested "has worked to the entire satisfaction of all."

The Superintendent renewed his recommendation relating to greater cooperation among the banks in fixing interest rates in each of his *Annual Reports* for some years thereafter. He called for voluntary interest rate regulation but also warned that rate competition could lead to a statute prohibiting the payment of interest on balances of less than specified amounts. This provision, however, was primarily associated not with interbank competition but with commercial bank competition with savings banks "for deposits naturally belonging to the latter." (The maximum deposit from one individual in a savings bank was limited by statute in New York to 3 thousand dollars in the early 1900s.)

With the organization of the Federal Reserve System, it was thought that bankers' balances would be substantially reduced and the interest payment problem would therefore be of little significance. But these expectations were not realized, and once again in 1915 and in 1916 the Comptroller of the Currency, in a discussion of ways to prevent bank failures, recommended that legislation be passed to curb interest payments.[35] In 1918 the Federal Reserve Board also became concerned over the increasing interest rates paid by banks, particularly on the deposits of other banking institutions. Governor Harding strongly criticized "reckless competition for deposits," and the Fed-

[35] Comptroller of the Currency, 53rd *Annual Report*, 1915, p. 33; and 54th *Annual Report*, 1916, pp. 16–17.

eral Reserve Board ". . . suggested that the Federal Reserve Banks wherever possible induce banks which were considering increases in interest rates to postpone such action, and also to persuade the institutions which had raised rates to reduce them."[36] The Board indicated that as it learned the names of cities where there was a "tendency toward an undue increase in the rate of interest" by the local banks, it planned to take the matter up with clearinghouses in those cities.[37] Thus, only a few years after the Pujo Committee had voiced its criticism of clearinghouse price fixing activities, the Federal Reserve Board and the District Banks were actively engaged in an effort to get the clearinghouses to adopt a schedule containing uniform rates of interest on deposits.[38]

In addition to the regulation of interest rates by clearinghouse agreements, during the 1920s and early 1930s some states established maximum rates of interest which could be paid on deposits.[39] Among these states was Virginia, the home of Senator Carter Glass, who was extremely important in shaping the banking reforms during the Great Depression. For a number of years Glass had displayed some concern regarding the deposit interest question, particularly as it applied to bankers' balances, and he included deposit interest restrictions in a number of bills he introduced. When the Banking Act of 1933 and the Banking Act of 1935 were passed, each contained provisions relating to deposit interest. The 1933 legislation prohibited the payment of interest on demand deposits, with certain exceptions, by members of the Federal Reserve System, and it empowered the Federal Reserve Board to limit the rate of interest that could be paid on time and savings deposits by these banks. The 1935 law made some minor changes in the powers of the Board and granted the Federal Deposit Insurance Corporation (FDIC) similar authority over non-member insured banks. Since February 1, 1936 the rates set by the

---

[36] Hales, *The Baltimore Clearing House,* p. 233.

[37] *Ibid.,* pp. 233–34.

[38] See various issues of the *Federal Reserve Bulletin,* 1918–1920.

[39] Willis, "Report of An Inquiry into Contemporary Banking in the United States," Volume V., p. 122. A vast amount of information concerning interest rate regulation is contained in recently completed dissertations on this topic by Albert H. Cox at the University of Michigan and Charles Linke at Indiana University. Part of Cox's study appears in the *Journal of Finance* (May 1967); and part of Linke's study appears in the *National Banking Review* (June 1966).

FDIC have been the same as those in effect for Federal Reserve member banks.[40]

*Legality of clearinghouse agreements.* The American Bankers Association (ABA) made a survey of deposit interest paid by the banks in 160 clearinghouse cities as of December 31, 1929.[41] One of the questions asked by the ABA concerned how the rates paid were determined by the responding banks.[42] The replies indicated the rates were set as follows: by clearinghouse rules, 58 percent; by agreement among the banks, 14 percent; by individual action, 14 percent; and by custom, 14 percent. These percentages leave little doubt regarding the significance of the clearinghouse agreement in establishing rates in leading cities by 1930.

During the 1920s some banks, fearing their agreements with other banks to set interest rates might violate federal antitrust laws, wrote the General Counsel of the American Bankers Association asking about the legality of this activity. Excerpts from several of the letters and their replies were included in *Paton's Digest* in 1926.[43] In this publication the ABA General Counsel indicated that an intercity agreement regarding maximum interest rates on savings deposits, and a clearinghouse agreement establishing a uniform rate for foreign exchange would not violate the Sherman Act. The Counsel's opinion read in part:[44]

In 1910 the rules of the New Orleans Clearing House Association, which establish a uniform minimum scale of charges for collection of out-of-town items, came into question. An individual who had been charged for collection of a draft on a Texas point laid the facts before the United States District Attorney at New Orleans, who presented the facts to the grand jury, being inclined to the view that the rules in question constituted a violation of the anti-trust act, but before finally so advising the grand jury, consented to give consideration to contrary legal opinions and also to be guided by the advice of the Attorney-General of the United

[40] Maximum rates are established under Regulation Q of the Board of Governors and under Section 329.6 of the Rules and Regulations of the FDIC. (12 CFR 329.6)

[41] See "Commercial Bank Competition for Savings," *American Bankers Association Journal* (October 1930), pp. 350 ff.

[42] *Ibid.*, p. 353. Cited in a draft of Albert Cox's University of Michigan dissertation noted above.

[43] *Paton's Digest* (New York: ABA, 1926), Vol. II, pp. 1452–54.

[44] *Ibid.*, 1940, Vol I, pp. 1196–98.

States. General Counsel of the American Bankers Association having been so requested, prepared an opinion upon the subject, in which he maintained there was no violation, which was submitted to Attorney-General Wickersham. The matter having been fully presented to the Attorney-General, the advice of the latter to the District Attorney at New Orleans was that the criminal prosecution be dropped and the grand jury thereupon so voted.

In 1916 the Superior Court of the State of Washington for King County rendered a decision in Peoples Savings Bank v. First National Bank et al. [affirmed 102 Wash. 436, 173 Pac. 52]. In that case the Seattle Clearing House adopted a rule fixing a maximum rate of interest on savings deposits and one of the members objecting, it thereafter proposed to dissolve and reorganize without the objecting member. The bank in question sought an injunction restraining the other member banks from enforcing this rule as to it fixing the rate of interest to be paid on deposits and also from organizing a new Clearing House. The court dismissed the action. It held that interest paid by the banks was not an article or commodity subject to the rule against restraint of competition "that in practice there has always existed among its members a common agreement in rates of interest, exchange and collection charges," and that each had agreed to abide by the rules adopted. The court held there was nothing unlawful in such an agreement.

Essentially the same philosophy prevailed through the early 1940s. For example, the 1940 edition of *Paton's Digest* included the following statement under the heading "Effect of Federal Antitrust Laws upon Uniform Clearinghouse Regulations and Agreements:"

The Sherman Anti-Trust Act, which declares illegal any combination in restraint of interstate commerce, has been interpreted many times by the courts. Although none of the court decisions deal squarely with the effect of the statute upon clearing house agreements or regulations, the analogous cases indicate that the act is not violated by such agreements or regulations, providing for uniform collection charges, or specifying a uniform service charge on small accounts, or adopting uniform interest rates. The furnishing of credit information to the member banks by the clearing house association does not seem to violate the federal antitrust laws, inasmuch as the Federal Government has specifically permitted the exchange of credit information among the members of other organizations in a similar situation. [footnotes omitted]

But this report warned the reader that the opinion was based upon a consideration of various decisions, interpreting the Sherman Antitrust Act, none of which involved the work of the clearinghouse, and until the Supreme Court ruled upon the application of this statute to clearinghouse associations the effect of the law upon uniform clearinghouse agreements could not be definitely stated.

From the above opinions of the General Counsel of the ABA, it is certainly understandable that bankers typically believed that they were not subject to the antitrust laws or that somehow the provisions of these statutes did not apply to banks in the same way that they did to most other industries. In fact the Comptroller of the Currency reported in 1963 that some state laws still "specifically and expressly" permitted banks to have agreed rates,[45] a practice which would appear to be a per se violation of the federal antitrust laws.

While this writer fully appreciates that bankers were encouraged and even coerced by the supervisory authorities into participating in price-fixing agreements, it would be unfair not to note also that bankers were told by the General Counsel of the ABA two decades ago that their clearinghouse rate agreements may violate the Sherman Act. *Paton's Digest* in September, 1946 warned that: [46]

The effect of clearinghouse rules fixing a minimum scale of uniform charges for collecting out of town checks is to control the price of this type of service in that locality. If this type of service is considered trade or commerce within the Sherman Act, then it would seem to be a violation per se under the above quoted language in the Socony Vacuum Oil Co. opinion [310 U. S. 150 (1940)]. . . . In view of the uncertainty, of the law and the trend of the decisions toward broadening the coverage of the Sherman Act, it would seem to be safer practice for clearinghouses not to attempt to establish uniform service charges by by-laws, rules or agreements.

Yet, until the bank price-fixing cases in the early 1960s received national publicity, it is doubtful that very many bankers were even aware that there was a possibility that charges might be brought against them for "cooperating" with other banks.

## THE PHILOSOPHY OF BANK COOPERATION

In the classrooms of the American Institute of Banking in the 1940s, young bank executives were taught that ". . . competition will be aggressive but honest and above board, with due regard for the

[45] U. S. Congress, House, *Meetings with Department and Agency Officials,* Hearings, 1963, p. 132.

[46] *Paton's Digest* (New York: ABA, 1946), Supplement, September 1946, Section 2, p. 5.

rights of other banks and the general good of the banking business. Cooperation will be extended whenever it is deemed necessary or is desired." [47] Therefore, it is not surprising that in the mid-1950s, when one of the leading scholars in the bank structure area, David Alhadeff, was preparing an analysis of bank pricing practices, he marvelled at the complete frankness with which collusive agreements in this industry were accomplished. He noted that bankers did not describe these arrangements as collusion but as "mutual assistance," "elimination of unhealthy competition," and "necessary coordination of activity."[48]

The Alhadeff study was one of the first works to consider banking from the viewpoint of public policy as well as monetary policy, and the ideas expressed were relatively new to the banking literature.[49] For example, one of the most popular college texts in use at the time the above comment was written included such clearinghouse agreements with "other useful services" whose general "purpose is to raise the plane of banking operations." [50] Moreover, the theme which one finds throughout the banking literature of two or three decades ago is that banks should compete but not too much. Alhadeff cited a line from a bank management book published in 1933 that aptly described this form of competition: "In soliciting new business, there should be 'nothing in the spirit of the bank's approach that can be interpreted as a bid for any considerable portion of the business of other banks.'"[51] James Trant, in his *Bank Administration,* also published in the early 1930s, voiced the same concern with the preservation of existing banks when he wrote:[52]

Competition for deposits is often so great as to cause banks to pay such high rates of interest on their balances left with them as to make a large part of the deposit business of banks unprofitable; particularly is that true of the marginal bank. As a means of preventing this ruinous competition clearinghouses have stepped in and prescribed the maximum rate of interest that may be paid on various minimum balances. This rule en-

[47] *Bank Administration,* p. 83.

[48] Alhadeff, *Monopoly and Competition in Banking,* p. 25.

[49] Chandler's "Monopolistic Elements in Commercial Banking" was one of the earliest efforts in this area.

[50] Peterson and Cawthorne, *Money and Banking,* pp. 344–45.

[51] *Bank Management,* p. 24. Cited in Alhadeff, *Monopoly and Competition in Banking,* p. 26.

[52] Trant, *Bank Administration,* p. 106.

forces conservative banking and prevents banks from breaking each other in an attempt to increase their deposits.

One might add that during this period the American Bankers Association actively promoted not only city clearinghouse associations but regional associations as well ". . . to make banking safer, to help expedite all phases of business, and . . . to lessen or eliminate all forms of losses, so the greater rewards may accrue to banking and better service to the public."[53]

If this cooperative competition reduced the number of bank failures, improved service, and so on, it may have provided certain social benefits, but it must also be acknowledged that it may have had social costs. For example, consider the words of a prominent banking authority in the 1920s, who in praising the operations of clearinghouses observed: "An undesirable customer is also less liable to force a concession from one bank under threat of going to the bank across the street. Instead of playing one bank against the other without profit to either, the customer and the bank usually get together, but upon terms *more favorable to the bank and less favorable to the customer.*"[54] [italics added] Although this quotation is probably a very poor choice when one considers the operation of clearinghouses in the 1960s, it does illustrate quite well the potential negative effects cooperative arrangements may have upon competition. Surely, this activity would not have been legal unless banks were exempt from prosecution under the antitrust laws or the "rule of reason" enjoyed a much broader application with respect to banking than it had to other industries.[55] Thus, while this form of competition may have been perfectly satisfactory to many bankers and bank supervisors, it would appear to have been "somewhat" below Sherman and Clayton Act standards—if these laws applied to commercial banks.

[53] "Regional Clearing House Associations," in *Commercial Bank Management,* preface. In addition, under Title One of the National Industrial Recovery Act a Bankers Code of Fair Competition was approved by the President. A part of the code included provisions directing clearinghouses to draft rules and regulations to deal with hours of banking, interest, service charges, and trust services. (Hales, *The Baltimore Clearing House,* pp. 270–73.) In *Schechter Poultry Corporation* v. *U. S.,* [295 U. S. 495 (1935)] the National Recovery Act was declared unconstitutional.

[54] Spahr, *The Clearing and Collection of Checks,* p. 133.

[55] Williams, "Banking and the Antitrust Laws," *The Banking Law Journal* (May 1964), p. 385.

## PRICE FIXING:
## FEDERAL BANK ANTITRUST CASES

Probably the prime example of a per se[56] violation of the Sherman Antitrust Act is price fixing. This action, whether by buyers or by sellers, has consistently been declared unlawful by the Supreme Court. In addition, the government agencies charged with the enforcement of the antitrust laws have always regarded this activity as the most serious of the various possible violations of these statutes. The vast majority of criminal convictions for violations of the antitrust laws have been based upon such practices, "and the possibility of a jail sentence for violation of the antitrust laws increases geometrically if the charge is price fixing."[57]

In the discussion of the *New York Mortgage Conference case*[58] at the beginning of this chapter, it was noted that the government filed an antitrust suit in 1945 against the members of a trade association which included one commercial bank. Three years later a case containing similar allegations was also brought against the Chicago Mortgage Bankers Association. Among the 35 defendants were 12 commercial banks.[59] As in the "New York case" the trade association and the corporate defendants were charged with violating Section 1 of the Sherman Act—in this instance for fixing minimum commissions, service fees, and interest rates in connection with making FHA construction loans. In 1954 the court dismissed the complaint after the trial was concluded, noting that all of the practices except those which were essentially local in nature had been terminated and that there was no threat or likelihood that they would be revived.[60]

[56] "Without refined analysis, it [per se doctrine] may be defined as the type of conduct which when proved forecloses those charged from any opportunity to seek to justify their conduct as a reasonable restraint of trade or as not in fact monopolistic in purpose or effect." Phillips, ed., *Perspectives on Antitrust Policy*, p. 22.

[57] Kintner, *An Antritrust Primer*, p. 31.

[58] *U. S.* v. *The Mortgage Conference of New York*, Civ. 37–247 (S.D.N.Y.); 1948–1949 *Trade Cases* ¶ 62,273.

[59] Williams, "Banking and the Antitrust Laws," *The Banking Law Journal* (May 1964), p. 384, n. 38.

[60] *U. S.* v. *Chicago Mortgage Bankers Association*, 123 F. Supp. 251 (1954).

## THE NEW JERSEY CASE[61]

In recent years there have been a number of commercial bank price-fixing cases brought by the Department of Justice. The first, which was filed December 26, 1961, involved three New Jersey banks: The First National Bank of Clinton (assets 3.3 million dollars), The Clinton National Bank (assets 12.1 million dollars), and Hunterdon County Trust Company (assets 4.7 million dollars). The complaint indicated the defendants agreed upon uniform charges for checks, checking accounts, collection of checks and drafts, and other banking services. It was alleged that representatives of these institutions in telephone conversations and in person discussed the desirability of uniform service charges, and as a result service charges of the three banks were raised, fixed, and maintained at high and artificial levels.[62]

The suit arose after the two Clinton, New Jersey banks had applied to the Comptroller of the Currency for permission to merge. It was reported that included among the papers filed with the banking agency was a pamphlet published jointly with the Hunterdon County Trust Company in nearby Califon, New Jersey, in 1957, listing the new service charges adopted at that time. When questioned regarding the existence of such an arrangement, an official of one of the three banks according to the *American Banker* conceded "that an agreement between the banks does exist."[63]

The Justice Department filed a civil suit under Section 1 of the Sherman Act asking the court to prohibit the banks from continuing to use common pricing schedules. In 1962 the case was terminated by a consent decree enjoining the defendants from engaging in any of the activities challenged in the complaint.[64] Under this procedure the

---

[61] *U. S.* v. *Hunterdon County Trust Company, First National Bank of Clinton,* and *Clinton National Bank,* 1962 *Trade Cases* ¶ 70,263. For a discussion of this case and other bank price-fixing cases, see Lifland, "Day-to-Day Banking Practices Under the Antitrust Laws," *The Bankers Magazine* (Summer 1964), pp. 38–43.

[62] *BNA's Antitrust & Trade Regulation Report* (January 2, 1962), A–3.

[63] "Banking Precedent Seen in New Jersey," *American Banker,* December 28, 1961. The merger was consummated March 16, 1962.

[64] The exact terms of the injunction may be found in *U. S.* v. *Hunterdon County Trust Company,* 1962 *Trade Cases* ¶ 70,263.

banks neither denied nor affirmed the original charges, but merely agreed not to engage in any such actions in the future.

## THE DALLAS CASE

An official of the Department of Justice indicated that the New Jersey case might be a forerunner of further actions against banking groups. Less than two weeks after charges in this case had been filed, a federal grand jury issued subpoenas to officers of seven major Dallas, Texas banks. While no indication was given by Justice at the time regarding the specific problem under investigation, the subpoenas ordered the officers to bring communications between the officers and employees of the banks concerning changes in service charges.[65]

The *American Banker* reported that the Comptroller of the Currency felt that any charges involving price-fixing by banks should be handled by his office, and he strongly criticized the action of the Justice Department in ordering the Dallas bankers to appear before a grand jury.[66] With the disclosure of the Dallas subpoenas, the Comptroller's office made public a letter sent to Deputy Attorney General (and now Associate Justice of the Supreme Court) Byron R. White by Deputy Comptroller W. M. Taylor on December 29, 1961, following the filing of the New Jersey suit. The letter stated: "Mr. Saxon regards matters such as this as coming within the jurisdiction of this office, and the examiners are being instructed to review the methods by which service and other charges are fixed by all national banks. Any price fixing by national banks of any charges will be appropriately dealt with by this office."[67] The Comptroller's office also issued an instruction to all national banks on February 28, 1962 indicating service charges must be determined independently. He noted agreements through clearinghouses or otherwise are not permitted, and it was the responsibility of each bank's board of directors to terminate promptly any such practices. The letter indicated national bank examiners had been instructed to determine whether appropriate action was taken to conform to this request.

Late in February, 1962 the grand jury which had heard testimony

[65] *BNA's Antitrust & Trade Regulation Report* (January 9, 1962), A–7.

[66] "Saxon Scores Secret Justice Move," *American Banker,* January 3, 1962.

[67] Quoted in *BNA's Antitrust & Trade Regulation Report* (January 9, 1962), A–7.

in the *Dallas case* was discharged and no action was taken against the banks. The United States Attorney according to the *Wall Street Journal* stated that he felt the investigation was finished and no further grand jury inquiry was contemplated.[68]

## THE MINNESOTA CASES[69]

In mid-September 1961 it was noted in the press that the Department of Justice had begun an investigation into the operations of three Minneapolis-based bank holding companies.[70] Subpoenas calling for detailed books and records were served on the officers of the group systems and more than thirty of their Minnesota subsidiaries. There was a considerable amount of speculation at the time regarding the reason for this probe, and a number of bankers concluded that it had something to do with possible antitrust violations since data concerning loan policies and interest rates were requested. The records were to be submitted to a federal grand jury which was to meet in Minneapolis on September 28.

After the federal grand jury had been investigating the operating practices of these banks and their affiliates for over fifteen months, it was rumored that it might be discharged without returning any criminal indictments.[71] However, within a few weeks, on February 8 and 11, 1963, both civil and criminal charges were filed against a total of eighteen commercial banks, one bank holding company, and one clearinghouse in Minnesota in six separate cases—three civil and three criminal. This was the first time that banks had been charged with criminally violating the antitrust laws.[72]

*United States v. the First National Bank of St. Paul.* The *St. Paul cases* were very similar to the New Jersey action discussed earlier. The defendants were charged with having violated Section 1 of the

---

[68] "U. S. Grand Jury Gives Clean Bill," *Wall Street Journal,* February 26, 1962.

[69] 3–63 Civ. 37; 3–63 Cr. 8; 5–63 Civ. 4; 5–63 Cr. 6; 4–63 Civ. 52; 4–63 Cr. 6 (D. Minn.).

[70] "Department of Justice Opens Probe," *American Banker,* September 14, 1961.

[71] "U. S. Jurors May Halt Minneapolis Probe," *American Banker,* January 8, 1962.

[72] Williams, "Banking and the Antitrust Laws," *The Banking Law Journal* (May 1964), p. 385.

Sherman Act by conspiring and combining to fix and maintain charges on checking accounts and charges for other bank services of depositors. The government indicated that this was supposedly accomplished through telephone discussions and meetings during which charges were agreed upon.

Considerable effort was exerted to reach a compromise settlement, and trial was postponed several times. Finally, in February 1964 the criminal proceeding was terminated when the defendants, seven banks and a bank holding company, were permitted to enter *nolo contendere* (no contest) pleas and were fined a total of 70 thousand dollars. The civil action was settled under the terms of a consent judgment which prohibited the banks "from fixing uniform service charges or exchanging information as to costs of service charges."[73]

*United States v. Northwestern National Bank of Minneapolis.* In this case an indictment was returned under Section 1 of the Sherman Act charging eleven national banks in Minneapolis, St. Paul, and Duluth, Minnesota with agreeing to fix the rates of interest, terms, and conditions on loans secured by bank stock; fix the rates of interest on livestock loans and to fix the amounts of rebate, kickback, or commission paid to banks which originate or service such loans; fix the rates of interest charged correspondent bankers for conventional loans; fix the amount of rebate, kickback, or commission to correspondent banks for placing general overline loans with the defendant banks; and other illegal acts.

One of the allegations which the bankers found very difficult to understand was the accusation that the banks had agreed to refrain from absorbing exchange charges for correspondent banks. (Exchange charges in this case referring to the discount that some banks which are not members of the Federal Reserve System make on their own checks when presented by another bank.) The bankers were confused because a provision of the Federal Reserve's Regulation Q prohibits the payment of interest on demand deposits, and if the banks had absorbed the charges themselves, except for a nominal 2

[73] Lifland, "Day-to-Day Banking Practices under the Antitrust Laws," *The Bankers Magazine* (Summer 1964), p. 39. The terms of the injunction may be found in *U. S. v. The First National Bank of St. Paul*, 1964 *Trade Cases* ¶ 71,021.

dollars per customer, per month, instead of passing them along to their customers they would have violated this regulation.[74] The attitude of many bankers regarding this particular charge in the Justice Department's complaint is exemplified by the following remark made by a bank executive: "How can we illegally conspire to refrain from doing something that is against the law to do?"[75]

After considerable delay the indictment against one defendant in the *Northwestern National Bank case* was dismissed and the remaining defendants entered no-contest pleas and were fined a total of 126 thousand dollars. The civil proceedings were terminated by entry of a consent decree which prohibited the banks "from agreeing to fix the rate of interest on loans, from restricting the solicitation of business by any correspondent bank, or from preventing the absorption of exchange charges or losses on securities for any third person."[76]

*United States v. Duluth Clearinghouse Association.* This was also an indictment under Section 1 of the Sherman Act. It charged a clearinghouse and four banks with agreeing: to fix rates, terms, and conditions of interest to be paid on savings accounts and other time deposits; to limit and refrain from advertising the interest rate paid on time deposits; to fix the rates for service charges; to fix the rates, terms, and conditions of interest to be charged for certain types of loans to borrowers; and to induce other banks in Duluth and in the surrounding territory to adopt the same or similar rates and charges to those used by the defendant banks.

As in the other cases, the banking institutions involved pleaded no contest in the criminal proceeding and fines of 57 thousand dollars were levied against them. The civil proceeding was terminated by a consent judgment which prohibited the defendants from fixing the interest rate paid to depositors or the terms or duration of installment loans, and from agreeing on service charges or exchanging information relating to them.[77]

---

[74] See *Published Interpretations of the Board of Governors of the Federal Reserve System* as of December 31, 1961, ¶¶ 3165–67.

[75] "Minnesota Banks Caught in Squeeze," *American Banker,* February 19, 1963.

[76] For the terms of the injunction, see 1964 *Trade Cases* ¶ 71,020.

[77] For the terms of the injunction, see 1964 *Trade Cases* ¶ 71,022.

SOME GENERAL OBSERVATIONS

The consent decree in the *New Jersey case* made many bankers aware that their cooperative actions with other banks, whether through the local clearinghouse or a less formal arrangement, may violate the antitrust laws. However, it was probably not until charges were filed in the *Minnesota cases,* with their extensive publicity and not only civil but criminal indictments, that the banking industry really became aware that some of the procedures commonly followed in day-to-day operations may have been illegal under provisions of the Sherman Act.

Naturally, the banking critic may point to the warnings by the ABA General Counsel regarding possible antitrust violations which appeared in *Paton's Digest* as early as the mid-1940s. Yet these were hardly sufficient to overcome a hundred years of precedent—precedent one might add which originated not only with the banks but with the bank supervisory agencies, both state and federal. As a result bankers simply could not believe that their industry was subject to the standard antitrust regulations until they were presented with convincing evidence in the form of the decision of the Supreme Court in the *Philadelphia National Bank case.* After this opinion was delivered, the change in the attitude of bankers was readily apparent. The Minnesota banks were prepared to capitulate and the president of the defendant bank holding company observed: "This decision by the United States Supreme Court was a most significant development and it seems clear that the banking industry of this country will conform its practices accordingly."[78]

Commercial bankers should have learned an important lesson from the *New Jersey* and *Minnesota cases* (and from the *Philadelphia* and *Lexington cases* to be discussed in the next chapter).[79] By now one would hope that bankers realize that if they engage in the ques-

[78] First Bank Stock Corporation, *Annual Report* for the year ended December 31, 1963, (p. 2) provides an excellent illustration of this.

[79] Some practices might have been sucessfully defended. Lifland, in his "Day-to-Day Banking Practices under the Antitrust Laws," *Bankers Magazine* (Summer 1964), states that the court might entertain the argument that certain restrictive agreements among commercial banks do not restrain trade, citing *U. S.* v. *Morgan,* 118 F. Supp. 621 (S.D.N.Y., 1953), and *Board of Trade of the City of Chicago* v. *U. S.,* 246 U.S. 231 (1918).

tionable activity discussed in this section they could face an antitrust suit which may result in costs running into the hundreds of thousands of dollars, injunctions, and extremely bad publicity. In addition, if criminal as well as civil indictments are filed, the next time the Department of Justice may decide to name individuals as well as firms (as in the early 1960s when 29 manufacturers of electrical equipment and 45 of their executives faced criminal charges) now that the banks should know they are subject to antitrust prosecution. Therefore, since it would certainly seem to be in the bankers' best interest not to forget this antitrust lesson, it might be advisable for the bank trade associations and the supervisory agencies[80] on occasion to remind bankers of the dangers in antitrust violations.[81]

## TYING ARRANGEMENTS AND EXCLUSIVE DEALING

Since the Minnesota cases, there have been no additional suits in which commercial banks have been charged with price-fixing violations under federal law. However, during the last few years litigation has been initiated under Sections 1 and 2 of the Sherman Act as a result of other forms of possible restraint of trade or monopolization by banking institutions. In 1964 two Utah banks sought damages and injunctive relief against a third Utah bank which they argued participated in tying arrangements and related activities. And in 1965 the Department of Justice filed suit against a Virginia bank because this institution was supposedly involved in exclusive dealing contracts.

Some readers who are familiar with the antitrust statutes may feel that the above-mentioned actions should have been initiated under Section 3 of the Clayton Act, which covers both exclusive dealing and tying agreements, as well as under the Sherman Act. However, both Sections 2 and 3 of the Clayton Act appear to cover only transactions in commodities, and there is considerable support for the view that therefore these Sections do not apply to most functions of commercial

[80] The Comptroller of the Currency through his examiners and legal staff, for example, has attempted to ensure that the banks under his supervision set rates independently. See U. S. Congress, House, *Meetings with Department and Agency Officials,* 1963, pp. 128–32.

[81] This has been done by the Comptroller of the Currency for national banks. See the Comptroller of the Currency, 101st *Annual Report,* 1963 p. 29.

banks. For example, a District Court decision in *U. S.* v. *Investors Diversified Services*[82] held that the making of a loan of money secured by a real estate mortgage was not a sale or lease within the meaning of Section 3. Furthermore, the opinion went on to note that ". . . the loaning of money is not a sale, leasing, or contract for sale of 'goods, wares, merchandise, machinery, supplies, or other commodities' within the meaning of Section 3 of the Clayton Act."[83]

Apparently, the question of the applicability of Sections 2 and 3 to some of the functions of commercial banks was one of the issues raised in the complaint in the Utah case discussed below, but the point was not considered in the decisions of the trial or appellate courts. The Supreme Court does not seem to have ever indicated its views on this question, although in *Times-Picayune Pub. Co.* v. *U. S.,* it referred to, but expressed no opinion concerning, the statutory interpretations of the term "commodity" given in the *Investors Diversified Services* case cited above.[84] Thus, since the more general provisions of Sections 1 and 2 of the Sherman Act are applicable to the practices enumerated in Sections 2 and 3 of the Clayton Act, whether or not "commodities" are involved,[85] the actions resulting from possible exclusive dealing or tying arrangements by banks to date have been brought only under the Sherman Act.[86]

THE UTAH CASE

In April 1964 the Bank of Utah and the Bank of Ben Lomond, both commercial banks located in Ogden, Utah, filed a complaint against a third bank in that city, The Commercial Security Bank,

---

[82] *U. S.* v. *Investors Diversified Services* 102 F. Supp. 645 (1951).

[83] *Ibid.,* at 649.

[84] *Times Picayune Pub. Co.* v. *U. S.,* 345 U.S. 594 (1953) at 609, note 27. It also mentioned *Fleetway Inc.* v. *Public Service Interstate Transportation Co.* [72 F. 2d 761 (1934)], in which the transportation of passengers for hire by motorbus was held not to involve a "commodity" within the meaning of Section 3 of the Clayton Act.

[85] Other cases relating to this point at least indirectly include: *Gaylord Shops Inc.* v. *Pittsburgh Miracle Mile,* 219 F. Supp. 400 (1963); *Centanni* v. *T. Smith & Son, Inc.,* 216 F. Supp. 330 (1963); and *Columbia Broadcasting System* v. *Amana Refrigeration Inc.,* 295 F. 2d 375 (1961), cert. denied, 369 U.S. 812 (1962).

[86] I am indebted to Larry Williams and William Lifland for their comments concerning the general question of banking as a commodity. They have no responsibility for any of the statements made, however.

claiming this institution had violated Sections 1 and 2 of the Sherman Antitrust Act and seeking damages and injunctive relief against the defendant. The specific charges resulted from contracts for payroll accounting services between the defendant and the Boards of Education of Ogden City and Weber County. The defendant, in turn, filed a counterclaim asserting the plaintiffs "tortiously induced" a breach of a similar contract with the St. Benedict's hospital.

The contracts involved what is referred to as a "no-check payroll plan," under which various payroll accounting procedures were performed by the Commercial Security Bank. The bank would mail to each employee covered by the plan a combination deposit receipt and earnings record. Also the bank would credit the net amount due each employee for the pay period to a special account set up in his name with that bank. The employee could make deposits to this account and use it as he would a regular checking account. In addition the employee could draw two checks against it each month without service charge, or he could arrange for the automatic transfer of the funds to any bank of his choice. (The last provision had been proposed by the plaintiff banks and adopted by the defendant.)

The trial court considered the plaintiffs' charges under Sections 1 and 2 of the Sherman Act and found the contracts did not amount to unlawful tying arrangements, did not involve unreasonable restraints of trade, and did not establish an attempt to monopolize commercial banking. Therefore, the plaintiffs' complaint was dismissed. In addition, the defendant was awarded 7,251 dollars on its counterclaim against the plaintiffs (Bank of Utah and Bank of Ben Lomond).[87] The judgment of the District Court was affirmed by the U. S. Court of Appeals, Tenth Circuit, on November 14, 1966,[88] and petition for certiorari was denied by the United States Supreme Court on April 24, 1967.

THE VIRGINIA CASE

On September 30, 1966, a civil antitrust case was brought by the Department of Justice against the Bank of Virginia.[89] The suit alleged that the bank maintained an exclusive dealing provision in the operation of its credit plan in violation of the restraint of trade and

[87] *Bank of Utah* v. *Commercial Security Bank*, 1965 *Trade Cases* ¶ 71,540.
[88] *Bank of Utah* v. *Commercial Security Bank*, 369 F. 2d 19 (1966).
[89] *U. S.* v. *The Bank of Virginia*, 1966 *Trade Cases* ¶ 71,947.

attempted monopolization sections (§§ 1 and 2) of the Sherman Act. A court order invalidating the requirement was sought by the suit.

The civil injunction complaint charged that the bank required merchants using its credit plan not to deal with any other regional credit service. Because of the Bank of Virginia's supposed dominant and established position among credit services in eastern Virginia, Justice contended the availability of the bank's plan was essential to many businessmen who wanted to participate in a credit plan type of operation. As a result, it was alleged that a number of businesses had stopped or refrained from dealing with other credit plans. This, it was asserted, denied businesses and the public the benefits of free and unrestricted competition in regional credit services in the area, while the bank's competitors in this field had been impeded.[90]

The Antitrust Division is reported to have stated that other banks were told "to stop this type of thing" and that they had responded without court action being necessary.[91] And, ultimately, the Bank of Virginia suit was also settled without a contest in the courts for, without admitting the truth of the Government's charges, on November 25, 1966 the bank entered into a proposed consent judgment in the Federal District Court for Eastern Virginia.[92] In very general terms, among other things the judgment prohibited the bank from requiring that merchants using its credit plan deal with no other regional credit service, and it stated that any exclusive dealing provisions in existing contracts with merchants were to be deleted. The Final Judgment in this action was entered December 27, 1966.

THE ANTITRUST DIVISION'S VIEWPOINT

The Department of Justice is attempting to spell out more clearly the practices which it feels might be illegal under the antitrust laws. For example, Assistant Attorney General Donald F. Turner in a speech at the Northwestern School of Law in the fall of 1966 provided a rough indication of the extent to which these statutes permit cooperative agreements among competitors. He observed:[93]

[90] BNA's Antitrust and Trade Regulation Report (October 4, 1966), A-4; and 1966 Trade Cases ¶ 71,947.

[91] "Justice Sues Va. Bank," American Banker, October 3, 1966.

[92] 1966 Trade Cases ¶ 71,947.

[93] Donald F. Turner, "Cooperation Among Competitors," speech before the Fifth Annual Corporate Counsel Institute, Northwestern University, October 13, 1966, pp. 13–14. (mimeographed)

(1) Agreements concerned with the dissemination of relevant market information are lawful, indeed encouraged, as long as there is no indication of a purpose to inhibit individual competitive decision making. (2) So long as there has been informed consumer choice, a voluntary agreement to take away certain product alternatives is unlawful unless essential to achievement of a strong, clear, overriding interest in the public health or safety, and then probably only until there has been an opportunity for appropriate legislative action. (3) There may be situations in which voluntary agreements to limit product alternatives are necessary to meet the incapacity of consumers to make a rational choice, but these are likely to be extremely rare and the burden of proof on proponents should be a heavy one.

While neither these remarks nor the more detailed antitrust guidelines reportedly being prepared by Justice are likely to reduce the need for competent legal counsel in this field, both the attorney and the businessman should welcome the establishment of at least some criteria to aid them in their decision making in this extremely complicated area.


## INTERLOCKING DIRECTORATES

By 1912 both major political parties had become committed to revisions in the antitrust law, including the strengthening of the prohibitions against interlocking directorates, and a number of bills were introduced which were designed to accomplish this objective. One of these bills, H. R. 15657, which was destined to become the Clayton Act, was introduced in April 1914, and Section 8 of this bill contained provisions which would have prohibited various forms of interlocking corporate managements. Numerous changes were made in the bill in the House and in the Senate. Of these revisions, one by the Senate Judiciary Committee was of particular importance to this study, for it would have struck out the entire provision relative to interlocking directorates that involved banks and trust companies. "The committee thought such prohibitions were more appropriately made by amendments to the banking laws and not the commerce acts."[94] However, in the Senate-House conference regarding the bill, the provisions applicable to bank directors which had been included in the House bill were restored with some modifications.

[94] U. S. Congress, House, *Interlocks in Corporate Management*, 1965, p. 19.

In essence, Section 8 of the Clayton Act as enacted into law in October 1914 read in part as follows:

That from and after two years from the date of the approval of this Act no person shall at the same time be a director or other officer or employee of more than one bank, banking association or trust company, organized or operating under the laws of the United States, either of which has deposits, capital, surplus, and undivided profits aggregating more than $5,000,000; and no private banker or person who is a director in any bank or trust company, organized and operating under the laws of a State, having deposits, capital, surplus, and undivided profits aggregating more than $5,000,000, shall be eligible to be a director in any bank or banking association organized or operating under the laws of the United States. . . . No bank, banking association or trust company, organized or operating under the laws of the United States, in any city or incorporated town or village of more than two hundred thousand inhabitants, as shown by the last preceding decennial census of the United States, shall have as a director or other officer or employee any private banker or any director or other officer or employee of any other bank, banking association or trust company located in the same place.

Exceptions to this section included mutual savings banks, 100 percent-owned affiliates, and Class A Federal Reserve Bank directors.

Between 1916 and 1935 there were numerous amendments to the provisions of Section 8 relating to banks.[95] In general these changes were designed to add exceptions to the interlocks prohibited and to provide standards that the Board of Governors could apply in granting its approval to such interlocks. The last amendments to the banking provisions of Section 8 were enacted on August 23, 1935 by Section 329 of the Banking Act of 1935, and the present Section 8 reads as follows:[96]

No private banker or director, officer, or employee of any member bank of the Federal Reserve System or any branch thereof shall be at the same time a director, officer, or employee of any other bank, banking association, savings bank, or trust company organized under the National Bank Act or organized under the laws of any State or of the District of

[95] These amendments are discussed in *ibid.,* pp. 23–25.

[96] The Federal Reserve Board's *Regulation L* (12CFR212) provides a much more detailed explanation of its interpretation of the Section 8 banking provisions. Also, see *Regulation R* (12CFR218) regarding similar appointment of directors, officers, and employees of dealers in securities restricted under the Banking Act of 1933, as amended.

Columbia, or any branch thereof, except that the Board of Governors of the Federal Reserve System may by regulation permit such service as a director, officer, or employee of not more than one other such institution or branch thereof; but the foregoing prohibition shall not apply in the case of any one or more of the following or any branch thereof:

(1) A bank, banking association, savings bank, or trust company, more than 90 per centum of the stock of which is owned directly or indirectly by the United States or by any corporation of which the United States directly or indirectly owns more than 90 per centum of the stock.

(2) A bank, banking association, savings bank, or trust company which has been placed formally in liquidation or which is in the hands of a receiver, conservator, or other official exercising similar functions.

(3) A corporation, principally engaged in international or foreign banking or banking in a dependency or insular possession of the United States which has entered into an agreement with the Board of Governors of the Federal Reserve System pursuant to section 25 of the Federal Reserve Act.

(4) A bank, banking association, savings bank, or trust company, more than 50 per centum of the common stock of which is owned directly or indirectly by persons who own directly or indirectly more than 50 per centum of the common stock of such member bank.

(5) A bank, banking association, savings bank, or trust company not located and having no branch in the same city, town, or village as that which such member bank or any branch thereof is located, or in any city, town, or village contiguous or adjacent thereto.

(6) A bank, banking association, savings bank, or trust company not engaged in a class or classes of business in which such member bank is engaged.

(7) A mutual savings bank having no capital stock.

Until February 1, 1939, nothing in this section shall prohibit any director, officer, or employee of any member bank of the Federal Reserve System, or any branch thereof, who is lawfully serving at the same time as a private banker or as a director, officer, or employee of any other bank, banking association, savings bank, or trust company, or any branch thereof, on the date of enactment of the Banking Act of 1935, from continuing such service.

The Board of Governors of the Federal Reserve System is authorized and directed to enforce complaints with this section, and to prescribe such rules and regulations as it deems necessary for that purpose.

It should be added that under Section 15 the Attorney General is granted concurrent enforcement responsibility with respect to all violations of the Clayton Act, and under Section 11 the Federal Reserve Board is granted specific authority to enforce Section 8 (as well as

Sections 2, 3, and 7) where applicable to banks, banking associations, and trust companies.[97]

## ENFORCEMENT EXPERIENCE

Despite the extensive criticism of interlocking corporate managements prior to the passage of Section 8 of the Clayton Act, there was little effort by the agencies charged with the enforcement of this provision to use this new power. From its enactment in October 1914 to January 1965 the Federal Trade Commission filed a total of thirteen complaints under Section 8 of the Clayton Act. Only one of these complaints resulted in a cease-and-desist order, and this was by consent; the remainder were dismissed when the directors who were involved discontinued the prohibited relationship. The Department of Justice did not undertake a systematic program with respect to interlocking directorates until after World War II, and the first case to be litigated to a decision was not filed until February 1952. As of January 1965 "Justice" had instituted a total of only ten cases to enforce Section 8.[98]

*Federal Reserve Board—interlocking bank directorates.*   A careful review of nearly seventy cases which "Shepard's Citator" and other legal sources[99] indicated contained at least some mention of Section 8 of the Clayton Act uncovered no court action directly involving a commercial bank under this section. This finding was correct in the opinion of the General Counsel of the Board of Governors. However, the counsel noted that the Board has held proceedings to determine whether violations under Section 8 of the Clayton Act have occurred, and it has issued orders based on its findings at these proceedings. But none of the orders issued was challenged through appellate review.[100]

[97] U. S. Congress, House, *Interlocks in Corporate Management*, 1965, p. 52.

[98] *Ibid.*, p. 57. This study contains an excellent summary of the experience under Section 8, and much of the material included herein was obtained from this source.

[99] *Shepard's United States Citations; American Law Reports Digest;* 83 *American Law Reports Annotated* 2d, 374; and *American Jurisprudence,* "Monopolies," §§ 101–18.

[100] Letter from Howard H. Hackley, General Counsel, Board of Governors of the Federal Reserve System, May 24, 1965.

The Antitrust Subcommittee of the Committee on the Judiciary of the House of Representatives recently requested that the Board of Governors provide statistics with respect to exceptions it has authorized under Section 8 of the Clayton Act. But, since the Board does not issue individual permits for such exemptions, no statistics could be supplied regarding the number of such interlocking relationships that presently exist.[101] To obtain at least some data concerning the general topic of bank interlocking directorates, the House committee's staff made a survey of the officer personnel and directors of the fifteen largest commercial banks in the United States as of December 31, 1962 (ranked by deposits). While the staff report showed no interlocks between the 15 commercial banks studied and other banks located in the same city, it did reveal that 68 direct officer or director interlocks with other commercial banks existed.[102] Although bankers would probably not be surprised that these relationships were found (and, considering the stature of many of the officers and directors of these large institutions, bankers might be surprised that there were not more), nevertheless, it requires little imagination to understand why the Department of Justice might be disturbed by these data.

*Federal Reserve Board—banks and dealers in securities.*[103]  The Board of Governors' enforcement authority is not limited to prohibiting (or exempting) certain types of interlocking bank directorates under Section 8 of the Clayton Act, for it has similar powers regarding bank-security dealer relationships as well. Under the provisions of Section 32 of the Banking Act of 1933, as amended, no officer, director, or employee of a firm primarily engaged in the issue, flotation, underwriting, public sale, or distribution of securities, can legally be at the same time an officer, director, or employee of any member bank of the Federal Reserve System (with numerous exceptions).

Considerable controversy has arisen regarding the meaning of the

[101] U. S. Congress, House, *Interlocks in Corporate Management*, 1965, p. 85.

[102] *Ibid.*, pp. 177–87.

[103] Section 8 of the Clayton Act was also amended by Section 33 of the Banking Act of 1933, which added Section 8A regarding interlocks between banks and firms which make loans secured by stock or bond collateral. The Banking Act of 1935, Section 329, strikes Section 8A of the Clayton Act.

expression primarily engaged, and unlike its experience under Section 8 of the Clayton Act, the Board has faced litigation because of its decisions under this section. In the mid-1940s certain directors of Paterson National Bank [New Jersey] were also employees of Eastman, Dillon & Company. Since less than one-half of Eastman, Dillon's gross income from all sources was derived from its brokerage business, the directors argued that their firm was not primarily engaged in this line of business. However, the Supreme Court, sustaining the Federal Reserve's view and overruling a lower court opinion, concluded the term primarily engaged required only that underwriting be an important part, but not necessarily the principal part, of the securities firm's business.[104]

In addition to requesting data concerning exemptions made by the Board of Governors under Section 8 of the Clayton Act, the House Antitrust Subcommittee also asked the Federal Reserve for statistical data with respect to the number of interlocking positions it has excepted from the requirements of Section 32 of the Banking Act of 1933. But, as in the case of Section 8, the Board replied there was no information available at the "Fed" to determine the frequency of exempted interlocking relationships since the Board can make exceptions to Section 32 only by general regulations, and it is not authorized to issue individual permits.[105]

## THE NEED FOR NEW LEGISLATION

For decades scholars have argued that Section 8 of the Clayton Act was not effective in the banking area because: it applied only to larger institutions and could not curb chain systems which were made up of small banks; the provisions in the law could be circumvented by appointing "dummy directors"; there were too many exceptions to Section 8's restrictions; the law was not actively enforced; and for numerous other reasons.[106] In recent years two studies of commercial banking operations prepared by federal agencies called for additional

[104] *Board of Governors of the Federal Reserve System* v. *Agnew*, 329 U.S. 441 (1947).

[105] U. S. Congress, House, *Interlocks in Corporate Management*, 1965, p. 84; and Board of Governors of the Federal Reserve System, *Regulation R*, n. 2.

[106] A few examples are: Chapman, *Concentration of Banking*, pp. 332–34; Willis, "Banking Inquiry of 1925," XIV, pp. 15–16; Cartinhour, *Branch, Group, and Chain Banking*, pp. 175–77; and *The Banking Situation in the United States*, p. 59.

legislation covering bank interlocking directorates. The report of the Advisory Committee on Banking to the Comptroller of the Currency (Saxon Report) published in the fall of 1962 observed: "The financial structure of the nation needs to be guarded against conflicts of interest." And the report recommended that "the prohibitions of the present law on interlocking directorates should be made applicable between banks, savings and loan associations, and mutual savings banks, whether chartered under state or federal law."[107] In a similar vein the April 1963 report of the Committee on Financial Institutions to the President of the United States (Heller Report) expressed concern because of Section 8's failure to cover ". . . interlocking relationships among nonmember banks, savings and loan associations, and other financial institutions." In addition, the report considered certain exemptions and exceptions to the law but it made no comment regarding them, except that the committee saw no reason why the limitation on interlocking relationships should apply only to commercial banks. The Heller Report also noted that the second part of Section 8 (dealing with corporations in general) needs clarification since banks are exempted and this might be interpreted as exempting an interlocking directorate between a bank and a competing financial institution. The report concluded: "The committee believes that the provisions of Section 8 of the Clayton Act which govern interlocking relationships involving financial institutions should be clarified and probably strengthened."[108]

Besides the above studies, which were primarily concerned with banks and other financial institutions, the general analysis of Section 8 of the Clayton Act prepared by the House Antitrust Subcommittee indicated this section needs revision. But the subcommittee's staff report expressed considerable uncertainty regarding the form such revision should take because its research found very little evidence of abuses resulting from management interlocks. The situation was summarized in the staff report as follows:[109]

There is virtually no reliable current information available that will demonstrate either acceptable or undesirable effects that have resulted from the fact that common management personnel participated in, or

[107] *National Banks and the Future*, p. 94.
[108] Heller Report, p. 53.
[109] U. S. Congress, House, *Interlocks in Corporate Management*, 1965, p. 229.

influenced, particular business transactions. Without factual information concerning the actual operation of interlocks, 'common sense,' presupposition, reliance on past proof, and abstract reasoning have been predominant in the analysis of both the virtues and evils attributed to corporate interlocks.

Despite the lack of evidence demonstrating specific abuses resulting from management interlocks, the report noted "commonsense, practical observation, and abstract reasoning all support the conclusion that such effects should follow."[110]

The staff report further indicated that in the absence of evidence bearing upon behavioral characteristics, as a framework for further investigation, a model bill that eliminates, from an analytical standpoint, known defects in existing law and proceeds from a theoretically consistent Government-wide policy would be helpful. A series of recommendations concerning the content of a model interlocking directorate bill was included in the study,[111] and legislation based upon these suggestions was introduced by Emanuel Celler late in 1965 (H. R. 11572), but no action was taken on the bill during the 89th Congress.[112]

Although the bill was not passed, it merits some additional consideration, for it points out a number of dangers in applying a general law of this type to commercial banking. Had the bill been enacted it would appear to have eliminated entirely all of the special banking provisions of § 8 of the Clayton Act listed earlier in this chapter. Thus, apparently it would have subjected banks to the same prohibitions that would have applied to other firms under this law; yet it would have retained Section 32 of the Banking Act of 1933 concerning relationships with securities firms. The potential impact of this statute was described in a recent legal periodical as follows:[113]

This change would not only prohibit management overlaps between most banks but also prohibit directors and executives of banks from serving in a responsible capacity with almost any other organization, since nearly every organization is a potential customer or creditor of a bank. A bank

[110] *Ibid.,* p. 230.

[111] *Ibid.,* p. 231.

[112] Comparable legislation was introduced by Representative Celler in the 90th Congress, H. R. 2509.

[113] Lombard, "Corporate Management Interlocks Bill," *Business Lawyer* (July 1966), p. 883.

director would apparently not even be permitted to serve as a director of a non-profit corporation, which would be a potential customer or creditor of the bank.

While the existing Section 8 of the Clayton Act as it applies to banks may be unsatisfactory, a bill such as H.R. 11572 if enforced as suggested above would not be an improvement. Clearly, considerable additional research in this area is needed not only to determine the effects of the existence of interlocking directorates but also the possible implications of legislation such as the Celler bill which might serve to eliminate them.[114]

[114] Public Law 89–175 (S.1240) approved September 9, 1965 provided an exemption from antitrust laws for banks and other lending institutions that voluntarily cooperate in the Administration's balance of payments program. (Exemption applies only to authorized activities under this program.) Exemption of participants in the program from the antitrust restrictions is conditioned on a review by the Attorney General and approval by the President of any agreement or program consummated under the act. This legislation [79 Stat. 674 (1965)] was recently extended to June 30, 1969. [81 Stat. 165 (1967)].

# CHAPTER 7

————◄─◆─►————

# Commercial Banking and the Federal Antitrust Laws: Mergers[1]

## INTRODUCTION

BETWEEN 1950 and 1960 there were approximately 1,500 mergers, consolidations, and absorptions of banks in the United States. Despite this pattern of acquisitions in an industry already characterized by relatively high levels of concentration in many geographic markets, at meetings of banking scholars and of operating bankers one rarely heard anyone even mention the anti-merger provisions of the antitrust laws. However, this was probably to be expected, for prior to the Supreme Court decision in *United States* v. *Philadelphia National Bank*[2] on June 17, 1963, there was general (though not unanimous) agreement that the antitrust laws probably did not cover mergers in this industry.[3] The District Court Judge who heard the *Manufacturers*

[1] In this chapter, as in earlier chapters, merger is merely used as a generic term referring to a statutory merger, consolidation, absorption, or acquisition.

[2] *U. S.* v. *Philadelphia National Bank,* 374 U.S. 321 (1963). Hereafter called the *Philadelphia case.*

[3] Two earlier cases, both involving bank holding companies, were challenged under § 7 but neither was heard by the Supreme Court—*Transamerica Corporation* v. *Board of Governors* and *U. S.* v. *Firstamerica Corporation.*

*Hanover case* described the attitude which prevailed as follows: ". . . In the decade 1950–1960, the Department of Justice, like Congress, the federal banking agencies, and most of the legal profession, believed that Section 7 did not apply to bank mergers accomplished by [what was presumed to be] the acquisition of assets, and there was doubt as to the applicability of the Sherman Act."[4] But, after *Philadelphia,* there was no longer any question—the antitrust laws applied to commercial banking, although two 1966 amendments to banking statutes did leave considerable doubt regarding the standards to be used in enforcing these laws.

The *Philadelphia case* was extremely significant not only to bankers but also to the Department of Justice, for its implications extended far beyond the banking community. The Assistant Attorney General in charge of the Antitrust Division at the time of the Philadelphia decision stated: "Certainly there is no disputing the fact that the *Philadelphia National Bank case* was the most important antitrust decision of the year and, perhaps, of the decade."[5] The Assistant Attorney General noted that this decision underscored the deep concern of the courts, the Congress, and of the public about the increasingly heavy concentration in some industries, and he warned that his division would continue to be vigorous in its attempts to enforce Section 7.

While the Supreme Court's opinion in the *Philadelphia case* affected many industries, naturally the effect was most immediate and the controversy was the greatest in the banking area. The criticism began with a 25-page dissenting opinion written by Mr. Justice Harlan of the United States Supreme Court, and, several years, dozens of journal articles, and hundreds of speeches later the debate still persists. In large part this activity has been beneficial to banking for it has stimulated an interest in research in the banking structure area, and it has encouraged a number of very able business organization

[4] Judge MacMahon's Opinion in *U. S.* v. *Manufacturers Hanover Trust Company,* Civ. 61–C–3194 (S.D.N.Y.), 240 F. Supp. 867, 949 (1965). Some lawyers, however, were quite certain the Sherman Act would apply. See "Federal Regulation of Bank Mergers: The Opposing Views of the Federal Banking Agencies and the Department of Justice," 75 *Harvard Law Review* 756, 760 (1962).

[5] Speech by William Orrick, Jr., before the Antitrust Section of the American Bar Association (August 12, 1963), p. 3. (mimeographed)

specialists to devote some of their time to a field which they have usually neglected in the past. But unfortunately, much of this work has been disappointing for it has been prepared by or for special interest groups, or it has been concerned primarily with the possible misapplication of the antitrust laws in the banking area rather than the more basic question of whether they should or should not be applied. This chapter and Chapter 8 consider the actions brought against bank mergers by federal authorities, the criteria used by the courts in determining the legality of these transactions, and the findings of banking structure research concerning a few of the more important issues raised in these cases.

## BANK MERGER CASES

Although the *Philadelphia National Bank case* was the first action involving a bank merger to be decided by the Supreme Court, it was not the first bank acquisition case brought under Section 7 of the Clayton Act or Section 1 of the Sherman Act. During the 1950s, two bank holding companies were charged with violating the antitrust laws because of their acquisition of commercial banks—Transamerica Corporation and Firstamerica Corporation.[6] Both of these cases will be discussed at some length in this section, while more detailed analysis of the recent series of bank cases, of which *Philadelphia* was the first, will appear in succeeding sections of this chapter.

*The Transamerica Case.*[7] On June 24, 1948, the Board of Governors of the Federal Reserve System initiated its first (and to date, its only) proceeding under Sections 7 and 11 of the Clayton Act.[8] The Board issued a complaint and notice of hearing to Transamerica

[6] Now called Western Bancorporation.

[7] For detailed analyses of this case and preceding and succeeding developments, see "Judicial Invalidation of Federal Reserve Policy Against Bank Holding Company Expansion," 57 *Yale Law Journal* 297 (1947); Neal, "The Clayton Act and the Transamerica Case," 5 *Stanford Law Review* 179 (1953); Herman, "Board of Governors v. Transamerica: Victory Out of Defeat," *Antitrust Bulletin* (July–August 1959) pp. 521–39; and "Transamerica—The Bankholding Company Problem," 1 *Stanford Law Review* 658 (1949).

[8] As was noted earlier, Section 11 (15 U.S.C. § 21) merely provides that the Federal Reserve Board has concurrent authority with the U. S. Department of Justice to enforce Sections 2, 3, 7, and 8 of the Clayton Act where applicable to banks.

Corporation, a West Coast holding company, charging that this firm and its predecessors violated Section 7 of the Clayton Act by continuously and systematically acquiring the stocks of independent banks in five states. This action by the Board was only one of a series of attempts by the federal banking agencies to restrain the expansion of this holding company. During the late 1930s and early 1940s moral suasion was employed, but it proved to be ineffective. Therefore the FDIC, the Comptroller of the Currency, and the "Fed" realized more definite action would have to be taken. As a result the three agencies agreed that they would not permit Transamerica (via its affiliates) to acquire additional branch offices,[9] and other ways of restricting the growth of this firm were considered. These included modification or cancellation of voting permits granted Transamerica for its member bank affiliates by the Board of Governors under the Banking Act of 1933 (12 U.S.C. § 61); passage of new group banking (bank holding company) legislation; and a possible antitrust suit by the Department of Justice under the Sherman Act or a similar suit by the Board under Section 7 of the Clayton Act.

Late in October, 1945, Justice informed the Board that there was inadequate evidence of abuse of power to sustain a Sherman Act charge.[10] Thereafter, the Board of Governors began to give more serious consideration to its initiating a Section 7 suit against Transamerica. Interest in a possible Clayton Act proceeding was further stimulated in 1946–1947 by the threatened breakdown of the gentlemen's agreement among the banking agencies under which they had attempted to restrict the expansion of branch offices by Transamerica banks.[11] The Federal Reserve realized that something would have to be done quickly to prevent the conversion of numerous Transamerica banks to branches, and, on November 7, 1947, the Board notified the other federal banking agencies and the Attorney General that it was investigating the possibility of instituting a Clayton Act suit against this holding company.[12]

After the Board's preliminary investigation was completed, its

[9] The holding company could still acquire banks but could not convert them into branches.

[10] Herman, "Board of Governors v. Transamerica," *Antitrust Bulletin* (July–August 1959), p. 524.

[11] Eccles, *Beckoning Frontiers,* p. 448.

[12] *Ibid.,* p. 450.

members voted to bring an action against Transamerica. A member of the Board was appointed hearing officer, and after reviewing a vast amount of evidence over a two-year period he concluded that the charges against Transamerica were valid. The Board of Governors agreed with the hearing officer's findings, and on March 27, 1952, it ordered Transamerica to divest itself completely of all capital stock in 47 majority-owned banks.[13] The holding company's attorneys immediately objected to this decision and sought relief through the United States Court of Appeals for the Third Circuit, and on July 16, 1953, the Court set aside the Board's order.[14] On November 30, 1953, the Supreme Court of the United States denied the Board of Governors' petition for certiorari to review the decision of the Court of Appeals,[15] and the Federal Reserve announced it would take no further action in this proceeding.[16]

The Circuit Court indicated that the Board's case was extremely weak in regard to the geographic market involved. The proceedings were conducted and the order was entered under the "old" Section 7 provisions which made competition between the acquired and the acquiring corporation a vital factor so far as substantial lessening of competition was concerned.[17] Yet, the Board's counsel emphasized the "tendency to create a monopoly clause," largely ignoring the question of competition between the firms involved and treating the case almost as though it were being tried under the amended Section

[13] "Clayton Act Proceeding," *Federal Reserve Bulletin* (April 1952), p. 391.

[14] *Transamerica Corporation* v. *Board of Governors of the Federal Reserve System,* 206 F. 2d 163 (1953).

[15] *Board of Governors of the Federal Reserve System* v. *Transamerica Corporation,* 346 U.S. 901 (1953).

[16] "Clayton Act Proceeding," *Federal Reserve Bulletin* (December 1953), p. 1329.

[17] Second paragraph of Section 7 of the Clayton Act as enacted October 15, 1914 by Ch. 323, § 7, 38 Stat. 731: No corporation shall acquire, directly or indirectly, the whole or any part of the stock or other share capital of two or more corporations engaged in commerce where the effect of such acquisition, or the use of such stock by the voting or granting of proxies or otherwise, may be to substantially lessen competition between such corporations, or any of them, whose stock or other share capital is so acquired, or to restrain such commerce in any section or community, or tend to create a monopoly of any line of commerce.

7.[18] As the case progressed, the Federal Reserve counsel gave more and more weight to competitive effects, until in the brief submitted by the Board to the Circuit Court ". . . the lessening of competition argument was elevated to virtual equality in importance with the allegation of tendency to monopoly. Nevertheless, much damage was done to the Board's case by the early de-emphasis of competitive effects, and the residue of inconsistencies and absurdities resulting from inadequate integration of these two major strands of argument."[19] Some years later, Assistant Attorney General Barnes in commenting on the preparation of the *Transamerica case* by the Federal Reserve noted that some of the men associated with the "Fed's" case had stated: "When we get into a situation like that we think we will do better to turn it over to somebody who has a little more experience in antitrust prosecution."[20]

The Board's case had attempted to show that the Transamerica Corporation controlled 41 percent of all commercial banking offices, 39 percent of all commercial bank deposits, and about 50 percent of all commercial bank loans in a five-state area (Arizona, California, Oregon, Nevada, and Washington). Using these aggregate data and without any findings as to the competitive effect of the group's acquisitions in the areas directly served by each of the acquired banks, the Board had reached its conclusion regarding the Section 7 violation and had ordered divestment. The Circuit Court judges indicated, however, that the Board in its own findings of fact [subparagraph (f) of Paragraph Seven][21] argued that the business of commercial banks

[18] Second paragraph of Section 7 of the Clayton Act as amended in 1950, 15 USCA § 18: No corporation shall acquire, directly or indirectly, the whole or any part of the stock or other share capital and no corporation subject to the jurisdiction of the Federal Trade Commission shall acquire the whole or any part of the assets of one or more corporations engaged in commerce, where in any line of commerce in any section of the country, the effect of such acquisition, of such stocks or assets, or of the use of such stock by the voting or granting of proxies or otherwise, may be substantially to lessen competition, or to tend to create a monopoly.

[19] Herman, "Board of Governors v. Transamerica," *Antitrust Bulletin* (July–August 1959), p. 526.

[20] U. S. Congress, Senate, *Report of the Attorney General's National Committee to Study the Antitrust Laws,* Hearings, 1955, p. 51.

[21] "Clayton Act Proceeding," *Federal Reserve Bulletin* (April 1952), p. 383.

was largely local and confined to the communities in which they operate and in which customers may conveniently visit them. Yet, the Board of Governors as noted above had selected a five-state area, not individual communities, as the relevant geographic market in which to analyze the competitive effects of the acquisitions, and it provided no valid reason for choosing this broad area. Hence, the court decided: "The Board's conclusion of a tendency to monopoly in the five-state area, therefore fails for want of a supporting finding that the five states constitute a single area of effective competition among commercial banks and flies in the face of its own finding that the local community is the true competitive banking area."[22] The court acknowledged that there might have been a tendency to monopoly in commercial banking by Transamerica in some of the areas in which the acquired banks were located, but the Board had not made any finding to indicate this had occurred.[23]

The *Transamerica case* left many questions unanswered, including such things as the possibility of competition between affiliates of the same group in the same market area, the ability of a holding company to control a bank (Bank of America N. T. & S. A.) by owning only a small minority interest in the institution in question, and the remedy which would be provided in a Section 7 case involving a series of bank acquisitions, primarily of noncompeting firms, when many of the transactions had taken place long before the proceeding was begun. On the other hand, the *Transamerica case* did clarify a number of points. First, the commercial banks involved were engaged in interstate commerce; second, the provisions of Section 7 did apply to commercial banks;[24] and, third, though not specifically indicated by the court, commercial banking could be employed as a distinct line of commerce, and "small customer banking" *may* determine the relevant geographic market.[25]

[22] *Ibid.,* (August 1953), p. 840.
[23] Although the Board lost the case in the courts, ultimately its objectives were achieved as Transamerica divested its shares in the Bank of America N. T. & S. A., and two years after the passage of the Bank Holding Company Act of 1956, the holding company had to separate its banking and nonbanking interests.
[24] 206 F. 2d 163, 165.
[25] 206 F. 2d 163, 167–68.

*The Firstamerica Case.*   On July 1, 1958, in order to comply with the provisions of the Bank Holding Company Act of 1956 which required the separation of the banking and nonbanking interests of registered bank holding companies, Transamerica transferred all of its directly held shares in majority-owned banks and 20 million dollars in cash to the newly created Firstamerica Corporation. In exchange Transamerica received over eleven million shares of Firstamerica's capital stock, which it immediately distributed to its shareholders. No corporate connection has existed between the two firms since that time.[26]

Less than two months after Firstamerica began operation it applied to the Board of Governors of the Federal Reserve System for approval of the proposed acquisition of California Bank, Los Angeles— a 1 billion dollar institution and the fifth largest bank in the state. This large holding company already held a controlling interest in the First Western Bank and Trust Company, San Francisco, the state's sixth largest bank, and it was indicated by the "Fed" at the time the transaction was approved that a merger of the two banks was contemplated.[27] Obviously this action could affect competition, and the Board's order approving the acquisition was accompanied by an opinion which analyzed the competitive factors involved and concluded the merger would not violate Section 7 of the Clayton Act. Nevertheless, the Department of Justice, which had become concerned because of the increasing number of bank mergers in the 1950s and which had managed to prevent a small number of bank acquisitions without litigation,[28] decided to test its antitrust powers in the banking area. By March 30, 1959, more than 97 percent of the outstanding shares of the California Bank had been irrevocably tendered pursuant to a Firstamerica exchange offer. On that day the Attorney General filed suit in the District Court charging that the agreement pursuant to which the exchange offer was made violated Section 1 of the Sherman Act and the holding company's acquisition

[26] *Prospectus, Western Bancorporation Capital Stock,* Blyth & Company, Inc., September 15, 1964, p. 2.

[27] "Law Department," *Federal Reserve Bulletin* (February 1959), pp. 134–46.

[28] U. S. Congress, Senate, *Financial Institutions Act of 1957,* Hearings, 1957, p. 1015.

of this stock violated Section 7 of the Clayton Act. This was the first time that the Justice Department had employed either of these sections in an action involving bank mergers or acquisitions.

At the time the litigation was announced, Firstamerica was the largest bank holding company in the United States, its aggregate deposits (3 billion dollars) and offices (over 320) representing approximately 9.3 percent and 11.1 percent of the deposits and offices respectively of all commercial banks in the eleven-state area served by this firm. However, it appears highly unlikely that the eleven states would have been chosen by Justice as the "relevant geographic market" in this case, especially after the Federal Reserve Board's disastrous experience in the *Transamerica case* in which it had attempted to use a five-state "market." Since both Firstamerica banks which planned to merge were located in one state but in different metropolitan areas, it is probable that the government would have argued that California was the proper section of the country in which to test the effects of the merger.[29]

Before the proposed merger with California Bank, Firstamerica's affiliate in California had 6.6 percent of total commercial bank offices and 4.3 percent of total commercial bank deposits in the state. After the merger the corresponding percentages would have been 10.9 percent and 9.3 percent, respectively. In addition, the two largest banks in California (Bank of America N. T. & S. A. and Security-First National Bank) held a substantial share of the remaining offices and deposits. The following breakdown provides some idea of the deposit concentration in the three largest banks in California before and after the proposed merger:[30]

[29] The writer does not mean to endorse the selection of the State of California (or any state) as a relevant geographic market in a situation such as this—the above is merely included for illustrative purposes. California may be a "more likely" choice than eleven states, but it may not be the best choice from the viewpoint of the banks' primary service areas. The State of California was used by David Alhadeff [*Monopoly and Competition in Banking*, p. 41] for intermediate-size borrowers as a "rough approximation to the relevant market for such borrowers."

[30] The three largest banks were selected to measure concentration merely to provide some perspective for the reader regarding the relative market shares involved in the *Firstamerica case* as contrasted with other recent bank antitrust cases.

| *Three Largest before Merger* | *Percentage of California Commercial Bank Deposits* |
|---|---|
| Bank of America | 44.9 |
| Security-First National | 13.1 |
| American Trust Company | 7.3 |
| Total | 65.3 |

| *Three Largest after Merger* | *Percentage of California Commercial Bank Deposits* |
|---|---|
| Bank of America | 44.9 |
| Security-First National | 13.1 |
| California Bank | 9.3 |
| Total | 67.3 |

From the above one may note that the increase in concentration resulting from the merger of the two Firstamerica affiliates (if California proved to be the relevant geographic market) would have been modest, but in the light of the existing high level of banking concentration in the state it may or may not have been "significant."

Following discussions with the Department of Justice in September 1960, Firstamerica adopted a plan under which the antitrust litigation that developed in connection with the acquisition of the stock of California Bank would be terminated. Under a stipulation between the holding company and the Justice Department, which was approved by the District Court, litigation was stayed pending applications for approval of the plan by the federal and state banking agencies concerned. In brief the plan involved merger of First Western Bank into California Bank to form United California Bank, as the group had desired, but the business of 65 of the offices of First Western was to be transferred to a new bank to be organized and operated under the title of First Western Bank and Trust Company, retaining whatever goodwill might be attached to this corporate name. However, Firstamerica was required to terminate the ownership of the new bank as promptly as possible after the new bank had been in operation for two years. In any event, Firstamerica had to divest itself of its shares in the new bank within six years of the Federal Reserve Board approval of the "old" First Western and California Bank merger, through a spin-off to the stockholders of Firstamerica if necessary. The required approvals to organize the new bank were obtained from the state authorities and the Federal Reserve by mid-January 1961,[31] and early in January 1963 the new First Western Bank and Trust Company was sold to Greatamerica Corporation of Dallas, Texas. Firstamerica (then called Western Bancorporation) thereby fulfilled its requirements under the 1960 agreement with the Department of Justice.[32]

Thus, the Department of Justice was reasonably successful in its first antitrust litigation to prevent a bank amalgamation; yet, the extent of its authority over such transactions remained an unknown quantity. There was considerable doubt in many quarters concerning the Government's ability to win a Sherman Act case, or more important a Clayton Act case involving a bank merger, despite its action against this holding company. In fact there was probably more uncertainty regarding this question after the Firstamerica suit was settled than there was before it began, for in the interim the Bank Merger Act of 1960 was passed, which many authorities suggested now clearly relegated Justice to an advisory role in this field. If the federal banking agencies had been more restrictive in approving merger proposals under this statute perhaps this uncertainty would remain even today, but they were not. It was only a matter of time before the Antitrust Division would find it necessary to determine the extent of its powers in this area.

## ANTITRUST LAW AND THE BANK MERGER ACT OF 1960

### BACKGROUND OF THE BANK MERGER CONTROVERSY

"In attempting to achieve this coordination, a closer liaison between our staff and the staffs of the *other banking agencies* of the government has been effected."[33] [Italics added] This comment was made

---

[31] "Orders under Section 3 of the Bank Holding Company Act," *Federal Reserve Bulletin,* (February 1961), pp. 157–59.

[32] "Western Bancorporation Completes Sale of Its First Western Holdings," *The Wall Street Journal,* January 3, 1963, p. 11.

[33] William Orrick, Jr., "Antitrust: Past and Future," speech before the Town Hall, Los Angeles, California, May 19, 1964, p. 3. (mimeographed)

not by an official of the FDIC or the Federal Reserve, nor by a staff member of the Comptroller's office; rather, it appeared in a speech by William Orrick, Jr., the head of the Justice Department's Antitrust Division, shortly after its Clayton Act Section 7 victory in the *Philadelphia case*. How different his views regarding the role of Justice in the banking area were from those of many of his predecessors. Only a few years earlier:[34]

Five distinguished representatives of the Justice Department—Attorney General Brownell in 1957, Deputy Attorney General Walsh in 1959, and three heads of the Antitrust Division: Judge Barnes in 1956, Judge Hanson in 1957, and Hon. Robert A. Bicks in 1960—recommended the enactment of a Bank Merger Act. They recommended that such an act should apply the principle of Section 7 to bank mergers. *All of them based their recommendations on their understanding that Section 7 did not apply.* [Italics added]

Surprisingly, in the interim between Mr. Orrick's remarks and the testimony of the other officials, the only legislation passed that was related to the banks' supposed exemption from Section 7 of the Clayton Act was the Bank Merger Act of 1960. And, if anything, the history and wording of this law would tend to support, not destroy, the exemption thesis.

At this point little can be accomplished by engaging in lengthy arguments regarding the question of whether or not banks were to be exempt from Section 7 prosecution. Nevertheless, since the terminology of the Celler-Kefauver amendment enacted in 1950 was the source of much of the confusion concerning the applicability of the Clayton Act to bank amalgamations, it might be worthwhile to review the history of some of the early bills which would have brought bank asset acquisitions under Section 7.[35] (The later, post-1950 bills, are reviewed in Chapter 4.) This may help to explain why both bankers

[34] Hearings on S. 1698 (1965), p. 36 and p. 329.

[35] For example, see the briefs of the government and the banks in the *Philadelphia case* and the *Manufacturers Hanover case;* "Government Regulation of Bank Mergers: The Revolving Door of the Philadelphia Bank," 62 *Michigan Law Review* 990 (1964); Ellis, "Antitrust, Bank Mergers, and the P.N.B. Decision," *The Banking Law Journal* (April 1964), p. 303; and "Comments on the Philadelphia-Girard Decision," *The National Banking Review* (September 1963), pp. 89–110.

and their counsels typically felt the Clayton Act did not apply to mergers in the banking industry.

## THE CELLER-KEFAUVER AMENDMENT[36]

Section 7 of the Clayton Act as it was originally passed in 1914 was primarily aimed at stock acquisitions by holding companies. Although asset acquisitions were not uncommon at the time the bill was being considered, they were not covered, and one authority concluded that Congress deliberately failed to prohibit them in the Clayton Act.[37] But, whether the omission was intentional or accidental, it was to lead to considerable controversy in later years. Twenty-one separate bills to amend Section 7 were introduced from 1921 through 1949,[38] as some groups attempted to (in their words) "plug the loophole" created by the emphasis upon stock acquisitions in the provisions of the law. In 1950 their efforts finally met with success when the Celler-Kefauver Act (which covered asset acquisitions) amended the Clayton Act.

During this period (1921–1950) the attitude of the Congress, the banking agencies, and the academic community toward the regulation of banking began to change. In the 1930s concern centered primarily on fear of "overbanking" and the need for safety and liquidity in our financial system; however, in more recent years the emphasis has begun to shift to concern over growing concentration and the possible lessening of competition.[39] This "new" approach to bank regulation may be noted as early as 1945. At that time Marriner Eccles, then Chairman of the Board of Governors of the Federal Reserve System, wrote to the House Judiciary Committee[40] requesting that one of Estes Kefauver's early antitrust bills (H.R. 2357) be amended to give the Federal Reserve control over both bank stock

[36] For a detailed analysis of the relationship of the Clayton Act to the Bank Merger Act, see Hearings on S. 1698 (1965), pp. 324 ff.

[37] Martin, *Mergers and the Clayton Act,* p. 240. Chapter Two of this work contains a detailed discussion of the "Legislative History of Section 7."

[38] *Ibid.,* p. 221.

[39] Phillips, ed., *Perspectives on Antitrust Policy,* "Mergers Among Commercial Banks," by George W. Mitchell, p. 225.

[40] Copies of the letter and suggested amendments appear in Senate Hearings on S. 1698 (1965), pp. 329–30. Also see the Federal Reserve Board's *Annual Report* for 1943 (p. 35), which discusses the need to control bank holding company expansion.

and bank asset acquisitions by expanding the Board's powers under Section 11 of the Clayton Act.[41]

On June 8, 1945, a committee print of the Kefauver bill was prepared and it was endorsed by representatives of the Federal Reserve Board.[42] This bill would have exempted acquisitions by banks from Section 7 of the Clayton Act but would have required that mergers be approved by the Comptroller of the Currency, the Board of Governors, or the FDIC. To obtain permission to merge two or more banks would have had to establish that the action in question would be in the public interest as determined by a set of criteria included in the bill.[43] However, when the bill was reported it mentioned only asset acquisitions subject to the Federal Trade Commission, and the various references to the exemption of banks and to supervision by the banking agencies were omitted. Similar bills were introduced from 1946 through 1949, but despite a number of requests by the Federal Reserve asking both House and Senate Committees to include Board approval of bank asset acquisitions in the provisions of the bills, this was not done.

Before the passage of H.R. 2734, which was to become the Celler-Kefauver Act, the Federal Reserve specifically called Congressman Celler's attention to the fact that this bill would not affect banks. Nevertheless, no effort was made to add a banking provision to the legislation, and the record does not reveal why banks were not included.[44] A report prepared by the staff of a House Antitrust Subcommittee in 1952 stated: "Because of the revisions made in subsequent versions of antimerger bills, . . . it became impracticable to include within the scope of the act [Celler-Kefauver] corporations other than those subject to regulation by the Federal Trade Commission."[45]

[41] U. S. Congress, House, Hearings on H.R. 2357, *To Amend Sections 7 and 11 of the Clayton Act,* 1945, p. 337 and p. 361.

[42] *Ibid.,* pp. 336–40.

[43] U. S. Congress, Senate, *Amend the Bank Merger Act of 1960,* Hearings on S. 1698 (1965), pp. 333–37.

[44] *Ibid.,* p. 326. See for details of the background of the law, "Section 7 of the Clayton Act: A Legislative History," 52 *Columbia Law Review* 766 (1952); Congressman Celler's views appear in Celler, "The New Antimerger Statute: The Current Outlook," 37 *American Bar Association Journal* 897 (1951).

[45] U. S. Congress, House, *Bank Mergers and Concentration of Banking Facilities,* 1952, p. viii.

However, a recent study by the staff of a Senate committee supports the conclusion reached by this writer after discussing the evolution of this law with a number of antitrust scholars—bank mergers may have been excluded for the simple reason that the addition of the necessary amendment might have resulted in the defeat of the bill.[46]

DEVELOPMENTS FROM 1950 THROUGH 1959

Following the passage of the Celler-Kefauver Amendment to the Clayton Act in 1950, members of Congress frequently expressed concern regarding the status of banks under this legislation. Therefore, as was discussed in Chapter 4, between 1950 and 1959 at least eleven bills were introduced in Congress which would have brought bank asset acquisitions under Section 7 of the Clayton Act. Two of these bills were passed by the House, which was much more favorably inclined toward this legislation than the Senate, while only one bill was voted out of the Senate Judiciary Committee. In the Senate the bank asset acquisition provision was deleted and a section in the Fulbright bill (S. 3911), which placed all bank mergers under the banking authorities, was substituted for it. This action provided some indication of the probable course of future developments, for after the Fulbright bill was introduced in Congress in the spring of 1956 it became quite evident that support for the antitrust approach to the regulation of bank mergers began to ebb. Hence, by the mid-1950s one could have been reasonably confident that if bank asset acquisitions were to be regulated by new legislation it would probably come through an amendment to a banking law, not through a change in the Clayton Act.

THE ENACTMENT OF S. 1062

As was noted earlier, in 1959 Senators Robertson, Capehart, and Fulbright introduced S. 1062, a bill to regulate bank mergers by amending the Federal Deposit Insurance Act. This bill was considered by the House and Senate Banking and Currency Committees—not the Judiciary Committees. It placed the authority over bank

---

[46] U. S. Congress, Senate, *Amend the Bank Merger Act of 1960,* Hearings on S. 1698, 1965, p. 326. The Celler-Kefauver Act did amend Section 11 of the Clayton Act to provide that any complaint issued by an administrative agency under Sections 2, 3, 7, and 8 had to be served by the Attorney General. Martin, *Mergers and the Clayton Act,* pp. 256–57.

mergers in the hands of the federal banking agencies, and unlike most[47] of the proposed amendments to the Clayton Act it specifically provided for the consideration of banking as well as competitive factors in weighing the merits of a given merger.

Those who supported the regulation of bank asset acquisitions under Section 7 of the Clayton Act offered a number of amendments to the bill, calling for public hearings, making consultation with the Department of Justice mandatory, seeking the adoption of an anti-trust saving clause, and numerous other things which they felt would strengthen the law. In addition several amendments were offered by the "antitrust advocates" when S. 1062 reached the Senate floor. Among these was an amendment sponsored by Senator O'Mahoney which would have replaced the competitive standard in the bill under consideration with that of Section 7 of the Clayton Act (with some important exceptions),[48] and an amendment by Senator Javits designed to change the wording of the competitive standard from "unduly" to "substantially" lessening competition.[49] Both amendments were defeated—the O'Mahoney amendment by a vote of 55 to 29.[50] In May 1959 S. 1062 was passed by the Senate, and by the House in April 1960. The Senate agreed to a number of House amendments, and the bill became Public Law 463 of the 86th Congress on May 13, 1960.

Before the Senate vote on the House amendments to S. 1062, Senator Lyndon Johnson asked that the following statement by him be inserted in the *Congressional Record:*[51]

This bill establishes uniform and clear standards, including both banking and competitive factors, for the consideration of proposed bank mergers. It eliminates a number of gaps in the statutory framework, which now permit many bank mergers to occur with no review by any federal agency. It provides for a thorough review by the appropriate federal bank supervisory agency, under these comprehensive standards, and with the benefit of any information which may be supplied by the Department of Justice in

[47] The O'Mahoney amendment, for example, contained a list of exceptions (a failing bank, incompetent management, etc.). 105 *Congressional Record,* p. 8113 (May 14, 1959).

[48] 105 *Congressional Record,* pp. 7826–31 (May 11, 1959); and *ibid.,* pp. 8112–14 (May 14, 1959).

[49] *Ibid.,* p. 8143 (May 14, 1959).

[50] *Ibid.,* p. 8139 and p. 8143 (May 14, 1959).

[51] 106 *Congressional Record,* pp. 9714–15 (May 6, 1960).

the report required from them, of the bank mergers by asset acquisitions and other means which are now and which will continue to be exempt from the antimerger provisions of Section 7 of the Clayton Antitrust Act.

But, had bank mergers in reality been exempted from prosecution under Section 7? Certainly the bills introduced during the 1950s and the discussions in committee reports and hearings on balance would lead one to believe that banks were not covered by this legislation. However, the supposed immunity of bank mergers (in this sense excluding stock acquisitions) from antitrust prosecution under Section 7 of the Clayton Act had yet to be tested in the courts. One could not be absolutely certain that the judges would agree (1) that banking is a regulated industry which is to be governed by banking agencies and banking statutes; (2) that banks were immune from prosecution under the antitrust laws because of the passage of the Bank Merger Act of 1960; or (3) that banks acquire other banks through the acquisition of assets which would not be covered in the banking field by Section 7. If the courts held that any one of these statements was true, bankers had little to fear from Section 7 of the Clayton Act, but if all were found to be false bankers could expect no special treatment under the antitrust laws. The answer was to come in the *Philadelphia case*.

## THE PHILADELPHIA NATIONAL BANK CASE

*Banking as a regulated industry.* One of the principal arguments made by the defense in the *Philadelphia National Bank case* was that commercial banking was subject to substantial government regulation; therefore, the industry should not be held to the strict letter of the antitrust laws.[52] This thesis was not only rejected; it was turned against the defendants.[53] Mr. Justice Brennan of the Supreme Court indicated: "The fact that banking is a highly regulated industry critical to the Nation's welfare makes the play of competition not less important but more so."[54] He warned that[55]

[52] For a fairly detailed analysis of this argument which supports the banks' position, see Backman and Sametz, *Workable Competition in Banking,* Bulletin No. 22, C. J. Devine Institute of Finance, p. 12.

[53] Handler, "Recent Antitrust Developments," 112 *University of Pennsylvania Law Review* 159, at 175 (1963).

[54] *U. S. v. Philadelphia National Bank,* 374 U.S. 321, 372 (1963).

[55] *Ibid.*

if the businessman is denied credit because his banking alternatives have been eliminated by mergers, the whole edifice of an entrepreneurial system is threatened; if the costs of banking services and credit are allowed to become excessive by the absence of competitive pressures, virtually all costs, in our credit economy, will be affected; and unless competition is allowed to fulfill its role as an economic regulator in the banking industry, the result may well be even more governmental regulation.

Perhaps it should have been expected that the Supreme Court would find that banking was not a "regulated industry," for even the basic goals of bank regulation, with their emphasis on preserving bank solvency and on controlling money creation, are vastly different from the objectives of public utility regulation, with their emphasis upon limiting the managerial discretion afforded by a monopoly position.[56] Charles Phillips, in his book *The Economics of Regulation,* observed that the term regulated industries refers to a diverse group of businesses which has been subjected over several decades to detailed local, state, and federal regulation as to rates and services. He cites a number of obligations of regulated industries, and among them were two particularly significant for banking:[57]

The regulated industries are obligated to charge only a 'just and reasonable' price for the services rendered. It is up to the various commissions and the courts to interpret this duty. Nonregulated businesses are under no such restraint, as competition is assumed to regulate prices in the public interest. . . . Also regulated industries have the obligation to serve all customers on equal terms. Unjust or undue discrimination among customers is forbidden.

Hence, the question to be answered in determining whether banking is in fact a regulated industry, it would seem, is whether or not the scope and cost of banking services as well as the price of credit are "sufficiently regulated." Certainly, one would have to concede at least that the numerous statutes and controls in the banking area set

[56] See Bain, *Industrial Organization,* pp. 589–602; Kaysen and Turner, *Antitrust Policy,* Chapter 6; and Pegrum *Public Regulation of Business,* Chapter 26.

[57] Phillips, *The Economics of Regulation,* pp. 81–82. See also Chapters 2–4. See also U. S. Congress, Hearings, *Employment, Growth, and Price Levels,* 1959, Part 7, pp. 2036–68.

boundaries within which competition may operate. But, to quote the opinion of the Supreme Court in the *Philadelphia case:*[58]

Bank regulation is in most respects less complete than public utility regulation, to which interstate rail and air carriers, among others, are subject. Rate regulation in the banking industry is limited and largely indirect; banks are under no duty not to discriminate in their services; and though the location of bank offices is regulated, banks may do business—place loans and solicit deposits—where they please. The fact that the banking agencies maintain a close surveillance of the industry with a view toward preventing unsound practices that might impair liquidity or lead to insolvency does not make federal banking regulation all-pervasive, although it does minimize the hazards of intense competition.

Many aspects of the court's regulatory test in the *Philadelphia case* could have been drawn from the "pervasive regulatory scheme" tests in *California* v. *Federal Power Commission*[59] and *United States* v. *Radio Corporation of America.*[60] These cases indicated "an immunity from the antitrust laws will not be implied when there is no express exemption, unless the agency is entrusted with the power both to administer a comprehensive regulatory scheme including rate control and to adjudicate antitrust issues."[61] Given these conditions, without attempting to judge their merits, it would certainly appear to have been consistent with its earlier decisions for the Supreme Court to conclude that mergers in banking should enjoy no special immunity from antitrust prosecution on the ground that this was a "regulated industry."[62]

[58] 374 U.S. at 352. See also *ibid.*, at 368.

[59] 369 U.S. 482 (1962).

[60] 358 U.S. 334 (1959).

[61] Sobel, "The Applicability of the Antitrust Laws to Combinations Approved Under the Bank Merger Act, Federal Power Act, and Natural Gas Act," 37 *New York University Law Review* 735, at 740 (1962). For a return to the doctrine of at least limited primary jurisdiction, see *Pan American World Airways, Inc.* v. *U. S.*, 371 U.S. 296 (1963); and *Seaboard Airline Railroad* v. *U. S.*, 382 U.S. 154 (1965).

[62] For excellent discussions of this topic, see Stokes, "A Few Irreverent Comments about Antitrust, Agency Regulation, and Primary Jurisdiction," 33 *George Washington Law Review* 529 (1964); and Hale and Hale, "Mergers in Regulated Industries," 59 *Northwestern University Law Review* 49 (1964); "Regulated Industries and the Antitrust Laws," 58 *Columbia Law Review* 673

*Effect of the Merger Act on the applicability of Section 7.*[63]   The defendants in commercial bank merger cases have customarily argued, at least in the District Court, that the approval of a merger by the proper authority was the final and exclusive determination of its legality, and that the Bank Merger Act of 1960 precluded a review of a proposed merger under the Clayton Act or Sherman Act. If this point were valid, bank mergers would have to be judged not only by the competitive criteria associated with the antitrust laws but also the so-called "banking factors"—financial history and condition of each of the banks involved; the adequacy of its capital structure; its future earnings prospects; the general character of its management; and the convenience and needs of the community to be served—would have to be considered as well.

Many people feel that the Supreme Court in the *Philadelphia case* completely ignored the fact that Congress clearly indicated on many occasions that it intended to leave control of bank expansion via the acquisition of other banks to the "Fed," the FDIC and the Comptroller of the Currency. One often hears that it is obvious that this was the goal of Congress, not only from the wording of the provisions of the Bank Merger Act, but also from statements in the *Congressional Record* and the Senate and House reports on this act, which provide considerable evidence in support of this position. For example, the opponents of Justice Department control of bank mergers note the provisions of the Bank Merger Act require that a report on the competitive factors involved be obtained from the Attorney General, but the Act states that this is only one of a number of items to be considered in deciding whether a transaction is in the public interest.

---

(1958); and Jaffe, "Primary Jurisdiction Reconsidered: The Antitrust Laws," 102 *University of Pennsylvania Law Review* 577 (1954).

[63] This question has been discussed at great length in many court opinions, briefs, hearings, and articles. See, for example, *U. S.* v. *Philadelphia National Bank* 374 U.S. 321 at 350 (opinion of the court) and *ibid.,* at 374 (dissenting opinion); Klebaner, "Federal Control of Commercial Bank Mergers," 37 *Indiana Law Journal* 287 (1962); "The Bank Merger Act and the Antitrust Law: Hopeless Conflict," 32 *University of Cincinnati Law Review* 505 (1963); Wemple and Cutler, "The Federal Bank Merger Law and the Antitrust Laws," 79 *The Banking Law Journal* 461 (1962); Ellis, "Antitrust, Bank Mergers, and the P.N.B. Decision," 81 *The Banking Law Journal* 303 (1964).

In addition, the "bank supporters" point out that since no saving provision such as that included in the Bank Holding Company Act of 1956[64] appears in the Bank Merger Act of 1960, Congress planned to exclude the application of the antitrust laws in this area.

Certainly there can be little doubt that the Bank Merger Act of 1960 was passed primarily because the banking agencies, the Congress, and the Department of Justice believed that bank asset acquisitions were not covered by existing legislation.[65] It is equally clear that the Congress expected that competitive factors were not to be controlling in the "public interest" determination to be made by the banking agency. For example, the Senate Report on the Bank Merger Act (p. 24) states:

Under S. 1062 the competitive factors involved in the merger are only one element of several to be considered in passing on the application. The committee wants to make crystal clear its intention that the various banking factors in any particular case may be held to outweigh the competitive factors, and that the competitive factors, however favorable or unfavorable, are not, in and of themselves, controlling on the decision.

The House Report on this bill (pp. 9–10) observes:

Because banking is a licensed and strictly supervised industry that offers problems acutely different from other types of business, the bill vests the ultimate authority to pass on mergers in the Federal bank supervisory agencies, which have a thorough knowledge of the banks, their personnel, and their types of business.

Yet, on page 9 of the House Report one finds: "S. 1062 would not in any way affect the applicability of the Sherman Act or the Clayton Act to bank mergers." On page 3 of the Senate Report one finds: "S. 1062 would not affect in any way the applicability of the Sherman Act to bank mergers or consolidations."

The District Court Judge in the *Philadelphia case* (Judge Thomas J. Clary), who found in favor of the banks on almost all points,

---

[64] 12 U.S.C. § 1841 et seq. "Nothing herein shall constitute a defense to any action, suit, or proceeding pending or hereafter instituted on account of any prohibited antitrust or monopolistic act, action or conduct."

[65] U. S. Congress, Senate, Report No. 196, *Regulation of Bank Mergers,* 1959, pp. 1–2; and U. S. Congress, House, Report No. 1416, *Regulation of Bank Mergers,* 1960, p. 9. Also see the earlier discussion of attempts to bring banks under Section 7, and U. S. Congress, Senate, *Amend the Bank Merger Act of 1960,* Hearings on S. 1698, 1965, pp. 295–330.

indicated that in the light of the difference of opinion even in the Congressional reports on this bill and the fact that creation of an exemption from the antitrust laws requires clear and explicit language in the exempting statute,[66] the Sherman and Clayton Acts would have to be held to be applicable to bank mergers.[67] (At this point Judge Clary had not as yet considered the "asset acquisition" question discussed below.) Essentially the same points were emphasized by the Supreme Court as it too rejected the argument that actions taken by the banking agencies under the provisions of the Bank Merger Act immunized approved mergers from challenge under the Federal antitrust laws.[68]

*Merger or asset acquisition.* The most disturbing part of the Philadelphia bank decision to a great many individuals was not the failure of the court to find that the Bank Merger Act protected the banks from prosecution under Section 7 but the Supreme Court's conclusion that banks acquire other banks through "merger," not via asset acquisition. The court specifically noted that ". . . if the proposed merger be deemed an assets acquisition, it is not within Section 7."[69] This finding was based on the fact that the "asset acquisition" provision of Section 7 of the Clayton Act is limited to corporations subject to the jurisdiction of the Federal Trade Commission (FTC), and the FTC under Section 5 of the Federal Trade Commission Act has no jurisdiction over banks.[70]

The court concluded that a "cash purchase of another bank's assets would not seem to be a fully effective method of corporate acquisition" because a bank's assets consist principally of cash and very liquid securities and loan receivables. "A cash purchase, in effect, only substitutes cash for cash."[71] But, on the other hand, the court indicated the Philadelphia-Girard merger did not involve a "pure stock acquisition," which would have been subject to the jurisdiction of the

---

[66] *U. S.* v. *Philadelphia National Bank* [374 U.S. 321, at 350, n. 28 (1963)] contains a list of cases on this point.

[67] *U. S.* v. *Philadelphia National Bank,* Civ. 29287 (E. D. Pennsylvania, 1962), 201 F. Supp. 348, 357 (1962).

[68] *Ibid.,* 374 U.S. 321, at 350–52.

[69] 374 U.S. 321, 336.

[70] 15 U.S.C. § 45 (a)(6).

[71] 374 U.S. 321, 344, n. 22.

Federal Reserve Board as well as the Department of Justice.[72] Instead, through a rather involved and sometimes confusing analysis, the court found that this amalgamation was somewhere between the "two ends of the spectrum" in a class of mergers which fits neither the "pure stock" nor "pure asset" acquisition categories perfectly,[73] but which is subject to the provisions of Section 7.

The decision to include bank mergers of the type involved in *U. S. v. Philadelphia National Bank* under Section 7 of the Clayton Act would appear to be the weakest element in the Supreme Court's decision in this case. One does not have to look far to find significant support for this conclusion, since three of the eight justices who considered the case dissented on this point.[74] In addition, Judge Clary in the District Court decision in *Philadelphia,* after analyzing the terms of the consolidation of the two banks involved in considerable detail, concluded: "This court is of the opinion that the Celler-Kefauver Anti-Merger Act of 1950 does not apply to a bank merger of this nature," because it involved the acquisition of assets, not the acquisition of stock as argued by the government. Judge Clary noted that "any extension of the statute is a function peculiar to the Congress of the United States."[75]

The decision of the Supreme Court, however, indicated that no revision of the law was necessary to bring bank mergers under Section 7. Mr. Justice Brennan in the opinion of the court stated that although "the legislative history is silent on the specific questions why the [Celler-Kefauver] amendment made no explicit reference to mergers, why assets acquisitions by corporations not subject to FTC jurisdiction were not included, and what these omissions signify," the majority of the court was able to discern "the basic Congressional design," and from that design it was able to infer answers to these questions.[76] The "answers," of course, confirmed that bank mergers

---

[72] *Ibid.*

[73] *Ibid.,* at 342. The Mercantile Trust Company acquired the Security Trust Company in St. Louis for cash under what Comptroller Saxon suggests is a "pure asset acquisition by merger," and he feels it is not covered by Section 7 of the Clayton Act. See the Comptroller's decision regarding the merger of these banks (June 24, 1965), pp. 4–6. (mimeographed)

[74] 374 U.S. 321, 386–97.

[75] 201 F. Supp. 348, 360 (1962).

[76] 374 U.S. 321, 341 (1962).

were covered by the Clayton Act. This conclusion proved to be quite shocking not only to the banking community but to the legal profession as well. In discussing this, a leading law journal commented: "Mr. Justice Brennan's interpretation of the statutory language, while highly sophisticated, was suggested neither by the arguments of the Antitrust Division, nor by the legislative history, nor by the precedents."[77] in the same vein Professor Handler of the Columbia University law school remarked: "The startling thing about this latest [Philadelphia] decision was the majority's conclusion that bank mergers are covered by Section 7 as well as the Sherman Act—not that the particular merger was unlawful once Section 7 was held to apply."[78]

Even the authors of the Celler-Kefauver bill were not aware that the Clayton Act covered bank mergers. Congressman Celler in discussing the 1966 Amendment to the Bank Merger Act noted that a degree of confusion developed as to whether the provisions of the amended Section 7 relative to merger by asset acquisition applied to banks. He then stated:[79]

I for one—and I was in a fairly good position to know—did not understand nor did Senator Kefauver of honored memory understand that the Celler-Kefauver amendment to Section 7 was to apply to acquisition of bank assets in cases of merger. . . . There was substantial confusion. Indeed, if I were a lawyer and some bank had come to me and said, "If I were to merge with this particular bank by asset acquisition, would I be violating the law?"—meaning the Celler-Kefauver Act—in good conscience I would have had to say "No," prior to the Philadelphia case.

Celler assumed bank mergers accomplished by what most people thought were "asset acquisitions" were not covered by the Clayton Act. Therefore, periodically during the 1950s, he introduced legislation "to close the gap insofar as banks are concerned [to] prohibit bank mergers achieved by asset as well as stock acquisition where the effect might be substantially to lessen competition or tend to create a monopoly."

It would surely be fair to state that even the Department of Justice

[77] "Government Regulation of Bank Mergers," 62 *Michigan Law Review* 990, 992.

[78] Handler, "Recent Antitrust Developments," 112 *University of Pennsylvania Law Review* 159, 173 (1963).

[79] *Congressional Record* (February 8, 1966), p. 2347.

had little hope that the court would rule that Section 7 applied to bank mergers. This is evident not only in its briefs but in the oral argument before the Supreme Court in which the government subordinated Section 7 to Section 1 of the Sherman Act. Former head of the Antitrust Division Judge Loevinger stated in his oral argument: "Section 7 is argued in the brief and we are relying on it. I don't have time to cover both sections. I am relying on Section 7 because I think the restraint is so clear that Section 1 clearly invalidates this merger and the court need proceed no further. Our point on Section 7 follows a fortiori." The makeweight argument the government advanced in regard to Section 7 was obviously apparent to Mr. Justice Harlan, for in his dissent in the *Philadelphia case* he remarked: "I suspect that no one will be more surprised than the government to find that the Clayton Act has carried the day for its case in this court."[80]

It is apparent that the Supreme Court in reaching its decision in *Philadelphia* was walking a tightrope "between judicial legislation—reaching a Congressionally unintended result—on the one hand and judicial impotence—forebearance from doing justice when justice can be done—on the other."[81] Certainly the majority of the court felt that the proscriptions of the Clayton Act should be applied in a market situation such as that encountered in the *Philadelphia case*. They also must have realized, considering the numerous unsuccessful attempts to bring bank mergers under Section 7 in the past, that if the court found that this acquisition was not subject to Clayton Act regulation it was very unlikely that the Congress would change the law to accomplish this in the foreseeable future. It is difficult to imagine that this did not affect the thinking of the court.

After reading the briefs, the opinions, the relevant case law, dozens of journal articles, and all of the works cited by the court in *Philadelphia,* this writer is tempted to conclude that the Supreme Court initially reached the decision that it was in the public interest to enjoin this merger (and set the precedent for future bank cases under Section 7) and then "molded" Section 7 to support the conclusion of the majority in this case. If this were true, it might be well to recall the admonition of Mr. Justice Brandeis: "When a court decides a case upon grounds of public policy, the judges become, in effect, legisla-

[80] 372 U.S. 321, 373 (1962).
[81] "Government Regulation of Bank Mergers," 62 *Michigan Law Review* 990, 1000–1001 (1964).

tors. The question then involved is no longer one for lawyers only. It seems fitting, therefore, to inquire whether this judicial legislation is sound."[82]

*The decision of the Supreme Court.* There was general, though not unanimous, agreement among public policy experts that after the High Court decided the legality of the consolidation of Philadelphia National Bank and Girard Trust Corn Exchange Bank was to be determined using conventional antitrust standards, little doubt remained that ultimately the merger would be enjoined. Of course, it could be argued that the relatively high banking concentration in the Philadelphia metropolitan area was the crucial element in the case and that if the alternative regional or national market had been selected this figure might have been reduced sufficiently to change the opinion of the Court. However, the Supreme Court decisions in Section 7 cases since *Philadelphia,* at least in retrospect, suggest that the findings would have been the same regardless of the section of the country chosen as relevant in analyzing the potential impact of the merger.

A rather lengthy analysis of the concept of the banking market is included in Chapter 8, which is devoted to banking concentration, and many of the elements of the *Philadelphia case* are reviewed in that chapter, where they can be readily compared with some of the major findings in other Section 7 antitrust suits in recent years. Therefore, to minimize the amount of repetition of the details of the judgment in the *Philadelphia case,* no further discussion of the factors weighed by the High Court in this action will be presented at this point.

SUMMARY OF BANK ANTITRUST CASES

During the past seven years the Department of Justice has brought sixteen bank merger suits against commercial banks or bank holding companies and their affiliates. (See Table 7.1) In all of these actions, with the exception of the *Lexington case,* charges were filed under Section 7 of the Clayton Act or under both this Section and Section 1 of the Sherman Act. In the earliest suits the Sherman Act was usually stressed and the Clayton Act played a secondary role in the Government's case (unless a bank holding company was in-

[82] *Ibid.,* at 1001.

TABLE 7.1. BANK ACQUISITIONS CHALLENGED BY THE DEPARTMENT OF JUSTICE OR BY THE FEDERAL RESERVE BOARD UNDER THE SHERMAN ACT AND THE CLAYTON ACT TO DECEMBER 10, 1967

| Date of Complaint | Principals and the Year of Acquisition | State | Position of Supervisory Agencies | | |
| | | | Federal Reserve | Comptroller of Currency | FDIC |
| --- | --- | --- | --- | --- | --- |
| 3/27/52 | Transamerica Corporation. 1904–1948 | n.a.† | n.a. | n.a. | n.a. |
| 3/30/59 | Firstamerica Corporation; California Bank. 1959 | Approved | APPROVED | n.a. | n.a. |
| 2/25/61 | Philadelphia National Bank; Girard Trust Corn Exchange Bank. 1960 | n.a. | Adverse | APPROVED | Adverse |
| 3/1/61 | First National Bank & Trust Company of Lexington; Security Trust Company. 1961 | n.a. | Adverse | APPROVED | Adverse |
| 3/2/61 | The Marshall & Ilsley Bank Stock Corporation; Northern Bank; Bank of Commerce; Marshall & Ilsley Bank. 1959–1961 | Approved | APPROVED | n.a. | n.a. |
| 8/29/61 | Continental Illinois National Bank & Trust Company; City National Bank & Trust Company of Chicago. 1961 | n.a. | Adverse | APPROVED | Adverse |

| Markets* | Supposed Concentration* | Status of Case |
|---|---|---|
| Five states: Arizona, California, Nevada, Oregon, and Washington | By 1948 Transamerica banks held 39% of all commercial bank deposits and 50% of all commercial bank loans in the five-state area. If Bank of America were not included the figures were 7% and 6.5% respectively | Board of Governors' order set aside by 3d Circuit Court 7/16/53. Petition for certiorari denied by Supreme Court 11/30/53 |
| Banking services in Los Angeles, State of California, and other Western states | Top four banks in Los Angeles had 82% of deposits and loans; in the state they had 66% of the banking offices, deposits, and loans | Consent decree filed 9/27/60 Firstamerica to set up new bank and divest itself of any interest in it. The new bank was sold to Greatamerica Corporation on 1/2/63 |
| Commercial banking in Philadelphia four-county metropolitan area | Five banks had 80% of assets in Philadelphia area | Merger enjoined by the Supreme Court 6/17/63 |
| Commercial banking in Lexington, Kentucky area | Merger would have given the defendants control over more than 50% of commercial bank assets, deposits, and loans, and 94% of trust accounts | Merger enjoined by the Supreme Court 4/6/64, but merger legal under Merger Act amendment. New action under § 2 begun 4/28/66; but a proposed consent judgment was filed 8/7/67 |
| Commercial banking in the City and County of Milwaukee | Four largest banks accounted for about 80% of total bank assets, deposits, and loans in city and 70% in county | Action dismissed by District Court, no jurisdiction, 6/15/66; reversed by the Supreme Court 5/22/67. Decision on merits pending |
| Commercial banking deposits and loans in Chicago; especially in the Loop | Top four banks in Chicago had 62% of deposits, 70% of loans, 83% of time deposits; top three in the Loop had 72% of deposits | Merger declared legal under 1966 Merger Act amendment. The case was never tried |

TABLE 7.1 (*continued*).

| Date of Complaint | Principals and the Year of Acquisition | State | Federal Reserve | Comptroller of Currency | FD |
|---|---|---|---|---|---|
| | | | | Position of Supervisory Agencies | |
| 9/8/61 | Manufacturers Trust Company; The Hanover Bank. 1961 | Approved | APPROVED | Favorable | Favor |
| 12/28/62 | The Valley National Bank of Arizona; Arizona Bank; Arizona Bancorporation. 1953 | n.a. | n.a. | n.a. | n.a |
| 10/8/63 | Crocker-Anglo National Bank; Citizens National Bank. 1963 | n.a. | Favorable (but some adverse factors) | APPROVED | None submit |
| 10/10/63 | The Calumet National Bank of Hammond and Mercantile National Bank of Hammond, Indiana.1963 | n.a. | Adverse | APPROVED | Favora |
| 8/10/64 | Third National Bank in Nashville; Nashville Bank & Trust Company. 1964 | n.a. | Adverse | APPROVED | Advers |
| 7/7/65 | Mercantile Trust Company, N.A.; Security Trust Company. 1965 | n.a. | Adverse | APPROVED | Favora |
| 4/1/66 | Provident National Bank; Central-Penn. National Bank. 1966 | n.a. | Adverse | APPROVED | None submitte |

| Markets* | Supposed Concentration* | Status of Case |
|---|---|---|
| Commercial banking in New York City | Top five banks had about 70% of assets, deposits, and loans | District Court ruled merger was illegal 3/10/65, but merger legal under Merger Act amendment |
| Commercial banking in Arizona | Four leading banks controlled nearly 94% of Arizona's bank resources; Valley National is first and the Arizona Bank was third largest in the state | Settled by consent decree. Final Judgment was entered 11/23/66. Valley National agreed to relinquish control of Arizona Bancorporation which had acquired a major interest in Arizona Bank |
| Commercial banking in California | Five largest commercial banks accounted for 80% of total loans and discounts | District Court found in favor of the banks 10/30/67 |
| Commercial banking in the Hammond, Indiana area | Five leading banks held 74% of the total loans held by all area banks | Dismissed; the merger was abandoned 11/6/63 |
| Commercial banking in the Nashville area | Three largest banks, including the resulting bank, would hold about 98% of the deposits and loans in the metropolitan Nashville area | District Court dismissed action 12/16/66; Justice appealed to Supreme Court 4/11/67. Case was argued 12/11/67; decision pending |
| Commercial banking in St. Louis | Merged bank had 35% of commercial bank deposits in the city; first and second largest banks had 56% of deposits in the city | District Court dismissed before trial on technical grounds; Justice appealed and the Supreme Court reversed and remanded 10/16/67 |
| Commercial banking in Philadelphia four-county metropolitan area | Merger of area's fifth and sixth largest banks with about 15% of deposits. Merger would increase deposit concentration among top 5 banks from 77% to 82% | District Court dismissed before trial; reversed by Supreme Court 3/27/67. Case was tried on merits in lower court. Oral arguments 12/6/67. Decision pending |

TABLE 7.1 (*continued*).

| Date of Complaint | Principals and the Year of Acquisition | State | Position of Supervisory Agencies | | |
|---|---|---|---|---|---|
| | | | Federal Reserve | Comptroller of Currency | FL |
| 6/10/66 | First National Bank of Hawaii; Cooke Trust Company, Ltd. 1966 | n.a. | No significant adverse effect | Favorable | APPR |
| 6/17/66 | First National Bank; Peoples National Bank; both of State College, Pa. 1966 | n.a. | Substantially adverse | APPROVED | Adve |
| 10/19/66 | First City National Bank; Southern National Bank. 1966 | n.a. | Adverse | APPROVED | Favo |
| 10/12/67 | National Bank and Trust Co. of Central Pennsylvania; Keystone Trust Co. 1967 | n.a. | Adverse | APPROVED | None submi |
| 11/24/67 | First National Bank; York Bank and Trust Co.; both of York, Pa. 1967 | Approved | Substantially adverse | Favorable | APPRO |

* N.A.—not applicable. CAPITAL LETTERS indicate the federal agency with primary j diction in a given merger or acquisition.

† There was no federal banking regulation which controlled holding company acquisitions of b before 1956.

| Markets* | Supposed Concentration* | Status of Case |
|---|---|---|
| Potential trust and banking competition in Hawaii. Without merger firms would probably move into each other's areas of business activity. | Merger of second largest bank (about one-third of Hawaii's bank assets) with the third largest trust company in the state | Automatic injunction lifted. Expected to be tried on merits in 1968 |
| Commercial banking in Centre County, Pa. | 3 largest banks in county will hold 85% of deposits, an increase of $\frac{1}{4}$; (merging banks had only $34 million of deposits) | Dismissed. Merger was abandoned 7/6/66 |
| Commercial banking in Harris County (Houston), Texas and the Houston metropolitan area | Largest and sixth largest banks involved; they control about one-fourth of assets and deposits in markets designated; with their "satellites" share exceeds 30% | District Court dismissed before trial; reversed by Supreme Court 3/27/67. Merger abandoned; Justice moved to dismiss suit 5/31/67 |
| Commercial banking in Harrisburg, Pennsylvania | Merger of largest and fourth largest banks in Harrisburg. Deposit concentration in 2 largest banks now 70% would increase to 75% after merger | Merger was abandoned 11/24/67 |
| Commercial banking in York County, Pa. | Merger of second and third largest banks in York with 28% and 11% of area's I.P.C. deposits | Banks' boards voted to abandon merger 12/5/67 |

* Whenever possible the Justice Department's descriptions of the product and geographic markets and concentration were used. They are obviously very brief and they have been included only to indicate something of the Justice Department's point of view on these questions, and the banks might object to them.

volved), for as has been noted there was serious doubt within the Department of Justice regarding the applicability of Section 7 to bank mergers or consolidations (in the technical sense). In fact, some years ago a Justice Department official indicated to this writer that this was the reason that Section 7 was not even mentioned in *Lexington,* since it appeared the Antitrust Division had a fairly strong Sherman Act case.

Prior to the passage of the 1966 amendments to the Bank Merger Act and Bank Holding Company Act, Justice had won one (*Manufacturers Hanover*) and lost two District Court decisions, and one case was dismissed on jurisdictional grounds. Both of the negative judgments, *Philadelphia* and *Lexington,* were reversed by the Supreme Court, and the jurisdictional question involving a bank holding company, M & I Bank Stock Corporation, was also reversed by the High Court. Two of the actions, the *Calumet National Bank of Hammond case* and *First National Bank of State College case,* were dropped since the merger plans were abandoned once Justice filed suit.

Of the above-mentioned actions which were decided by the courts using conventional antitrust standards (before the 1966 amendments) the most unusual from the viewpoint of the law was probably the *Marshall and Ilsley Bank Stock case,*[83] for it involved a possible conflict of jurisdiction between Justice and the Federal Reserve Board regarding the enforcement of Section 7. It has sometimes been suggested that Justice was precluded from attacking bank stock acquisitions under the Clayton Act because Section 11 of this statute gave express authority to enforce the banking industry's compliance with the Sections 2, 3, 7, and 8 of the Act to the "Fed"—"a delegation which could easily have been read as exclusive."[84] This would not have eliminated all of Justice's antitrust powers, however, for the Sherman Act makes no such distinction between banks and other defendants.[85]

[83] *U. S.* v. *Marshall & Ilsley Bank Stock Corporation,* Civ. 61–C–54 (E.D. Wisc.).

[84] "The 1966 Amendment to the Bank Merger Act," *The Banking Law Journal* (September 1966), p. 756.

[85] Berle, "Banking under the Antitrust Laws," *Columbia Law Review* (May 1949), p. 606. This study also contains a discussion of the jurisdictional issue.

The jurisdictional issue did not develop in the first of the two earlier bank holding company cases, *Transamerica,* but it did arise in the second, the *Firstamerica case.* In the latter action, the District Court denied a motion by the holding company to dismiss the antitrust complaint because of prior adjudication by the Board of Governors of the Federal Reserve System involving the same issues, the same facts, and the same parties. (The Clayton Act Section 7 and Sherman Act Section 1 charges respectively were to be dismissed on the grounds of *res judicata* and collateral estoppel.) This question was also raised in a petition to the Supreme Court for a writ of certiorari but the petition was denied.[86] Thus, the High Court's position on this point still was not established.

In *M & I Bank Stock* the *res judicata* issue arose once again. In this instance the trial court held that it was without jurisdiction in the case. This conclusion stemmed from the observations made by the Supreme Court in the *Philadelphia case* when it addressed itself to a related question and stated:[87]

Section 11 of the Clayton Act, 15 U.S.C. § 21, vests the FRB with authority to enforce § 7 "where applicable to banks." This provision has been in the Act since it was first passed in 1914 and was not changed when § 7 was amended. The Bank Merger Act of 1960, assigning roles in merger applications to the FDIC and the Comptroller of the Currency as well as to the FRB, plainly supplanted, we think, whatever authority the FRB may have acquired under § 11, by virtue of the amendment of § 7, to enforce § 7 against bank mergers. Since the Bank Merger Act applies only to mergers, consolidations, acquisitions of assets, and assumptions of liabilities but not to outright stock acquisitions, the FRB's authority under § 11 as it existed before the 1950 amendment of § 7 remains unaffected.

In analogous fashion the U. S. District Judge in the *M & I case* concluded Congress intended that the Federal Reserve Board, while ruling on an acquisition subject to the Bank Holding Company Act,

---

[86] *Firstamerica* v. *U. S.,* 361 U.S. 928 (1960), certiorari denied. A denial by the U. S. Supreme Court of a petition for a writ of certiorari means, and means only, that fewer than four members of the Court in the exercise of its discretionary power to review thought it should be granted. Such a denial carries with it no implication whatever regarding the Court's views on the merits of a case which it has declined to review. *Maryland* v. *Baltimore Radio Show,* 338 U.S. 912 (1949).

[87] *U. S.* v. *Philadelphia National Bank,* 374 U.S. 321 at 344, note 22.

simultaneously perform its duties under the Clayton Act and that the Board alone retain its jurisdiction with respect to acquisitions subject to the Bank Holding Company Act. Thus, in effect, the District Judge decided that § 15 of the Clayton Act, which gave Justice concurrent jurisdiction with the Board in enforcing § 7 of the Clayton Act, was repealed as to acquisitions subject to the Bank Holding Company Act of 1956 because of the "plain repugnancies between the two provisions."[88] Therefore, the Judge ruled that the District Courts have no jurisdiction in such matters, and he dismissed the action against M & I Bank Stock Corporation. Justice appealed the case to the Supreme Court on January 30, 1967.[89] On May 22, 1967, in a brief unsigned order which cited Section 11 (e) of the Bank Holding Company Act of 1966 (80 Stat. 236) and *U. S.* v. *First City National Bank of Houston* (386 U.S. 361), the High Court reversed the District Court decision. In effect the Supreme Court reinstated the case against Marshall & Ilsley Bank Stock Corporation, indicating that the merger standards which applied to banks would be equally applicable to bank holding companies. The case was returned to the Lower Court for a decision on the merits under the tests enacted by the 1966 Amendment to the Bank Holding Company Act.

## ANTITRUST IMPLICATIONS OF THE
## 1966 AMENDMENTS

### BANK MERGER ACT[90]

If the status of banks under the antitrust laws was not changed through new legislation, doubtless the Supreme Court would have continued to emphasize only competitive factors in weighing the legality of mergers in this industry. In effect this would have meant

---

[88] *U. S.* v. *Marshall & Ilsley Bank Stock Corp.,* 255 F. Supp. 273, 285 (1966). The Court subsequently indicated that it would not reconsider its judgment because of the 1966 amendment to the Bank Holding Company Act. [1966 *Trade Cases* ¶ 71,827; 1967 *Trade Cases* ¶ 71,992.] Appeal was filed January 30, 1967. Some additional observations relevant to the question of the Fed's primary jurisdiction appear in *U. S.* v. *Manufacturers Hanover,* 240 F. Supp. 867, 911, note 134.

[89] Supreme Court of the United States, October Term, 1966, No. 1017. Decided May 22, 1967.

[90] 12 U.S.C. 1828 (c) as amended February 1966; 80 Stat. 7 (1966).

that concentration in a given market or the status of the firms in question as "major competitive factors in a relevant market" would have remained the primary (or perhaps only) consideration in determining whether a bank merger was to be enjoined. Exceptions to this rule might have arisen if one of the banks involved was a "failing firm" or if the consolidation involved two relatively and absolutely small banks seeking to compete more successfully with the leading firms in the market.[91] Although both of these situations have been mentioned by the Supreme Court in its opinions as illustrations of types of mergers which may be afforded special treatment under the antitrust laws, one cannot be certain just how (or if) these different standards would have been applied.

The more typical approach of the Supreme Court in the past to bank merger litigation was spelled out by the majority in the *Philadelphia case:*[92]

We are clear, however, that a merger the effect of which "may be substantially to lessen competition" is not saved because, on some ultimate reckoning of social or economic debits and credits, it may be deemed beneficial. A value choice of such magnitude is beyond the ordinary limits of judicial competence, and in any event has been made for us already, by Congress when it enacted the amended § 7. Congress determined to preserve our traditionally competitive economy. It therefore proscribed anticompetitive mergers, the benign and the malignant alike, fully aware, we must assume, that some price might have to be paid.

This approach to the evaluation of the legality of a bank merger certainly differs from the "public interest criteria" which Congress included in the Bank Merger Act and which it directed the bank supervisory agencies to consider in evaluating the merits of a given bank consolidation. Moreover, the history of the Bank Merger Act shows beyond any reasonable doubt that the lawmakers did not expect that under any circumstances bank acquisitions would be judged solely on the basis of the factors considered by the Supreme Court in the *Philadelphia* and *Lexington cases.* Thus, a new law clearly spelling out the attitude of the federal legislators on this question was badly needed, and early in 1966 the Congress amended

[91] *U. S.* v. *Philadelphia National Bank,* 374 U.S. 321, 370–72 (1963); and *U. S.* v. *First National Bank of Lexington,* 376 U.S. 665, 671–72 (1964).
[92] *U. S.* v. *Philadelphia National Bank,* 374 U.S. 321, 371.

the Bank Merger Act supposedly with the intention of stating more clearly its position on this issue.

The 1966 amendment to the Bank Merger Act contained provisions which were both favorable and unfavorable from the viewpoint of a bank facing antitrust litigation. Several of its more important paragraphs are as follows:

(5) The responsible agency shall not approve—

(A) any proposed merger transaction which would result in a monopoly, or which would be in furtherance of any combination or conspiracy to monopolize or to attempt to monopolize the business of banking in any part of the United States, or

(B) any other proposed merger transaction whose effect in any section of the country may be substantially to lessen competition, or to tend to create a monopoly, or which in any other manner would be in restraint of trade, *unless it finds that the anticompetitive effects of the proposed transaction are clearly outweighed in the public interest by the probable effect of the transaction in meeting the convenience and needs of the community to be served.* [Emphasis added]

In every case, the responsible agency shall take into consideration the financial and managerial resources and future prospects of the existing and proposed institutions, and the convenience and needs of the community to be served.

(6) The responsible agency shall immediately notify the Attorney General of any approval by it pursuant to this subsection of a proposed merger transaction. If the agency has found that it must act immediately to prevent the probable failure of one of the banks involved and reports on the competitive factors have been dispensed with, the transaction may be consummated immediately upon approval by the agency. If the agency has advised the Attorney General and the other two banking agencies of the existence of an emergency requiring expeditious action and has requested reports on the competitive factors within ten days, the transaction may not be consummated before the fifth calendar day after the date of approval by the agency. In all other cases, the transaction may not be consummated before the thirtieth calendar day after the date of approval by the agency.

(7) (A) Any action brought under the antitrust laws arising out of a merger transaction shall be commenced prior to the earliest time under paragraph (6) at which a merger transaction approved under paragraph (5) might be consummated. The commencement of such an action shall stay the effectiveness of the agency's approval unless the court shall otherwise specifically order. In any such action, the court shall review de novo the issues presented.

(B) In any judicial proceeding attacking a merger transaction ap-

proved under paragraph (5) on the ground that the merger transaction
alone and of itself constituted a violation of any antitrust laws other than
section 2 of the Act of July 2, 1890 (section 2 of the Sherman Antitrust
Act, 15 U.S.C. 2), the standards applied by the court shall be identical
with those that the banking agencies are directed to apply under paragraph (5).

(C) Upon the consummation of a merger transaction in compliance
with this subsection and after the termination of any antitrust litigation
commenced within the period prescribed in this paragraph, or upon the
termination of such period if no such litigation is commenced therein, the
transaction may not thereafter be attacked in any judicial proceeding on
the ground that it alone and of itself constituted a violation of any
antitrust laws other than section 2 of the Act of July 2, 1890 (section 2 of
the Sherman Antitrust Act, 15 U.S.C. 2), but nothing in this subsection
shall exempt any bank resulting from a merger transaction from com-
plying with the antitrust laws after the consummation of such transaction.

(D) In any action brought under the antitrust laws arising out of a
merger transaction approved by a Federal supervisory agency pursuant to
this subsection, such agency, and any State banking supervisory agency
having jurisdiction within the State involved, may appear as a party of its
own motion and as of right, and be represented by its counsel.

(8) For the purposes of this subsection, the term 'antitrust laws' means
the Act of July 2, 1890 (the Sherman Antitrust Act, 15 U.S.C. 1–7), the
Act of October 15, 1914 (the Clayton Act, 15 U.S.C. 12–27), and any
other Acts in pari materia.

Considering the high degree of regulation in banking, the service
nature of this industry, and the technical problems encountered in this
area, it is very doubtful that a purely competitive standard could
possibly have been completely satisfactory as the only test of the
legality of all bank mergers. Surely in at least some instances more
than a concentration ratio or the fact that the banks involved may
have been "major competitors" in a market would have to be weighed
in determining the lawfulness of a merger, if "the convenience and
needs of the community were to be served." With this in mind the
Congress in drafting the 1966 amendment to the Bank Merger Act
(hereafter termed simply "the 1966 amendment") directed the courts
to consider both "banking factors" and competitive factors in determining the legality of a merger, no doubt assuming that in a very
limited number of cases a bank merger would still be in the public
interest, although competition might be significantly reduced.

This amendment was also expected to eliminate the cause of much of the confusion which has developed as a result of the different standards found in the Bank Merger Act of 1960 and the antitrust laws, for under this new legislation the courts have been directed to use the same criteria as those employed by the banking agencies in paragraph 5 cited above. But, contrary to what is frequently believed, this change could make the status of competition in a given market a more important, not a less important consideration in this field than it was before this legislation was passed. Under the original Bank Merger Act, the banking agencies were directed to consider competition, but this was merely one of seven factors to be weighed in deciding whether a merger should be approved. Today, however, the banking agency must make a substantive antitrust judgment, and where it finds a substantial lessening of competition may occur the merger is to be approved only if this factor is clearly outweighed by the positive benefits which are expected to accrue to the community, assuming the merger is authorized. Thus, since it is difficult for Justice to try an antitrust suit and only a few are instituted each year and it is relatively easy for the banking authorities to reject a merger application, if this standard is employed by the banking agencies in the manner Congress appears to have intended,[93] it could prove to be a far more effective weapon against bank amalgamations than Section 1 or Section 7 might ever have been.

The 1966 amendment eliminated retroactive application of Section 1 of the Sherman Act or Section 7 of the Clayton Act to any merger involving an insured bank, which relieved the uncertainty regarding

[93] See the discussion of the bill in the *Congressional Record,* February 8, 1966, pp. 2332–60; *Ibid.,* February 9, 1966, pp. 2537–51; and U. S. Congress, House, Report 1221, *Bank Merger Act Amendment,* 1966. There can be little doubt that the Federal Reserve Board is giving greater weight to competitive factors. In fact the Board has begun to reject mergers on the basis of potential competition as well as existing competition (formation of Allied Bankshares and the acquisition of Liberty National Bank by BT New York Corporation), which means that the Board has moved ahead of the Supreme Court for none of the actions involving conglomerate bank mergers (*Crocker–Citizens, First National City–Carte Blanche, First National Bank of Hawaii–Cooke Trust*) has been decided as yet. Details of the two Fed decisions are included in the *Federal Reserve Bulletin* (May 1967). Jerome W. Shay, Assistant General Counsel of the Federal Reserve Board indicated the Fed is now considering not only direct competition but concentration levels and potential competition that may be ended by mergers. "Crosse says Application of Antitrust Laws Ignores Competitive Strength," *American Banker,* June 12, 1967.

the validity of a large number of past bank mergers. This provision may seem to be of little importance for under present policy few banks were likely candidates for a belated Section 7 suit[94] of the type brought against duPont.[95] Nevertheless, there appears to be a growing interest in Congress and in the Department of Justice with the reduction of existing high levels of concentration in some industries, and in time suits designed to accomplish this objective could become more common.

Although there was general agreement concerning the exemption of past mergers which had not been challenged,[96] a bitter controversy developed concerning the treatment of acquisitions already found to violate the antitrust laws. This conflict arose because the 1966 amendment provided that two mergers which had been enjoined by the courts, *Lexington* and *Manufacturers Hanover,* were held to be conclusively presumed to have not been in violation of Section 1 of the Sherman Act and Section 7 of the Clayton Act, along with the still pending *Continental Illinois* merger. In addition any unchallenged bank merger consummated between June 16, 1963, and February 21, 1966, the law provided, could not now be attacked in any judicial proceeding "on the ground that it alone and of itself constituted a violation of the antitrust laws other than Section 2 of the Sherman Act." Ironically, the Philadelphia banks, which unlike the other institutions sued never merged but instead waited until the issues had been adjudicated, not only were not permitted to merge but the rather clumsy drafting of the law has even "obscured Congress' intent as to whether these banks are to be given a second chance."[97]

While the 1966 amendment contained a number of provisions which the Antitrust Division found objectionable, it also included provisions Justice long desired. For example, under this new legislation Justice will receive premerger notification essentially as it did under the original Bank Merger Act of 1960, but in addition the

[94] "The 1966 Amendment to the Bank Merger Act," *The Banking Law Journal* (September 1966), p. 768. This article was reprinted from the April 1966 *Columbia Law Review.*

[95] *U. S.* v. *E. I. du Pont,* 353 U.S. 586 (1957).

[96] Attorney General Katzenbach noted that Justice did not strongly object to this exemption. House Report 1221, January 24, 1966, pp. 8–10, 16–18.

[97] "The 1966 Amendment to the Bank Merger Act," *The Banking Law Journal* (September 1966), p. 771, n. 92.

Attorney General has been given the power to enjoin a merger by merely commencing an action against it. Prior to this amendment of the 1960 legislation, the Justice Department had to seek an injunction in the courts to stop a bank acquisition, but now the injunction is "automatic," and it can be removed only if the courts issue *a specific order* permitting the consummation of the merger. Thus, the burden has been shifted from the plaintiff (Justice Department) to the defendant (banks)—the plaintiff now being granted the injunction and the defendant being required to convince the court to set it aside.

Some authorities argued that the courts would find this remedy to be too extreme and that judges would usually rule in favor of the banks on this question, and this position appeared to be the correct one based upon the statements and decisions of the District Courts through early 1967. However, in its opinion regarding the procedural issues in the *First City National Bank of Houston* and *Provident National Bank cases,* the Supreme Court directed that "the stays continue until the hearings below are completed and any appeal is had." The Court observed:[98]

A stay is not mandatory under any and all circumstances. But absent a frivolous complaint by the United States, which we presume will be infrequent, a stay is essential until the judicial remedies have been exhausted. . . . The legislative history is replete with references to the difficulty of unscrambling two or more banks *after* their merger. The normal procedure therefore should be maintenance of the *status quo* until the antitrust litigation has run its course, lest consummation take place and the unscrambling process that Congress abhorred *in the case of banks* be necessary.

Thus, the Justice Department's injunction powers under the 1966 amendment appear to have much greater force than the Trial Courts had indicated.

[98] *U. S.* v. *First City National Bank of Houston* and *U. S.* v. *Provident National Bank,* 386 U.S. 361 (1967), 18 L. ed. 2d 151, 158 (1967). Nevertheless, some bankers found solace in the wording of this paragraph because it placed such great emphasis upon the difficulty of dividing merged banks. Assistant Attorney General Donald Turner noted he expects the three banks whose mergers have been completed (Third National Bank of Nashville, Mercantile Trust Company of St. Louis, and Crocker Citizens National Bank of San Francisco) and which are now being tested in the courts to "push that point pretty hard." "I would if I were in their place," he remarked. "Turner: Key Questions Unanswered," *American Banker,* March 29, 1967.

In addition to the provisions discussed above there are a number of confusing or questionable elements in this legislation which its critics decried during the Congressional debates on the bill. For example, paragraph (7) (D) permits a federal supervisory agency and a state agency to appear as a party in bank merger antitrust litigation. This has resulted in two federal government executive agencies opposing each other in a court of law in all bank merger cases tried since the new law was enacted.[99]

Furthermore, this legislation, under certain circumstances, apparently provides "special treatment" for banks under Section 7 of the Clayton Act and Section 1 of the Sherman Act but *not* under Section 2 of the Sherman Act. Yet, it is Section 2 which has not been tested in bank merger litigation, for although both Section 1 and 2 violations were charged in the *Lexington case* the Supreme Court's decision was based solely on the former.[100] And, in April 1966, the Section 2 issue was reopened by Justice. The District Judge declined to overrule the 1962 decision in this case [263 F. Supp. 268 (1967)], and this denial was being appealed by the Antitrust Division. However, on August 7, 1967, a consent judgment was filed which in time should bring this action to a close.[101]

Another rather unusual aspect of the 1966 amendment to the Bank Merger Act is its omission of any reference to a product market (line of commerce). While the Clayton Act refers to a potential lessening of competition in any line of commerce in any section of the country,

[99] See, for example, *U. S.* v. *I. C. C.*, 337 U.S. 426, 431–32 (1949) for an earlier example of litigation involving two opposing government agencies.

[100] The *Report of the Attorney General's National Committee to Study the Antitrust Laws,* 1955 (p. 43) interpreted Section 2 of the Sherman Act as follows: "Monopolizing under Section 2 consists of monopoly in the economic sense—that is, power to fix prices or to exclude competition—plus a carefully limited ingredient of purpose to use or preserve such power. Economic monopoly becomes illegal monopolization not only (1) if it was achieved or preserved by conduct violating Section 1 but also (2) if it was, even by restrictions not prohibited by Section 1 deliberately obtained or maintained. This element of 'deliberateness' or 'purpose,' distinguishing economic monopoly from the offenses of monopolization, differs from the more demanding concept of 'specific intent' relevant where the offense alleged is an attempt to monopolize."

[101] The constitutionality of the "foregiveness" provisions of the Bank Merger Act of 1966 was attacked by another Kentucky bank and by a First Security National Bank of Lexington stockholder in September 1967. See *American Banker,* September 22, 1967; and *ibid.,* October 4, 1967.

only the latter standard is included in this new legislation. Senator Robertson in the Congressional debate on the bill noted this omission was made so that the criteria to be considered would closely resemble those found in the Bank Merger Act. Hence, he indicated:

> The banking agencies and the courts, in other words, are not intended and are not permitted to select some single, perhaps minor aspect of the banks' business and to say that, because there is some lessening of competition in this element of the business, the overall effects of the merger—the increase of competition in the entire field of banking and in the broader field of financial institutions which may result from other aspects of the merger—are irrelevant and may not be considered.

And the House Report on the bill noted that one of its objectives was "the promotion of healthy competition among *financial institutions.*" [Emphasis added] Therefore, some people argue that a merger must be evaluated from the viewpoint of the banking business as a whole, including other financial institutions, and not merely considering small customer banking or such as the relevant product. To this the Justice Department has responded that since this is an amendment to the Federal Deposit Insurance Act: "It was quite unnecessary and indeed would have been inappropriate for the phrase 'in *any* line of commerce' to have been included in so obviously a statute concerned exclusively with banks."[102] The March, 1967 decision of the Supreme Court in the *First City National* and *Provident National cases* was limited to procedural issues and provided no indication of the Justices' position on this point.

### BANK HOLDING COMPANY ACT[103]

Some time after the Bank Holding Company Act of 1956 was signed, Senator Robertson remarked that it had required eighteen years to pass the Act, and no doubt largely in jest he noted it would probably require eighteen more years to amend it. However, on July 1, 1966, only a little over a decade after the original bill was enacted, some major revisions were made in this legislation.[104]

---

[102] *U. S.* v. *Crocker-Anglo National Bank,* 63 C. 41808 (N. D. Calif.), *Plaintiff's Supplementary Post-Trial Reply Brief,* p. 12A.

[103] 80 Stat. 236 (1966).

[104] In Chapter 3 a number of the general provisions of the new law were reviewed; therefore, in this section, only those parts of the revised statute which are directly related to antitrust questions will be discussed.

Under the 1966 amendments, the Federal Reserve Board is required to apply the same tests in judging acquisitions by bank holding companies as the three federal banking agencies employ under the amended Bank Merger Act.[105] The antitrust standards are also essentially the same, with only minor changes in terminology to cover the operations of a group system, as opposed to actions which may be undertaken by a single bank. The main elements of paragraphs 5(A) through 8 quoted in the previous discussion of the Bank Merger Act amendment are all included in the new holding company law. These paragraphs cover the standards to be applied by the agency: the notification of the Attorney General of any approval of an acquisition; the "automatic injunction"; the requirement that action under Section 1 and Section 7 be initiated within thirty days of approval; the establishment of identical standards to be applied by the courts and the Board; the provision that a transaction may later be attacked under Section 2 of the Sherman Act; and the statement that the Board and any State supervisory agency having jurisdiction may appear as a party in an antitrust action arising out of any acquisition they approved.

Unlike the Merger Act, however, there was no exemption for bank holding companies involved in antitrust litigation under Section 1 or Section 7 prior to June 17, 1963 (the date of the Supreme Court decision in the *Philadelphia case*). This was to be expected, since bank stock acquisitions by group systems were specifically covered by the original Clayton Act, and there could be no argument that confusion existed on this point, in contrast to the "asset acquisition" question which arose in the case of bank "mergers."[106] Nevertheless, any bank acquisition by a group system which was consummated prior to the date of the 1966 amendment to the Bank Holding Company Act (July 1, 1966) and "as to which no litigation was initiated by the Attorney General" is conclusively assumed not to have been in violation of any antitrust laws other than Section 2 of the Sherman Act.

[105] 80 Stat. 7 (1966).

[106] Of course, the District Court decision in the *Marshall & Ilsley Bank Stock case* raised some questions about the power of Justice to attack a holding company acquisition approved by the Board of Governors, but in May 1967 the Supreme Court reversed the Lower Court decision. [387 U.S. 238 (1967)]

COURT DECISIONS AFTER THE 1966 AMENDMENTS[107]

"The 1966 Act was the product of powerful contending forces, each of which in the aftermath claimed more of a victory than it deserved." This comment by the Supreme Court in the *Houston* and *Provident National cases* was addressed to the Bank Merger Act amendment but it could also have been directed toward the Bank Holding Company Act amendment since much of the language in the latter was drawn from the former. This section considers the actions taken by the Courts between the passage of the Bank Merger Act amendment (February 1966) and the decision of the Supreme Court in *Houston* and *Provident National* (March 1967), and it examines some of the implications (actual and expected) of this decision.

*The Crocker case.*    The basic positions to be taken by the Antitrust Division and the banks under this new legislation were immediately apparent in the replies to the request of the Court in the *Crocker-Citizens case* for further briefs after the 1966 amendment to the Bank Merger Act was approved. Justice took the point of view, which it subsequently held in all of the cases filed since that time, that the 1966 legislation made no substantial change in the law or the standards to be applied in passing upon the issues presented in these actions. In the Department's words:[108]

It is, of course, the essential position of the Government . . . that the 1966 amendment to the Bank Merger Act (P.L. 89–356; 80 Stat. 7) has not resulted in substantial change in substantive antitrust law or in the standards used by the courts in determining the legality of bank mergers.

However, the District Court in the *Crocker case* did not accept this thesis, and it stated: "The legislative history of the Act [1966 amend-

---

[107] Some of the main facts concerning each of these cases are summarized in "Developments under the Bank Merger Act of 1966," *Bank Stock Quarterly,* M. A. Schapiro & Co., December 1966, pp. 10–11.

[108] One writer observed: "A clear demonstration of the political power of large banking institutions is provided by the provisions in the 1966 amendment exempting the three challenged pre-*Philadelphia* mergers. The lobbying campaign in favor of the banks involved in litigation and the need to resolve a dispute as to committee authority may have distracted Congress from a thoughtful analysis of the bank merger problem." "The 1966 Amendment to the Bank Merger Act," *The Banking Law Journal* (September 1966), p. 787.

ment to the Bank Merger Act] most emphatically contradicts the position now taken by the Government."[109]

Following an analysis of the provisions in the 1966 legislation, the Court remarked: "It seems clear that what we are now called upon to do is to review a decision and determination of the Comptroller of the Currency."[110] But the law stipulated the Court was to "review *de novo* the issues presented," and the Judges in the *Crocker case* questioned the extent to which this could be done. They indicated no difficulty would be presented in reviewing *de novo* the competitive effects of the merger, since this has been the courts' traditional function. But the statute also called for a weighing of the anticompetitive effects (if any) of the transaction against its probable benefits in meeting the convenience and needs of the community to be served. The Trial Court indicated the latter decision ". . . is plainly and unquestionably a legislative or administrative determination of a type which this court, as a constitutional court, is prohibited from deciding."[111]

On October 30, 1967, the District Court dismissed the Government's complaint, finding that the merger of the two California banks was not in violation of the Bank Merger Act of 1966, Section 7 of the Clayton Act, or Section 1 of the Sherman Act. The judges ruled that

[109] *U. S.* v. *Crocker-Anglo National Bank,* 263 F. Supp. 125, 128 (1966).

[110] *Ibid.,* at 131. However, the Court noted the Comptroller's decision was not based on the new language of the law and it also antedated the decisions of the Supreme Court in *U. S.* v. *El Paso Natural Gas,* 376 U.S. 651 (1964) and *U. S.* v. *Penn Olin,* 378 U.S. 158 (1964). These decisions, the court observed, developed Section 7 of the Clayton Act to an extent not previously announced, indicating it is designed to preserve not only present but potential competition in the market in question. Thus, before the Court would "review the action of the Comptroller" under the new law, they remanded the matter to him for consideration under the provisions of the 1966 Act. [263 F. Supp. 125, 139 (1966)] The new Comptroller of the Currency, William B. Camp, in his finding requested by the Court indicated there was no "actual or potential anticompetitive effect" from the merger. "Crocker Merger," *American Banker,* December 28, 1966.

[111] *U. S.* v. *Crocker-Anglo National Bank,* 263 F. Supp. 125, 132–33 (1966). This would seem to follow from the comment of the Supreme Court in *Philadelphia* 374 U.S. 321 at 371: "We are clear, however that a merger the effect of which 'may be substantially to lessen competition' is not saved because, on some ultimate reckoning of social and economic debits and credits, it may be deemed beneficial. A value choice of such magnitude is beyond the ordinary limits of judicial competence . . ."

the Government failed to prove that the merger had a substantial adverse effect on actual or potential competition in the business of banking in any economically significant section of the country. Furthermore, the Court indicated that if the merger had resulted in a substantial lessening of competition, such anti-competitive effects were clearly outweighed in the public interest by the probable effects of the merger in meeting the convenience and needs of the community. The decision also noted the Bank Merger Act of 1966 permitted an assessment of the competitive effect of a merger, not in the narrow market of commercial banks, but in the wider and more realistic field of all institutions which compete either for the savings or investment dollar. In regard to geographic markets the Court concluded that the State of California as a whole was not a relevant market in which to measure competitive effects. (1967 *Trade Cases* ¶72,258) No doubt the decision will be appealed.

*The Nashville case. U. S.* v. *Third National Bank in Nashville* was a case which, like *Crocker,* was pending when the 1966 amendment was enacted; however, unlike the California suit, this action was tried after the amendment was enacted. The opinion of the Court, the first to be handed down under the new law, was entered November 22, 1966, and it was based upon the amended Bank Merger Act, not upon the Clayton or Sherman Acts as desired by Justice. As in the *Crocker case* the decision indicated ". . . the amendment introduces new standards to be applied by the banking agencies, by the Department of Justice, and by the courts alike."[112] And the opinion went on to note that the legality of bank mergers must be weighed in terms of the antitrust standards prescribed in the amendment since "the banking industry is . . . recognized as occupying a unique place in our national economy requiring a specialized set of antitrust standards. . . ."[113] Furthermore, the Court stated that while Justice had "established an arguable case for condemnation of the merger under the pre-1966 standards of the *Lexington, Philadelphia,* and other cases" . . . "the merger is not violative of the new antitrust standards of the 1966 amendment."[114] Justice appealed the case to the Supreme Court

[112] *U. S.* v. *Third National Bank in Nashville,* 260 F. Supp. 869, 871 (1966).
[113] *Ibid.,* at 872.
[114] *Ibid.,* at 878.

on April 11, 1967. Briefs were filed late in the fall; and the High Court's decision is expected in 1968.

*Mercantile Trust case.*   The third suit which was pending at the time the Bank Merger Act was amended was *U. S.* v. *Mercantile Trust Co. National Association.*[115] This case was not tried on its merits since the District Judge ordered the Government attorneys to refile their suit under the provisions of the amended bank merger statute but they did not do so, and therefore he dismissed the action early in 1967. On April 14, 1967, Justice appealed the decision to the Supreme Court, arguing the dismissal was based on the identical reasoning found in the First City National Bank of Houston and the Provident National Bank dismissals which were reversed by the Supreme Court. This argument was accepted by the High Court, and on October 16, 1967 the case was remanded to the lower court for trial. (1967 *Trade Cases* ¶72,237)

*Provident National and First City National cases.*[116]   Both the *Provident National*[117] and *First City National*[118] suits were dismissed by the District Courts before they were tried. In very general terms, the dismissals resulted from the Government's failure to sue under the Bank Merger Act, rather than Section 7 of the Clayton Act, and from its refusal to carry the burden of establishing that the "convenience and needs factors" do not outweigh any anticompetitive effects of the proposed mergers. Justice appealed both decisions to the Supreme Court where they were argued consecutively since they involved identical procedural questions. Oral arguments on the points in dispute were heard on February 20 and 21, 1967, and five weeks later, on March 27, 1967, Mr. Justice Douglas delivered the opinion of the Court.[119]

[115] *U. S.* v. *Mercantile Trust Company,* 263 F. Supp. 340 (1966).

[116] Three other suits were instituted (see Table 7.1) but in each case the planned amalgamation was abandoned when the suit was initiated. In addition, the Hawaii case is still pending. Stay vacated. *U. S.* v. *First National Bank of Hawaii,* 257 F. Supp. 591 (1966).

[117] *U. S.* v. *Provident National Bank,* 1967 *Trade Cases* ¶ 71,985; 262 F. Supp. 397 (1966).

[118] *U. S.* v. *First City National Bank of Houston,* 1967 *Trade Cases* ¶ 71, 970. (The decision was not reported in F. Supp.)

[119] 1967 *Trade Cases* ¶ 72,048; 386 U.S. 361 (1967), 18 L. ed. 2d 151, 158 (1967).

The main issues raised in the lower courts included: (1) the proper statute under which a bank merger action was to be brought; (2) the party who was to carry the burden of proof; (3) the meaning of the expression *de novo* review used in the 1966 Amendment; and (4) the role of the "automatic injunction" provision in this law.

(1) The Supreme Court found that the 1966 Amendment did not require that a government antitrust suit be brought against a bank merger under the Bank Merger Act. The action, the Justices observed, is to be brought under the antitrust laws, and the Bank Merger Act merely provides a new defense or justification to the merger's proponents. (2) The Court indicated that the burden of proof is on the defendant banks to establish that the anticompetitive effects of a proposed merger are clearly outweighed by the probable benefits of the transaction in meeting the convenience and needs of the community to be served. Furthermore, the Court found that the decision as to whether or not the benefits do clearly outweigh any anticompetitive effects belongs to the courts, rather than to the banking agency. (3) Thus, *"review de novo"* under the 1966 Amendment involves a judgment of the issues by the courts, not merely a judicial review of an administrative ruling which is sustained unless the agency's action was clearly not supported by substantial evidence. (4) The Court's position regarding the injunction, as was discussed earlier in this chapter, was that the statutory stay provided for under the 1966 Amendment is essential until judicial remedies in antitrust litigation have been exhausted.

The Justices expressed no views on the merits of either the Provident National–Central Penn or the First City National–Southern National mergers; they merely overruled the pre-trial dismissals by the lower courts and remanded the cases to the District Courts for trial on their merits.

Shortly after the Supreme Court decision was handed down, the First City National Bank of Houston and Southern National Bank announced they were abandoning their merger plans.[120] However, the Provident National Bank and Central Penn National Bank continued the litigation,[121] and a decision is expected in 1968.

[120] "Houston Banks Call Off Merger," *American Banker,* April 21, 1967.
[121] "Provident, Central Penn Will Fight," *American Banker,* April 28, 1967.

THE FUTURE OF BANK MERGERS AND ACQUISITIONS

The Supreme Court's decision in the *Provident National* and *First City National cases* left two vital questions unanswered. First, it is clear that the "convenience and needs" element may serve as a new defense or justification for a bank merger in antitrust litigation; but what factors will the Court consider as relevant to the convenience and needs of a community, and how much weight will they actually be given? And, second, the Supreme Court in a footnote in the Provident National and First City National decision noted the omission in the 1966 Amendment of the phrase "in any line of commerce," which is present in Section 7 of the Clayton Act. This change in wording could be very significant in determining the product market in an antitrust suit, but the Court gave no indication of how this terminology will be interpreted.

With these important issues still to be decided, it is impossible to predict the ultimate significance of the 1966 Amendment to the Bank Merger Act at this time. However, in light of the decisions of the Supreme Court in recent years, in banking and in other fields, it is very difficult to imagine that the impact of the "convenience and needs"[122] defense or the effect of the possible change in market definition[123] will be very great. From the viewpoint of the merged or merging bank, it would seem that the major gain from this legislation stems from the provisions preventing attack upon past mergers under Section 1 of the Sherman Act and Section 7 of the Clayton Act or upon present mergers after a 30-day waiting period.[124] The major loss on the other hand, results from the "automatic injunction" now available to Justice and, as was noted earlier, from the increased emphasis which the banking agencies are expected to give to antitrust factors in considering merger applications. Perhaps these observations

---

[122] The *Philadelphia case*, with its 30 percent "test," and the *Lexington case*, in which mergers involved major competitors in a relevant market, brought at least some bank mergers very close to the status of per se violations, and at least these acquisitions are now definitely one step removed from the per se rule.

[123] This may make it more difficult for the Government to move successfully to a "line within a line" of commerce test in bank merger litigation.

[124] Continental-Illinois National Bank and Manufacturers-Hanover, and perhaps First National Bank and Trust of Lexington, enjoyed the most immediate benefits from this legislation, of course.

far understate the significance of the 1966 Amendment, but this will not be known until a body of case law relating to this statute is developed.[125]

[125] Care must be taken in weighing the significance of the findings of many of the cases now in litigation. *Crocker-Citizens* and *First National Bank of Hawaii* involve future competition; *Third National Bank in Nashville* may present a "floundering bank" defense; and *Marshall & Ilsley Bank Stock* raises some unanswered questions regarding competition among holding company affiliates. [The "floundering bank" concept is discussed in the House Report (No. 1221, 89th Cong., 2d Sess.) on the 1966 Bank Merger Act Amendment.]

# CHAPTER 8

## Banking Concentration

IT IS OFTEN SUGGESTED that the bank merger movement which has been in progress in this country in recent decades has resulted in a substantial increase in banking concentration, and numerous studies can be cited to support this contention. But many investigators remain far from convinced that this argument is valid; and, as is so often true in the social sciences, it is reasonable that this difference of opinion should not only arise but persist. The problem develops in this case primarily because either explicitly or implicitly the investigator in computing a concentration ratio must decide which markets, both product and geographic, are relevant for the problem at hand. Therefore, since the boundaries of these markets for economic analysis are not fixed, the limits ultimately designated will often depend very heavily upon the judgment of the researcher, and the ratios computed by two individuals may disagree considerably. Moreover, even in bank antitrust cases, in which the courts have had to compromise in order to secure a "workable" market definition, both the product and geographic markets employed in two studies may be identical; yet, they can legitimately reach far different conclusions about concentration depending upon the number of firms included in the numerator of the ratio and the period selected as the base for which changes are to be measured.[1]

[1] Data which are relevant for analysis of specific markets are not available in published form. The FDIC has developed statistics by size of depositor and by

*Terminology.* Concentration, as the term is employed in this book, simply means the degree to which a relatively small number of banks account for a large proportion of some line of the banking business in a given area. In industrial studies numerous indexes have been developed to measure concentration in this general sense, using a variety of bases including business assets or income, employment statistics, value added data, and shipments figures.[2] However, in banking most of the analysis has been restricted to major balance sheet items, and in this chapter only total deposit data will be employed in computing the ratios.

*Measurement.* If a person is faced with the problem of compiling banking concentration statistics, he soon discovers that the computation of really meaningful ratios is far from the simple, mechanical procedure often expected. Naturally anyone with access to bank directories could quickly sum the deposits, loans, or investments held by a number of banks and note the percentage controlled by a particular institution or by several institutions. Yet, these figures may have little or no relevance to the case at hand unless they relate to the specific product and geographic markets being investigated by the economist or by the court.

For example, banks are multi-product firms which serve a vast array of different markets. In the banking literature these institutions are often termed "department stores of finance," which is somewhat indicative of the numerous different lines in which they operate. Furthermore, since they deal in a relatively homogeneous product which may be transported from one area to another at modest expense, a large number of banks may effectively compete not only in many different product markets but also in numerous geographic markets.

---

type of institution within metropolitan areas, including areas in statewide branching states, but even these figures are subject to dispute. (For the purposes of economic analysis, what is a "large" depositor?)

[2] Many of these ratios are discussed in Rosenbluth, "Measures of Concentration," in *Business Concentration and Price Policy,* pp. 57–95. For current analysis, see Bock and Farkas, *Concentration in Manufacturing;* and for a new approach to concentration see Finkelstein and Friedberg, "Application of an Entropy Theory of Concentration," 76 *Yale Law Journal* 677 (1967).

This point may be illustrated by considering the limits of a few of the bank customer markets:[3]

In general, the banking market is essentially local for the typical household savings or demand deposit, for consumer instalment and residential real estate loans, and for loans and other services to small business customers. Some of these customers may have potential alternatives beyond the local market area, but for most the forces of ignorance, inertia, local ties, the relative disinterest of outside banks in non-local small customers, and the costs and other disadvantages of locating and maintaining outside relationships, render non-local banking facilities poor alternatives. Larger business customers, however, have effective options outside the local community, sometimes encompassing a neighboring metropolitan area and sometimes going well beyond that.

Banks too could be divided into those which deal primarily in local markets or in national markets, and depending upon how the expression "local" is defined there may be some banks which would be classified in an intermediate category.[4]

Viewed very broadly, the trends in banking concentration since the turn of the century in all three of the above-mentioned customer markets were found to be very similar by Jack Guttentag and Edward Herman in their study of bank structure prepared for the Pennsylvania State Banking Department.[5] They noted that concentration decreased during the 1900–1921 period as a result of the great expansion in the number of banks. After 1921, however, they found that it tended to increase, with much of this growth occurring as a result of the sharp advance in commercial bank mergers and suspensions between 1921 and 1934. During World War II this trend was temporarily reversed, but after the war banking concentration began to rise once again at all levels—in the nation, states, and financial centers.

---

[3] Guttentag and Herman, *Banking Structure and Performance*, p. 10.

[4] See Alhadeff, "Bank Mergers: Competition Versus Banking Factors," *Southern Economic Journal* (January 1963), pp. 218–30; and his standard work *Monopoly and Competition in Banking* for a discussion of bank customer markets.

[5] Guttentag and Herman, *Banking Structure and Performance*, p. 11. This writer is not firmly convinced that their conclusion regarding the 1900 to 1921 period is entirely correct if chain systems are considered in the concentration data and the usual ("larger" bank) measures of concentration are used.

Nevertheless, its growth in this most recent period has been very limited when contrasted with that of the twenties and early thirties.

*Market shares of large banks: the nation.* Developments in the "national market" are often gauged by analyzing data relating to the combined market shares of the 100, 200, or 300 largest banks. This writer has some very serious reservations regarding the relevance of such statistics since most banks are not significant competitors in this market and the data included may be drawn from national, regional, or local markets.[6] Nevertheless, as an aid to those who may be interested in very general changes in the banking industry the figures in Table 8.1 were compiled.

These statistics show that of the total commercial bank deposits in the United States, approximately 49, 58, and 63 percent respectively were held by the 100, 200, and 300 largest banks at the end of 1966. While the share of the total deposits controlled by the banks ranking from 101 to 300 has been relatively stable since the 1930s, the percentage held by the largest banks has varied tremendously. These institutions increased their share from 32 percent in 1923 to 57 percent in 1940. Thereafter the ratio of the deposits of the 100 largest banks to all commercial bank deposits fell considerably, reaching 46 percent, its 1930 level, in 1950. During the last sixteen years this figure has moved within a very narrow range but has increased by 3 percentage points, and it currently stands at 49 percent, which is almost the same as it was in 1945.

Even this rather small relative increase in the deposits in the very large banks may be misleading, for data compiled by the FDIC from the late 1950s to the present time for the 100 largest commercial banks indicate there has been almost no change in the market shares of these institutions. (It has remained at about 46 percent.) The difference between the *American Banker* data cited earlier which showed a small increase in concentration and the FDIC statistics it would seem stems primarily from the inclusion of reciprocal demand deposit balances and deposits in foreign branches by the former and the ex-

---

[6] In addition, the choice of 100 or more firms is not common to say the least, since it is unusual to find the "top 20" firms in an industry included in such analyses.

TABLE 8.1. THE GROWTH OF LARGE AND SMALL COMMERCIAL BANKS IN THE UNITED STATES YEAR-END OR DATE OF FINAL CALL SELECTED YEARS, 1935–1966 (DEPOSITS IN $ MILLION)

| Rank by Deposit Size[a] | 1966 | 1965 | 1960 | 1955 | 1950 | 1945 | 1940 | 1935 |
|---|---|---|---|---|---|---|---|---|
| 1–100 | | | | | | | | |
| Deposits | 172,602 | 160,783 | 109,024 | 90,498 | 71,690 | 72,538 | 37,637 | 25,102 |
| Percent | 49 | 48 | 47 | 47 | 46 | 48 | 57 | 55 |
| 101–200 | | | | | | | | |
| Deposits | 32,208 | 30,772 | 21,014 | 17,552 | 13,505 | 12,952 | 5,203 | 3,603 |
| Percent | 9 | 9 | 9 | 9 | 9 | 9 | 8 | 8 |
| 201–300 | | | | | | | | |
| Deposits | 17,505 | 16,638 | 11,715 | 9,560 | 7,887 | 7,487 | 2,828 | 1,986 |
| Percent | 5 | 5 | 5 | 5 | 5 | 5 | 4 | 4 |
| over 300 | | | | | | | | |
| Deposits | 132,813 | 125,586 | 88,780 | 75,595 | 63,006 | 58,199 | 20,082 | 14,677 |
| Percent | 37 | 38 | 39 | 39 | 40 | 38 | 31 | 32 |
| all commercial banks[b] | | | | | | | | |
| Deposits[c] | 355,128 | 333,779 | 230,532 | 193,205 | 156,088 | 151,176 | 65,750 | 45,368 |
| Percent | 100 | 100 | 100 | 100 | 100 | 100 | 100 | 100 |

[a] At the end of 1966 the 100th, 200th, and 300th largest banks in the United States respectively had deposits of $457 million, $226 million, and $146 million.

[b] Columns may not add exactly to the totals given because the figures were rounded.

[c] "U. S. and Other Areas" reported by FDIC.

Source: *American Banker* for individual bank data and the FDIC for aggregate data.

clusion of them by the latter.[7] Both of these items are of questionable significance, but not necessarily of no significance,[8] in evaluating the extent of deposit concentration in the United States.[9]

In all fairness to those who support the "increasing concentration thesis," however, it should be noted that the years of uncertain economic conditions in the 1930s favored the relative growth of large banks.[10] And, by the mid-1940s, as a result of war financing and in part no doubt because of the greater confidence in smaller banks, deposits became more evenly distributed. Thus, the comparison of 1966 data with 1940 or 1935 may be rather unfair. On the other hand, when one considers the number of mergers by and among the largest banks during the past sixteen years (the latter requiring the addition of new banks to the 100 largest banks' totals to replace those acquired) it must be conceded that the smaller banks have shown a remarkable capacity to compete with the bigger institutions and to retain their relative market shares.

*Market shares of large banks: the states.* Although existing studies have not conclusively established there is an "intermediate" bank or customer market, and it seems rather doubtful that it would be conterminous with state boundaries, some state "concentration" statistics were compiled for this book merely for the purpose of illustration. Using data for the three largest banks in each state, for example, one finds a decline in their relative position during the war and early postwar period; but after 1950 the market shares of these institutions

[7] The FDIC uses call report data which exclude these items, while apparently the *American Banker* uses questionnaire responses which do not call for these adjustments. This tends to exaggerate slightly the percentage controlled by the largest banks, since the latter publication uses "gross" data in the numerator and the FDIC "adjusted" total deposit data in the denominator in computing the ratios.

[8] For example, economic power may be enhanced in one market by gains achieved in another, as in the case of a conglomerate merger where the overall power of the firm may be directed to particular markets.

[9] For a much more detailed analysis of the changing market shares of large banks, see Alhadeff and Alhadeff, "Growth of Large Banks, 1930–1960," *Review of Economics and Statistics* (November 1964), pp. 356–63.

[10] U. S. Congress, House, *Banking Concentration and Small Business*, Staff Report, 1960, pp. 2–3.

began to rise once again.[11] By the early 1960s the average of the state concentration ratios computed on this basis had returned to its prewar level, and the distribution of the ratios as described by such measures as the mean, the quartiles, the standard deviation, and skewness was virtually identical to that of 25 years earlier.

The Board of Governors on several occasions in the past has compiled state concentration statistics on a somewhat different basis than the above, choosing the same fixed percentage of banks rather than using the same number of banks for each state. These data were revised slightly by this writer to make them uniform for all periods and the most recent figures available (Table 8.2) were compiled for this study. The changes in concentration using this measure were very similar to those found in the other state and national studies discussed above.[12] (Since metropolitan areas have usually been selected as the relevant section of the country in bank antitrust cases, the discussion of the market shares of large banks in the cities is included in the following section of this chapter.)

## CONCEPT OF THE BANKING MARKET

A market is conveniently defined as a closely interrelated group of sellers and buyers. This concept has been a vital element in merger antitrust suits, yet the word does not even appear in Section 7 of the Clayton Act. The statutory test under this section is whether the effect of a merger may be substantially to lessen competition in any line of commerce in any section of the country. However, in 1957, in the *du Pont–General Motors case,* the Supreme Court held that a proper definition of "the market" was essential to any finding of a Clayton

[11] For detailed analysis of state concentration data, see FDIC *Annual Report,* 1960, pp. 54–55, 101; and *ibid.,* 1962, p. 55.

[12] Rank correlation coefficients (Spearman's) were computed to measure the strength of the relationship between the positions of the states in one time period and another. The coefficients were very high, ranging between .93 and .97 for the three shorter periods (1939–1951, 1951–1960, 1960–1965), and the corresponding figure for the much longer interval, 1939–1965, was .79. As one might expect, using a T-test upon the rank correlation coefficients, the null hypotheses were all rejected, even at the .0005 level. For the tests employed see Siegel, *Nonparametric Statistics,* pp. 202–13.

TABLE 8.2. RATIO OF DEPOSITS OF SELECTED LARGE COMMERCIAL BANKS TO ALL COMMERCIAL BANKS, BY GEOGRAPHIC AREA, YEAR-END 1939, 1951, 1960, AND 1965*

| Geographic Area | 1939 | 1951 | 1960 | 1965 | Geographic Area | 1939 | 1951 | 1960 | 1965 |
|---|---|---|---|---|---|---|---|---|---|
| New England | 45.5 | 41.8 | 47.3 | 48.3 | South Atlantic | 46.8 | 39.3 | 40.0 | 38.3 |
| Maine | 14.7 | 15.2 | 25.3 | 25.3 | Delaware | 48.8 | 43.4 | 47.4 | 39.1 |
| New Hampshire | 14.7 | 11.7 | 11.5 | 11.9 | Maryland | 48.2 | 40.8 | 48.0 | 52.4 |
| Vermont | 12.0 | 11.8 | 17.6 | 21.8 | D. C. | 45.4 | 44.3 | 57.0 | 53.3 |
| Massachusetts | 55.7 | 49.5 | 50.7 | 52.7 | Virginia | 41.6 | 34.6 | 33.1 | 41.9 |
| Rhode Island | 55.3 | 65.4 | 85.8 | 85.1 | West Virginia | 27.0 | 25.1 | 20.3 | 18.0 |
| Connecticut | 27.8 | 29.0 | 42.5 | 41.5 | North Carolina | 47.8 | 41.6 | 56.8 | 64.2 |
|  |  |  |  |  | South Carolina | 41.9 | 39.2 | 43.1 | 47.8 |
| Middle Atlantic | 74.7 | 72.0 | 75.0 | 74.8 | Georgia | 68.4 | 57.3 | 53.7 | 53.4 |
| New York | 86.2 | 85.9 | 87.9 | 85.0 | Florida | 41.5 | 27.0 | 20.3 | 17.1 |
| New Jersey | 26.5 | 25.7 | 29.1 | 27.6 |  |  |  |  |  |
| Pennsylvania | 51.6 | 50.9 | 57.7 | 62.4 | East South Central | 45.9 | 40.3 | 39.7 | 40.6 |
|  |  |  |  |  | Kentucky | 41.0 | 38.6 | 37.7 | 39.8 |
| East North Central | 62.4 | 53.4 | 50.8 | 50.6 | Tennessee | 54.2 | 47.7 | 45.0 | 46.0 |
| Ohio | 56.4 | 53.9 | 52.8 | 52.5 | Alabama | 53.8 | 44.1 | 40.6 | 37.4 |
| Indiana | 39.6 | 34.9 | 38.1 | 35.2 | Mississippi | 21.5 | 18.9 | 28.8 | 33.8 |
| Illinois | 74.2 | 58.7 | 52.7 | 54.2 |  |  |  |  |  |
| Michigan | 60.1 | 59.2 | 58.6 | 57.4 | West South Central | 49.0 | 42.9 | 43.5 | 37.2 |
| Wisconsin | 45.7 | 38.9 | 36.7 | 33.0 | Arkansas | 35.9 | 26.4 | 23.5 | 22.0 |
|  |  |  |  |  | Louisiana | 53.3 | 40.7 | 34.4 | 31.1 |
| West North Central | 53.2 | 42.7 | 38.4 | 35.1 | Oklahoma | 50.5 | 49.7 | 46.8 | 44.3 |
| Minnesota | 59.7 | 50.7 | 44.9 | 42.4 | Texas | 48.8 | 43.7 | 47.0 | 41.3 |

| | | | | |
|---|---|---|---|---|
| Iowa | 31.5 | 27.5 | 26.8 | 24.4 |
| Missouri | 66.3 | 54.5 | 46.3 | 43.1 |
| North Dakota | 31.0 | 25.4 | 23.6 | 19.9 |
| South Dakota | 34.1 | 26.6 | 27.0 | 27.1 |
| Nebraska | 53.7 | 42.2 | 42.2 | 38.9 |
| Kansas | 31.4 | 29.0 | 27.8 | 26.5 |
| Pacific | 80.5 | 81.0 | 88.4 | 84.3 |
| Washington | 56.8 | 58.1 | 60.8 | 61.2 |
| Oregon | 77.4 | 77.0 | 84.7 | 83.7 |
| California | 84.6 | 85.8 | 93.6 | 88.4 |
| Alaska | 15.6 | 25.1 | 28.6 | 32.0 |
| Hawaii | 45.0 | 47.7 | 44.9 | 41.9 |
| Mountain | 38.2 | 35.1 | 40.2 | 39.0 |
| Montana | 24.5 | 15.8 | 15.8 | 16.5 |
| Idaho | 28.1 | 29.5 | 35.9 | 35.5 |
| Wyoming | 22.0 | 18.7 | 21.2 | 19.7 |
| Colorado | 48.5 | 38.7 | 44.0 | 41.7 |
| New Mexico | 31.0 | 27.9 | 30.7 | 30.4 |
| Arizona | 45.9 | 51.2 | 47.8 | 46.3 |
| Utah | 31.2 | 39.2 | 50.8 | 47.9 |
| Nevada | 77.9 | 66.8 | 63.1 | 55.7 |
| United States | | | | |
| Total | 65.0 | 57.7 | 59.1 | 58.1 |

* The largest commercial banks were selected in each state; the number used for each year was 2% of the total number of commercial banks in the state in 1951 (with all fractions raised)—except in Rhode Island, District of Columbia, New York, and California, where a larger number was used, which was the number included in the 100 largest banks in 1951. Although the same number of banks was used in each year (329), the banks were not necessarily identical, because of mergers and changes in the relative sizes of the banks.

Source: U. S. Congress, Senate, Staff Report of the Board of Governors of the Federal Reserve System Submitted to the Subcommittee on Monopoly of the Select Committee on Small Business, *Concentration of Banking in the United States*, 82d Cong., 2d Sess., 1952, Committee print 7, pp. 17–18; and U. S. Congress, Senate, Special Staff Report of the Federal Reserve System Submitted to the Select Committee on Small Business, *Recent Developments in the Structure of Banking—A Supplement to Concentration of Banking in the United States*, 87th Cong., 2d Sess., 1962, pp. 19–21. Some minor revisions were made in the Board's figures for 1939 using data obtained from *Polk's Bank Directory* (March 1940) to make them uniform for all years. The 1965 data were compiled, using the same procedure followed by the Federal Reserve, from reports in the *American Banker* (March 15, 1966), pp. 11–60; *Polk's Bank Directory* (March 1966); and from information supplied by the FDIC.

Act violation. This interpretation was carried a step further in 1958 by the District Court in *Bethlehem Steel* and in 1962 by the Supreme Court in *Brown Shoe*,[13] as the judges found that the "line of commerce" phrase in Section 7 signified a product market and the term "section of the country" referred to a geographic market.

The problem of defining the relevant market has become especially difficult during the past few years, for the courts have begun to interpret the expressions *"any* line of commerce" and *"any* section of the country" to mean some rather than all markets in which the acquired and acquiring companies operate. This approach was followed in lower court rulings in *Bethlehem Steel, Crown Zellerbach, Reynolds Metals,* and *Brown Shoe,* and it was accepted by the Supreme Court as it affirmed the judgment of the District Court in *Brown Shoe.*[14] This was especially important to banking so long as this industry was not given special treatment under the antitrust laws, for recent court decisions seem to indicate that if potential anticompetitive effects in any market may result from a merger it is highly unlikely that they could be offset by showing the amalgamation would produce procompetitive effects in other markets. For example, in *Philadelphia National Bank* the Supreme Court found that the merger might tend to lessen competition in the small- and medium-sized customer markets, and it gave little consideration to the banks' argument that the increased lending limit of the resulting bank would enable it to compete with major out-of-state banks for very large loans.[15]

A number of scholars in the public policy area have indicated in their publications that the introduction of this "submarket" approach in antitrust proceedings has not eliminated the formal requirement to

[13] *U. S. v. E. I. du Pont de Nemours & Co.,* 353 U.S. 586 (1957); *U. S. v. Bethlehem Steel Corporation,* 168 F. Supp. 576 (1958); and *Brown Shoe Company v. U. S.,* 370 U.S. 294 (1962).
[14] *U. S. v. Bethlehem Steel Corporation,* 168 F. Supp. 576 (1958); *Crown Zellerbach Corporation* v. *Federal Trade Commission,* 296 F. 2d 800 (1961), cert. denied, 370 U.S. 937 (1962); *Reynolds Metals Company* v. *Federal Trade Commission,* 309 F. 2d 223 (1962); *U. S. v. Brown Shoe Company,* 179 F. Supp. 721 (1959); and *Brown Shoe Company* v. *U. S.,* 370 U.S. 294 (1962). This question is discussed in Lewyn and Mann, "Some Thoughts on Policy and Enforcement of Section 7," 50 *American Bar Association Journal* 154 (February 1964).
[15] *U. S. v. Philadelphia National Bank,* 374 U.S. 321, 370–71 (1963).

define both product and geographic markets, despite the fact that it appears to have noticeably altered this procedure.[16] However, this conclusion may have to be modified in future bank antitrust litigation, in regard to the product market, as a result of the 1966 amendments to the Bank Merger and Bank Holding Company Act, and in all cases as a result of the Supreme Court's decision in *U. S.* v. *Pabst Brewing Company*.[17] The revisions in the banking acts established identical standards to be employed by the banking agencies and by the courts in considering bank amalgamations; yet neither law included any reference to a line of commerce (product market) test, although both statutes noted that a merger's effect upon competition in "any section of the country" (geographic market) was to be analyzed. On the other hand, the Pabst decision raised serious doubt regarding the importance of the geographic market concept in antitrust litigation, for in this case the Court held that the Government under Section 7 of the Clayton Act was not required to show a "relevant geographic market" but merely to prove that the merger of the corporations had a substantial anticompetitive effect "somewhere in the United States."

Since the significance to be attached to the apparent omission of the line of commerce in the banking legislation and the seemingly diminished importance of the "section of the country test" in the *Pabst case* will not be clear for some time, the following discussion will not attempt to take these actions into account, for they only serve to emphasize further the problems involved in trying to predict the courts' choice of relevant markets in a Sherman Act or Clayton Act case. Even without the addition of these new variables, the courts had tremendous flexibility in regard to market definition, for as was pointed out by George Hall and Charles Phillips:[18]

The Brown Shoe and Philadelphia National Bank decisions have established that there are markets-within-markets and that the narrowest reasonable market is the relevant one. That this situation is an intellectual monstrosity does not prevent it from being judicially useful by providing almost unlimited authority to the courts in choosing a market.

[16] See for example Hale and Hale, "Mergers in Regulated Industries," 59 *Northwestern University Law Review* 49, 50 (1964).

[17] *U. S.* v. *Pabst Brewing Company*, 384 U.S. 546 (1966).

[18] Hall and Phillips, "Antimerger Criteria: Power, Concentration, Foreclosure, and Size," 9 *Villanova Law Review* 211, 219 (1964).

Thus, although commercial banking may have been chosen as the relevant product market and the intrastate portion of a standard metropolitan statistical area (SMSA) as the relevant geographic market in the "last" case, one should not forget that they may not necessarily be selected in the next.[19]

## THE PRODUCT MARKET[20]

Commercial banking is a multiproduct (or multiservice) industry. Bank attorneys in antitrust cases have typically argued that each of these product lines faces competition to some degree from other institutions. Therefore, they state that insurance companies, small loan companies, finance companies, and numerous other intermediaries must be considered in weighing the probable effects of a given merger upon competition. To this argument both the Supreme Court and the District Courts have replied[21]

that the cluster of products (various kinds of credit) and services (such as checking accounts and trust administration) denoted by the term "commercial banking," composes a distinct line of commerce. Some commercial banking products or services are so distinctive that they are entirely free of effective competition from products or services of other financial institutions; the checking account is in this category. Others enjoy such cost advantages as to be insulated within a broad range from substitutes furnished by other institutions. . . . Finally, there are banking facilities which, although in terms of cost and price they are freely competitive with the facilities provided by other financial institutions, nevertheless enjoy a settled consumer preference, insulating them to a marked degree, from competition; this seems to be the case with savings deposits. In sum, it is clear that commercial banking is a market "sufficiently inclusive to be meaningful in terms of trade realities."

Thus, the courts do not ignore that other financial intermediaries compete with commercial banks; they merely indicate that the com-

[19] For a brief but very good summary of the market concept in antitrust, see Hall and Phillips, *Bank Mergers and the Regulatory Agencies,* pp. 239–55; for greater detail see Betty Bock's periodic research reports published by the National Industrial Conference Board, Studies in Business Economics, Nos. 93, 87, 85, 77, and 69.

[20] An excellent discussion of this topic is found in Shull's "Commercial Banking as a Line of Commerce," *The National Banking Review* (December 1963), pp. 187–206.

[21] *U. S.* v. *Philadelphia National Bank,* 374 U.S. 321, 356–57, and 326, n. 5.

mercial banks' "package" of services—the "full-service" concept so actively publicized by the Foundation for Commercial Banks—sets these firms apart from other financial institutions. The Supreme Court in *Philadelphia,* for example, did not indicate banks were immune from the competition of savings and loan associations and mutual savings banks; it simply cited a defense witness who indicated that for fifty years or more in his area the mutual savings banks had offered an interest rate ½ percent or more higher than that paid by commercial banks; yet, the rate of increase in savings accounts in commercial banks had kept pace with (and in some cases exceeded) the rate of increase of deposits in mutual savings banks. The witness observed that "habit, custom, personal relationships, convenience doing all your business under one roof appear to be factors superior to changes in the interest rate level."[22] Thus, to the extent that commercial banks are "department stores of finance" and a convenience factor stimulates the transaction of financial matters with one institution, a leading law journal concluded, "commercial banking is a relevant line of commerce."[23] [However, notwithstanding the above-mentioned testimony in the *Philadelphia case,* there is still considerable disagreement among academicians regarding the effects of interest rate differentials of various magnitudes on savings flows into competing financial intermediaries.[24]]

Even if one were to assume that commercial banking was the correct choice as the relevant product market under Section 7 as it is

[22] *Ibid.,* 357. Some savings and loan executives have reached a similar conclusion regarding the interest differential needed to avoid "stiff" competition with banks. See *1963 Conference on Saving and Residential Financing* (Chicago: U. S. Savings and Loan League, 1963), pp. 75–76.

[23] "Federal Bank Merger Policy and the Philadelphia National Bank Decision," 25 *University of Pittsburgh Law Review* 563, 571 (1964).

[24] See, for example, Alhadeff and Alhadeff, "The Struggle for Commercial Bank Savings," *Quarterly Journal of Economics* (February 1958), pp. 1–22; Werboff and Rozen, "Market Shares and Competition among Financial Institutions," pp. 278–83; and Horvitz, "Economies of Scale in Banking," pp. 40–43, both in *Private Financial Institutions;* Friend, "The Effects of Monetary Policies on Non-monetary Financial Institutions and Capital Markets," *Private Capital Markets,* pp. 29–33; Fiege, *The Demand For Liquid Assets, A Temporal Cross-Section Analysis,* pp. 37–38; Cohen and Kaufman, "Factors Determining Bank Deposit Growth by State: An Empirical Analysis," *Journal of Finance* (March 1965), p. 67; and Gray, "Some Implications of Higher Interest Rates on Time Deposits," *Journal of Finance* (March 1964), pp. 64–67, 75.

currently interpreted, in terms of actual bank operations the definition is at least several decades out of date. The Supreme Court in the *Philadelphia case* discussed the banking industry at some length, especially emphasizing the importance of the demand deposit function of commercial banks and their role in supplying short-term funds to business. This concept of commercial banking, while not uncommon, neglects the tremendous change in this financial intermediary in recent years. Today, some banks are predominantly savings institutions in terms of their deposit liabilities and sources of consumer credit (including mortgages) in terms of their assets. In addition, commercial banks differ significantly in size, which is a material factor with respect to a bank's ability to compete for the business of the large wholesale customer.[25]

Of course, one can argue that the composition of a litigant bank's assets or liabilities is irrelevant, for the Supreme Court has found[26] that the products of a commercial bank viewed collectively have "sufficiently peculiar characteristics and uses" to set them apart from similar products and services of other firms.[27] And, if the merger is between a relatively large and a small bank whose functions or service areas differ considerably (in effect a conglomerate merger),[28] size itself may some day be the deciding factor in a Section 7 suit. If the two banks operated largely in different product lines or different geographic markets, conventional market share statistics would have little or no significance; hence, total assets or total deposits may possibly be substituted as an indicator of market power.[29] Nevertheless, if concentration in banking is to be measured in an economically

[25] This point will be considered later in the discussion of the *Manufacturers Hanover case*.

[26] Some attorneys still feel the Supreme Court has not specifically ruled that commercial banking is distinct from other types of financial institutions. See "Trial to Split Crocker-Citizens," *American Banker,* June 1, 1965.

[27] *Brown Shoe Company* v. *U. S.,* 370 U.S. 294, 325 (1962). See also *U. S.* v. *E. I. du Pont de Nemours,* 353 U.S. 586, 593–94 (1957).—the "General Motors case"—as contrasted with *ibid.,* 351 U.S. 377, 404 (1956)—the "Cellophane case."

[28] This topic is discussed in detail in Turner, "Conglomerate Mergers and Section 7 of the Clayton Act," 78 *Harvard Law Review* 1313 (1965).

[29] The court might even find that entry by merger into other markets affects the degree of market power in existing markets. See Martin, "The Brown Shoe Case and the New Antimerger Policy," *American Economic Review* (June 1963), pp. 355–56.

as well as a legally relevant product market, the variation in bank size and type of customer served cannot be ignored. To bulk all commercial banking institutions together for antitrust purposes merely because they accept demand deposits and grant short-term business loans may be very convenient for the courts but it clearly ignores the realities of the present-day operations of these firms.[30]

Some improvement in the product market definition may be found in the *Manufacturers-Hanover case*. In this action the District Judge (Lloyd F. MacMahon) in determining the line of commerce acknowledged that banks serve different types of customers and that the impact of a merger on these customers and on other banks may vary. He concluded that there were two relevant product markets involved in the case—wholesale and retail commercial banking. However, he did not consider the question of whether or not "commercial banking" is a distinct line of commerce, since the problem was solved by the defendants who conceded that it was. This concession by the banks was "inspired, if not compelled," the judge observed, by the findings of the Supreme Court in the *Philadelphia case*.

Although the 1966 amendments to the Bank Merger Act and Bank Holding Company Act appear to suggest that financial institutions other than banks should be included in analysis of banking markets, the Supreme Court did not reach this question in the *Provident* and *First City National cases*. Therefore, it is still not certain how (or if) the High Court will broaden its product market definition in commercial banking cases. Moreover, Section 2 of the Sherman Act seems to remain relatively unaffected by the new legislation. It is not difficult

---

[30] The court's analysis of the commercial banking industry contained a number of perhaps minor but disturbing inaccuracies. For example, the District Courts and the Supreme Court have all indicated: "Commercial banks are unique among financial institutions in that they alone are permitted by law to accept demand deposits." [374 U.S. 321, 326 (1963).] Yet, the FDIC *Report of Call No. 78*, December 31, 1966, showed mutual savings banks held 386 million dollars of IPC demand deposits. Moreover, in one recent action relating to these deposits the Trial Court held it was lawful for the savings bank in question to accept and maintain deposits that are subject to withdrawal by depositor's check. See *Hudson County National Bank* v. *Provident Institution for Savings*, 80 N.J. Super. 339 (Ch. Div. 1963). Affirmed by Supreme Court of New Jersey, February 15, 1965. For a much different decision regarding this general question, see *Savings Bank of Baltimore* v. *Herbert R. O'Connor, Bank Commissioner of the State of Maryland*, Circuit Court of Baltimore City, No. A-48274. Memorandum Opinion filed January 26, 1967.

to visualize a Government victory in an antitrust action under this section if the Supreme Court were to decide a case based upon sub-products in commercial banking. The concept of a line within a line of commerce was the basis for the Section 2 charges which were brought in the reopened *Lexington case.* In this instance the banks involved played dominant roles in the trust business in the area, but a similar action could also develop as a result of the merger of a commercial bank and another type of institution such as a savings bank or savings and loan association.

## THE GEOGRAPHIC MARKET

The Supreme Court in the *Philadelphia case,* like the District Court in *Manufacturers Hanover,* did not have to consider many of the problems discussed earlier in regard to the selection of the product market, for the appellees did not contest the use of commercial banking as the relevant line of commerce.[31] However, the court did face the difficult task of defining the appropriate section of the country. In determining this relevant geographic market, the Supreme Court stated:"The proper question to be asked in this case is not where the parties to the merger do business or even where they compete, but where, within the area of competitive overlap, the effect of the merger on competition will be direct and immediate. This depends upon the geographic structure of supplier-customer relations."[32] Both in *U. S.* v. *Philadelphia National Bank* and in *U. S.* v. *First National Bank of Lexington* (the latter involving only Sherman Act charges), the Supreme Court decided that the appropriate location in which to test the effects of the merger was the area in which the banks had branches, which in each of these cases closely approximated the intrastate portion of a standard metropolition statistical area (SMSA). In the *Philadelphia case,* four southeastern Pennsylvania counties were chosen as the geographic market[33] (this state permits branching in contiguous counties), but in the *Lexington case* the analysis was limited to Fayette County, Kentucky[34] (this state permits

[31] *U. S.* v. *Philadelphia National Bank,* 374 U.S. 321, 335 (1963).
[32] *Ibid.,* at 357.
[33] *Ibid.,* at 361.
[34] *U. S.* v. *First National Bank of Lexington,* 376 U.S. 665, 668 (1964).

branching within the county or in an adjacent county where there is no existing bank).[35]

The Supreme Court did not limit its market analysis in the two bank antitrust suits which it has heard to a review of branch bank lines. The court indicated that an important factor in its decisions regarding the relevant geographic markets in these cases was the fact that:[36]

In banking, as in most service industries, convenience of location is essential to effective competition. Individuals and corporations typically confer the bulk of their patronage on banks in their local community; they find it impractical to conduct their banking business at a distance. The factor of inconvenience localizes banking competition as effectively as high transportation costs in other industries. [Notes omitted]

Also, the Supreme Court noted that its "relevant geographic market" in both cases closely approximated the regions which the majority of the federal banking agencies designated as the "area of effective competition" for the banks in question. Another point of at least some significance was that the available statistics provided no indication of the amount of business done within the market by banks located beyond its perimeter. Therefore, the judges felt that by using metropolitan area data they could be reasonably confident that most of the business done in this market by banks not included in the "local banking statistics" would be primarily large customer oriented. As a result, the geographic area chosen would still be valid in assessing the competitive effect of the proposed merger upon the bank facilities available to the smaller customer—"a perfectly good line of commerce in light of Congress' evident concern in enacting the 1950 amendments to §7 with preserving small business."[37]

The District Court opinion in the *Manufacturers Hanover case*,[38] which was decided some time after the Supreme Court cases discussed

[35] In two pending cases, banks in states which prohibit branching are involved. *U. S.* v. *Marshall and Ilsley Bank Stock Corporation,* Civ. 61–C–54 (E.D. Wisc.); filed March 2, 1961 and *U. S.* v. *Mercantile Trust Company, N.A.,* Civ. 65–C–54 (E.D. Mo.); filed July 7, 1965.

[36] *U. S.* v. *Philadelphia National Bank,* 374 U.S. 321, 357–58 (1963).

[37] *Ibid.,* at 360, n. 37.

[38] *U. S.* v. *Manufacturers Hanover Trust Company,* 240 F. Supp. 867 (1965).

344 CHAPTER 8

above, provides an interesting variation in the choice of the relevant markets. As was noted earlier, the court in this instance found that banking in metropolitan New York City could be divided into two distinct subproducts—"wholesale" and "retail" accounts. The findings of the court indicated:[39]

In the parlance of the industry, a wholesale bank is one handling a small number of large accounts, concentrating its efforts primarily on large corporations, governmental bodies, financial institutions, and wealthy individuals, while a retail bank is one handling a large number of small and intermediate accounts, catering to the mass needs of the general public and small business. The economic scale of the customer, size of account, size of the bank, specialized nature of the service, tradition, reputation, and public image determine whether the pattern of a bank's business is wholesale, retail, or wholesale-retail.

Given this definition of wholesale and retail banking, the District Judge then tried to determine the relevant geographic market for each of the two lines of commerce. After reviewing the testimony at the trial, he concluded "When the area of effective competition is confined to the customer's own locality, as is the case with retail customers, so is the relevant geographic market, but when the area of effective competition embraces the nation, as is the case with wholesale customers, so does the relevant geographic market."[40]

Before concluding this short review of the geographic market concept, it would seem to be essential that some additional detail concerning the *Pabst Brewing Company case,* mentioned earlier, be included, since it appears that this decision implies that the Government does not necessarily have to prove the section of the country in which the claimed effect of the acquisition will occur. To quote from the opinion of the Supreme Court in this action:[41]

The language of [Section 7 of the Clayton Act] requires merely that the Government prove the merger may have a substantial anti-competitive effect somewhere in the United States—"in *any* section" of the United States. This phrase does not call for the delineation of a "section of the country" by metes and bounds as a surveyor would lay off a plot of ground. The Government may introduce evidence which shows that as a result of a merger competition may be substantially lessened throughout the country, or on the other hand it may prove that competition may be

[39] *Ibid.,* at 896.
[40] *Ibid.,* at 913.
[41] *U. S.* v. *Pabst Brewing Co.,* 384 U.S. 546, 549–50 (1966).

substantially lessened only in one or more sections of the country. In either event a violation of § 7 would be proved. Certainly the failure of the Government to prove by an army of expert witnesses what constitutes a relevant "economic" or "geographic" market is not an adequate ground on which to dismiss a § 7 case. Compare *United States* v. *Continental Can Co.,* 378 U.S. 441, 458. Congress did not seem to be troubled about the exact spot where competition might be lessened; it simply intended to outlaw mergers which threatened competition in any or all parts of the country. Proof of the section of the country where the anti-competitive effect exists is entirely subsidiary to the crucial question in this and every § 7 case which is whether a merger may substantially lessen competition anywhere in the United States.

Thus, while the Government will no doubt continue to attempt to establish the relevant geographic market in banking cases, its inability to do so may not necessarily mean a merger cannot be enjoined under Section 7.

THE NEED FOR IMPROVED MARKET DATA

Earlier in this chapter the concept of the banking market developed by the Supreme Court in *Philadelphia National Bank* and in *Lexington* was criticized. It was stated that in the light of present-day banking operations the product market chosen was much too narrow and that the court should not completely rule out the possibility that in some cases competition with other financial institutions may be relevant. In addition, it was suggested that the *Manufacturers Hanover* approach to market analysis may be superior to the method employed by our highest court, since it would appear to provide a better indication of the probable effects an acquisition may have upon bank customers.

Judge MacMahon in *Manufacturers Hanover* defined retail deposit accounts as those under 100 thousand dollars.[42] The FDIC has applied this standard to the deposits of banks in leading cities in an attempt to obtain a more meaningful measure of concentration in the local market, and the results are quite impressive. Table 8.3 contains a summary of the findings for some of the largest cities in the nation,

---

[42] Expecting criticism regarding the criteria used to subdivide customers into wholesale and retail, Judge MacMahon stated: "These are ordinary terms used to express ideas in common usage and understanding and certainly are no fuzzier than norms applied by courts and juries every day giving concrete expression to imprecise concepts." 240 F. Supp. 867, 919.

TABLE 8.3. PERCENTAGE OF THE DEPOSITS IN THE LARGEST INSURED
COMMERCIAL BANK AND IN THE THREE LARGEST INSURED COMMERCIAL
BANKS BY SELECTED STANDARD METROPOLITAN STATISTICAL AREAS IN
THE UNITED STATES, NOVEMBER 18, 1964

| | *Percentage of Deposits of All Commercial Banks in* | | | |
| | *The Largest Bank* | | *The Three Largest Banks* | |
| *Area\** | *Total* | *Deposits under $100,000* | *Total* | *Deposits under $100,000* |
|---|---|---|---|---|
| New York, N. Y. (L) | 20 | 17 | 50 | 46 |
| Chicago, Ill. (P) | 22 | 10 | 49 | 28 |
| Philadelphia, Pa. (L) | 18 | 14 | 48 | 36 |
| Detroit, Mich. (L) | 34 | 26 | 67 | 60 |
| Boston, Mass. (L) | 36 | 24 | 60 | 45 |
| Cleveland, Ohio (L) | 36 | 41 | 74 | 72 |
| Washington, D. C. (D) | 18 | 16 | 46 | 36 |
| St. Louis, Mo. (P) | 18 | 10 | 40 | 24 |
| Pittsburgh, Pa. (L) | 50 | 36 | 81 | 70 |
| Minneapolis, Minn. (P) | 21 | 14 | 55 | 39 |
| Houston, Texas (P) | 24 | 16 | 62 | 42 |
| Miami, Fla. (P) | 27 | 17 | 39 | 28 |
| Arithmetic Mean | 27 | 20 | 56 | 44 |

* Letters following each name indicate the status of branch banking: L—limited,
P—prohibited, and D—districtwide. The cities were chosen by population rank but
those in statewide branch banking states were dropped because deposit figures for all
banks, including those with branches throughout a state were reported on a consolidated basis and are attributed to the county in which the head office is located. This
could also affect the data for other areas with widespread branch banking.

*Source:* FDIC, "Concentration Measures for Local Banking Markets," mimeographed release dated May 6, 1965, for the banking data; and *Rand McNally Cosmo-
politan World Atlas*, 1962, p. 199, for the population data. The status of branching
was designated by the author.

and these data reveal that on the average the concentration in the
largest bank in each of these cities was approximately 27 percent for
all deposits but only 20 percent for deposits under 100 thousand
dollars, and the corresponding figures for the three largest banks were
56 percent and 44 percent respectively. Thus, the average of the
concentration ratios declined by about one-fourth when only the
"local market" (under 100 thousand dollars) deposits were included.[43]

[43] See *Annual Report of the Federal Deposit Insurance Corporation* for the
year ended December 31, 1964, "Survey of Deposit Accounts and Insurance
Coverage," which includes recent work by the FDIC in this area.

Despite the substantial reduction in concentration which would have resulted if the revised product definitions in *Manufacturers Hanover* had been used, it would seem safe to conclude that this would not have affected the decisions of the Supreme Court in *Philadelphia National Bank* or *Lexington* (or in litigation which might develop in most other cities in this country). If this conclusion is correct then one might logically ask why such great concern was expressed earlier regarding the delimitation of the product and the geographic markets. The obvious answer is that these cases are precedents for future litigation, but this is not the only consideration, for the importance of market share statistics extends far beyond the courtroom. These data are considered by the academic writing about the competitive conditions in the industry, by the banking agencies in evaluating the merits of a proposed merger, and by the Congress in weighing the need for new antitrust legislation. Thus, if the market concepts mentioned above would provide better concentration data, it is in the best interest of commercial banking that this be done, for many individuals who use these statistics never question how they were computed.

## THE IMPORTANCE OF BANKING CONCENTRATION

Professor Bain, in his standard work *Industrial Organization,* uses a more formal definition of "concentration" than that employed earlier in this chapter. When he discusses concentration he refers to ". . . the ownership or control of a large proportion of some aggregate of economic resources or activity either by a small proportion of the units which own or control the aggregate, or by a small absolute number of such units." [44] Thus, in very general terms, in banking his primary concern probably would be with the number of banks providing a given service in the area in question and with their relative and absolute sizes.[45] The most popular measures of banking concentration, of course, combine these factors to obtain some indication of the percentage of the market controlled by the largest bank, the three

[44] Bain, *Industrial Organization,* p. 85.
[45] Near-bank financial institutions should be included in some analyses. (That is, a case primarily emphasizing mortgages and/or savings deposits should not ignore S & Ls.)

CHAPTER 8

largest banks, or some other number which the court or the investigator feels is significant in a particular situation.

THE RELEVANCE OF CONCENTRATION DATA

In recent years concentration data and market share statistics have been relegated to a subsidiary role in a number of Supreme Court antitrust decisions.[46] Nevertheless, even in these cases, the general development of concentration in the economy or in the particular industry involved has not been ignored. For example, the following comments are found in two 1966 Supreme Court opinions in cases in which specific market share data appear to have been given relatively little consideration by the majority. In *U. S.* v. *Von's Grocery Company* the Court stated: [47]

As we said in *Brown Shoe Co.* v. *United States,* 370 U.S. 294, 315. "The dominant theme pervading congressional consideration of the 1950 amendments was a fear of what was considered to be a rising tide of economic concentration in the American economy." To arrest this "rising tide" toward concentration into too few hands and to halt the gradual demise of the small businessman, Congress decided to clamp down with vigor on mergers. It both revitalized § 7 of the Clayton Act by "plugging its loophole" and broadened its scope. . . .

And in the *Pabst Brewing Company case* the Court noted: [48]

We hold that a trend toward concentration in an industry, whatever its causes is a highly relevant factor in deciding how substantial the anticompetitive effect of a merger may be.

From these statements it would appear that concentration remains as a general if not a specific consideration in Supreme Court decisions.[49]

Furthermore, before any broad conclusions regarding the relevance of concentration statistics in antitrust litigation are drawn from current Supreme Court opinions, the very unusual market situations in many of these actions should be examined. In some of these cases the Government has successfully attacked conglomerate mergers and ac-

[46] This change was noted by an antitrust scholar some years ago. See Martin, "The Brown Shoe Case and the New Antimerger Policy," *American Economic Review* (June 1963), p. 356. The term "market share" refers to the percent of the transactions of all companies in a market accounted for by an individual company.
[47] *U. S.* v. *Von's Grocery Company,* 384 U.S. 270, 276 (1966).
[48] *U. S.* v. *Pabst Brewing Company,* 384 U.S. 546, 552–53 (1966).
[49] *U. S.* v. *Philadelphia National Bank* at 364 provides some indication of their importance in *Philadelphia.*

quisitions in which only potential rather than existing competition was involved, and this problem is far different from the conventional bank merger suit which might be decided almost solely on the basis of market share statistics.

Some writers have suggested that under the amended Bank Merger and Bank Holding Company statutes, which appear to require that courts weigh "convenience and needs" factors against anticompetitive effects, concentration in a market will be much less significant in bank merger cases. To the contrary, it might be more, not less important, since the first consideration for both the banking agency and the courts must be the impact of the merger on competition. To quote from the Provident and First City National decision: "Congress intended that a defense or justification be available once it had been determined that a transaction would have anticompetitive effects, *as judged by the standards normally applied in antitrust actions.*" [50] [Emphasis added]

The concentration ratios considered by the High Court in a few of its recent decisions were as follows:[51]

| | | *Post-Merger Market Shares of* [52] | | |
| | | *Litigant Firm,\* percent* | *Largest Firm, percent* | *Three Largest Firms, percent* |
| *Year* | *Case* | | | |
|---|---|---|---|---|
| 1963 | U. S. v. Philadelphia National Bank | 36(15) | 36 | 68 |
| 1964 | U. S. v. First National Bank of Lexington | 52(12) | 52 | 82 |
| 1964 | U. S. v. Aluminum Co. of America | 29(1) | 29 | 68 |
| 1964 | U. S. v. Continental Can | 25(3) | 27 | 63 |
| 1966 | U. S. v. Von's Grocery Company | 8(4) | 8 | 20 |

* Data in parentheses indicate the market share of the smaller of the two merging firms in each case before merger.

[50] *U. S.* v. *First City National Bank of Houston,* 1967 *Trade Cases* ¶ 72,048, p. 83,727; 386 U.S. 361 (1967).

[51] 374 U.S. 321 (1963); 376 U.S. 665 (1964); 337 U.S. 271 (1964); and 375 U.S. 893 (1964). These data were computed from statistics in U. S. Congress, Senate, Hearings on S. 1698, *Amend the Bank Merger Act of 1960,* 1965, pp. 549–51, statistics in the Opinion of the Court in the *Lexington case* at 669, and in *U. S.* v. *Von's Grocery Company,* 384 U.S. 270, 280–82 (1966).

[52] Share of total commercial bank deposits in bank cases; aluminum conductor production in *Alcoa;* metal and glass container shipments in *Continental Can;* and retail grocery sales in Los Angeles in *Von's.*

These percentages would seem to suggest that under the "standards normally applied in antitrust actions" few bank mergers could be successfully defended against an attack under Section 7 of the Clayton Act or under Section 1 of the Sherman Act.

*The conglomerate merger: a special case.* The Justice Department's actions against mergers involving the Crocker-Anglo National Bank and Citizens National Bank; the First National Bank of Hawaii and Cooke Trust Company; and the First National City Bank of New York acquisition of the Carte Blanche[53] credit card business of Hilton Credit Corporation differ considerably from most of the other bank antitrust suits. These cases involve potential rather than existing competition and the acquisitions have many of the characteristics of mixed-conglomerate mergers[54] in contrast to the simple horizontal mergers of direct competitors typically encountered in the banking field.

Although both banks in the *Crocker-Citizens case* were located in California they were based in different metropolitan areas and there was almost no overlap in the locations of their branch systems. Therefore Justice made some effort to try to establish the entire State of California as the relevant geographic market, instead of some more limited "section of the country" following the pattern of *Philadelphia National Bank* or *Lexington.* Unless this was done, little existing competition between the two banks could be shown.

To the government lawyers the question of diminished potential competition raised by this merger was far more vital than any reduction in existing competition, and it was this point which they emphasized. In effect, Justice was trying to establish whether its powers in the bank merger area extended to cases where there was a reasonable

[53] *U. S.* v. *Crocker-Anglo National Bank,* Civ. 41808, (N. D. Calif.), October 8, 1963; *U. S.* v. *First National City Bank of New York,* Civ. 65–3963 (S.D.N.Y.), December 30, 1965; and *U. S.* v. *First National Bank of Hawaii,* Civ. A.2540 (D. Hawaii), June 10, 1966.

[54] A conglomerate merger involves companies that neither compete directly nor stand in a buyer-seller relationship. In a mixed-conglomerate merger the firms may produce the same product but sell in different geographic markets or produce different but related products (that is, they could be produced with the same facilities or be marketed through the same distribution channels). Turner, "Conglomerate Mergers and Section 7 of the Clayton Act," 78 *Harvard Law Review* 1313, 1314–1315 (1965).

probability that at some future time, if the merger were enjoined, the firms may become direct competitors. To quote from the Antitrust Division's *Supplementary Post-Trial Brief:* ". . . one or both of the defendant banks, absent the merger, would have become large state-wide banking institutions in due course via the *de novo,* or more modest acquisition, route." [55]

As in other bank antitrust suits, the Department of Justice attempted to obtain a preliminary injunction to halt the proposed merger, but this was denied by the District Court. The judges, in explaining the reasons for their decision, noted the Supreme Court in the *Philadelphia National Bank case* indicated that in "banking as in most service industries convenience of location is essential to effective competition." [56] Yet, they observed, in the *Crocker-Citizens case* the only place in which the banks both had offices was Ventura County, California, and any reduction in competition there was such a small part of the banks' total business that it would be *de minimis.* The judges also concluded that the evidence available to them at that time (prior to the trial) was wholly insufficient to permit the Court to find any lessening of potential competition. The case has since been tried by the District Court which found in favor of the banks. [57]

In the *First National Bank of Hawaii* and the *First National City Bank cases* the basic problem was also one of potential competition, but the debate revolved around the product market, not the geographic market which was stressed in *Crocker-Citizens.* Following a 1965 revision in state law which permitted Hawaiian commercial banks to operate trust departments for the first time, [58] the First

[55] *Plaintiff's Supplementary Post-Trial Brief* (p. 3) in the *Crocker-Citizens case.* Justice emphasized potential competition so much that the District Court judges presiding observed: "The Government's showing seems to indicate that this point represents its entire case." *U. S.* v. *Crocker-Anglo National Bank,* 223 F. Supp. (N. D. Calif., 1963). And in its *Supplementary Post-Trial Reply Brief* (p. 52) Justice states: "While *Von's* and Pabst involved direct 'horizontal' mergers, and the primary issue in the instant case [*Crocker-Citizens*] revolves more about potential competition. . . ."

[56] *U. S.* v. *Crocker-Anglo National Bank,* 223 F. Supp. 849 (N. D. Calif., 1963).

[57] The Court ruled that the Government failed to prove the merger had a substantial adverse effect on actual or potential competition. 1967 *Trade Cases* ¶72,258.

[58] "Hawaii Merger," *American Banker,* August 24, 1966. *U. S.* v. *First National Bank of Hawaii,* 257 F. Supp. 591 (1966).

National Bank of Hawaii and the Cooke Trust Company Limited entered into negotiations which resulted in an agreement to merge the two firms. First National, the second largest bank in the state, reportedly did no trust business and Cooke, the third largest trust company, did no banking business.

The merger involved a national bank and a noninsured trust institution. Therefore final authority would rest with the FDIC under Section 18(c)(1) of the Federal Deposit Insurance Act, but apparently the Corporation made its approval contingent on a favorable ruling by the Comptroller of the Currency.[59] Both of these agencies approved the amalgamation, and the Federal Reserve submitted a favorable report on the competitive factors involved. Nevertheless, in June 1966 Justice filed suit to enjoin the merger, indicating that if this acquisition did not occur the First National, with one-third of Hawaii's bank assets, and Cooke with one-eighth of the state's trust assets, would probably expand into each other's area of business.

Under the provisions of the 1966 amendment to the Bank Merger Act, an injunction automatically went into effect halting the merger when the Department of Justice filed suit. However, at the request of the banks, the injunction was lifted by the District Court with the understanding that certain conditions would be met to expedite divestiture if Justice should win the antitrust case.[60] The suit is expected to be tried beginning in spring 1968.[61]

In *U. S.* v. *First National City Bank of New York* the Justice Department's suit, filed December 30, 1965,[62] was designed to prevent the New York bank from acquiring control of the Carte Blanche

[59] 12 U.S.C. 1828(c). See "Hawaii Merger," *American Banker*, July 25, 1966, for a brief comment concerning Comptroller Saxon's role in approving the merger.

[60] The agreement in some ways was similar to the one reached some months earlier when the First National City Bank was allowed to acquire the Carte Blanche credit card business.

[61] The suit has been described by a leading state official as an attack on Hawaii's sovereignty, and it is reported the State may file a brief *amicus curiae*. "Justice Department Decides Not to Appeal," *American Banker*, July 25, 1966.

[62] *U. S.* v. *First National City Bank*, Civ. 65–3963 (S.D.N.Y.), December 30, 1965. This transaction did not involve the acquisition of one insured bank by another, and therefore it was not covered by the provisions of the Bank Merger Act.

general credit card business of Hilton Credit Corporation. The Government indicated that First National City was especially qualified to enter this field on a national and international scale on its own and that such entry was likely if the merger was enjoined. Justice argued the proposed acquisition would eliminate potential competition between the two firms and would tend substantially to lessen competition in the general purpose credit card field.

The Antitrust Division stated the acquisition would violate Section 7 of the Clayton Act, and it called for temporary and permanent injunctions against the merger. A temporary restraining order was issued by the Court but this was removed a few days later, and First National City was permitted to acquire operating control of Carte Blanche. This was done under the terms of an agreement in which the bank stipulated that pending the final decision in the case Carte Blanche would be maintained and operated so as to permit its disposition as a going business should the final decision so require. However, some authorities suggest there is a remote possibility that the case will never require a "final decision," for the crowded calendar in the Federal Court in New York could delay the trial for several years and the number of national credit card plans is growing rapidly. It has been suggested that this change in the product market may persuade the current senior Justice Department officials, who appear to have a more liberal philosophy regarding such questions than some of their predecessors, to drop the suit, despite the fact that the action would probably be decided largely on the basis of the market as it existed at the time the case was initiated.

In attacking these three mergers, the Justice Department stressed the "fact" that they would each result in a substantial reduction in potential competition, for if they were enjoined Crocker might open branches in the area served by Citizens (or vice versa), the First National Bank of Hawaii might establish its own trust services, and the First National City Bank of New York might develop its own general credit card plan. Many people who find it difficult to accept the arguments of Justice when they are based upon existing competition will surely find this potential competition thesis to be incredible, but some leading antitrust scholars have long argued that this approach is logical under Section 7 of the Clayton Act. While the potential competition approach appeared to suffer a significant setback in the December, 1967 decision of the Supreme Court in the Penn-Olin case, this concept would still appear to be compatible with most of the current thinking of the High Court.[63]

The *Penn-Olin case,* which was cited quite often in the Crocker-Citizens litigation, is of particular importance to those who are concerned with suits involving potential competition. In this case Pennsalt Chemicals and Olin Mathieson set up a joint venture, Penn-Olin Chemical Company, to construct a sodium chlorate plant. The Government brought suit charging, among other things, that this joint venture would substantially lessen competition in sodium chlorate. The District Court held that the formation of Penn-Olin would not substantially lessen competition, noting there was no evidence that both companies would have gone into the southeastern sodium chlorate market at the same time.[64] On review the Supreme Court held the District Court had not applied the proper criteria and that a joint venture could substantially lessen competition in violation of the Clayton Act if either parent might have gone into the relevant market, while the other remained a significant potential competitor.[65]

On remand the District Court found that it had not been shown as a reasonable probability that, in the absence of a joint venture, either Pennsalt or Olin Mathieson on its own would have built a sodium chlorate plant in the southeastern market. Justice appealed this case to the Supreme Court, and as a result of a deadlocked (four-to-four) vote, the lower court opinion that the merger was legal was left standing.[66]

It is possible that in a similar action in the future the High Court might find in favor of Justice,[67] and this could have far-reaching effects upon the overall development of commercial banking.

[63] *U. S.* v. *Penn-Olin Chemical Company,* 378 U.S. 158 (1964). *U. S.* v. *Continental Can Co.,* 378 U.S. 441 (1964); *U. S.* v. *El Paso Natural Gas Co.,* 376 U.S. 651 (1964); *Federal Trade Commission* v. *Procter and Gamble,* 386 U.S. 568, 18 L. ed. 2d 303 (1967).

[64] *U. S.* v. *Penn-Olin Chemical Company,* 217 F. Supp. 110 (1963).

[65] *Ibid.,* 378 U.S. 158 (1964).

[66] Associate Justice Marshall took no part in the hearing since he was Solicitor General when the case was prepared.

[67] *U. S.* v. *Penn-Olin Chemical Company,* 246 F. Supp. 917 (1965). The District Court in the *Crocker case,* in October 1966, called for further consideration of the merger by the Comptroller of the Currency in light of the

A joint venture by two Maryland banks, under which they had planned to form a new bank in a proposed "city of the future" was abandoned in mid-1967 because of federal regulatory agency warnings about the antitrust implications.[68] This could also impede bank entry into new markets such as credit cards, data processing, equipment leasing, mortgage servicing, and numerous others, which many authorities predict will be the source of much of the growth of "commercial" banks in the years ahead.

The potential competition question could also be of considerable importance to the development of branch banking in the future, for the relaxation of branch restrictions in state laws in recent years has not been accompanied by the removal of the "home office protection" rules[69] against *de novo* branching. The 1963 law permitting limited branch banking in New Hampshire, for example, states that no bank should open a branch in a contiguous town if there is an operating bank in such town, and no bank shall open a branch in a noncontiguous town if there is an operating bank within a radius of ten miles of the proposed location of such branch, except where banks in such areas are acquired by merger or purchase of assets.[70] A similar provision appears in the New York statutes revised in 1960,[71] and the 1962 Virginia branch banking legislation indicates that branches may be established in counties contiguous to the city in which the parent is located provided such branches in the contiguous county may not be established more than five miles outside the city limits,

passage of the 1966 Amendment to the Bank Merger Act and the *El Paso* (376 U.S. 651) and *Penn-Olin* (378 U.S. 158) decisions by the Supreme Court. In findings submitted to the District Court on December 27, 1966, the Comptroller stated the *Crocker case* was clearly distinguished from both *El Paso* and *Penn-Olin since his office had foreclosed the possibility of de novo branching* on a statewide scale by either of the two banks involved in the merger, and Crocker-Anglo was unable, for financial and administrative reasons, to move into the Los Angeles area without a merger.

[68] "Danger of Antitrust Suit Prompts Md. Banks to Drop Joint Venture," *American Banker,* May 15, 1967.

[69] "Home office protection" generally implies that any community containing the head office of a bank is closed to the entry of another bank by a *de novo* branch.

[70] *Encyclopedia of Banking Laws,* "New Hampshire," p. 1.

[71] *Ibid.,* "New York," p. 5.

and they may be established elsewhere by merger with banks located in any other county, city, or town.[72]

CONCENTRATION: THREE VIEWPOINTS

*The viewpoint of the courts.*[73] The Supreme Court in the 1920s in the *U. S. Steel* and *International Harvester cases* handed down decisions which reflected the Court's opinion that size in and of itself was no offense to the law.[74] However, by 1932 Mr. Justice Cardozo in the *Swift and Company case* proclaimed that "size carries with it an opportunity for abuse that is not to be ignored when the opportunity is proved to have been utilized in the past."[75] From this point on, a long series of decisions, including *American Tobacco, Alcoa,* and *United Shoe,* has laid increasing emphasis on market power, until two antitrust authorities were led to conclude that "monopoly (or market power) 'without more' is still no offense under the antitrust laws, but the 'more' is being attenuated into what mathematicians might call the second order of smalls."[76]

In 1960 in the *Brown Shoe case* the Supreme Court indicated that "the market share which companies may control by merging is one of the most important factors to be considered when determining the probable effects of the combination on effective competition.[77] But the court went on to say that while market share statistics were the primary index of market power, only a further examination of the structure, history, and the probable future of a particular market could provide an appropriate setting for judgment.[78] Thus, it would

[72] *Ibid.,* "Virginia," pp. 1–2.

[73] For a thought-provoking discussion of recent Supreme Court decisions, see Handler "Polarities of Antitrust," 60 *Northwestern University Law Review* 751 (1966); and Handler, "Atonality and Abstraction in Modern Antitrust Law," 52 *American Bar Association Journal* 621 (1966).

[74] *U. S.* v. *United States Steel,* 251 U.S. 417 (1920); *U. S.* v. *International Harvester Company,* 274 U.S. 693 (1927). The developments in this period are discussed in Baldwin, *Antitrust and the Changing Corporation,* pp. 50–77.

[75] *U. S.* v. *Swift and Company,* 286 U.S. 106, 116 (1932).

[76] Kaysen and Turner, *Antitrust Policy,* xiii–xiv.

[77] *Brown Shoe Company* v. *U. S.,* 370 U.S. 294, 343 (1962).

[78] An excellent review of antitrust policy and philosophy may be found in Joel B. Dirlam's "The Celler-Kefauver Act: A Review of Enforcement Policy," in *Administered Prices: A Compendium on Public Policy,* U. S. Congress, Senate, 1963.

appear that the percentage of the market foreclosed could not itself be decisive. Yet, some authorities feel the opinion of the court in *Brown Shoe* really fell back on the substantiality doctrine, and the analysis is "clearly in conformity with an approach to the enforcement of Section 7 that rejects broad economic inquiry, and applies, as a touchstone for illegality, a limited battery of structural tests."[79]

If any doubt remained regarding the significance of concentration and market share data in antitrust suits, this was certainly removed by the 1963 and 1964 decisions of the Supreme Court. In 1963, in *U. S. v. Philadelphia National Bank,* which was only the second case to be decided by the High Court under the Clayton Act since it was amended in 1950 (*Brown Shoe* was the first), the court noted that a merger which produces a firm controlling an undue percentage share of the relevant market should be enjoined unless evidence clearly indicates it will not lessen competition. The Court then observed: "Without attempting to specify the smallest market share which would still be considered to threaten undue concentration, we are clear that 30 percent presents that threat."[80] Later in the same opinion, one finds: "There is nothing in the record in this case to rebut the inherently anticompetitive tendency manifested by these percentages."[81] In the 1964 decisions under Section 7, the Supreme Court considered the degree of concentration and oligopoly in the markets in all four cases tried and found them to be high.[82] In addition, in several of the opinions, as was noted earlier, the court warned that if concentration is high in a given market, it is vital that even slight increases be prevented.

In addition to the Clayton Act litigation in 1964, the Supreme Court heard a Sherman Act merger case—*U. S. v. First National Bank of Lexington.* In this action the Court concluded: "Where, as here, the merging companies are major competitive factors in a relevant market, the elimination of significant competition between them constitutes a violation of Section 1 of the Sherman Act."[83] William

[79] *Ibid.*, pp. 106–107; and Phillips, ed., *Perspectives on Antitrust Policy,* pp. 182–83.

[80] *U. S. v. Philadelphia National Bank,* 374 U.S. 321, 363–64 (1963).

[81] *Ibid.,* at 366.

[82] Bock, *Mergers and Markets: An Economic Analysis of the 1964 Supreme Court Decisions,* p. 68.

[83] 376 U.S. 665, 673 (1964).

Orrick, Jr., head of the Antitrust Division at the time the Court decided the *Lexington case,* stated that he could not overestimate the importance of this decision. Citing the above quotation from the opinion of the Court, he observed: "Thus history has returned to the antitrust division the antimerger weapon in Section 1 of the Sherman Act which it once had and which may well be easier to deal with than the weapon Congress fashioned in Section 7 of the Clayton Act."[84]

In any event, this decision at least went a long way toward bringing the interpretation of the Sherman Act into line with the merger policy enunciated by Congress in amending Section 7 of the Clayton Act. For example, "the ruling was based on the effect of the merger rather than specific intent to monopolize and the effect was judged in a rather small geographical area." Furthermore, "no predatory purpose was found."[85] Regarding the substantiality of competition between the two merging banks, the court considered that the relative degree of overlap in their business was irrelevant.[86] (At this point one might ask—if this is the Sherman Act, why was there so much concern about whether or not Section 7 of the Clayton Act applied to bank mergers? This writer can only answer that most people did not recognize that "this" could be the Sherman Act; not because this interpretation of the law was so new but, rather, because it was so old.)

Mr. Justice Harlan in his dissent in the *Lexington case* observed: "But for the court's return to a discarded theory of antitrust law, this case would have little future importance." The "discarded theory" to which he refers is, of course, the application of the per se rule to horizontal mergers "if the participants are major competitive factors in a relevant market." Numerous articles in the antitrust literature written after *Lexington* appear to endorse the conclusion that "bigness, at least insofar as mergers are concerned, is now embraced within the per se rule,"[87] and Judge MacMahon followed essentially

[84] Speech by William H. Orrick, Jr., "The Impact of the Federal Antitrust Laws on Corporate Mergers," prepared for delivery before the Association for Corporate Growth, Inc., May 12, 1964, p. 11. (mimeographed)

[85] David D. Martin, "Economic Implications of Recent Merger Cases," in *Economic Concentration,* Hearings, U. S. Congress, Senate, 1965, Part 2, p. 697.

[86] *Ibid.*

[87] von Kalinowski, "The Per Se Doctrine—An Emerging Philosophy of Antitrust Law," 11 *U.C.L.A. Law Review* 569 (1964); Schlesinger, "Merger

this approach in reaching his decision concerning the wholesale (national) banking market in *Manufacturers Hanover*. After stating that in the local market the merger violated Section 7 of the Clayton Act in so many ways that "to allow it to stand would be to ignore the statute altogether," he noted that in *Columbia Steel* (334 U.S. 527–28) the Supreme Court held that the validity of a horizontal merger under Section 1 of the Sherman Act depended on assessment of many factors other than the mere cessation of competition between former competitors. The District Judge then proceeded to analyze the national market situation in *Manufacturers Hanover,* using the tests found in *Columbia Steel* as follows:[88]

Looking to the factors specified in Columbia Steel, we find; the dollar volume great, but not of compelling significance; defendant does not control an undue, dominant, or decisive share of the national market; the merger springs from legitimate business requirements to enable defendant to satisfy the credit needs of very large customers and to compete more vigorously as a lead bank against larger competitors; there is no purpose to monopolize, curtail competition, or control prices; the structure of the national market is one of many enterprises, none of which has any significant advantage over its next smaller competitor; newcomers abound; the relative aggregate share of the six largest banks has remained fairly consistent since 1950 and has declined since the merger; the market is not oligopolistic, and this merger does not threaten monopoly or oligopoly; the government has failed to prove a merger trend toward concentration in the national market; small competitors flourish; and the national market and number of competitors is growing by leaps and bounds. Defendant's increased lending limits reduced the advantage of the three larger competitors, but handicapped smaller competitors, though the advantage over smaller competitors did not threaten to become decisive, for the Federal Reserve Board found that the pro-competitive effect outweighed the anticompetitive effect in the same market. We incline to agree.

There is neither need nor purpose, however, to consider or determine whether the Columbia Steel factors just enumerated offset the anticompetitive effect resulting from the elimination of substantial competition between major competitors, the elimination of a substantial factor from competition as a whole, and the customers loss of an important alternative lead bank. That course has been foreclosed by Lexington.

---

Litigation under the Sherman Act—Choice or Echo," 18 *Southwestern Law Journal* 712 (1964); "Recent Decisions," *University of Illinois Law Forum* 667 (Fall 1964).

[88] 240 F. Supp. 867, 953–56 (1965).

Hence, the judge concluded that the elimination of substantial competition which previously existed between the two New York banks in the national market itself constituted an unreasonable restraint of trade in violation of Section 1 of the Sherman Act. *A fortiori*, this established a reasonable probability of a substantial lessening of competition in violation of Section 7 of the Clayton Act.[89]

In addition to the principles which seem to have been laid down by the High Court and applied by the District Court in *Manufacturers-Hanover*, the Supreme Court has established a number of other standards in antitrust litigation. From a careful review of the Court's decisions during the past few years Larry Williams, a former official of the Justice Department's Antitrust Division, summarized these criteria as follows:[90]

(1) Immunity from the antitrust laws is frowned upon. (2) A merger that results in the acquiring company having 20 percent to 30 percent of a market is presumptively unlawful. (3) Proponents of a merger involving a leading member of a concentrated industry will have great difficulty showing that an acquisition of even a very small competitor is lawful. (4) A merger between substantial competitors that eliminates significant competition between them may be unlawful even though that competition is but a small part of their total business and without regard to probable effects it will have on others. (5) Legality of certain types of merger is suspect without elaborate inquiry into the nature of the industry. (6) Proof of actual effects on competition is not necessary to establish a violation in a merger case. (7) And in some instances it is not necessary for merging companies to be either competitors or in a buyer-seller relationship to run afoul of the antimerger provisions of the antitrust laws.

*The viewpoint of the economist.* J. M. Clark in his classic essay on "workable competition" noted that perfect competition "does not and cannot exist and has presumably never existed."[91] If an exception to this statement were to be revealed, it would certainly not be found in the commercial banking industry. Yet, the conclusions of the Supreme Court regarding the potential effects of bank mergers in *Lexington* and in *Philadelphia*—insofar as these conclusions are based on economic theory—would seem to require that something

[89] *Ibid.*

[90] Williams, "Some Significant Recent Developments in Antitrust Law," *Corporate Practice Commentator* (February 1966), p. 331.

[91] John M. Clark, "Toward A Concept of Workable Competition," in *Readings in the Social Control of Industry*, p. 453.

approaching pure or perfect competition[92] existed before the mergers in the markets in question occurred, or that if these mergers (and no doubt future mergers) were prevented it would be reasonably probable that this form of competition would ultimately evolve. Both suppositions would appear to be false.

Texts in economic theory almost invariably indicate that if the pure competition model is to be used to attempt to predict the results of a particular action the market in question must have certain characteristics. For example, among the half dozen or so "fundamental prerequisites" for the existence of pure competition, one usually finds the following (in much oversimplified form): a large number of firms in the market; their products are homogeneous; and anyone who wished to enter the industry must be allowed to do so.[93] Conclusions drawn on the basis of such assumptions would seem to have little relevance in determining the probable effects of a given bank merger since the number of competing firms involved is usually small, their products or services are far from homogeneous, and entry is severely restricted.[94]

The Supreme Court in its decisions in bank cases seems to place particular emphasis upon the number of competitors, although this is only one of a number of factors which may affect a market. J. M. Clark pointed out the danger in stressing one factor as opposed to another when he stated:[95]

If there are, for example, five conditions, all of which are essential to perfect competition, and the first is lacking in a given case, then it no

[92] The terms perfect, pure, and atomistic competition will be used interchangeably. There are technical differences between pure and perfect competition, such as reference in the latter to "perfect knowledge." Other assumptions include complete mobility of factors between industries, "no transport costs," and the ever-present *ceteris paribus* (other things being equal).

[93] Stonier and Hague, *A Textbook of Economic Theory*, pp. 123–26.

[94] The competitive situation in most banking markets might better be described as "monopolistic competition with oligopoly" because of the product differentiation which exists between banks. But, for simplicity, the term oligopoly will be used. The banking market was discussed at some length in Lester V. Chandler, "Monopolistic Elements in Commercial Banking," *Journal of Political Economy* (February 1938); and David Alhadeff, "The Market Structure of Commercial Banking in the United States," *Journal of Political Economy* (February 1951).

[95] John M. Clark, "Toward A Concept of Workable Competition," in *Readings in the Social Control of Industry*, p. 454. The Court has also cited the problem of entry in banking, but it did not argue restrictions should be eased.

longer follows that we are necessarily better off for the presence of any one of the other four. In the absence of the first, it is *a priori* quite possible that the second and third may become positive detriments; and a workably satisfactory result may depend on achieving some degree of "imperfection" in these other two factors.

In 1964 the Federal Deposit Insurance Corporation published an analysis of the market shares of large banks which revealed that in about one-half of the 65 metropolitan areas in this country with a population of 400 thousand or over the largest bank held 35 percent or more of the deposits of all commercial banks and the three largest banks held 75 percent or more of the deposits of all commercial banks.[96] In addition, a more detailed survey of banking facilities prepared by the Federal Reserve Board as of June 30, 1962 showed that in 9,972 centers in the United States with populations under fifty thousand, 99 percent had three banking institutions or less, 95 percent had two or less, and 77 percent had only one.[97] Therefore, it must be recognized in evaluating bank performance and bank structure that if somehow the number of banks serving each of these communities were doubled or even tripled the local market would still be oligopolistic. Hence, great care must be taken in drawing conclusions about banking markets using conventional economic models for there is no reasonable probability that even the harshest antitrust policy can offer the banking customer in most areas the opportunity to enjoy the "benefits" of pure competition; it can only present him with the possibility of facing another shade of oligopoly. And, although this writer would agree that other things being equal usually ten competitors is better than five, five is better than three, and so on, it must be recognized that the selection of the better form of oligopoly, unlike the choice of many as opposed to a few competitors, is based primarily on intuition and not on economic theory.

The Supreme Court in the *Philadelphia National Bank case*[98] made

[96] FDIC, *Annual Report* for the year ended December 31, 1964, pp. 142–43.

[97] "Changes in Banking Structure," *Federal Reserve Bulletin* (September 1963), p. 1197. The expression "banking institutions" refers to the number of independent managements available to bank customers whether through the head office of a local bank or a branch of a bank from outside the community.

[98] 374 U.S. 321, 363–64 (1963).

a number of references to the desirabilty of having a comparatively large number of competitors in a market. In one instance the majority observed that it is commonly accepted by most economists that "competition is likely to be greatest when there are many sellers none of which has any significant market share." And, in the same opinion the Court indicated that the 1950 Clayton Act amendments were intended "to arrest anticompetitive tendencies in their incipiency." If one keeps these comments in mind, it is not difficult to understand why the Supreme Court concluded that its decisions in cases such as *Von's Grocery*[99] and *Brown Shoe*[100] were consonant with economic theory.[101] But, on the other hand, it is extremely difficult to visualize an analogous competitive situation either existing or developing in the short or the long run in most local banking markets with entry limited and with Justice unable to attack past amalgamations under Section 1 or Section 7.[102]

In the *Philadelphia case* the Supreme Court did not consider the national market because of the "local nature" of banking service. Instead the Court based its decision on the local market in which the five largest banks held 77 percent of the area's deposits and the other 37 banks averaged only a little over 0.6 percent each. Furthermore, only one new bank opened there between 1951 and 1961, and at the end of ten years' operation it had 1/3 of 1 percent of the area's deposits. The five largest banks, it should be noted, had held over two-thirds of the deposits for thirty years. Thus, there seemed to be little prospect that a market with many sellers, none with a significant market share, was likely to exist in Philadelphia in the foreseeable future.

It is surely fair to assume that the choice in banking markets is not really between pure competition and oligopoly, but between one form of oligopoly and another. Therefore, any theoretical analysis must

[99] 384 U.S. 270 (1966).

[100] 370 U.S. 294 (1962).

[101] In the sense that the concentration in the markets in question and the market shares of the leading firms, by and large, were relatively low.

[102] Both the Bank Merger Act Amendment (80 Stat. 7) and the Bank Holding Company Act Amendment (80 Stat. 236) presume past bank mergers and acquisitions to have not been in violation of any antitrust laws other than Section 2 of the Sherman Act, and current amalgamations must be attacked (except under Section 2) within thirty days of agency approval.

draw upon studies indicating the significance of various degrees of relatively high concentration and not between "insignificant" concentration and "high" concentration. The Supreme Court itself found the latter market structure difficult to analyze, for in its opinion in *Philadelphia,* the Court stated: "In an oligopolistic market [which accurately describes virtually every major banking market in the United States][103] small companies may be perfectly content to follow the high prices set by the dominant firms, yet the market may be profoundly anticompetitive."[104] This would certainly be acknowledged by many (or most) antitrust and business organization specialists. On the other hand, S. Chesterfield Oppenheim, a leading antitrust scholar, remarked in a recent law review article: "My position, for which I find ample support in the writings of authoritative economists, is that oligopoly competition can be viable as in markets where a large number of firms struggle for customers."[105] Professor Oppenheim noted that the court cited only two books and a comment in the *Yale Law Journal* in support of its generalization; and he quoted from studies by Corwin Edwards, J. K. Galbraith, and Dirlam and Kahn, and added numerous other references to corroborate his findings.

Once the problem has been switched from pure competition v. oligopoly to oligopoly "A" v. oligopoly "B," economic theory provides little assistance to the investigator. To quote Professor Jesse Markham, from one of four articles the court cited in support of its "30 percent is too large" conclusion in the *Philadelphia case:*[106]

In brief, economic *analysis* may reveal with absolute precision that a given merger reduces the number of independent sellers in a market from eleven to ten and raises (say) the third largest seller's share of the market from

[103] This refers to what Kaysen and Turner (*Antitrust Policy,* p. 25) call "structurally oligopolistic markets—those which show a small number of large sellers supplying a large part of the output."

[104] 374 U.S. 321, 367, n. 43 (1963).

[105] Oppenheim, "Antitrust Booms and Boomerangs," 59 *Northwestern University Law Review* 33, 42 (March–April 1964). See Edwards, *Big Business and the Policy of Competition,* p. 38; Galbraith, *American Capitalism,* p. 58; Dirlam and Kahn, *Fair Competition: The Law and Economics of Antitrust Policy* pp. 33–34. Other citations appear in the Oppenheim article. Some of the problems in this analysis are spelled out in Andrews, *On Competition in Economic Theory,* pp. 43–63.

[106] Markham, "Merger Policy under the New Section 7," 43 *Virginia Law Review,* 489, 491–92 (1957).

17 percent to 20 percent. However, economic theory cannot predict a priori *how much* this affects competition, or even whether it affects competition substantially. Moreover, the historical evidence on merger yields no stochastic laws which may be used to predict the precise competitive effects of such a merger; that is, no correlations have been calculated which show that within a certain probability range the merger can be expected to reduce (or increase) competition by a substantial amount.

Professor Joe Bain, also cited by the court in its opinion in *Philadelphia,* has remarked "the whole idea of change in concentration, as a statistical concept, is inherently complicated and potentially ambiguous."[107] Professor Edward Mason, one of the three authors cited by the Supreme Court in defense of its thinking regarding the benefits of "many sellers," has noted the situation is quite different when the market is oligopolistic. He has indicated: "Despite Stigler's [another author quoted by the court] observation that an 'industry that does not have a competitive structure will not have competitive behavior,' a study of structure is not enough. . . . Many if not most of the markets with which antitrust is concerned do not approach very closely *the only two models,* pure competition and pure monopoly, that permit us to infer with assurance—at least under equilibrium conditions—behavior from structure."[108] [Italics added] Professor Richard Hefflebower has written: "Economists have not been able to develop a theory of price behavior for such markets for when sellers are few they tend to be 'jointly acting oligopolists' because of 'conjectural interdependence' among them. . . . In one industry there may be more conjectural restraint with ten sellers than in another with four."[109] Finally, George Hall and Charles Phillips, in reviewing the Supreme Court's apparent "switch" from a rule which considered an action's impact on structure to a rule under which concentration alone was sufficient to declare a merger illegal, commented: "The issue is whether concentration is an adequate proxy for all of the determinants of economic behavior. If it were the tasks of the economists

[107] Bain, *Industrial Organization,* p. 190.

[108] Kaysen and Turner, *Antitrust Policy,* "Preface," by Edward S. Mason, xviii. See also, Neale, *The Antitrust Laws of the U. S. A.,* pp. 477–79, 421–22.

[109] Richard B. Hefflebower, "Conscious Parallelism and Administered Prices," in Phillips, ed., *Perspectives on Antitrust,* pp. 89–90.

would be much simpler, but the history of industrial organization studies indicates that it is not. More importantly the vagueness of the concept of a market in merger laws leaves concentration with little meaning."[110]

To return to the *Philadelphia opinion,* once the Supreme Court "had established" that its action was "consonant with economic theory," it then moved to a decision regarding how much concentration was too much. This raises a third question regarding the court's analysis in *Philadelphia.* The majority opinion stated:[111]

Kaysen and Turner suggest that 20 percent should be the line of prima facie unlawfulness; Stigler suggests that any acquisition by a firm controlling 20 percent of the market after the merger is presumptively unlawful; Markham *mentions* 25 percent. Bok's principal test is [an] increase in market concentration, and he suggests a figure of 7 or 8 percent. . . . We intimate no view on the validity of such tests for we have no need to consider percentages smaller than those in the case at bar, but we note that such tests are more rigorous than is required to dispose of the instant case. [Italics added]

Let us consider each of the works cited, in turn, as they may relate to commercial banking. Kaysen and Turner list commercial banking as an exempt industry, which they noted was "that part of the economy to which antitrust policy does not apply because of legislative exemptions, expressed or implicit."[112] They described the present market structure as oligopolistic in the national market and in most local markets, and indicated that in the absence of regulation "concentration might be reduced but oligopolistic structures would probably still dominate."[113]

Although Professor Stigler was properly quoted by the court, the judges might have mentioned that the market situation in *Philadelphia* did not appear to be quite what he had in mind when he presented his 20 percent standard.[114] In the same article he remarked:[115]

[110] Hall and Phillips, "Antimerger Criteria: Power, Concentration, Foreclosure, and Size," 9 *Villanova Law Review* 211, 218 (Winter 1964). They cite a number of industrial organization studies which support their thesis.

[111] 374 U.S. 321, 364, n. 41 (1963).

[112] Kaysen and Turner, *Antitrust Policy,* pp. 41, 291.

[113] *Ibid.,* 290–91.

[114] I do not mean to suggest that Kaysen, Turner, Stigler, and others would not accept the Court's standard (they may or may not); I am simply questioning

The level of concentration which seriously threatens competition still eludes precise determination by the economist. We all recognize that in a properly defined industry, if the largest firm has less than 10 percent of the output, competition will be effective—in the absence of collusion. . . . And when one firm has 40 to 50 percent or more, or two to five firms have 75 percent or more of the industry's output competition will seldom plague the industry.

But, isn't the latter case the typical market situation in banking?

Professor Markham merely "mentioned" (to use the Supreme Court's expression): "The antitrust agencies appear to have used a cut-off point of 25 percent;"[116] Therefore, it is difficult to explain why his name was included. It should be added that at the time his article was written (1957), Markham said: "A not altogether hasty survey of the recent literature turned up only one suggested quantitative measure of market power for the administration of Section 7—Professor Stigler's.[117]

Professor Bok's "8 percent change figure"[118] seems to have been developed "as a consequence of his disillusionment with the usefulness of more sophisticated economic measures" and "in the interest of providing simple rules that would relieve uncertainty and reduce delays."[119] He remarks in his article: "Unfortunately, as any economist would concede, there is no ascertainable magic size or number of firms which divides competition from oligopoly or any other less desirable form of market behavior. At best, economists might conclude long after the fact that behavior in any industry had deteriorated substantially from a competitive standpoint."[120] Bok quotes Professor Bain, who said: "So far as I know, oligopoly theory does not tell us

---

whether the High Court's conclusion is supported by the *specific* "evidence" cited in its opinion.

[115] Stigler, "Mergers and Preventative Antitrust Policy," 104 *University of Pennsylvania Law Review* 176, 181 (1955).

[116] Markham, "Merger Policy under the new Section 7," 43 *Virginia Law Review* 489, 522 (1957).

[117] *Ibid.*

[118] Since these comments could be misinterpreted, it should be noted that Bok has made it very clear that he has a very high regard for the contributions of economists.

[119] Joel Dirlam, "The Celler-Kefauver Act: A Review of Enforcement Policy," in U. S. Senate, *Administered Prices,* 1963, pp. 103–104.

[120] Bok, "Section 7 of the Clayton Act and the Merging of Law and Economics," 74 *Harvard Law Review* 226, 241–42 (1960).

the maximum number of firms among which competitive behavior will still be oligopolistic";[121] and he provides other references supporting this position. Bok cites Stigler, and Kaysen and Turner, as the court did, to indicate control of one-fifth of the market by a single firm was too much.[122] He also stated: "While these suggestions do not purport to reflect any certain knowledge, they nevertheless fall within the range of competent opinion."[123] Thus, as in the other illustrations, competent opinion—or, perhaps more accurately, the competent opinion of some experts—not economic theory, wins the day!

*The viewpoint of banking structure research.* The decision of the Supreme Court in the consolidated *Provident* and *First City National Bank of Houston cases* clearly indicated that the burden of proof is on the defendant banks to show an anticompetitive merger, "as judged by the standards normally applied in antitrust actions," meets the requirements of the convenience and needs exception included in the 1966 Amendment to the Bank Merger Act.[124] But, in light of the oligopolistic nature of most local banking markets, providing this evidence may prove to be a difficult and in some instances an impossible task since the predictive value of economic models is severely limited when there are only a few competitors, and to date most empirical studies of banking competition have produced rather divergent results. In this section some of the findings of banking structure research in three areas which may be of some importance in the evaluation of the convenience and needs of a community in bank antitrust litigation (pricing, operating efficiency, and resource allocation) are very briefly reviewed.[125]

*Pricing.* In considering various forms of bank structure, one of the most crucial elements to both the customer and the bank supervi-

[121] *Ibid.,* 242, n. 73.

[122] *Ibid.,* 328, n. 300.

[123] *Ibid.,* 328.

[124] *U. S.* v. *First City National Bank of Houston,* 1967 *Trade Cases* ¶ 72,048; 386 U.S. 361 (1967).

[125] The *Report of the Attorney General's National Committee to Study the Antitrust Laws,* p. 315, indicated such evidence was of prime importance, for economic prediction as to market consequences of certain conduct ". . . is persuasive only in the absence of evidence of actual market behavior."

sor is the effect this variable may have upon the pricing practices and performance of competing firms in a given market. Unfortunately, there are substantial problems involved in obtaining dependable evidence relating to this question. This point is well-illustrated by the work of three researchers who have contributed substantially to this area: Franklin Edwards, Theodore Flechsig, and George Kaufman. Edwards found a statistically significant relationship between business loan rates and banking concentration in major metropolitan areas;[126] however, Flechsig questioned these findings on the grounds that differences in the supply and demand conditions in local or regional markets and differences in loan characteristics are important explanations of variations in rates on short-term business loans and that there is no significant association between rates and the degree of deposit concentration in each area when the foregoing are taken into account.[127] Edwards prepared a second study using a somewhat different approach, and he again found a relationship between the degree of banking concentration and interest rates. But, as in his previous research, a very sizable change in concentration was associated with a very small change in interest rates.[128]

George Kaufman has prepared a number of papers on this topic at the Federal Reserve Bank of Chicago. His published work includes a detailed analysis of Iowa banking data,[129] which revealed the greater the number of banks or the lower the percentage of deposits held by the largest bank in the study: the lower were effective interest rates charged on loans, the higher were interest rates paid on time deposits and the greater the ratio of time to total deposits. In addition, higher banking concentration was also associated with greater pre-tax earnings on assets. But, while Kaufman found these relationships to be statistically significant, he noted that the effect of structure on performance was not strong. He observed that large changes in structure were associated with relatively small changes in performance, which

---

[126] Edwards, *Concentration and Competition in Commercial Banking.*

[127] Flechsig, *Banking Market Structure and Performance,* p. 7.

[128] Edwards, "The Banking Competition Controversy," *National Banking Review* (September 1965).

[129] Kaufman, "Bank Market Structure and Performance: The Evidence from Iowa," *The Southern Economic Journal* (April 1966), p. 438.

apparently led him to conclude from his findings that "structure affects bank performance, although possibly not greatly."[130]

The inability of statistical analysis to provide any really convincing evidence regarding the influence of structural factors upon the performance of commercial banks probably should be expected, since nearly all banking markets have relatively high levels of concentration. The Federal Deposit Insurance Corporation studies of banking concentration in recent years have indicated that in the principal county or counties in nearly all large metropolitan areas in the United States, the three leading banks in each area held over 50 percent of the deposits. As a result there may be too few nonconcentrated markets to provide an adequate foundation for statistical inference. Thus, in reality the studies which have been done in this field have been attempting to measure the effects of varying high levels of concentration not merely varying levels of concentration, and from the existing research about all that one can conclude is that though a movement from a relatively high to a higher degree of concentration appears to be associated with an increase in interest rates charged by banks in absolute terms the magnitude of this change seems to be very small.[131]

*Operating efficiency.* In weighing the merits of one form or size of bank organization as opposed to another, the question of operating efficiency must be considered.[132] In banking, this expression in turn is usually translated into some measure of the real cost of producing a given financial service. In other words, to cite but one example, would a banking system composed of a few large institutions produce bank-

---

[130] A study published early in 1967 suggested that "the number of banks was insignificant" in determining loan rates in metropolitan areas. The author found that "loan rates are a parabolic function of average bank size, statistically the most significant bank structure variable." Meyer, "Price Discrimination, Regional Loan Rates, and the Structure of the Banking Industry," *Journal of Finance* (March 1967), pp. 37–48.

[131] Almarin Phillips' article, "Evidence on Concentration" [*Federal Reserve Bulletin* (June 1967)], objectively examines the differences in the findings of the various bank interest rate studies. He suggests further work which might be undertaken and states that "meanwhile, the conclusion remains that the available evidence indicates positive concentration effects."

[132] Guttentag and Herman, *Banking Structure and Performance*, Chapter 5, contains an enlightening discussion of this topic.

ing services at a lower real cost to the community than a system composed predominantly of small banks?[133]

Numerous studies have been conducted to try to determine the answers to such questions as this, beginning with David Alhadeff's work in 1954.[134] Since then a series of other investigators have expended considerable effort in trying to solve this problem, among them Paul Horvitz, Lyle Gramley, George Benston, and Stuart Greenbaum.[135] The Guttentag and Herman monograph prepared for the Pennsylvania Banking Commission summarized the results of these studies as follows: "Our major conclusion from reviewing this literature is that we do not know very much more about bank operating efficiency today than we did before 1954." Nevertheless, the authors concluded that significant scale economies exist in the bank size range up to about 10 million dollars; in the intermediate size range from 10 to 50 million dollars to 100 to 500 million dollars the evidence is less clear but it seems there is no change or a small reduction in unit costs; and for larger banks over 500 million dollars Guttentag and Herman noted nothing useful could be said about scale economies or diseconomies.[136]

The March and April 1967 issues of the *Business Review* of the Federal Reserve Bank of Boston included an analysis of "Economies of Scale in Banking" based upon the functional cost data collected by the Boston, New York, and Philadelphia Reserve Banks.[137] This study concluded that expanding operations within existing banking facilities results in significantly lower unit costs, but for many banks the savings

[133] Greenbaum, "Costs and Production in Commercial Banking," *Monthly Review*, Federal Reserve Bank of Kansas City, March–April 1966, presents one of the finest summaries of the approaches to this problem being employed and their alternatives.

[134] Alhadeff, *Monopoly and Competition in Banking.*

[135] Paul M. Horvitz, "Economies of Scale in Banking," in *Private Financial Institutions;* Gramley, *A Study of Scale Economies in Banking;* Benston, "The Cost of Bank Operations;" Benston, "Branch Banking and Economies of Scale," *The Journal of Finance* (May 1965); and Benston, "Economies of Scale and Marginal Costs in Banking Operations," *The National Banking Review* (June 1965): and Greenbaum, "Banking Structure and Costs: A Statistical Study of the Cost-Output Relationship in Commercial Banking."

[136] Guttentag and Herman, *Banking Structure and Performance*, pp. 106–24.

[137] "Economies of Scale in Commercial Banking," *New England Business Review*, Federal Reserve Bank of Boston (March 1967); *ibid.* (April 1967); and "A Simplified Method of Judging Bank Performance," *ibid.* (March 1965).

are offset by the greater expenses of branch operations. This would seem to be consistent with the findings of a number of other investigations in this field.

However, it could be argued that studies which compare the relative costs of a unit bank and a branch bank of equal size are biased in favor of the unit bank since they ignore the elements of accessibility and convenience which are usually associated with a branch institution.[138] For many years bank location specialists have stressed the importance of these factors, and their significance was pointed out once again in a recent series of bank customer surveys made by the Federal Reserve Bank of Chicago which revealed that accessibility was the primary factor in determining the selection of banks by both business firms and households.[139] Therefore, it may be more meaningful from the viewpoint of public policy to devote much greater research effort to the analysis of the costs of operating a branch bank and a number of small banks which might be combined to form a comparable branch institution to marginal cost studies of branch and unit banks, and to similar studies in which the impact of the convenience variable is minimized.[140]

Despite the importance of this subject and the great interest in it, analyses of bank operating efficiency (or scale economies), not unlike those concerning pricing practices, have encountered problems which to date have proved to be insuperable. Much of the difficulty stems from the multiproduct and service nature of banking output. (What is the output of a commercial bank and how do you measure it?) Furthermore, in banking there are also numerous alternatives in the specification of inputs.

Stuart Greenbaum has observed that the complexity of the prob-

---

[138] This is not a new idea, and it is not meant as a criticism of the Fed study, for the Federal Reserve Bank of Boston researchers noted that "the higher costs of branching are not necessarily detrimental either to banks or to consumers." *Ibid.* A small study of this type was undertaken under the direction of Howard Crosse while he was with the Federal Reserve Bank of New York some years ago, but the results were somewhat disappointing.

[139] The large majority of the households and, to a somewhat lesser extent, business firms use a primary bank that is most convenient to them. "Bank Markets and Services," *Business Conditions,* Federal Reserve Bank of Chicago (May 1967). Several of the individual city surveys have also been published by the Federal Reserve Bank of Chicago.

[140] Guttentag and Herman, *Banking Structure and Performance,* pp. 124–25.

lems in this area has led economists to study returns to scale at an analytical level once removed from the production function (employing cost functions instead). Greenbaum remarked:[141]

If the output of commercial banks could be defined and measured unequivocally, and if the more important factors impinging on the production of bank output also could be specified and measured accurately, and finally, if the structure of the functional relationship between output and the factors of production could be specified accurately, the analysis of economies of scale would be a simple matter. Unfortunately, none of the above "ifs" [has] evoked many affirmative responses from students of banking structure.

Recommending a new approach to this question, at least in regard to banking studies, he has suggested that greater use be made of production theory in this type of research. However, this work is in its early stages, and it will surely be some time before substantial advances are made in the measurement of operating efficiency in this industry.[142]

*Resource allocation*.[143] In addition to the pricing policies and operating efficiency of banks in various market situations, another extremely important factor to be considered in evaluating the merits of different forms of bank organization is the relationship between bank structure and resource allocation. Guttentag and Herman in their monograph for the Pennsylvania Banking Law Commission analyzed this problem, focusing on three questions: Which type of structure (1) provides more office facilities; (2) produces a wider range of auxiliary banking services; and (3) does a better job in meeting local credit demands? Each of these factors is considered below.

(1) In general, existing studies support the hypothesis that branch banks provide more offices in small communities than unit banks.[144]

[141] Greenbaum, "Costs and Production in Commercial Banking," *Monthly Review*, Federal Reserve Bank of Kansas City (March–April 1966).

[142] The functional cost studies are now being prepared in most of the Federal Reserve Districts, and in time, with these data available, better results may also be obtained using more conventional methods.

[143] The general format for the summary of developments in this area is drawn largely from Guttentag and Herman, *Banking Structure and Performance* [pp. 26–29, 126–68], but this does not imply they would endorse the conclusions in this study.

[144] *Ibid.*, pp. 21–22. For discussions of this topic see Anderson, "What Price Branching," *New England Business Review* (August 1964), pp. 2–8; Horvitz,

For example, it has been found that suburban municipalities within major metropolitan areas with populations of 20,000 to 30,000 persons averaged 1.5 banking offices per community in unit banking states and 3.0 offices in branch banking states. Furthermore, in moderate- and larger-sized nonmetropolitan communities of roughly 10,000 and over, the number of banking offices under branch banking was not only greater but tended to grow as the size of the locality increased. And it was only in the smallest communities, which typically had few banking outlets regardless of the form of banking structure, that the differences between branch and unit bank areas were negligible. Unfortunately, the economic significance of these findings for the general public is virtually impossible to determine, for as yet no optimum relationship between the number of branch offices in a market and other relevant variables has been established.[145]

(2) It is customarily conceded that wider branch banking usually results in some net expansion in the number of bank services offered to the customer.[146] However, as might be expected, this difference is

Concentration and Competition in New England Banking, pp. 133–36; Jacobs, "The Interaction Effects of Restrictions on Branching and Other Bank Regulations," The Journal of Finance (May 1965), pp. 332–48; Schweiger and McGee, "Chicago Banking," Journal of Business, University of Chicago (July 1961), pp. 203–366; and Horvitz and Shull, "The Impact of Branch Banking and Bank Performance," The National Banking Review (December 1964), pp. 301–41.

[145] Thomas G. Gies, "Book Reviews," The National Banking Review (December 1966), p. 238. This task is further complicated by the fact that not only the number of offices but among other things their location, costs, and array of services offered must be considered. For example, Robert F. Lanzillotti prepared a detailed study of state legislation and bank structure for the Michigan Bankers Association, and in this research he found banking laws affected primarily the composition (the mix between branches and main offices), not the total number of bank offices. But it would seem that in order to circumvent existing statutory restrictions, bankers placed main offices and branches in locations which were not necessarily the most economical. Lanzillotti, Banking Structure in Michigan, 1945–1963, pp. 70–71; and "Summary of Discussion: Conference on Bank Markets and Competition," Federal Reserve Bank of Chicago, October 21, 1965, pp. 15–16. (mimeographed)

[146] This topic is reviewed in Robert Weintraub and Paul Jessup, A Study of Selected Banking Services by Bank Size, Structure, and Location, U. S. Congress, House, 1964. Some additional analysis of this question may be found in Ernest Kohn, Branch Banking, Bank Mergers and the Public Interest, New York State Banking Department, 1964, Chapter VII; and Horvitz and Shull, "The Impact of Branch Banking on Banking Performance."

most apparent when a large branch bank and a small unit bank are analyzed, and it is much less pronounced when the two types of institutions are of similar size. Nevertheless, the first form of comparison seems fairly reasonable, for wider branch banking in this country would probably mean that many small banks would be absorbed or combined into larger institutions.

Commercial banks serve not only the general public but other banks, and an effort has been made to try to determine the effect mergers may have upon the services supplied to these institutions. Ira Scott, in his questionnaire survey concerning correspondent banking for the House Banking and Currency Committee, asked the banks in his sample whose "city" correspondent(s) either (a) merged or consolidated with another bank, or (b) joined a holding company to indicate whether the services received from their "city" depositary subsequently improved. From the sample results it was concluded that if replies had been received from all 13,103 insured banks in 1963, about one-tenth would have reported a correspondent merged or consolidated, and of these nearly one-half would have indicated services had improved. On the other hand, only 1 percent of the banks would have noted a correspondent was acquired by a holding company, and of these approximately one-eighth would have stated service improved.[147]

Although these findings reveal little change under group banking, they do appear to give some support to the argument that within limits at least branch banking may lead to better or expanded customer services. But existing research provides little information regarding the extent to which new or improved services made available following an amalgamation of two or more banks might have been supplied before a merger or the extent to which the new services were actually used. Thus, even within very broad limits, the contribution to the general welfare of the additional banking services which might result from a change in bank structure remains an unknown quantity.

(3) Local credit demands are usually given a high social priority, as one may note from the emphasis upon them in antitrust suits, in Congressional debates, and in bank structure studies. Therefore, it is of some importance that "there is clear evidence that branch banks

[147] U. S. Congress, House, *A Report on the Correspondent Banking System*, 1964, pp. 7, 33, 39.

have higher loan-to-asset ratios than unit banks, even in given bank size categories"; and, "with some important exceptions (mainly in the large business loan category), higher loan ratios imply larger credit extensions to the local community."[148] Part of this difference may be explained by the fact that branch banks are primarily located in the rapidly growing western states, but this by no means is the only explanation.

Guttentag and Herman noted that the higher loan ratios of branch banks[149]

also appear to result from their wider network of offices, which places them in closer proximity to local customers; from a willingness to maintain a less liquid position than unit banks; and from the greater ability of branch banks to maintain more offices in specialized locations in urban areas, which generate only selected types of business. Branch banks also possess an automatic mechanism for channeling funds from offices where loan demand is light to offices where it is heavy. This is reflected in the much wider range of loan-deposit ratios for individual branch offices than for individual unit banks.

In addition, recent investigations have failed to uncover evidence to support the charge that branch systems neglect rural areas in favor of the cities or that large banks neglect small business customers in favor of large firms.[150] In regard to the latter point, however, it should be mentioned that one study indicated that the "growth of total bank deposits beyond 100 million dollars, and perhaps to as much as 250 million dollars, has the effect of increasing the loans to small business." But beyond 250 million dollars in total deposits increasing bank size seemed to reduce the volume of loans to small business.[151]

[148] Guttentag and Herman, *Banking Structure and Performance,* p. 26.

[149] *Ibid.* An excellent attack upon the conventional view of deposit mobility under branch banking (including some of the arguments noted in this section) appears in Galbraith, *The Economics of Banking Operations: A Canadian Study,* pp. 195–214.

[150] The general topic of bank structure and local credit demands is discussed in Schweiger and McGee, "Chicago Banking"; Kohn, "Branch Banking, Bank Mergers and the Public Interest," Chapter IV; Laudadio, "Size of Bank, Size of Borrower, and the Rate of Interest," *The Journal of Finance* (March, 1963), pp. 20–28; Hodgman, *Commercial Bank Loan and Investment Policy;* and Federal Reserve Board, *Financing Small Business,* 1958. It should be noted that not all of these sources necessarily agree with the above conclusions.

[151] Guttentag and Herman, "Do Large Banks Neglect Small Business," *Journal of Finance* (September 1966), p. 538. Banks below the 100 to 250

## SOME GENERAL OBSERVATIONS ON BANKING CONCENTRATION

*Concentration in a service industry.* Not too many years ago a treatise on American antitrust law included the following comment concerning the applicability of these statutes to banks:[152]

> Banking is primarily the furnishing of personal services. It is basically impossible to consider a question of 'tendency to create a monopoly' in a business, in which monopoly is impossible. Antitrust laws should not be applied to banking in the absence of evidence of predatory practices, agreements or combinations, which are in themselves restrictive and illegal, regardless of the question of monopoly.

While the Supreme Court, in determining the legality of bank amalgamations under the Sherman and Clayton Acts, appears to have accepted a considerably different view of monopoly in banking from that suggested above,[153] this quotation does contain a substantial element of truth. It also pinpoints one of the major weaknesses of banking structure statistics—namely their failure to account for the possible variations in the quality (used in a very broad sense) of the outputs of different banks. In a service industry such as banking these differences may be substantial,[154] and it is possible that because of this variation many of the "products" of a billion dollar bank cannot be compared with the corresponding "products" of a 10 million dollar bank, or perhaps even with those of a 100 million dollar bank.

From the viewpoint of public policy the differences which may exist in the quality of the outputs of different-sized banks is particu-

---

million dollar size class showed a declining ratio of loans to small business borrowers to all business loans, but the increasing ratio of business loans to deposits more than offset the decline.

[152] Toulmin, *A Treatise on the Antitrust Laws of the United States,* Vol. 5, § 2.2.

[153] For example, in *Philadelphia* the Court observed: "So also we reject the position that commercial banking . . . because it deals in the intangibles of credit and services rather than in the manufacture or sale of tangible commodities is somehow immune from the anticompetitive effects of undue concentration." 374 U.S. 321, 368 (1963).

[154] This does not mean to imply that large qualitative differences exist only in the personal service area. They are found in any field, but it would seem that for the purposes of statistical analysis it is especially difficult to determine the value of advice from Bank A's trust or loan officer as opposed to Bank B's. Their salaries are of little help since no single specialist from the large institution may be able to do the work of the generalist in the small bank and vice versa.

larly significant. In studying economies of scale, for example, if qualitative changes are associated with changes in bank size, either positively or negatively, this could bias research findings[155] since an investigator may draw conclusions regarding supposed economies (or diseconomies) of scale from data which relate to the production of two very different products. Similarly, studies of banking structure which ignore qualitative factors may either understate or overstate both the degree of competition in banking markets and the probable impact a given change in concentration may have upon price.

On the other hand, while the personal service nature of commercial banking and the lack of information regarding the qualitative aspects of bank output may reduce the value of certain banking statistics, this does not mean that they have no value. To paraphrase the concluding remarks in a study published early in 1967 by the Federal Reserve Bank of Chicago: "Bank performance is far from being uniquely determined by bank size or structure or even the intensity of external rivalry [it depends] heavily on the qualities of individual bank managements and personnel—factors that are not suitable for statistical investigation. Imperfect knowledge, nevertheless, is greatly to be preferred to total ignorance."[156] This writer would be inclined to endorse this statement if the last sentence were amended to read: Imperfect knowledge, *when it is employed by individuals who appreciate its limitations,* is greatly to be preferred to total ignorance.

*Concentration: a pragmatic approach.* The problem of applying economic models to oligopolistic markets was recently discussed by Assistant Attorney General Donald F. Turner, who is both a lawyer and an economist. He stated in a speech in March 1967:[157]

[155] Somewhat related to this point, this writer found, in studying banking operations in a number of communities, that banks which reached certain levels began to take on additional functions and began to employ specialists "because a bank their size was expected to have these services or personnel," not necessarily because of their profitability. How universal this practice is this writer cannot state, but if it is widespread it might be worthwhile in some scale economies studies to divide banks into several broad size classifications and to stress analysis of economies of scale of banks within these tiers rather than between banks in different tiers.

[156] Mote, "Competition in Banking: What is Known? What is the Evidence?" *Business Conditions,* Federal Reserve Bank of Chicago (February 1967), p. 16.

[157] Donald F. Turner, "The Merits of Antimerger Policy," reprinted in 1967 *Trade Regulation Reports* ¶ 50, 165.

Taken literally, Section 7 asks for a predictive economic judgment, a conclusion about the probability of various possible economic consequences of the merger, and an assessment of how substantial those effects are likely to be. The main difficulty with this is that except in the most obvious cases economic theory and economic analysis simply do not permit confident judgments on these issues even when all of the relevant facts can be duly assembled. I suppose there would be general agreement that the merger of two out of only three firms in a well-defined market, with high barriers to entry, would probably have substantial anticompetitive effects. Perhaps most of us would be equally confident in reaching the same conclusion about a merger of two out of four or five firms of more or less equal size in the same market circumstances. . . . Beyond that, one is sure to get well-nigh unresolvable dispute. Indeed, when one gets into the range of mergers between two of ten or more comparable competitors, I would not be surprised to find that a good many economists would be unable to testify that such a merger, in and of itself, would probably substantially lessen competition.

Dr. Turner indicated that antimerger law cannot turn on a case by case evaluation of all of the relevant economic facts; instead, he called for relatively simple, general rules which are "rationally conceived." He cited as an example the rule proposed by Justice and apparently accepted by the Supreme Court in the *Von's Grocery case* that a merger between direct competitors is presumptively unlawful, even in a market still relatively unconcentrated, if (1) the market is threatened with undue concentration, and (2) the challenged merger increases market concentration substantially.[158]

This writer would be inclined to agree with Professor Turner regarding the need for the establishment of such simple, general rules, with their emphasis on concentration, even though indexes of concentration are not necessarily indexes of monopoly,[159] and a knowledge of market behavior (conduct) and market performance, in addition to information relating to market structure, usually is needed to try to determine whether workable competition is likely to exist in a given

---

[158] In the *Von's case* [384 U.S. 270 (1966)] the Supreme Court found the companies were substantial, growing, and reasonably healthy competitors "in a market characterized by a long and continuous trend toward fewer and fewer owner-competitors." Before merger each of the firms involved in the litigation had about 4 percent of the Los Angeles' grocery market, and the share of the eight largest competitors was about 40 percent. The High Court ordered divestiture.

[159] Wilcox, *Public Policies Toward Business*, p. 303.

market situation.[160] However, if such rules are to be applied to determine the legality of mergers in a quasi-regulated industry such as commercial banking, it seems that they would have to undergo at least a modest amount of modification.

With the high level of concentration in most local commercial banking markets, if Justice files suit under Section 1 of the Sherman Act or Section 7 of the Clayton Act and the participating banks are major competitors;[161] the banks' chance of winning an action brought against them if conventional antitrust standards are employed would be virtually nil.[162] Therefore, in light of the significant amount of regulation in banking and the particular importance of this industry to the nation, the apparent decision of the Congress to provide the banks with a second line of defense in antitrust litigation through the convenience and needs test[163] was surely warranted.

Nevertheless, the simple general rules of legality in merger cases which are based largely on concentration will no doubt continue to play a vital role in deciding the lawfulness of bank consolidations and acquisitions, and the "convenience and needs exception" is not expected to ease greatly restrictions on bank amalgamations. In fact some authorities argue that this provision will have almost no impact. These experts suggest that, with the possible exception of a case involving a failing or "floundering bank," the merging institutions will find it is nearly impossible to prove that their transaction should be approved if the court finds it has an anticompetitive effect. If this is true the 1966 Amendments will be just another milestone in a continuing controversy over the application of the antitrust laws to the banking industry.

There is still at least a possibility that this pessimistic view will not prevail, for the Supreme Court has not as yet revealed its position on

[160] Bain, *Industrial Organization,* pp. 3–4; and Massel, *Competition and Monopoly,* p. 191.

[161] A "major competitor" may have only a relatively small share of the relevant market.

[162] Barring a failing firm defense which may be accepted.

[163] The Amendment to the Bank Merger Act provides: "That the anticompetitive effects of the proposed merger are clearly outweighed in the public interest by the probable effect of the transaction in meeting the convenience and needs of the community to be served [12 U.S.C. § 1828 (c)(5)(B)]; and similar language is found in the Bank Holding Company Act Amendment [12 U.S.C. § 1842 (c)(2)].

the convenience and needs question. However, it would have to be conceded that the pattern of decisions by the High Court in the antitrust field in recent years would hardly lead one to expect that it will be very lenient with bank mergers because of the 1966 Amendments. Perhaps the one hope of those who advocate special treatment for bank amalgamations under the Sherman Act and Clayton Act is the fact that the High Court acknowledged the 1966 Amendments provided "a new defense or justification to the merger's proponents,"[164] and if bank mergers are not *sui generis* there can be no new defense. Therefore, if these statutes place a heavy burden on the banks to prove a given transaction is an exception to the general rule, it is surely reasonable to assume that this legislation places no less a burden on the judiciary to give real weight to any valid convenience and needs arguments the banks may present.

[164] *U. S.* v. *First City National Bank of Houston*, 1967 *Trade Cases* ¶ 72,048.

# CHAPTER 9

---◄◆►---

# *Closing Observations*

IN THE INTRODUCTION to this book, it was mentioned that this study was written to provide background material for investigations of banking structure such as those which are being carried out by the National Bureau of Economic Research (NBER) and by other organizations and individuals. In fact, as Charls Walker notes in the Foreword, this study is itself the first step in a research program designed to provide information that would be needed for an intelligent appraisal of the bank structure problem.

Since this work was supposed to be objective, providing general knowledge which would be useful to all regardless of their views on the questions discussed, and since it is to be followed by a series of studies concerning the effects of structure, no policy recommendations or broad conclusions will be included in this book. Instead, this final chapter will be limited to some closing observations regarding banking structure and banking structure research, and those limited conclusions which are drawn have been included in the individual chapters, where the reader may carefully review this writer's assumptions and any related analysis of a particular point. This writer is well aware that this procedure will no doubt be criticized, but, in light of the preliminary nature of many of the findings in this book, it was decided that this was the better format.

A far more difficult problem than that posed by the location of the conclusions was faced by this writer when the decision had to be made to concentrate on the evolution and regulation of banking structure and to include only a modest amount of discussion or analysis of its impact. The last topic is certainly much more exciting and many people would argue it is much more vital. Furthermore, a substantial amount of data to be used in the evaluation of structural effects had been gathered before the decision was made to limit the scope of this book, and detailed analyses of measures of concentration, market concepts, and related factors had been planned (and much preliminary work had already been done) which now would have no place in this work.

Nevertheless, since this writer had available *Banking Structure and Performance* prepared by Guttentag and Herman for the Pennsylvania Banking Commission, which provided a detailed examination of research in this area done to date, and since it was highly probable that in the near future the American Bankers Association would make a fairly substantial grant to the NBER to undertake a series of studies of the impact of banking structure, I agreed to restrict this book to the evolutionary and regulatory aspects of this question. It is impossible at this juncture to be objective regarding the wisdom of this choice. Therefore, any decision on this point will have to rest with the student of banking structure, who may, or may not, find this book of some value.

SANCTITY OF THE PRESENT SYSTEM

This book on a number of occasions has entered an extremely controversial area, for it has raised questions regarding the inviolability of the present so-called unit banking system in the United States. To some groups in this country, any work containing such heresy would automatically suggest that its author is "big bank" oriented and that the findings are undoubtedly biased. This writer would have to concede he is in favor of at least some form of limited branching, which is surely reflected in this study by the lengthy examination of the proposition that large banks and not necessarily branch banks were opposed by our forebears, and that branch and unit banks should both be considered as legitimate local banking alternatives. But this acceptance of limited branching should not be misinterpreted as a vote in favor of the eventual establishment of a handful of nationwide branch banks or even as a vote for widespread branch banking.

It is suggested in this book that limited branching will not necessarily lead to large-scale branching; in fact, quite to the contrary, it is very likely that the introduction of some branches in areas where they are now prohibited would make the passage of broader branch banking laws more (not less) difficult. For example, President Kennedy's Committee on Financial Institutions (Heller Committee) expressed great fear concerning any increase in banking concentration that might occur under unrestricted branching; yet the Committee observed:[1]

> Extreme limitations on authority to permit branching by commercial banks in some states may operate to the detriment of the interest of businesses and consumers in those states. . . . Leaving aside considerations involving the relationship between the federal and state governments, it is difficult to defend the extreme disparity among the states in the prevalence of branch banking. It is likely that the public interest would be better served by a more consistent policy among the states regarding branches.

This comment would seem to lend support to the argument that if in the foreseeable future there is any broadening of national bank branch powers beyond those granted under state law, a development greatly feared and opposed by independent bankers' groups for over half a century, this would probably come not because some states had given the proverbial "inch" to the branch forces but rather because some states had continued to prohibit branching.

The Heller Committee suggested that "federal and state governments, within their respective authorities, should review present restrictions on branching with a view to developing a more rational pattern, subject to safeguards to avoid excessive concentration and preserve competition,"[2] and the conclusions of this book would be essentially the same. Naturally, some groups stanchly oppose such investigations, for they fear that they will disturb the status quo. Yet, it must be realized that whether research is underaken or not, change

[1] Heller Report, p. 51.
[2] *Ibid.*, p. 52.

will come, and in reality the fundamental question is whether this change is to occur by design or by accident.[3]

## PERFORMANCE CRITERIA ARE NEEDED

As was noted earlier, until very recently bank structure research was undertaken by only a few economists and the banking agencies produced an occasional paper devoted to this topic. Inevitably the work was highly descriptive and contained a minimum of analysis, but today the situation is much different. Numerous studies have been completed in this area relating to a variety of questions both practical and theoretical. In fact, a sufficient amount of work has been done to require two very able economists, Jack Guttentag and Edward Herman, to write a 200 page volume merely to summarize the findings of the existing research in this area.[4]

With this background material and a host of experienced investigators available who are extremely knowledgeable in this field, it would appear that the time has arrived not only to assess where structure research has been (through a survey of the literature) but where it is going. It might be generally accepted that the aim of banking structure studies should be to provide the best possible banking system for this country from the viewpoint of the general public. However, there may be considerable disagreement regarding the standards which should be employed in selecting the optimum system. Yet, either implicitly or explicitly a decision-maker is working toward some goal, even when his objective is the status quo. Therefore, it would appear to be of vital interest to the bank supervisor, the banker, the legislator, and the researcher to have some of the resources now being used to try to determine the effects of selected structure variables channeled into a careful examination and evaluation of the numerous criteria which might be used to measure the performance of a banking system. The findings of such a study would be helpful, for they could point out the various alternatives in banking structure and their

[3] It might be argued that the market should decide, but this is a quasi-regulated industry and the consumer cannot realistically be given a choice among alternative banking systems. (To vote on the question is not to give it a market test, for the political power, goodwill, and finances would typically rest with the existing system.)

[4] Guttentag and Herman, *Banking Structure and Performance.*

possible impact, and they could give added direction to the investigations undertaken in this area. But, more important, until this is done decisions affecting bank structure must continue to be made largely on an ad hoc basis and there can be no bank structure policy worthy of the name.[5]

A SOCIAL AND POLITICAL PROBLEM

At present the total deposits of the five largest banks in the United States exceed the aggregate deposits of the 10,000 smallest. Nevertheless, the small, local bank remains a powerful political force (notwithstanding some recent setbacks) whose opposition to change in bank structure can still have a substantial influence upon legislation, particularly at the state level and in the House of Representatives. Thus, in establishing criteria to be employed in evaluating the merits of various banking structures, great care must be taken not only to consider the economic implications of this problem but political and social questions must be examined as well.

About 50 percent of the American banks have less than 5 million dollars of deposits and 90 percent have deposits of less than 25 million dollars. Of the branch institutions approximately four-fifths with roughly two-thirds of all offices have no branches beyond the head-office county. Therefore, despite the thousands of bank mergers which have occurred since World War II and the furor which has arisen concerning banking concentration in recent years, the activity of the vast majority of the banks of this nation continues to be dominated by a single community or a very limited primary-service area. This local orientation of commercial banking is considered by some to be a part of the American heritage, and in an era when the federal government has usurped local authority in many fields, states' rights in regard to bank structure continue to be defended by numerous groups and many lawmakers with almost as much vigor as local control over education.

[5] Professor Charles Williams suggested to this writer several years ago that the best initial project in the ABA study of bank structure would be "Public Policy and the Structure of Commercial Banking—Criteria for Evaluating Performance." He, of course, is not responsible for any comments made above. A pioneering effort in this general area is Benjamin H. Beckhart's "Criteria of a Well-Functioning Financial System," a study prepared for the Commission on Money and Credit, May 1, 1960. (mimeographed)

Thus, any realistic appraisal of the desirability of effecting changes in this country's banking structure because they appear to be economically sound must also consider that they have to be politically sound since the continued existence of local banks in the short run does not stem solely from small bank performance. As a result, even if cost data were available and they provided convincing evidence that widespread branching was substantially more efficient than local banking (which may or may not be the case) it would still be extremely difficult for the legislator and bank supervisor to choose the type of banking structure which would be of maximum overall benefit to the general public, for in making this decision they would still face many complex problems. Not the least of their difficulties would involve attempts to weigh the possible economic cost of unit banking against the "social cost" of widespread branch banking, for the advocates of local banks insist that unit banking or very limited branch banking is what the public really desires.

## A DIM FUTURE FOR UNIT BANKING?

Since World War II there has been a vast expansion of *de novo* branch offices in metropolitan areas and a substantial number of small suburban unit banks were acquired by larger city institutions and converted into branches. This development is reflected in the aggregate branch and unit bank data for the past two decades which show a decline in the number of unit banks of approximately 2,500 and an increase in the number of branch offices (excluding head offices) of about 13,000. Thus, the importance of the unit bank in the American financial system has diminished tremendously since 1945, and there appears to be no reason to expect a reversal of this trend in the future.

The role of the general public in the expansion of branch banking and in the decline of the unit bank is extremely difficult to assess. Nevertheless, this writer's research in this field and the findings of others would seem to lead to the conclusion that the role of the general public in most of these transactions was that of a passive observer. This point was noted by George Mitchell of the Federal Reserve Board when he remarked:[6]

[6] Speech by Governor George W. Mitchell before the Bank Presidents' and Senior Officers' Policy Seminar of the Independent Bankers Association of the Twelfth District. Reprinted in the *American Banker*, March 17, 1966.

Seldom indeed do the submissions to the merger record before our Board contain evidence of community preference for a locally-owned and operated institution. On occasion we do get a vigorous advocate of local banking, but it is usually a one man crusade. . . .

Governor Mitchell strongly emphasized the fact that working control in a vast number of small banks is held by only a few families, many of which may no longer even live in the town in question; and he concluded that given the very limited community participation in the ownership of local banks: "it does not seem surprising . . . that community banks fail to generate a ground swell of local opposition to mergers with non-local interests."

Without this "ground swell of local opposition," one would have to expect the erosion of the position of the small unit bank in this country to persist. This point is well-illustrated in a speech made by Oscar Brown, the 1966–1967 President of the Kansas Bankers Association.[7] In a commentary on his year in office, Brown remarked:

This success of the Kansas Development Credit Corp. in creating more jobs, especially in rural areas of Kansas, is becoming more important all the time. It seems to me that many of our small towns face the problem of survival, what with school construction; fewer railroad trains stopping at smaller towns; decreasing populations; fewer but larger farmers, whose credit needs will probably increase by as much as two-and-one-half times by 1980; fewer successful local merchants; constantly improving roads and the ease of automobile transportation, etc.

We should be thinking about how best to provide banking service in the future to these smaller communities which now may have a bank or which perhaps have already lost their local bank.

The factors cited by this Kansas banker are indicative not only of the situation in his section of the country but in many other parts of the nation and the list of problems of small banks he has compiled might be expanded considerably to include: the reapportionment of legislatures which in time could lead to the expansion of branch banking powers; bank entry into new lines as the customer's demand for standard banking services is reduced with the growth of credit cards and other "cashless society" techniques; the seemingly endless expansion of automation (which is also reflected in the previous factor);

[7] Oscar Brown, "President's Address," *American Banker,* May 19, 1967.

the increased use of capital notes, federal funds, and negotiable
certificates of deposit by larger banks to meet liquidity needs under
highly competitive money market conditions;[8] the ever-present management succession problems which are particularly burdensome to
the small bank; the better marketability of the shares of large banks,[9]
and the gradual termination of nonpar banking in the United States. It
is through the solution (if possible) of many of these problems, not
through stricter enforcement of the banking or the antitrust laws, that
large numbers of small local banks will be preserved in this country.

## THE ANTITRUST LAW–BANKING LAW PARADOX

There is considerable disagreement regarding the significance of the
threat which strict antitrust law enforcement may hold for the future
development of commercial banking in the United States. In the early
1960s Justice filed suit in a handful of bank price-fixing cases, but
there has been no other litigation in this area in several years. And in
the future, now that bankers are well aware that certain practices are
in violation of the antitrust laws, one would hope there will be no
court action involving bank price fixing unless it relates to acts
supposedly performed some years ago or to a test case in which the
circumstances are such that there is no clear per se violation.[10] In the

[8] This may be countered somewhat by greater freedom at the discount
window for Fed members and perhaps even nonmembers as a part of a possible
major change in Fed discount policy. Paul Nadler, "Fed May Change Discount
Role," *American Banker,* June 15, 1967.

[9] "Since the late 1950s, the market prices of big-bank shares have moved to a
permanently higher plateau based in [David Cates'] opinion, on earning power
rather than the older benchmark of book value. . . . Since small-bank shares
on the contrary, typically are quoted at book value or less, the wide market
disparity between big and small is creating a powerful economic incentive to
merge. . . ." Cates, "Trends in the Organization of U. S. Banking," (Bank
Stock Department, Salomon Bros. and Hutzler, March 20, 1964). (mimeographed) Also see U. S. Congress, House, Committee on Banking and Currency, *The Market for Bank Stock,* 88th Cong., 2d Sess., 1964; and for an
analysis of small-bank shares see Van Horne and Helwig, *The Valuation of
Small-Bank Stocks.*

[10] This writer would argue that in the future Justice should warn the banking
agencies that a given act may violate the antitrust laws. The agencies in turn
should notify the banks of this fact, and if there is reasonable doubt regarding
the validity of the Government's position a test case should be tried with no
criminal charges.

bank amalgamation field, on the other hand, it can be expected that banks will continue to be charged with Section 7 (Clayton Act) violations, covering a variety of situations ranging from conglomerate mergers and potential competition cases to simple horizontal combinations.

In terms of absolute numbers the sixteen suits which Justice filed against bank mergers or acquisitions since 1961 amounted to only about 1 percent of the amalgamations approved by the Fed, the FDIC, and Comptroller during the past seven years; and even if one were to include the number of planned amalgamations which were cancelled because of possible antitrust action the percentage of mergers prevented would probably still not be too impressive. Thus, the odds are high that if a merger is approved by the banking agencies it will not be prevented by Justice. Nevertheless, with nearly all local banking markets characterized by oligopoly and with banks finding it essential to enter a variety of new fields in which merger or partnership with existing firms or cooperation with other banks or organizations may be essential to successful operation, there could be a substantial impact from a relatively small number of unfavorable (from the viewpoint of the banks involved) antitrust decisions.

Before closing this last discussion of antitrust, some mention should be made of the strange paradox which appears to result from the strict application of the antitrust laws to a quasi-regulated industry such as banking. The opinions of the Supreme Court in recent years suggest the majority of the present High Court strongly opposes increasing concentration and advocates the preservation of small business. Yet, in commercial banking, using the type of market analysis employed by the Court in the *Philadelphia National Bank case,* banking concentration is typically highest where the banks are the smallest.

Some antitrust scholars have indicated that, despite the potential sacrifice of local automony, to introduce some additional competition in the more than 9,000 one- and two-bank communities in this country a considerable expansion of branch banking should be permitted. And the two major revisions in state branching laws since 1960 (New Hampshire and Virginia) have resulted in some increase in branching powers. But, ironically in the light of the application of antitrust laws to bank amalgamations, both new statutes include "home office protection"[11] provisions under which the greatest branching authority is granted in cases involving the establishment of a branch by acquiring an existing bank via merger and the laws are most restrictive in cases involving the organization of a *de novo* branch.[12]

A High Court decision in the *Crocker-Citizens case*, the *Hawaii case*, or the *First National City Bank case* which involve potential competition, may be helpful both in evaluating the possible impact of this apparent conflict between federal antitrust and state banking philosophy and the effect the Clayton Act may have upon bank entry into new product markets via merger. But this writer has learned not to be too optimistic regarding the outcome of a bank antitrust suit nor to place too much weight upon precedent in such litigation, for as Supreme Court Justice Stewart observed in his dissent in the *Von's Grocery Company case*: ". . . the Court pronounces its work consistent with the line of our decisions under § 7 since the passage of the 1950 [Celler-Kefauver] amendment. The sole consistency that I can find is that in litigation under § 7, the Government always wins."[13]

## THE NEED FOR A BANK STRUCTURE POLICY

Earlier in this chapter the desirability of establishing goals and standards in the bank structure area was mentioned. This task would not be easy and the limits of any criteria decided upon would have to be very broad. But banking agencies implicitly or explicitly have objectives in mind and requirements which must be met before mergers are approved, charters are granted, and other decisions affecting banking structure are made. This study would merely plead for a

---

[11] An illustration of this would be the requirement that an outside bank cannot enter a community when the head office of another bank already exists there.

[12] For example, the Virginia law states that branches may be established within the limits of the city, town, or county in which the parent is located, or in cities contiguous to the county or city in which the parent is located, or in counties contiguous to the city in which the parent is located provided such branches in the contiguous county may not be established more than 5 miles outside the city limits or elsewhere by merger with banks located in any other county, city, or town.

[13] *U. S. v. Von's Grocery Co.*, 384 U.S. 270, 301 (1966). This comment was made before the December 1967 Penn-Olin decision.

careful analysis of the future implications of these present decisions to
see if they are likely to achieve long-run goals which appear to be in
the best interest of the general public.

However, the testing of short-run decisions against long-run objectives and the development of a bank structure policy will be of little
value unless the agencies whose actions affect bank structure generally agree upon goals and cooperate in attempting to attain them.
Certainly, internecine conflict among federal government agencies
concerning mergers and branching is not the means to this end. It has
been suggested that a "super-agency" be created whose decisions
relating directly to bank structure would be final, but should such
extreme measures really be necessary? A senior officer of a relatively
small bank which was recently caught in this bureaucratic web has
remarked: "As president of our bank and a former employee of the
Comptroller's Office, I am very concerned that the Comptroller's
Office, the Federal Reserve Board, the Federal Deposit Insurance
Corporation, and the Department of Justice, for the good of banking
in general, get together and talk over their apparent problems." This
writer would heartily endorse this statement with two small
changes—these agencies should get together not only for the good of
banking but for the good of the general public and their apparent
problems should not only be discussed, they should be solved.

# BIBLIOGRAPHY[1]

Alhadeff, Charlotte, and David Alhadeff. "Growth of Large Banks, 1930–1960," *Review of Economics and Statistics*, November 1964.
——— "Recent Bank Mergers," *Quarterly Journal of Economics*, November 1955.
——— "The Struggle for Commercial Bank Savings," *Quarterly Journal of Economics*, February 1958.
Alhadeff, David A. "Bank Mergers: Competition Versus Banking Factors," *Southern Economic Journal*, January 1963.
——— "The Market Structure of Commercial Banking in the United States," *Journal of Political Economy*, February 1951.
——— Monopoly and Competition in Banking. Berkeley, University of California Press, 1954.
——— "A Reconsideration of Restrictions on Bank Entry," *Quarterly Journal of Economics*, May 1965.
Allen, Frederick L. The Big Change. New York, Harper and Brothers, 1952.
American Bankers Association. The Bank Chartering History and Policies of the United States. New York, American Bankers Association, 1935.
——— Banking Legislation in the Second Session, 87th Congress. New York, American Bankers Association, 1962.
——— The Commercial Banking Industry. Englewood Cliffs, New Jersey, Prentice-Hall, 1962.
——— Present Day Banking, 1958. New York, American Bankers Association, 1958.
——— Report of the Economic Policy Commission. New York, American Bankers Association, 1932.
——— State Bank Supervision: Ninth Quinquennial Survey, 1964. New York, American Bankers Association, 1965.
Anderson, Paul S. "What Price Branching," *New England Business Review*, August 1964.
Andrews, P. W. S. On Competition in Economic Theory. London, Macmillan and Company, Ltd., 1964.

[1] University law journal articles are listed in standard legal form—volume, title, first page of article, and year of publication.

"Are Branch Banking Limitations Applicable to Approved Bank Holding Company Operations," *Banking Law Journal,* April 1965.

Arrington, Frank J. "A Factual Study of the Deficiency of Rural Bank Management in Georgia and the Problem of Managerial Succession," Unpublished thesis, The Graduate School of Banking, Rutgers University, 1958.

Auburn, H. W. (ed.). Comparative Banking. London, Waterlow and Sons, Ltd., 1963.

Backman, Jules. The Bank Holding Company Act. Bulletin No. 24–25. New York, C. J. Devine Institute of Finance, Graduate School of Business, New York University, 1963.

Backman, Jules, and Arnold Sametz. Workable Competition in Banking. Bulletin No. 22. New York, C. J. Devine Institute of Finance, Graduate School of Business, New York University, 1962.

Bain, Joe S. Barriers to New Competition. Cambridge, Massachusetts, Harvard University Press, 1956.

——— Industrial Organization. New York, John Wiley and Sons, 1959.

Baldwin, William L. Antitrust and the Changing Corporation. Durham, North Carolina, Duke University Press, 1961.

Bank Administration. New York, American Bankers Association, 1938.

"Bank Charter, Branching, Holding Company and Merger Laws: Competition Frustrated," *Banking Law Journal,* August 1962.

The Bankers' Handbook. Homewood, Ill., Dow Jones–Irwin, Inc., 1966.

"Bank Holding Companies: Ten Years Later," *Bank Stock Quarterly,* M. A. Schapiro and Company, Inc., June 1966.

The Banking Situation in the United States. National Industrial Conference Board. New York, National Industrial Conference Board, Inc., 1932.

Bank Management. New York, American Institute of Banking, 1933.

"The Bank Merger Act and the Antitrust Law: Hopeless Conflict," 32 *University of Cincinnati Law Review* 505, 1963.

Bank Mergers. Bulletin No. 18. New York, C. J. Devine Institute of Finance, Graduate School of Business, New York University, 1962.

Barnett, George E. "State Banks and Trust Companies Since the Passage of the National Bank Act," in State Banks and Trust Companies and the Independent Treasury System. National Monetary Commission Publications, Washington, Government Printing Office, 1911.

Barnett, Robert. "The National Bank of the United States," *Bankers Magazine,* October 1882.

Beckhart, Benjamin H. "Criteria of a Well-Functioning Financial System," a study prepared for the Commission on Money and Credit, May 1960. (mimeographed)

——— (ed.). The New York Money Market. 4 vols. New York, Columbia University Press, 1932. Vols. I and II.

Bell, James F. "National Bank Branches—The Authority to Approve and to Challenge," *Banking Law Journal,* January 1965.

Benson, Lee. The Concept of Jacksonian Democracy: New York as a Test Case. Princeton, Princeton University Press, 1961.

Benston, George. "Branch Banking and Economies of Scale," *Journal of Finance,* May 1965.

————— "The Cost of Bank Operations," doctoral dissertation, University of Chicago, 1964.

————— "Economies of Scale and Marginal Costs in Banking Operations," *National Banking Review,* June 1965.

Berle, Adolph A., Jr. "Banking under the Antitrust Law," 49 *Columbia Law Review,* 589, 1949.

BNA's Antitrust and Trade Regulation Report. Washington, Bureau of National Affairs, Inc., 1962–1966.

Board of Governors of the Federal Reserve System publications are listed under Federal Reserve Board.

Bock, Betty. Mergers and Markets: An Economic Analysis of the 1964 Supreme Court Merger Decisions. Studies in Business Economics No. 87. New York, National Industrial Conference Board, 1965.

Bock, Betty, and John Farkas. Concentration in Manufacturing. Studies in Business Economics No. 92. New York, National Industrial Conference Board, 1966.

Bok, Derek C. "Section 7 of the Clayton Act and the Merging of Law and Economics," 74 *Harvard Law Review,* 226, 1960.

"Branch Banking—Restrictive State Laws and the Public Interest," 38 *Notre Dame Law Review* 315, 1963.

Bremer, C. D. American Bank Failures. New York, Columbia University Press, 1935.

Bryan, Alfred C. History of State Banking in Maryland. Baltimore, Johns Hopkins Press, 1899.

Burr, Anna R. The Portrait of a Banker: James Stillman. New York, Duffield and Company, 1927.

Business Concentration and Price Policy. Princeton, New Jersey, Princeton University Press, 1955.

Cannon, James G. Clearing Houses. New York, D. Appleton and Company, 1900.

Carson, Deane (ed.). Banking and Monetary Studies. Homewood, Illinois, Richard D. Irwin, Inc., 1963.

Cartinhour, Gaines T. Branch, Group and Chain Banking. New York, The Macmillan Company, 1931.

Catterall, Ralph C. H. The Second Bank of the United States. Chicago, The University of Chicago Press, 1903.

Celler, Emanuel. "The New Antimerger Statute: The Current Outlook," 37 *American Bar Association Journal* 897, 1951.

Chandler, Lester. "Monopolistic Elements in Commercial Banking," *Journal of Political Economy*, February 1938.

"Changes in Banking Structure," *Federal Reserve Bulletin*, September 1963.

Chapman, John M. Concentration of Banking. New York, Columbia University Press, 1934.

Chapman, John M., and Ray B. Westerfield. Branch Banking. New York, Harper and Brothers, 1942.

Cohen, Bruce C., and George G. Kaufman. "Factors Determining Bank Deposit Growth by State: An Empirical Analysis," *Journal of Finance*, March 1965.

Collins, Charles W. The Branch Banking Question. New York, The Macmillan Company, 1926.

———— Rural Banking Reform. New York, The Macmillan Company, 1931.

Collins, N. R., and L. E. Preston. "The Size Structure of the Largest Industrial Firms, 1909–1958," *American Economic Review*, December 1961.

"Comments on the Philadelphia-Girard Decision," *National Banking Review*, September 1963.

"Commercial Bank Competition for Savings," *American Bankers Association Journal*, October 1930.

Comptroller of the Currency. *Annual Reports*, 1st (1863) through 103d (1965).

———— Instructions and Suggestions Relative to the Organization and Management of National Banks, 1909.

———— Studies in Banking Competition and the Banking Structure, 1966.

Corey, Lewis. The House of Morgan. New York, G. Howard Watt, 1930.

"Correspondent Banking," *Monthly Review*, Federal Reserve Bank of Kansas City, March–April 1965.

Cox, Albert H., Jr. Regulation of Interest Rates on Bank Deposits. University of Michigan, Michigan Business Studies, 1966.

Coyle, William F. "Comments: Banks and Banking—A Century Long Conflict between National Banks and State Banks over Branch Banking," 8 *Villanova Law Review* 209, 1962–1963.

Crick, W. F., and J. E. Wadsworth. A Hundred Years of Joint Stock Banking. London, Hodder and Stoughton, 1936.

"Critical Problems Concerning Country Bankers," *The Analyst*, September 23, 1929.

Crosse, Howard D. "Banking Structure and Competition," *Journal of Finance*, May 1965.

———— Management Policies for Commercial Banks. Englewood Cliffs, New Jersey, Prentice-Hall, 1962.

Crowder, Walter. The Structure of American Industry. Temporary National Economic Committee Monograph 27, 1941.

Curtis, J. G. "The Turning Financial Worm," *The Nation,* April 23, 1930.

Darnell, Jerome C. "Chain Banking," *National Banking Review,* March 1966.

——— "Chain Bank Ownership and Operation," *National Banking Review,* December 1966.

Davis, Andrew M. The Origin of the National Banking System. National Monetary Commission, 1910.

Davis, Lance E., and Jonathan R. T. Hughes. American Economic History. Homewood, Illinois, Richard D. Irwin, 1965.

Dewey, Davis R. Financial History of the United States. New York, Longmans, Green and Company, 1911.

——— State Banking Before the Civil War. National Monetary Commission. Washington, Government Printing Office, 1910.

Dirlam, Joel B., and Alfred E. Kahn. Fair Competition: The Law and Economics of Antitrust Policy. Ithaca, New York, Cornell University Press, 1945.

Donaldson, Elvin F. Corporate Finance. New York, The Ronald Press Company, 1957.

Dorset, David C. "Bank Mergers and Holding Companies and the Public Interest," *Banking Law Journal,* September 1963.

Dunbar, Charles. "The Bank Note Question," *Quarterly Journal of Economics,* October 1892.

Eccles, Marriner. Beckoning Frontiers. New York, Alfred Knopf, 1951.

Eckardt, H. M. P. A Rational Banking System. New York, Harper and Brothers, 1911.

Edwards, Corwin. Big Business and the Policy of Competition. Cleveland, Cleveland Press of Western Reserve University, 1956.

Edwards, Franklin R. "The Banking Competition Controversy," *National Banking Review,* September 1965.

——— Concentration and Competition in Commercial Banking: A Statistical Study. Federal Reserve Bank of Boston, Research Report No. 29, 1964.

Eliason, Adolph O. The Rise of Commercial Banking in the United States. Minneapolis, The University of Minnesota Press, 1901.

Ellis, Charles D. "Antitrust, Bank Mergers, and the P.N.B. Decision," *Banking Law Journal,* April 1964.

Encyclopedia of Banking Laws. Boston, Banking Law Journal, 1964.

"Federal Bank Merger Policy and the Philadelphia National Bank Decision," 25 *University of Pittsburgh Law Review* 563, 1964.

Federal Deposit Insurance Corporation. *Annual Reports,* 1934–1966.

"Federal Regulation of Bank Mergers: The Opposing Views of the Federal Banking Agencies and the Department of Justice," 75 *Harvard Law Review* 756, 1962.

Federal Reserve Board. *Annual Reports,* 1st (1913) through 53rd (1966).

—— Bank Holding Company Act. Report of the Board of Governors of the Federal Reserve System Pursuant to the Bank Holding Company Act of 1956. Washington, Government Printing Office, 1958.

—— Banking Studies, 1941.

—— Committee on Branch, Chain, and Group Banking, "Committee Reports," 1933. (mimeographed)

—— Concentration of Banking in the United States. Report to the Subcommittee on Monopoly of the Select Committee on Small Business, U. S. Senate. Washington, Government Printing Office, 1952.

—— Financing Small Business. Report to the Committees on Banking and Currency and the Select Committees on Small Business, U. S. Congress. Washington, Government Printing Office, 1958.

—— Recent Developments in the Structure of Banking. Report to the Select Committee on Small Business, U. S. Senate. Washington, Government Printing Office, 1962.

Federal Trade Commission. The Merger Movement, A Summary Report. Washington, Government Printing Office, 1948.

Feige, Edgar L. The Demand for Liquid Assets, A Temporal Cross-Section Analysis. Englewood Cliffs, New Jersey, Prentice-Hall, 1964.

Fillmore, Millard. "The Banking System of New York," *Bankers Magazine,* June 1848.

"Financial Facts and Opinions," *Bankers Magazine,* January 1892.

Finkelstein, Michael O., and Richard M. Friedberg. "The Application of an Entropy Theory of Concentration to the Clayton Act," 76 *Yale Law Journal* 677, 1967.

Finney, Katherine. Interbank Deposits, the Purpose and Effects of Domestic Balances, 1934–1954. New York, Columbia University Press, 1961.

Fischer, Gerald C. Bank Holding Companies. New York, Columbia University Press, 1961.

—— *"U. S. v. M & I Bank Stock Corporation," Banking Law Journal,* September 1965.

Flechsig, Theodore G. Banking Market Structure and Performance in Metropolitan Areas, A Statistical Study of Factors Affecting Rates on Bank Loans. Washington, Board of Governors of the Federal Reserve System, 1965.

Funk, Carl W. "Antitrust Legislation Affecting Bank Mergers," *Banking Law Journal,* May 1958.

Galbraith, John A. The Economics of Banking Operations: A Canadian Study. Montreal, McGill University Press, 1963.

Galbraith, John K. American Capitalism. Boston, Houghton Mifflin, 1952.

Gilbart, James W. The History of Banking in America. London, Longman, 1837.

Goldsmith, Raymond W. Financial Intermediaries in the American Economy since 1900. Princeton, New Jersey, Princeton University Press, 1958.

Golembe, Carter. "The Deposit Insurance Legislation of 1933," Political Science Quarterly, June 1960.

"Government Regulation of Bank Mergers: The Revolving Door of the Philadelphia Bank." 62 Michigan Law Review 990, 1964.

Gramley, Lyle E. A Study of Scale Economies in Banking. Federal Reserve Bank of Kansas City, 1962.

Gray, H. Peter. "Some Evidence on Two Implications of Higher Interest Rates on Time Deposits," Journal of Finance, March 1964.

Greenbaum, Stuart I. "Banking Structure and Costs: A Statistical Study of the Cost-Output Relationship in Commercial Banking." Unpublished doctoral dissertation, Johns Hopkins University, 1964.

———— "Costs and Production in Commercial Banking," Monthly Review, Federal Reserve Bank of Kansas City, March–April 1966.

Gresham, Otto. The Greenbacks. Chicago, Book Press, Inc., 1927.

Guttentag, Jack M., and Edward S. Herman. Banking Structure and Performance. Bulletin No. 41–43. New York, Institute of Finance, Graduate School of Business, New York University, 1967.

———— "Do Large Banks Neglect Small Business?" Journal of Finance, September 1966.

Hackley, Howard H. "Our Baffling Banking System," 52 Virginia Law Review 565, 1966.

Hald, Earl C. Business Cycles. New York, Houghton Mifflin Company, 1954.

Hale, G. E., and Rosemary Hale. "Mergers in Regulated Industries," 59 Northwestern University Law Review 49, 1964.

Hales, Charles A. The Baltimore Clearing House. Baltimore, The Johns Hopkins Press, 1940.

Hall, George R. "Bank Holding Company Regulation," Southern Economic Journal, April 1965.

Hall, George R., and Charles F. Phillips, Jr. "Antimerger Criteria: Power, Concentration, Foreclosure, and Size," 9 Villanova Law Review 211, 1964.

———— Bank Mergers and the Regulatory Agencies. Board of Governors of the Federal Reserve System, 1964.

Handler, Milton. "Atonality and Abstraction in Modern Antitrust Law," 52 American Bar Association Journal, 621, 1966.

Handler, Milton. "Polarities of Antitrust," 60 *Northwestern University Law Review* 751, 1966.

―――― "Recent Antitrust Developments," 112 *University of Pennsylvania Law Review* 159, 1963.

Hanson, J. J., and J. O. von Kalinowski. "Status of State Antitrust Laws with Federal Analysis," 15 *Western Reserve Law Review* 9, 1963.

Hartsough, Mildred L. The Twin Cities as a Metropolitan Market. Minneapolis, University of Minnesota Press, 1925.

Hayes, F. W. "A Plan for Bank Consolidation," *Banking Law Journal,* July 15, 1892.

Helderman, Leonard C. National and State Banks: A Study of Their Origins. New York, Houghton Mifflin Company, 1931.

Herman, Edward S. "Board of Governors v. Transamerica: Victory Out of Defeat," *Antitrust Bulletin,* July–August 1959.

Hershkowitz, Leo. "The Locofoco Party of New York," *New York Historical Society Quarterly,* 1962.

Historical Statistics of the United States, Colonial Times to 1957. Department of Commerce. Washington, Government Printing Office, 1960.

Historical Statistics of the United States, 1789–1945. Department of Commerce. Washington, Government Printing Office, 1949.

Hodgman, Donald R. Commercial Bank Loan and Investment Policy. Champaign, Illinois, University of Illinois Press, 1963.

"The Holding Company in Banking," *American Bankers Association Journal,* October 1927.

Holdsworth, John T., and Davis R. Dewey. The First and Second Banks of the United States. National Monetary Commission. Washington, Government Printing Office, 1910.

Holland, Robert C. "Research Into Banking Structure and Competition," *Federal Reserve Bulletin,* November 1964.

Horvitz, Paul M. Concentration and Competition in New England Banking. Federal Reserve Bank of Boston, Research Report No. 2, 1958.

―――― "Stimulating Bank Competition through Regulatory Action," *Journal of Finance,* March 1965.

Horvitz, Paul M., and Bernard Shull. "The Impact of Branch Banking and Bank Performance," *National Banking Review,* December 1964.

Hugon, James H. "Federal Regulation of Bank Holding Companies." Unpublished doctoral dissertation, University of Washington, 1964.

Iinkai, Kosei Torihiki. Antitrust Legislation of the World as of 1960. Tokyo, Eibun-Horei-Sha, 1960.

Independent Banking: An American Ideal. Sauk Center, Minnesota, Independent Bankers Association, 1965.

"Investment Affiliates Thrive," *American Bankers Association Journal,* May 1930.

Isbell, Wilbur H. "Management Succession in Smaller Banks." Unpublished thesis, The Graduate School of Banking, Rutgers University, 1956.

Jacobs, Donald. "The Framework of Commercial Bank Regulation: An Appraisal," *National Banking Review*, March 1964.

——— "The Interaction Effects of Restrictions on Branching and Other Bank Regulations," *Journal of Finance*, May 1965.

Jacobs, Donald, and Eugene Lerner. "Chicago Banking: A Critical Review," *Journal of Business*, October 1962.

Jaffe, Louis. "Primary Jurisdiction Reconsidered: The Antitrust Laws," 102 *University of Pennsylvania Law Review* 577, 1954.

James, F. Cyril. The Growth of the Chicago Banks. New York, Harper and Brothers, 1938.

James, Marquis, and Bessie James. Biography of a Bank. New York, Harper and Brothers, 1954.

Johnson, Harry L. "Commercial Bank Markets: A Case Study," *Business and Government Review*, University of Missouri, July–August 1966.

Jollie, Rose Marie. On the Grow with Cleveland. Cleveland, Central National Bank, 1965.

"Judicial Invalidation of Federal Reserve Policy against Bank Holding Company Expansion," 57 *Yale Law Journal* 297 (1947).

Kane, Thomas P. The Romance and Tragedy of Banking. New York, The Bankers Publishing Company, 1922.

Kaufman, George G. "Bank Market Structure and Performance: The Evidence from Iowa," *Southern Economic Journal*, April 1966.

Kaysen, Carl, and Donald F. Turner. Antitrust Policy: An Economic and Legal Analysis. Cambridge, Massachusetts, Harvard University Press, 1959.

Kefauver, Estes. "Affront to Free Enterprise," *The Independent Banker*, March 1963.

Kent, Raymond P. Money and Banking. New York, Rinehart and Company, 1956.

Kettering, Charles F., and Allen Orth. The New Necessity. Baltimore, Williams and Wilkins, 1932.

Kintner, Earl W. An Antitrust Primer. New York, The Macmillan Company, 1964.

Klebaner, Benjamin J. "Bank Mergers, Business Loans, and the Structure of Banking Markets," *The American Journal of Economics and Sociology*, October 1963.

——— "Federal Control of Commercial Bank Mergers," 37 *Indiana Law Journal* 287, 1962.

Knox, John Jay. A History of Banking in the United States. New York, Bradford Rhodes and Company, 1900.

Kohn, Ernest. Branch Banking, Bank Mergers and the Public Interest. New York State Banking Department, 1964.

Kohn, Ernest. The Future of Small Banks. New York State Banking Department, December 1966.

Laibly, C. T. "Supervisory Control of Commercial Banks." Unpublished thesis, The Graduate School of Banking, Rutgers University, 1946.

Lamb, W. Ralph. Group Banking. New Brunswick, New Jersey, Rutgers University Press, 1962.

Lanzillotti, Robert F. Banking Structure in Michigan, 1945–1963. East Lansing, Michigan State University Bureau of Business Research, 1966.

Laudadio, Leonard. "Size of Bank, Size of Borrower, and the Rate of Interest," *Journal of Finance,* March 1963.

Lawrence, Robert J. The Performance of Bank Holding Companies. Washington: Board of Governors of the Federal Reserve System, 1967.

Lewis, Lawrence. A History of the Bank of North America. Philadelphia, J. B. Lippincott, 1882.

Lewyn, Thomas M., and Stephen Mann. "Some Thoughts on Policy and Enforcement of Section 7," 50 *American Bar Association Journal* 154, 1964.

Lifland, William T. "Banking and the Antitrust Laws," *Harvard Business Review,* May–June 1967.

——— "Day-to-Day Banking Practices under the Antitrust Laws," *Bankers Magazine,* Summer 1964.

Lightner, Otto C. The History of Business Depressions. New York, Northeastern Press, 1922.

Linke, Charles M. "Interest Rate Regulation on Commercial Bank Deposits: Its Evolution and Impact in the State of Indiana." Unpublished doctoral dissertation, Indiana University, 1965.

——— "The Evolution of Interest Rate Regulation on Commercial Bank Deposits in the United States," *The National Banking Review,* June 1966.

Lombard, Richard S. "Corporate Management Interlocks Bill," *Business Lawyer,* July 1966.

McCulloch, Hugh. "The National Banking Law of 1863," *Bankers Magazine,* July 1863.

Markham, Jesse. "Merger Policy Under the New Section 7," 43 *Virginia Law Review,* 489, 491–92, 1957.

Martin, David D. "The Brown Shoe Case and the New Antimerger Policy," *American Economic Review,* June 1963.

——— Mergers and the Clayton Act. Los Angeles, University of California Press, 1959.

Massel, Mark S. Competition and Monopoly: Legal and Economic Issues. Washington, Brookings Institution, 1962.

Meyer, Paul A. "Price Discrimination, Regional Loan Rates, and the Structure of the Banking Industry," *Journal of Finance,* March 1967.

Miller, Harry E. Banking Theories in the United States before 1860. Cambridge, Massachusetts, Harvard University Press, 1927.

Mitchell, Mary T. "New Yardsticks in Measuring Bank Competition for Demand Deposits," *Bankers Magazine,* Summer 1966.

Money and Credit—Their Influence on Jobs, Prices, and Growth. Englewood Cliffs, New Jersey, Prentice-Hall, 1961. (CMC Report)

"More on Correspondent Banking," *Monthly Review,* Federal Reserve Bank of Kansas City, July–August, 1965.

Morison, Samuel E., and Henry S. Commager. The Growth of the American Republic. New York, Oxford University Press, 1942.

Mote, Larry R. "Competition in Banking: The Issues," *Business Conditions,* Federal Reserve Bank of Chicago, January 1967.

———— "Competition in Banking: What is Known? What is the Evidence?" *Business Conditions,* Federal Reserve Bank of Chicago, February 1967.

Motter, David C. "Bank Formation and the Public Interest," *National Banking Review,* March 1965.

Motter, David, and Deane Carson. "Bank Entry and the Public Interest: A Case Study," *National Banking Review,* June 1964.

Mussey, Henry R. (ed.). Reform of the Currency. New York, Academy of Political Science, Columbia University, 1911.

Nadler, Marcus, and Jules Bogen. The Bank Holding Company. New York, Graduate School of Business, New York University, 1959.

Nadler, Paul. "The Coming Change in Correspondent Relationships," *Banking,* April 1966.

National Association of Supervisors of State Banks. Report of the Committee to Evaluate Responses to a Survey of State Banker Opinion made by the Association. Washington, NASSB, 1963. (NASSB 1963 Report)

National Banks and the Future. Report of the Advisory Committee on Banking to the Comptroller of the Currency. 1962. (Saxon Report)

Neal, Phil C. "The Clayton Act and the Transamerica Case," 5 *Stanford Law Review* 179, 1953.

Neale, A. D. The Antitrust Laws of the United States of America. Cambridge, England, Cambridge University Press, 1960.

Nelson, Ralph L. Merger Movements in American Industry, 1895–1956. Princeton, New Jersey, Princeton University Press, 1959.

"The 1966 Amendment to the Bank Merger Act," *The Banking Law Journal,* September 1966.

Noyes, Alexander. Forty Years of American Finance. New York, G. P. Putnam's Sons, 1909.

Nussbaum, Arthur. A History of the Dollar. New York, Columbia University Press, 1957.

O'Connor, J. F. T. The Banking Crisis and Recovery under the Roosevelt Administration. Chicago, Callaghan and Company, 1938.

"Official Bulletin of New National Banks," *Bankers Magazine,* August 1877.

Oppenheim, S. Chesterfield. "Antitrust Booms and Boomerangs," *59 Northwestern University Law Review* 33, 1964.

Palyi, Melchior. The Chicago Credit Market. Chicago, University of Chicago Press, 1937.

"The Patman Report," *Bank Stock Quarterly,* M. A. Schapiro and Company, Inc., March 1963.

Peach, W. Nelson. The Security Affiliates of National Banks. Baltimore, The Johns Hopkins Press, 1941.

Pegrum, Dudley F. Public Regulation of Business. Homewood, Illinois, Richard D. Irwin, 1965.

Peltzman, Sam. "Entry in Commercial Banking." Unpublished doctoral dissertation, The University of Chicago, 1965.

Pennsylvania Banking Law Commission. Commission's Statement of Issues and Reports of Commission's Economic Consultants, January 1967.

Peterson, J. Marvin, and D. R. Cawthorne. Money and Banking. New York, The Macmillan Company, 1949.

"Petrol Solus Agreements: British Common Law of Restraint of Trade in a New Context," *52 Virginia Law Review* 690 (1966).

Phillips, Almarin. "Competition, Confusion and Commercial Banking," *Journal of Finance,* March 1964.

——— "Evidence on Concentration in Banking Markets and Interest Rates," *Federal Reserve Bulletin,* June 1967.

——— (ed.). Perspectives on Antitrust Policy. Princeton, New Jersey, Princeton University Press, 1965.

Phillips, Charles F., Jr. The Economics of Regulation. Homewood, Illinois, Richard D. Irwin, 1965.

Pontecorvo, Giulio. "Patterns of Ownership of Commercial Banks," *Bankers Magazine,* Winter 1966.

Popple, Charles S. Development of Two Group Banks in the Northwest. Cambridge, Massachusetts, Harvard University Press, 1944.

Private Capital Markets. Englewood Cliffs, New Jersey, Prentice-Hall, 1964.

Private Financial Institutions. Englewood Cliffs, New Jersey, Prentice-Hall, 1963.

Readings in the Social Control of Industry. Philadelphia, The Blakiston Company, 1949.

"Recent Bank Failures—Why," *Monthly Review,* Federal Reserve Bank of Richmond, September 1965.

"Recent Decisions," *1964 University of Illinois Law Forum* 667.

"Regional Clearing House Associations," in Commercial Bank Management. New York, Bank Management Commission, American Bankers Association, 1931.

"Regulated Industries and the Antitrust Laws," *58 Columbia Law Review* 673, 1958.

The Report of the Attorney General's National Committee to Study the Antitrust Laws. Washington, Government Printing Office, 1955.

Report of the Committee on Financial Institutions to the President of the United States, April 1963. (Heller Report)

Report of the Monetary Commission of the Indianapolis Convention. Chicago, University of Chicago Press, 1898.

Robb, Thomas B. The Guaranty of Bank Deposits. New York, Houghton Mifflin, 1921.

Rostow, Eugene V. "British and American Experience with Legislation Against Restraints of Competition," 23 *Modern Law Review* 477, 1960.

"Saxon versus the Status Quo," *Bank Stock Quarterly*, M. A. Schapiro and Company, Inc., June 1963.

Schlesinger, Anthony D. "Merger Litigation under the Sherman Act— Choice or Echo," 18 *Southwestern Law Journal* 712, 1964.

Schweiger, Irving, and John S. McGee. "Chicago Banking," *Journal of Business*, University of Chicago, July 1961.

Scott, Ira, Jr. "Correspondent Banking in the USA," *The Banker*, August 1965.

"Section 7 of the Clayton Act: A Legislative History," 52 *Columbia Law Review* 766, 1952.

Shull, Bernard. "Commercial Banking as a Line of Commerce," *National Banking Review*, December 1963.

—— "Competition in Banking: A New Old Problem," *Business Review*, Federal Reserve Bank of Philadelphia, January 1963.

Shull, Bernard, and Paul Horvitz, "Branch Banking and the Structure of Competition," *National Banking Review*, March 1964.

Siegel, Sidney. Nonparametric Statistics. New York, McGraw-Hill, 1956.

Smith, James G. Trust Companies in the United States. New York, Henry Holt, 1928.

Smith, Tynan. "Research on Banking Structure and Performance," *Federal Reserve Bulletin*, April 1966.

Smith, William Paul. "Measures of Banking Structure and Competition," *Federal Reserve Bulletin*, September 1965.

Sobel, Gerald. "The Applicability of the Antitrust Laws to Combinations Approved under the Bank Merger Act, Federal Power Act, and Natural Gas Act," 37 *New York University Law Review* 735, 1962.

Southworth, Shirley D. Branch Banking in the United States. New York, McGraw-Hill Book Company, 1928.

Spahr, Walter E. The Clearing and Collection of Checks. New York, The Bankers Publishing Company, 1926.

Spaulding, Elbridge. History of the Legal Tender Paper Money. Buffalo, Express Printing Company, 1869. Extra Sheets from Spaulding's History were published separately in 1875.

Sprague, O. M. W. History of Crises Under the National Banking System. National Monetary Commission, 1910.

Starnes, George T. Sixty Years of Branch Banking in Virginia. New York, The Macmillan Company, 1931.

"Status of Group, Chain, and Branch Banking in the United States," American Bankers Association Journal, July 1930.

Stigler, George J. "Mergers and Preventative Antitrust Policy," 104 University of Pennsylvania Law Review 176, 1955.

Stokes, Edwin. "Public Convenience and Advantage in Applications for New Banks," Banking Law Journal, November 1957.

Stokes, John M. "A Few Irreverent Comments about Antitrust, Agency Regulation, and Primary Jurisdiction," 33 George Washington Law Review 529, 1964.

Stonier, Alfred W., and Douglas C. Hague. A Textbook of Economic Theory. New York, John Wiley and Sons, 1964.

"Summary of Discussion: Conference on Bank Markets and Competition," Federal Reserve Bank of Chicago, October 21, 1965. (mimeographed)

Sumner, William. A History of Banking in the United States. Vol. I of A History of Banking in All Leading Nations. New York, The Journal of Commerce and Commercial Bulletin, 1896.

"Thaw on Bank Holding Companies," Bank Stock Quarterly, M. A. Schapiro and Company, June 1965.

Thiemann, Charles L. "The Bank Merger Act of 1960." Unpublished doctoral dissertation, Indiana University, 1964.

Thomas, R. G. "Concentration in Banking Controls through Interlocking Directorates as Typified by Chicago Banks," Journal of Business, January 1933.

Thorp, Willard L., and Walter Crowder. The Structure of American Industry. Temporary National Economic Committee Monograph 27, 1941.

Toulmin, Harry A., Jr. A Treatise on the Antitrust Laws of the United States. Cincinatti, W. H. Anderson, 1950.

Trade Cases, New York, Commerce Clearing House, Inc., 1950–1967.

"Transamerica—The Bank Holding Company Problem," 1 Stanford Law Review 658, 1949.

Trant, James B. Bank Administration. New York, McGraw-Hill, 1931.

Trescott, Paul B. Financing American Enterprise. New York, Harper and Row, 1963.

The Triple Banking System. New York, M. A. Schapiro and Company, 1956.

Turner, Donald F. "Conglomerate Mergers and Section 7 of the Clayton Act," 78 Harvard Law Review 1313, 1965.

U. S. Congress,[2] House, Strengthening the Public Credit, 55th Cong., 2d Sess., 1898, Report No. 1575, Part I.

────── House, To Secure to the People a Sound Currency, 55th Cong., 2d Sess., Report No. 1575, Part II.

────── House, Committee on Banking and Currency, Report of the Committee Appointed Pursuant to House Resolutions 429 and 504 to Investigate the Concentration of Control of Money and Credit, 62d Cong., 3rd Sess., 1913. (Pujo Committee Report)

────── Senate, Hearings, on S. 1782 and H. R. 2, Consolidation of National Banking Associations, 69th Cong., 1st Sess., 1926.

────── House, Committee on Banking and Currency, Hearings, on H. Res. 141, Branch, Chain and Group Banking, 71st Cong., 2d Sess., 1930. (House Hearings, 1930)

────── Senate, Committee on Banking and Currency, Hearings, on S. Res. 71, Operation of the National and Federal Reserve Banking Systems, 71st Cong., 3rd Sess., 1931.

────── Senate, Operations of the National and Federal Reserve Banking Systems, 72d Cong., 1st Sess., 1932, Report No. 584.

──────House, Committee on the Judiciary, Hearings, on H. R. 2357, To Amend Sections 7 and 11 of the Clayton Act, 79th Cong., 1st Sess., 1945.

──────Senate, Committee on Banking and Currency, Hearings, on S. 2318, Bank Holding Bill, 81st Cong., 2d Sess., 1950.

──────House, Antitrust Subcommittee of the Committee on the Judiciary, Bank Mergers and Concentration of Banking Facilities, 82d Cong. 2d Sess., 1952.

──────Senate, Joint Committee on the Economic Report, Monetary Policy and the Management of the Public Debt, 82d Cong., 2d Sess., 1952.

──────House, Antitrust Subcommittee of the Committee on the Judiciary, Hearings, Bank Mergers, 84th Cong., 1st Sess., 1955.

──────House, Committee on the Judiciary, Amending an Act Approved October 15, 1914, 84th Cong., 1st Sess., 1955, House Report No. 1417 to accompany H. R. 5948.

──────Senate, Select Committee on Small Business, Hearings, Report of the Attorney General's National Committee to Study the Antitrust Laws, 84th Cong., 1st Sess., 1955.

──────Senate, Committee on the Judiciary, Mergers and Price Discrimination, 84th Cong., 2d Sess., 1956, Senate Report to accompany H. R. 9424.

──────Senate, Subcommittee on Antitrust and Monopoly of the Commit-

[2] Publications of the United States Congress are listed in chronological order. If a very abbreviated title is used in the text (for example, House Hearings, 1930), it follows the full citation.

tee on the Judiciary, Legislation Affecting Corporate Mergers, 84th Cong., 2d Sess., 1956.

U. S. Congress, Senate, Subcommittee on Banking of the Committee on Banking and Currency, Hearings, on S. 3911, Regulation of Bank Mergers, 84th Cong., 2d Sess., 1956.

————House, Committee on Banking and Currency, Hearings, on S. 1451 and H. R. 7026, Financial Institutions Act of 1957, 85th Cong., 1st Sess., 1957.

————Senate, Subcommittee on Banking of the Committee on Banking and Currency, Hearings, on S. 1451, Financial Institutions Act of 1957, 85th Cong. 1st Sess., 1957.

————Senate, Subcommittee on Antitrust and Monopoly of the Committee on the Judiciary, Hearings, Legislation Affecting Sections 7, 11, and 15 of the Clayton Act, 85th Cong., 2d Sess., 1958.

————Joint Economic Committee, Hearings, Employment, Growth, and Price Levels, 86th Cong., 1st Sess., 1959.

————Senate, Committee on Banking and Currency, Hearings, on S. 1062, Regulation of Bank Mergers, 86th Cong., 1st Sess., 1959.

————Senate, Committee on Banking and Currency, Regulation of Bank Mergers, 86th Cong., 1st Sess., 1959, Report No. 196.

————House, Committee on Banking and Currency, Regulation of Bank Mergers, 86th Cong., 2d Sess., 1960, Report No. 1416.

————House, Select Committee on Small Business, Banking Concentration and Small Business, 86th Cong., 2d Sess., 1960, Staff Report Committee Print.

————House, Subcommittee No. 2 of the Committee on Banking and Currency, Hearings, Regulation of Bank Mergers, 86th Cong., 2d Sess., 1960.

————House, Select Committee on Small Business, Mergers and Superconcentration, 87th Cong., 2d Sess., 1962, Staff Report.

————House, Committee on Banking and Currency, Hearings, Meetings with Department and Agency Officials and Trade Organizations, 88th Cong., 1st Sess., 1963.

————House, Committee on Banking and Currency, Hearings, Conflict of Federal and State Banking Laws, 88th Cong., 1st Sess., 1963.

————House, Select Committee on Small Business, Chain Banking: Stockholders and Loan Links of 200 Largest Member Banks, 88th Cong., 1st Sess., 1963. (Patman's *Chain Banking Report*)

————Senate, Committee on Banking and Currency, Federal Banking Laws and Reports, 88th Cong., 1st Sess., 1963.

————Senate, Subcommittee on Antitrust and Monopoly of the Committee on the Judiciary, Administered Prices: A Compendium on Public Policy, 88th Cong., 1st Sess., 1963.

————House, Committee on Banking and Currency, Correspondent Relations: A Survey of Banker Opinion, 88th Cong., 2d Sess., 1964.

U. S. Congress, House, Committee on Banking and Currency, Hearings, on H. R. 10668 and H. R. 10872, Bank Holding Company Legislation, 88th Cong., 2d Sess., 1964.

———House, Committee on Banking and Currency, The Market for Bank Stock, 88th Cong., 2d Sess., 1964.

———House, Committee on Banking and Currency, A Report on the Correspondent Banking System, 88th Cong., 2d Sess., 1964.

———House, Committee on Banking and Currency, The Structure of Ownership of Member Banks and the Pattern of Loans Made on Hypothecated Bank Stock, 88th Cong., 2d Sess., 1964, Staff Analysis to the Subcommittee on Domestic Finance.

———House, Committee on Banking and Currency, Twenty Largest Stockholders of Record in Member Banks of the Federal Reserve System, 88th Cong., 2d Sess., 1964.

———House, Committee on Government Operations, Crimes Against Banking Institutions, 88th Cong., 2d Sess., 1964, Report No. 1147.

———House, Hearings, on H. R. 12267 and H. R. 12268, Notice of Change in Control of Management of Insured Banks, 88th Cong., 2d Sess., 1964.

———House, Subcommittee on Domestic Finance of the Committee on Banking and Currency, A Report on the Correspondent Banking System, 88th Cong., 2d Sess., 1964.

———House, Subcommittee on Domestic Finance of the Committee on Banking and Currency, A Study of Selected Banking Services by Bank Size, Structure, and Location, 88th Cong., 2d Sess., 1964.

———Senate, Subcommittee on Antitrust and Monopoly of the Committee of the Judiciary, Hearings, on S. Res. 262, Economic Concentration, 88th Cong., 2d Sess., 1964–1965.

———House, Committee on Banking and Currency, Hearings, on H. R. 7371, To Amend the Bank Holding Company Act, 89th Cong., 1st Sess., 1965.

———House, Committee on Banking and Currency, Hearings, on H. R. 7372, Amending the Bank Holding Company Act with Respect to Registered Investment Companies, 89th Cong., 1st Sess., 1965.

———House, Committee on the Judiciary, Interlocks in Corporate Management, 89th Cong., 1st Sess., 1965, A Staff Report to the Antitrust Subcommittee.

———House, Subcommittee on Domestic Finance of the Committee on Banking and Currency, Hearings, To Amend the Bank Merger Act, 89th Cong., 1st Sess., 1965. 4 Vols.

———Senate, Committee on Banking and Currency, Amendments to the Bank Holding Company Act of 1956, 89th Cong., 1st Sess., 1965, Analyses of S. 2353, S. 2418 and H. R. 7371.

———Senate, Permanent Subcommittee on Investigations of the Committee on Government Operations, Hearings, Investigation into Federally Insured Banks, 89th Cong., 1st Sess., 1965.

U. S. Congress, Senate, Subcommittee on Antitrust and Monopoly of the Committee on the Judiciary, Hearings, Economic Concentration, 89th Cong., 1st Sess., 1965.

————Senate, Subcommittee on Antitrust and Monopoly of the Committee on the Judiciary, Hearings, Foreign Trade and the Antitrust Laws, 89th Cong., 1st Sess., 1965.

————Senate, Subcommittee of the Committee on Banking and Currency, Hearings on S. 1698, Amend the Bank Merger Act of 1960, 89th Cong., 1st Sess., 1965.

————House, Bank Merger Act Amendment, 89th Cong., 2d Sess., 1966, Report No. 1221.

————House, Committee on Banking and Currency, Bank Stock Ownership and Control, 89th Cong., 2d Sess., 1966, Staff Report.

————Senate, Committee on Banking and Currency, Amendments to the Bank Holding Company Act of 1956 (Lists of Bank Holding Companies and of Organizations that Would Apparently be Covered by the Bank Holding Company Act Incorporated in S. 2353), 89th Cong., 2d Sess., 1966.

————Senate, Committee on Banking and Currency, Hearings, on S. 2353, S. 2418, and H. R. 7371, Amend the Bank Holding Company Act of 1956, 89th Cong., 2d Sess., 1966.

————Senate, Subcommittee on Investigations of the Committee on Government Operations, Investigation into Federally Insured Banks, 89th Cong., 2d Sess., Report No. 1103, 1966.

————House, Committee on Banking and Currency, Hearings, Meetings with Department and Agency Officials, 90th Cong., 1st Sess., 1967.

———— House, Staff Analysis for the Subcommittee on Domestic Finance of the Committee on Banking and Currency, Acquisitions, Changes in Control, and Bank Stock Loans of Insured Banks, 90th Cong., 1st Sess., 1967.

Van Horne, James C., and Raymond C. Helwig. The Valuation of Small Bank Stocks. East Lansing, Michigan, Graduate School of Business, Michigan State University, 1966.

von Kalinowski, Julian. "The Per Se Doctrine—An Emerging Philosophy of Antitrust Law," 11 U. C. L. A. Law Review 569, 1964.

Waller, Leslie. "Our Unique Correspondent Banking System," Banking, August 1961.

Watkins, Leonard L. Bankers Balances. Chicago, A. W. Shaw and Company, 1929.

———— Commercial Banking Reform in the United States. Ann Arbor, Michigan, University of Michigan, 1938.

Welldon, Samuel A. Digest of State Banking Statutes. National Monetary Commission, 1910.

Wemple, William, and Kenneth Cutler. "The Federal Bank Merger Law and the Antitrust Laws," *Banking Law Journal*, June 1962.

Wernette, John P. Government and Business. New York, The Macmillan Company, 1964.

Weston, J. Fred. The Role of Mergers in the Growth of Large Firms. Berkeley, University of California Press, 1961.

White, Horace. Money and Banking. Boston, Ginn and Company, 1902.

Wilburn, Jean A. Biddle's Bank: The Crucial Years. New York, Columbia University Press, 1967.

Williams, Larry. "Banking and the Antitrust Laws," *Banking Law Journal*, May 1964.

———"Some Significant Recent Developments in Antitrust Law," *Corporate Practice Commentator*, February 1966.

Willis, H. Parker. "The Demand for Centralized Banking," *Sound Currency*, March 1902.

———Report of an Inquiry into Contemporary Banking in the United States. An unpublished study prepared under the direction of H. Parker Willis. Vols. V and VI, 1925. (On file in the Graduate School of Business Library, Columbia University)

# INDEX

Acquisitions, bank, *see* Mergers, bank

*Acquisitions, Changes in Control, and Bank Stock Loans of Insured Banks,* 94n

Act of 1864, *see* National Bank Act (1864)

Advisory Committee on Banking to the Comptroller of the Currency (1962), *see* Saxon Report (1962)

Affiliate banking, 83

"Agreement" corporation, 110n

Agricultural land values: in 1920s, 199

Alhadeff, David, 254, 371

Allen, Frederick Lewis: quoted, 37

*Amend the Bank Merger Act* (1960) hearings, 141

American Bankers Association (ABA), 2, 6; branch banking discussion (1903–1916), 43; resolution (1930), 49; study of bank chartering, 198; study of state bank supervision, 214; survey of deposit interest rates, 251

American Bankers Association General Counsel: opinions on clearinghouse agreements, 251–53, 262

American Bar Association, 156

American Smelting and Refining Company, 124

American Tobacco Company, 124

Anaconda Copper, 124

Antitrust concept, 239, 243

Antitrust laws: in England and Germany, 238–39; flexibility of, and diversity of interpretations, 239; assumptions of banking immunity from, 239 ff.; state statutes, 243; per se violations, 256; bank cases, 256–63, 301–10, 302T; applicability to banks, 276 ff., 377; Bank Merger Act (1960) and, 286–310, 302T; 1966 Amendments, 310–26, 380; in relation to future commercial banking developments, 389–91

Antitrust policy: formulation of, 245; court interpretations, 245, 356–60; market concept as element in merger antitrust litigation, 333 ff.; "submarket" approach, 336; product market and geographic market tests, 337; in conglomerate mergers, 350–56; the economist's viewpoint, 360–68

*Argument in Favor of the Organization of a Financial Corporation and Union of Banks, An,* 76

Arkansas: limited-service offices in, 56

Asset acquisitions, bank, 150, 151, 154, 155, 156; applicability of Sec. 7 of Clayton Act to, 297–301; *see also* Mergers, bank

Association of Registered Bank Holding Companies, 107

Atomistic competition, *see* Competition, pure

413

Automobile transportation: effect on intracity branching, 34

Bain, Joe S.: quoted, 234, 347, 365, 367–68
Baker, George F., 77, 78
Bancitaly Corporation, 79
*Bank Administration* (Trant), 254
Bank failures and suspensions, 64; in the twentieth century: 67, 96; 1921–1935, 198–203, 204T; 1921–1966, 210; 1934–1966, 223–28, 225T; correlation with mergers, 128; before 1838, 175; in free banking era, 181; Panic of 1907, 186 ff.; in 1890s, 192; rural banks, 200 ff.; statistical summary, 203; changes in underlying causes, 226 ff.; effect on bank chartering, 229–30
Bank holding companies, 50; definitions, 72–73, 105; formation of, in Northwest, 76; statistics, 80; contributing factors to development of, 95; correlation with restrictions on branch banking, 96, 102; growth (1930–1966), 96–99, 97T; fifteen leading groups, 98n; operations, 99–101; loans and interest rate policies, 100–01; bank acquisitions, 134 ff., 168–73, 169T; *Transamerica case*, 241–42, 278–82; merger cases under antitrust laws, 278 ff.; *Firstamerica case*, 283 ff., 309; applicability of Sec. 7 of Clayton Act, 288; summary of antitrust cases, 301–10, 302T
Bank Holding Company Act (1956), 82, 84, 99; definition of chain banking based on, 91; purpose and provisions, 104–07, 143–49, 147T, 149T; revision, through amendment to Small Business Investment Act

(1958), 105; 1966 amendments, 106–07, 164, 308, 318–19, 337, 341, 349; applicability of antitrust laws under, 296
Bank Holding Company Act (New York State), 110n
Bank holiday (1933), 202
Bank Merger Act (1960), 123; origin and proposed legislation, 149–58; provisions, 158–59; administration of, 159–62, 162T, 163T; disputes between Justice Department and supervisory agencies, 164; 1966 amendments, 164, 308, 310–18, 337, 341, 349; applicability of Sec. 7 of Clayton Act under, 242, 295–97; antitrust law and, 286 ff.; background of merger controversy, 286–88
"Bank Mergers and the Concentration of Banking Facilities" (Judiciary Committee Report), 150
Bank of Albany (1792), 15
Bank of America (Los Angeles), 79
Bank of America N. T. & S. A., 99, 282, 284
Bank of Ben Lomond (Utah), *see Utah case* (1964–1965)
Bank of California National Association, The, 64n
Bank of Indiana: as branch bank, 16, 74
Bank of Iowa: as branch bank, 16, 74
Bank of Italy (California), 79
Bank of Massachusetts (1784), 9, 15
Bank of Missouri: as branch bank, 16
Bank of New York (1784), 9, 15
Bank of North America (1781), 9, 10

Bank of Ohio: as branch bank, 16, 74

Bank of Pennsylvania (1780), 9n

Bank of Pennsylvania (1793), 15

Bank of Providence (1791), 15

Bank of South Carolina (1792), 15

Bank of the United States (First), 11, 74

Bank of the United States (Second), 11 ff., 74

Bank of the United States (Third): bill vetoed by Tyler, 14–15

Bank of Utah (Ogden), see Utah case (1964–1965)

Bank Stock Ownership and Control, 90n

Bank Stock Quarterly (periodical), 86–87

Bankers' balances, 117 ff., 187, 248

Banking Act (1933), 23, 39, 51, 53, 82, 96; regulation of bank holding companies, 102–04, 106; establishment of FDIC, 202; deposit interest provisions, 250

Banking Act (1935), 52, 96; bank chartering provisions, 203–10; new banks and branches, 212T; deposit interest provisions, 250; interlocking directorate provisions, 268–69

Banking industry, 177; expansion and regulation of, 220, 222, 232 ff.; condition of entry, 230 ff., 234; correlation between number of new banks formed and bank failures, 232; federal antitrust cases, 256–63; applicability of antitrust laws in mergers, 276 ff.; Supreme Court opinions on, 293, 294, 340; markets of, 328 ff.; market shares of large banks, 330–33; definition of

wholesale and retail banking in relation to geographic market, 344, 345; as a service industry, 377 ff.

Banking offices, commercial: changing patterns in number of, 30 ff., 31T, 35T

Banking officials, state: preference for status quo, 2

Banking structure: studies of, 3, 6, 166 ff.; concept of, 4; in colonial period, 8; as multi-product firms, 328; oligopolistic character of local market, 362; research findings on pricing, operating efficiency, and resource allocation, 368–76; weakness of statistics, 377; need for performance criteria, 385–86; social and political problems, 386–87; need for policy, 391–92

Banking Structure and Performance (Guttentag and Herman), 168n, 383

Banking system, dual, 2, 178–79

"Banking under the Antitrust Laws" (Berle), 241n; cited, 231

Banks: early opposition to, 9 ff., 17

Barnes, Stanley, 153; quoted, 154

Barnett, George, 180

Barr, Joseph W.: quoted, 227

Beckhart, Benjamin H., 386n

Benston, George, 371

Berle, Adolf, 241n; quoted, 231

Biddle's Bank (Wilburn), 12

Big Change, The (Allen): cited, 37

Bok, Derek C.: quoted, 367

Branch banking, 2; before 1900, 9 ff., 15 ff., 25 ff.; hostility toward, 10, 28; in First and Second Bank of the United States, 11 ff.; national banking law provisions, 19 ff.; 1865 amendment to National Bank Act, 24; growth and changing role of,

Branch banking (*Continued*)
29 ff., 31T; intracity, 33–37; intercity, 37–41; metropolitan area branches, 40; operations, 41–42; federal legislation and regulation, 42–56; limited-service offices, 44–46, 47; trade-area concept, 50; vs. deposit insurance, 50–52; intrastate, 52; Supreme Court emphasis on equality under state and federal law, 56; state legislation and regulation, 56–66, 59T, 62T, 68T, 69F; as aid to rural credit, 61; current status, 66–67; future prospects, 67–71; in New York City, 77; correlation with chain banking, 92; correlation with bank holding companies, 96, 102; in mergers, 127, 132, 133T; de novo branches, 212T; potential competition aspect, 355; operating costs, 372; services offered by, 373 ff.; as alternative to unit banking, 383 ff.; dominated by single-community type, 386

*Branch Banking* (Chapman and Westerfield), 176

"Branch Banking" (Federal Reserve Board, Committee Reports): cited, 23

*Branch Banking Question, The* (Collins), 43

Brandeis, Louis D.: quoted, 300–01

Bremer, C. D.: quoted, 185

Brennan, William J.: quoted, 292–93, 298

Brown, Oscar: quoted, 388

*Brown Shoe Company* v. *U. S.* (1962), 336, 356, 357, 363

Burr, Anna R.: quoted, 188

Burt, Hollis W.: quoted, 223

Business cycles: correlation with mergers, 125–26

*Business Review* (periodical), 371

Buyer concentration, 5n

California: branch banking statute (1909), 60

California Bank, Los Angeles, 283

*California* v. *Federal Power Commission* (1962), 294

Cannon, Henry W., 247

Capehart, Homer E., 152, 156, 290

Cardozo, Benjamin N.: quoted, 356

Carson, Deane: quoted, 235

Carte Blanche credit card business, 350, 352–53

Celler, Emanuel, 150–51, 274; quoted, 151, 299

Celler-Kefauver Act (1950): as amendment to Clayton Act, 150, 151, 244, 287, 288–90, 298

Chain banking, 64; definitions, 72–73, 84, 85–87, 90, 91; development of, 82 ff., 90–92; Patman's Report (1963), 85–90; current dimensions, 91–92; correlation with restrictions on branch banking, 92; operations, 92–93

*Chain Banking: Stockholder and Loan Links of 200 Largest Member Banks, see* Patman's Chain Banking Report (1963)

Chapman, John M.: quoted, 176

Chartering, bank: before 1838, 175; 1838–1900, 176–79; development of dual banking system, 178–79; philosophy, 179–84; developments (1900–1935), 184–210; discretionary powers of state supervisory officials, 188 ff.; authority of Comptroller of the Currency, 191–98; of national banks, 192 ff., 196T, 215–17; of rural banks, 201; Banking Act (1935), 203–10; developments (1936–1966), 210–37, 204T, 212T, 219T; during Saxon administration, 217–23, 219T, 229; impact of failures and suspensions on, 229–30

Chase Manhattan Bank (New York City): interbank deposits, 120

Chase Manhattan–Liberty National Bank, 109n–10n

Check clearing, 112

Checking deposits: prevalence of, 36

Chicago: multiple-unit banking in, 76 ff.; concentration of bankers' balances in, 120

Chicago Mortgage Bankers Association: antitrust suit against, 256

Chicago Plan (multiple-unit banking), 76

Clark, John M.: quoted, 360, 361–62

Clark, Tom C.: quoted, 55–56

Clarke, Freeman, 19

Clary, Thomas J., 296, 297; quoted, 298

Clay, Henry, 14

Clayton Anti-Trust Act (1914), 82, 93; assumptions of commercial banking immunity from, 239 ff.; additions to (1936, 1950), 244; provisions, 245–46, 268; in *Firstamerica case*, 284; Sec. 7, 288 ff., 295–97, 308 ff., 353; bank acquisitions challenged under, 302T; market test, 333–36, 337

Clearinghouse agreements: inconsistencies in recommendations of regulatory agencies, 247 ff., 262; legality of, 251–53, 262

*Clearing-Houses* (Cannon), 248n

CMC Report, 67, 70

Collins, Charles W., 43

Commerce: federal regulation of, 240

"Commerce immunity thesis," 240

Commercial banks, 4; mergers and acquisitions, 122, 126–37, 130T, 133T, 136T, 204T; federal legislation and regulation of mergers before 1956, 137–43; growth, 179, 331T; number of state and national (1880–1920), 192; analysis of changes in number of, 204T, 212T; failures and suspensions (1934–1966), 223 ff., 225T; market situation for, 234; immunity from antitrust prosecution, 239–42; price-fixing violation charges against, 259–61, 262, 263; tying arrangements and exclusive dealing, 263–67; interlocking directorates, 267–75; significance of *Transamerica case* to, 282; summary of antitrust cases, 301–10, 302T; ratio of deposits of selected large banks to all banks, 334T; as multiproduct (multiservice) industry, 338 ff.; geographic market, 342–45; percentage of deposits, by selected standard metropolitan statistical areas, 346T; services provided, 375, 378; local orientation, 386

Commercial Security Bank (Utah), see *Utah case* (1964–1965)

Commerzbank (West Germany), 101

Commission on Money and Credit (1958–1961), see CMC Report

Committee on Financial Institutions, Report to the President of the United States, see Heller Report (1963)

"Commodity": statutory interpretation of term, 264

Competition, bank: as factor in mergers, 148–49, 296, 313 ff.; as test, in proposed legislation, 150; court interpretations, 174; condi-

Competition (*Continued*)
tion of entry in banking industry, 230 ff.; interest rates and voluntary regulation, 248 ff.; attitudes toward, 253 ff.; concern over lessening of, 288; Supreme Court opinion in *Philadelphia case,* 292 ff.; market concept as element in antitrust suits, 333 ff.; financial intermediaries as competitors, 338 ff.; determination of geographic market, 342 ff.; oligopoly type, 363 ff.

Competition, potential, 353 ff.

Competition, pure, 360 ff.

Comptroller of the Currency: administrative ruling of 1922, 36; authority in connection with mergers, 138, 140, 162T, 163T; role in bank chartering, 178, 180 ff., 191–98, 216; Saxon administration, 217–23, 219T, 229; legislative recommendation, 249

Concentration in banking, 126 ff.; terminology, 328; measurement of, 328–30, 340–41; trends, 329; market shares of large banks, 330–33, 331T, 334T; percentage of deposits, commercial banks, by selected standard metropolitan statistical areas, 346T; relevance of concentration data, 348–56; court interpretations, 356–60; economist's viewpoint, 360–68; as statistical concept, 365; viewpoint of banking structure research, 368–76; general observations, 377–81

Cooperation, interbank: philosophy of, 253–55

Cootner, Paul: quoted, 235

Corn Products Company, 124

Correspondent banking: operations, 111–17, 114T; statistics, 117–21, 119T; role of, 121

Country banks, *see* Rural banks

Credit accommodation, 112, 375 ff.

Crissinger, Daniel R., 44, 61; quoted, 195

*Crocker-Citizens case,* see *U. S.* v. *Crocker–Anglo National Bank* (1966)

Crosse, Howard, 4n; quoted, 117, 137

Crowley, Leo T.: quoted, 208

*Crown Zellerbach Corporation* v. *Federal Trade Commission* (1961), 336

Currency circulation, 182 ff.

Customer, small, 36, 38, 329

Customer, wholesale, 33, 38, 340

*Dallas case* (1962), 258–59

Darnell, Jerome C., 91n, 93n

Davis, Archie K.: quoted, 1

Dawes, Charles G.: quoted, 28

Dawes, Henry M., 45

Defalcation: as cause of bank failures, 226 ff.

Demand: cross elasticity of, 5

"Department stores of finance," 328, 339

Deposit banking, 34, 231, 340

Deposit insurance: vs. branch banking, 50–52; acceptance of concept of, 209

Deposits, bank: interbank, 111, 117 ff.; share of New York City banks, 126 ff.; interest rates, 248 ff.; in commercial banks, 330, 331T, 334T; ratio of, selected large commercial banks to all commercial banks, 334T; distinction between retail and wholesale banking measured by, 345, 346T

Depression, Great: banking structure reorganization during, 32; merger correlation with, 126;

bank failures and suspensions, 202 ff., 204T

Deutsche Bank (West Germany), 101

*Development of Two Group Banks in the Northwest* (Popple), 75n

Devine (C. J.) Institute of Finance: merger study cited, 131

Dillon, Douglas: quoted, 222

Directorates, interlocking, 127; antitrust aspects, 267–70, enforcement of regulatory legislation, 270–72; need for new legislation, 272–75

Dirlam, Joel B., 356n

District Bank (United Kingdom), 101

Douglas amendment to Bank Holding Company Act (1956), 145

Dresdner Bank (West Germany), 101

du Pont (E. I.) de Nemours & Company, 124, 333 ff.

*du Pont–General Motors case* (1957), see *U. S.* v. *E. I. du Pont de Nemours & Company* (1957)

Eccles, Marriner, 288

Eckels, James H., 191

Economic models: pure competition, 361; as applied to oligopolistic markets, 378 ff.

Economic theory: oligopoly, 363 ff.

Economic time series: correlation with mergers, 125–26

*Economics of Banking Operations* (Galbraith), 171n

*Economics of Regulation, The* (Phillips): cited, 293

Edwards, Franklin, 369

Efficiency, operating: as element in banking structure, 370–73

Emergency Banking Act (1933), 202

England: antitrust legislation, 238–39

Entry into market, 4, 230 ff.; by merger, 340n; potential competition aspect, 355

Equal Rights (Locofoco) Party, 18n

Exclusive dealing, 263–67

Farm economy: collapse of (1921–1923), 61

Farm products prices, 199

Farmers Exchange Bank (Gloucester, R. I.), 186

Federal Deposit Insurance Act, 158; cited, 139

Federal Deposit Insurance Corporation: influence on bank mergers, 129, 138, 139; action on merger applications, 161, 162T, 163T; licensing powers, 207 ff.; authority to limit interest rates of nonmember insured banks, 250–51; analysis of market shares of large banks, 362; studies of banking concentration, 370

Federal Deposit Insurance Corporation *Report* (1960): cited, 32

Federal Reserve Act, 110n

Federal Reserve Board: recommendation for branching legislation, 43; surveys of chain banking, 80, 90; questionnaire on stockholder and loan links, 85 ff.; recommendations for amendments to Bank Holding Company Act, 106, 107; mergers and acquisitions, 138–39, 143 ff., 147T, 149T, 161, 162T, 163T; interest rate regulation,

Federal Reserve Board (*Continued*)
249–50; proceedings *re* interlocking directorates, 270; authority in bank-security dealer relationship, 271–72; bank acquisitions challenged by, 302T; survey of banking facilities, 362

Federal Reserve System: compilations of state branch banking laws, 59

Federal Trade Commission (FTC): statistics for manufacturing and mining mergers, 125–26

Fillmore, Millard: quoted, 21

Financial Institutions Act (1957), 155, 156

Financial Institutions Supervisory Act (1966), 94, 228

Financial intermediaries: as part of banking structure, 4; interlocking directorates, 273; as competitors of commercial banks, 338 ff.; product market definition, 341

Financial system: public and private investigations of, 67 ff.

*Firstamerica case* (1959–1961), 283–86, 309

Firstamerica Corporation, 278, 283 ff.

First Bank of the United States, *see* Bank of the United States (First)

First Camden National Bank and Trust Company (New Jersey), 64n

*First National Bank in St. Louis* v. *State of Missouri* (1924), 23, 46–47, 63

*First National Bank of Logan* v. *Walker Bank and Trust Company;* etc. (1966), 54–56

First National City Bank (New York City), 120, 350, 352–53

First Western Bank and Trust Company, San Francisco, 283

Flechsig, Theodore, 369

Florida East Coast Railway, 107

Forgan, James B., 76

Fortas, Abe: quoted, 239

Franklin National Bank (Mineola, New York), 214n, 235–36

Free banking: legislation, 18; geographical extent, 24–25; as antimonopoly device, 176; bank failures in era of, 181; under National Banking System, 182 ff.; Panic of 1907, 193; end of era, 198, 210

Fulbright, J. William, 152, 156, 290

Fulbright bill (S. 3911), 152ff.

"Full-service" concept, 339

*Future of Small Banks, The* (Kohn), 172

Germany: antitrust legislation, 239

Giannini, Amadeo P., 79

Gidney, Ray M., 218, 219; quoted, 53, 141

Gilbart, James: quoted, 165–66

Glass, Carter, 49, 50, 250

Glass-Steagall Act (1932), 202

Gold Standard Act (1900), 27, 185

Goldsborough, T. A.: quoted, 51

Golembe, Carter H., 50n; quoted, 52

Gramley, Lyle, 371

Greenbaum, Stuart, 371, 372; quoted, 373

Group banking, 64, 73; *see also* Bank holding companies; Chain banking

Guttentag, Jack M., 167, 168, 329, 373, 383, 385; quoted, 371, 376

Hall, George R., 161n; quoted, 145, 148, 337, 365

Hamilton, Alexander, 9n, 10

Hammond, Bray: quoted, 177

Handler, Milton, 356n; quoted, 299

Harlan, John M.: dissenting opinions: in *Philadelphia case,* 277, 300; in *Lexington case,* 358

Harrison, William Henry, 14

Hartford Bank (1792), 15

Hefflebower, Richard: quoted, 365

Heller Report (1963), 67, 70; cited, 273, 384

Herman, Edward S., 167, 168, 329, 373, 383, 385; quoted, 371, 376

*History of Crises Under the National Banking System* (Sprague), 187

Holding companies, *see* Bank holding companies

Holland, Robert: quoted, 7

"Home office protection," 355, 391

Hooper, Samuel, 18n

Horvitz, Paul, 371

House Banking and Currency Committee: 1930 hearings, 50, 80

House Judiciary Committee Report (1952), 150

Howard Corporation (Dallas), 84

Howell, Charles R.: quoted, 231–32

Illinois: early banking laws, 16; satellite and affiliate banking systems, 84

Indiana: early banking laws, 16; "over-banking," 207

Industrial organization: merger movements, 123–26

*Industrial Organization* (Bain), 234

Industries, regulated, 233, 293, 294

*Instructions in Regard to the Organization, Extension, and Management of National Banks* (various eds.): cited, 191, 194–95

Insurance business, 240

Interbank deposits, *see* Deposits, bank

Interest rates: of bank holding companies, 101; on deposits, 248 ff.; clearinghouse agreements on, 250; differentials of, as competitive factor, 339

International Harvester Company, 124

Interstate offices, 64n

Investments: of branch institutions, 32, 33

Iowa: "over-banking," 206

Jackson, Andrew, 13

Jacobs, Donald, 233n

Javits, Jacob K., 291

Jennings, L. A.: quoted, 153

Johnson, Lyndon B.: quoted, 291–92

Joint Economic Committee Report (U. S. Congress; 1952), 211, 215, 217

Jordan, Edward, 18n

Kane, Thomas: quoted, 194

Kansas: prohibition of branching, 56n

Kansas Development Credit Corporation, 388

Katzenbach, Nicholas deB.: quoted, 239

Kaufman, George, 369

Kaysen, Carl: quoted, 366

Kefauver, Estes: quoted, 245

Kennedy, John F., 67

Kintner, Earl: quoted, 244–45

Knickerbocker Trust Company (New York City), 187
Knox, John Jay: quoted, 183, 247
Kohn, Ernest: quoted, 172–73

Lacey, Edward S., 191
Law Against Restraints of Competition (Germany; 1957), 239
Lawrence, Robert, 170n
Legislation and regulation (federal): anti-trust, 239 ff.; bank chartering, 177, 207 ff.; bank holding companies, 101–07; banking, 53; branch banking, 42–56; chain banking, 93–95; commercial banks, 137–43; mergers and consolidations, 137–43, 143–49, 147T, 149T, 149–62, 286–310, 310–26; multiple-unit banking, 81–82
Legislation and regulation (state): branch banking, 56–66, 59T, 62T, 68T, 69F, 355; multiple-unit banking, 81
Lexington case, see U. S. v. First National Bank and Trust Company of Lexington (1964)
Liberty Bank of San Francisco, 79
Liberty National Bank (Buffalo), 109n–10n
Limited-service offices: state laws, 56
Loans: of branch institutions, 32, 33; in chain banking, 85 ff.; on bank stock, 88–90; by bank holding companies, 100; city-country bank arrangements, 112–13; expansion emphasized by holding company affiliates, 171 ff.; ratios of unit and branch banks, 376
Locofocos, see Equal Rights (Locofoco) Party
Loevinger, Lee: quoted, 300

Louisiana: state branch bank legislation, 58

M & I Bank Stock Corporation, 308–10; see also U. S. v. Marshall and Ilsley Bank Stock Corporation (1967)
MacMahon, Lloyd F., 341, 345, 358; quoted, 359
Management, 94; problem of succession, in relation to mergers, 135, 136T; as factor in failures and suspensions, 201, 226 ff.
Management Policies for Commercial Banks (Crosse), 4n
Manufacturers Hanover (New York City): interbank deposits, 120
Market: definitions, 333, 336, 337; need for improved data, 345–47; power of, emphasized by courts, 356; oligopolistic structure of, 366 ff.
Market, banking: shares of large banks, 330–33, 331T; concept of, 333–47; percentage of deposits, commercial banks, by selected standard metropolitan statistical areas, 346T; choice between forms of oligopoly, 363
Market, geographic: definition, 327; commercial bank deposits by geographic area, 334T; interpretations, 336, 337, 342 ff.; commercial banking as line of commerce, 342
Market, product: interpretations, 327, 336, 337, 341–42
Market structure: defined, 4
Markham, Jesse: quoted, 364–65, 367
Martin, William McChesney, Jr.: quoted, 88
Maryland Bank (1790), 15

Mason, Edward: quoted, 365
Mass distribution: correlation with branch banking, 36
Massachusetts: state branch bank legislation, 58
Massachusetts Land Bank, 9n
McClellan, John L.: quoted, 218
McCulloch, Hugh, 21
McFadden Act (1927), 23, 37, 47–49, 63
McIntosh, J. W.: quoted, 197
Memorials to Congress, 13
Mercantile Bank (New York City), 187
Mergers, bank: definitions, 31n, 123; in commercial banking, 122, 126–37, 130T, 133T, 136T, 204T; correlation with restrictions on branch banking, 127; federal legislation and regulation before 1956, 137–43; Bank Holding Company Act (1956), 143–49, 147T, 149T; Bank Merger Act (1960), 149–62; varying attitudes of supervisory agencies, 160–61, 162T, 163T; state controls, 164–65; effects of, 165–73, 169T, 327; court cases under antitrust laws, 276–86, 301–10, 302T; background of controversy, 286–88; developments (1950–1959), 290–92; implications of 1966 amendments, 310 ff.; issues still undecided, 325–26; market concept, 333 ff., 342; conglomerate, 340, 348, 350–56; court interpretations of concentration, 356–60; pure competition theory, 360 ff.; economic models as applied to, 378 ff.; *see also* Asset acquisition, bank
Mergers, nonbank, 123–26
Metropolitan area data, 343

Michigan: limited branching legislation (1945), 64, 66; free banking act (1837), 176
*Minnesota cases* (1963–1964), 259–61, 262
Missouri: branch bank legislation, 56n, 58; bank holding company status, 81
Mitchell, George W.: quoted, 388
*Money and Credit—Their Influence on Jobs, Prices, and Growth, see* CMC Report
*Monopoly and Competition in Banking* (Alhadeff), 254n
Montana: "over-banking," 206
Morgan, J. P., 77, 78
Morris, Robert, 9n
Morse-Heinze banking chain, 77, 81, 187
Mote, Larry R.: quoted, 378
Multiple-unit banking: development, 73–82; statistics, 79–81; federal and state legislation and regulation, 81–82; forecast, 108–09; *see also* Bank holding companies; Chain banking
Murray, Lawrence O., 43, 193; quoted, 194

*Nashville case, see U. S. v. Third National Bank in Nashville* (1966)
*Nathan v. Louisiana* (1850), 240
National Association of Supervisors of State Banks, 189, 206
National Bank Act (1864): provisions, 19 ff., 22, 42; amendment of 1865, 23, 24; Supreme Court interpretation (1966), 54–56; effect on state bank chartering, 179; goals of, 180 ff.; capital requirements, 181; cited, 181
National Bank Consolidation Act (1918), 44

National Banking System, 182 ff.
National banks, 2; free bank principle, 18; branching status under National Bank Act, 42; branching powers under Consolidation Act (1918), 44; intrastate branching, 52; interstate offices, 64n; affiliates organized by, 76 ff.; federal regulation of mergers, 140; currency distribution, 182 ff.; chartering (1900–1966), 192 ff., 196T; chartering (1936–1966), 212T, 216; chartering during Saxon administration, 217–23, 219T
*National Banks and the Future*, see Saxon Report (1962)
National Bureau of Economic Research (NBER), 2, 6, 167
National Credit Corporation (1931), 202
National Currency Act (1863), 15, 18, 21, 22, 177, 180 ff.
National Monetary Commission (1909), 58
National Monetary Commission *Report* (1912), 27–28
Neale, A. D.: quoted, 238
Nebraska: branching prohibition, 56n; "over-banking," 206
Nelson, Ralph: quoted, 124
New Hampshire: branch banking law (1963), 355, 390
New Jersey: legislation on corporation stock ownership, 75
*New Jersey case*, see *U. S. v. Hunterdon County Trust Company, First National Bank of Clinton and Clinton National Bank* (1962)
New York City: branch banking, 77 ff.; banking concentration, 120, 126; banks in, during Panic of 1907, 187; division of banking into subproducts in, 344

*New York Mortgage Conference case*, see *U. S. v. Mortgage Conference of New York* (1946)
New York State: branch banking, 58, 65, 355; chain banking, 74, 81; multiple-unit banking, 108; bank chartering, 175; discretionary powers of state supervisory officials, 188 ff.
New York State free banking act (1838), 18, 20, 22n, 176
New York State Superintendent of Banks report (1905): cited, 248–49
Nominee registration of securities, 86n, 88
North, the: branch banking in, 17
North Central states: bank failures and suspensions in, 203
North Dakota: limited-service offices in, 56; "over-banking," 206
Northwest, the: multiple-unit banking system, 76
Northwest Bancorporation, 76

Oklahoma: branching prohibition, 56n, 64, 66
*Old Kent Bank and Trust Company v. Martin*, 141–43
O'Mahoney, Joseph C., 291
Oppenheim, S. Chesterfield: quoted, 364
Orrick, William, Jr.: quoted, 245, 277, 286, 358
"Over-banking," 201, 203 ff., 288

Panic of 1839, 175
Panic of 1873, 247
Panic of 1884, 247
Panic of 1907, 77, 186–88; *see also* Depression, Great
Patman, Wright, 85, 107
Patman's Chain Banking Report (1963), 85–90, 91; cited, 86

*Paton's Digest* (1926 ed.), 251–52
*Paton's Digest* (1940 ed.), 252
*Paton's Digest* (1946 ed.), 253, 262
Per se violation doctrine, 256 ff.
Perfect competition, *see* Competition, pure
Personnel, bank: problems of, 135; *see also* Management
"Pervasive regulatory scheme" tests, 294
*Philadelphia case,* see *U. S.* v. *Philadelphia National Bank* (1963)
Phillips, Charles F., Jr., 161n; quoted, 293, 337, 365
Platt, Edmund: quoted, 200
Pluralism, doctrine of, 244
Pole, John W., 50; quoted, 197
Price fixing: attitudes of supervisory authorities, 246 ff.; federal bank antitrust cases, 256–63
Pricing: as element in banking structure, 368–70
Private banks, 177, 178n
Product differentiation, 4
*Promise of Free Enterprise, The* (Saxon), 218n
Provincial Bank (United Kingdom), 101
Public Bank of Detroit, 228
Public Utility Holding Company Act (1935), 96
Pujo Committee Report (1913), 78, 82, 102, 128, 250; cited, 247

Railway Executives Association, 107
Randall, K. A.: quoted, 227n
Reconstruction Finance Corporation (1932), 202
*Report of the Committee on Financial Institutions to the President of the United States* (1963), *see* Heller Report (1963)
Republic National Bank (Dallas), 84
Republic National Company (Dallas), 84
Reserve requirements, 111
Resource allocation: as element in banking structure, 373–76
*Reynolds Metals Company* v. *Federal Trade Commission* (1962), 336
Ridgely, William B.: quoted, 29
Robertson, A. Willis, 155, 156, 290; quoted, 318
Robinson-Patman Act (1936), 244
*Romance and Tragedy of Banking, The* (Kane), 194n
Roosevelt, Franklin D., 104, 202
"Rule of reason," 244
Rural banks: reserve requirements, 111; personnel problems in relation to mergers, 135, 136T; economic and financial problems of 1920s, 199 ff.; "overbanking," 201
Rural credit, 61

Satellite banking, 83
Saxon, James J., 54, 214n; as Comptroller of the Currency, 217–23, 219T, 229
Saxon Report (1962), 67 ff.; cited, 273
Schapiro (M. A.) & Company, 86
Scott, Ira, 375; quoted, 113
Second Bank of the United States, *see* Bank of the United States (Second)
Security dealers, 271–72
Security-First National Bank (California), 284
Seller concentration, 4

Senate Banking and Currency Committee: hearings of 1931 and 1932, 50

Senate Committee on Government Operations, 229

Senate Investigation into Federally Insured Banks (1965), 218

Service charges: of bank holding companies, 101

Service industry: banking as, 377 ff.

"Shaving shops," 21

Shay, Jerome: quoted, 141

"Shell corporations," 84

Sherman Antitrust Act (1890), 239, 240, 243; provisions, 245–46; in *Firstamerica case,* 283; bank acquisitions challenged under, 302T; market test, 337; importance of *Lexington case* to interpretation of, 358

Shull, Bernard, 338n

Small Business Investment Act (1958), 105

Smith, Adam, 17

South, the: branch banking in, 17

South Dakota: contest between national and state bank systems, 206

*South-Eastern Underwriters case,* see *U. S.* v. *South-Eastern Underwriters* (1944)

Southwest: state bank chartering, 211

Sparkman, John J., 152

Spaulding, E. G., 18, 21n; quoted, 23n

Specie Resumption Act (1875), 183

Sprague, O. M. W.: quoted, 187

*St. Louis case,* see *First National Bank in St. Louis* v. *State of Missouri* (1924)

Standard metropolitan statistical area (SMSA), 342

State banks, 15 ff., 177 ff., 179 ff.; growth, 184 ff.; supervisory officials, 188–91; chartering, 211 ff., 212T

*State Banks and Trust Companies since the Passage of the National Bank Act* (Barnett), 180

States' rights: as issue in Bank Holding Company Act, 144; emphasized in bank structure debates, 386

Stephens Branch Banking Bill (1934), 65

Stewart, Potter: dissent in *Von's Grocery Company case,* 391

Stigler, George J.: quoted, 367

Stillman, James, 77, 78

Stilwell, Silas, 18n

Stockholders Auxiliary Corporation, 79

Stockholding: in chain banking, 85 ff.; in holding company affiliation, 135, 136T; equity, 181

"Structure of Competition of Commercial Banking in the United States, The" (Carson and Cootner), 235

*Structure of Ownership of Member Banks and the Pattern of Loans Made on Hypothecated Bank Stock, The,* 90n

Study Commission for Indiana Financial Institutions, Report: cited, 207

*Study of Group and Chain Banking* (ABA); cited, 6

Suburban growth, 38

Sumner, William: quoted, 22n

Supervisory authorities: discretionary chartering powers of state officials, 188–91, 207, 211–15; powers of Comptroller of the Currency, 191–98;

chartering powers of federal officials, 215 ff.; Saxon administration, 217–23, 219T, 229; need for review of standards employed by, 234; status of banks under antitrust laws made uncertain by, 246, 262

Texas: branch legislation, 56n; satellite and affiliate banking system, 84
Third Bank of the United States, *see* Bank of the United States (Third)
Thorp, Willard: quoted, 125
*Times-Picayune Pub. Co. v. U. S.* (1953), 264
"Tobey bill," 104
Toulmin, Harry A., Jr.: quoted, 377
Trade-area branching, 50; legislative recommendations, 70
Transamerica Corporation, 99, 104, 242, 278 ff.
*Transamerica v. Board of Governors of the Federal Reserve System* (1953), 241–42, 278–82
Trant, James: quoted, 254–55
Trust companies, 186, 187
Turner, Donald F.: quoted, 267, 366, 379
*Twenty Largest Stockholders of Record in Member Banks of the Federal Reserve System,* 92n
*Twin Cities as a Metropolitan Market, The* (Hartsough), 75n
Tying arrangements, 263–67
Tyler, John, 14

Union Bank of Boston (1792), 15
Union Investment Company, 76
Unit banking, 2, 9 ff., 19; growth and changing role of, 29 ff., 31T; as "local banking system," 33; deposit insurance as bulwark of, 51; significance of correspondent banking to, 121; services offered by, 373 ff.; inviolability of, 383; future trends, 387–89
United Kingdom: bank holding companies in, 101
United States Congress: regulation of commerce, 240 ff.
United States Court of Appeals (D. C.): *Old Kent Bank and Trust Company* v. *Martin* (1960), 141–43
United States Department of Justice: vs. banking agencies, 162–64, 302T; viewpoint of Antitrust Division, 266–67; role of, in banking industry, 286 ff.; bank acquisitions challenged by, 302T; powers under 1966 amendments to Bank Merger Act, 315–16; potential competition thesis, 353 ff.; suits filed against bank mergers since 1961, 390
United States Steel Corporation, 124
United States Supreme Court cases:
  *Board of Governors of the Federal Reserve System* v. *Agnew* (1947), 272
  *Brown Shoe Company* v. *U. S.* (1962), 336, 356, 357, 363
  *First National Bank in St. Louis* v. *State of Missouri* (1924), 23, 46–47, 63
  *First National Bank of Logan* v. *Walker Bank and Trust Company; etc.* (1966), 54–56

United States Supreme Court Cases (*Continued*)

*Nathan* v. *Louisiana* (1850), 240

*Times-Picayune Pub. Co.* v. *U. S.* (1953), 264

*U. S.* v. *Aluminum Company of America* (1964), 349

*U. S.* v. *Continental Can* (1964), 349

*U. S.* v. *E. I. du Pont de Nemours & Co.* (1957), 333–36

*U. S.* v. *First City National Bank of Houston* (1967), 316, 318, 320, 323–25, 349, 368

*U. S.* v. *First National Bank and Trust Company of Lexington* (1964), 164, 242, 342, 349, 357–58

*U. S.* v. *Marshall & Ilsley Bank Stock Corporation* (1967), 308–10, 319n

*U. S.* v. *Pabst Brewing Company* (1966), 337, 344–45, 348

*U. S.* v. *Penn-Olin Chemical Company* (review), 354

*U. S.* v. *Philadelphia National Bank* (1963), 164, 174, 242, 262, 276 ff., 292–301, 309, 311, 336, 338 ff., 342 ff., 349, 357, 362 ff., 366

*U. S.* v. *Provident National Bank* (1967), 316, 318, 320, 323–25, 349, 368

*U. S.* v. *South-Eastern Underwriters* (1944), 240–41

*U. S.* v. *Von's Grocery Company* (1966), 348, 349, 363, 379

United States Supreme Court interpretations: branch banking, 23, 24; banking industry, 293, 294, 340; concentration data and market share statistics, 348; size and market power, 356 ff.; standards in antitrust litigation, 360; competition and concentration, 380 ff.

*U. S.* v. *Aluminum Company of America* (1964), 349

*U. S.* v. *Bank of Virginia,* see *Virginia case* (1966)

*U. S.* v. *Bethlehem Steel Corporation* (1958), 336

*U. S.* v. *Chicago Mortgage Bankers Association* (1954), 256

*U. S.* v. *Continental Can* (1964), 349

*U. S.* v. *Crocker-Anglo National Bank* (1966), 320–22, 350 ff., 391

*U. S.* v. *Duluth Clearinghouse Association,* see *Minnesota cases* (1963–1964)

*U. S.* v. *E. I. du Pont de Nemours & Co.* (1957), 333–36

*U. S.* v. *First City National Bank of Houston* (1967), 316, 318, 320, 323–25, 368

*U. S.* v. *First National Bank and Trust Company of Lexington* (1964), 164, 242, 342, 349, 357–58

*U. S.* v. *First National Bank of Hawaii* (1966), 350, 351 ff., 391

*U. S.* v. *First National Bank of St. Paul,* see *Minnesota cases* (1963–1964)

*U. S.* v. *First National City Bank of New York* (1965), 352 ff., 391

*U. S.* v. *Hunterdon County Trust Company, First National Bank of Clinton and Clinton National Bank* (1962), 257, 262

*U. S.* v. *Investors Diversified Services* (1951), 264

*U. S.* v. *Manufacturers Hanover Trust Company* (1965), 276–77, 341, 343 ff.

*U. S.* v. *Marshall & Ilsley Bank Stock Corporation* (1967), 308–10, 319n

*U. S.* v. *Mercantile Trust Co. National Association* (1967), 323

*U. S.* v. *Morgan* (1953), 241–42

*U. S.* v. *Mortgage Conference of New York* (1946), 241, 256

*U. S.* v. *Northwestern National Bank of Minneapolis,* see *Minnesota cases* (1963–1964)

*U. S.* v. *Pabst Brewing Company* (1966), 337, 344–45, 348

*U. S.* v. *Penn-Olin Chemical Company* (1964), 354

*U. S.* v. *Philadelphia National Bank* (1963), 164, 174, 242, 276 ff., 292–301, 309, 311, 336, 338 ff., 342 ff., 349, 357, 362 ff., 366

*U. S.* v. *Provident National Bank* (1967), 316, 318, 320, 323–25, 368

*U. S.* v. *Radio Corporation of America* (1959), 294

*U. S.* v. *South-Eastern Underwriters* (1944), 240–41

*U. S.* v. *Third National Bank in Nashville* (1966), 322

*U. S.* v. *Von's Grocery Company* (1966), 348, 349, 363, 379

Urbanization, 34 ff.

Utah: branch banking laws, 55

*Utah case* (1964–1965), 264–65

Vermont State Bank (1806), 15

Virginia: branch banking legislation (1948), 64; branch banking law (1962), 355, 390, 391n

*Virginia case* (1966), 265–66

Voting permits (holding company affiliates), 103

West Germany: bank holding companies in, 101

Westerfield, Ray B.: quoted, 176

Western Bancorporation, *see* Firstamerica Corporation

Whitney Holding Corporation, 109n

Wickersham, George W.: branching powers opinion (1911), 43, 46, 47

Wilburn, Jean, 12; quoted, 13–14

"Wildcat banks," 21

Williams, Charles, 386n

Williams, Larry: quoted, 360

Willis, H. Parker: quoted, 29

Wisconsin: prohibition of branching, 56n, 64, 66; chain and group legislation, 81

Witham, William S., 75

World War II: market shares of largest and smaller banks during, 32